AN OHIO READER

RECONSTRUCTION TO THE PRESENT

edited by

THOMAS H. SMITH
Director, Ohio Historical Society

977.1
OHI
v.2
Co

William B. Eerdmans
  Publishing Company   Grand Rapids, Michigan

Copyright © 1975 by Wm. B. Eerdmans Publishing Company
All rights reserved
Printed in the United States of America

Library of Congress Cataloging in Publication Data
Main entry under title:

An Ohio reader.

Includes bibliographical references.
CONTENTS: v. 1. European settlement to the Civil
War.—v. 2. 1865 to the present.
1. Ohio—History—Sources. I. Smith, Thomas H.,
1936-
F491.039   977.1   75-11606
ISBN 0-8028-7034-1 (v. 2)

All Ohio State documents reprinted by permission of the Ohio Historical Society.

to my maternal grandparents

c.3

ACKNOWLEDGMENTS

An effort of this size is never accomplished without help. I would like to thank the library staff of the Ohio Historical Society, especially Conrad Weitzel, the library staff of the Cincinnati Historical Society, and the staff of the Ohio State Library; Professor Harry R. Stevens who offered helpful suggestions and encouragement; Marcia Smith and Bret Smith who helped with the manuscript; Pat Smith who made corrections; and Joanne who watched, waited and typed.

CONTENTS

INTRODUCTION

THIS IS NOT merely a history readings book; it is also a documentary history of the development of a geographical area limited by man-made boundaries—the state of Ohio. The first state to be formed from the Northwest Territory, Ohio struggled from a crude frontier existence to maturity in the modern world. The general movement of the Ohio experience was not unique: it was repeated countless times throughout the Midwest and across the nation; taken by itself, it loses meaning, but considered within the general context of national history, it is reflective of the entire nation's past. Perhaps, if there is a national experience, it is the sum total of all local experiences; and it is through an appreciation of local history that one can discover a patient and tolerant vehicle for understanding matters on a broader scale.

Thus, Ohio history can be seen as a microcosm of national history. Before the coming of Europeans, culturally rich prehistoric Indians had thrived across the state; numerous historic Indians hunted and farmed its productive land and experienced the despair of removal. Like many states, Ohio had its bloody frontier war and muddled through the frustrations of territorial government. Its people developed a stable constitutional government and sought an economic stability upon which Western culture could flourish. Ohioans participated at all levels of western expansion, debated the issues of slavery, and fought to keep the nation one. During the period between the American Civil War and the turn of the century, urbanization and industrialization introduced problems that affected the lifestyle of man and the environment. Ohioans sought a better life, both economic and governmental, and the impact of the state's reform movement extended far beyond its political boundaries. The two world wars in the twentieth century, and the turmoil of reconstruction that followed both, were disruptive and challenging experiences that Ohioans shared with America and the rest of the world. By mid-twentieth century, the issues that faced modern society— including racial strife, educational development, economic expansion, population growth, social welfare, inflation, and governmental finance—were full-blown. Ohioans searched for their own solutions, but not independently of the national experience. Thus, the experiences of Ohioans were shared by Americans of all races, creeds, and political beliefs. What happened in Ohio affected the national scene, and the historical processes at the national level had their impact on the Buckeye State as well.

An Ohio Reader is intended to be many things to many people; its potential uses are numerous and varied. The increasing interest in local history among professional historians over the past twenty years has manifested itself in numerous articles and monographs that have been published on topics limited to specific eras and geographical areas. But the interest goes beyond the needs of the professional. Ohio history has been taught in the public schools of the state at the elementary, secondary, and college level for years, and a genuine fascination with local history has grown among the general public. The current popular search for nostalgia's wonderland in the mass media is one evidence of that fact. The collection of documents and materials in these volumes is intended to be both instructive and interesting to the general reader. At the same time, these volumes are also intended for use in the classroom. Teaching Ohio history for several years and listening to and talking with students and teachers has convinced me of the need for more available sources on local history. Though textbooks currently in use in the state certainly serve a purpose and give students an outline of the flow of events, they fail because of space limitations to provide materials for in-depth study and substantive inquiry.

Four criteria were used to compile the selections in these volumes. First, particular attention was paid to the major issues in Ohio's history that have occupied the time of both historians and laymen. Second, each document selected was intended to stand alone: no reader need have a special expertise in any particular field to understand the meaning of each issue. Consequently, the selections were chosen because they contained both pertinent survey and specific material relative to each topic. Third, a problematic approach was employed when the topic and materials permitted. For instance, during the 1912 Ohio Constitutional Convention the issue of women's suffrage was debated with regularity and vigor; arguments pro and con echoed throughout the convention chamber. The selected segments of the debate from the convention, therefore, air both sides of the women's suffrage issue, which occupied the thoughts of Ohioans for several decades. Fourth, in each instance the documents had to be contemporaneous and represent eyewitness accounts or descriptions of the particular issues that faced each generation. It is only through the participants' record that one can gain an appreciation for historic issues in their own time. Accordingly, each document's authenticity has been preserved, even though many contain archaic spellings and grammatical constructions.

Most of the selections come from state documents and newspaper accounts. The reports made to the governor by the heads of the various state agencies, departments, bureaus, and commissions are taken from the Ohio Executive Documents series. Prior to World War I, these reports were compiled and published as single volumes. Descriptive in construction, they contain data and information found nowhere else. Following World War I, however, the state reports were no longer gathered and published as single volumes but were printed independently by each agency. The majority of these later reports contain informative and descriptive reviews, but they are outlines of the agencies' work for the year. During the Depression of the 1930s, many of the agencies—in order to save money—stopped quality production of their reports and issued mimeographed outlines of their activities. Although printed reports returned during the 1940s, the practice of each agency's printing its own report continued. At the same time, many of the reports became less informative and appeared to be printed for in-house consumption rather than for informing the general public.

Newspaper reporting has also changed substantially since Ohio's early years. In the late nineteenth and early twentieth centuries, newspaper reporters were eyewitnesses to newsworthy events and gave the reading public descriptive accounts of what they observed. This is clearly evident in the articles concerning labor, urban conditions, and bossism. Consequently, newspapers of that period have been highly useful in the compilation of this volume. In the twentieth century, however, newspaper reporting lost much of its narrative dimension in favor of personal interpretations of events. Admittedly, the narrative is still present in modern newspaper reporting; yet the reporter often stands between the reader and the event, and the newspaper becomes a less important source for a collection of this nature.

It may appear to some that the issues and readings selected make for a discouraging picture of the state's history. This may be true, yet the editor believes that the intrinsic meaning of historical processes operates on various levels. While the annual messages of the governors to the general assembly contained glowing accounts of the accomplishments and successes of their respective administrations, the agency reports hit at the problems within the state that had yet to be remedied. To identify a problem at the state executive or legislative level is one thing, but to be personally involved with a problem where it affects the quality of human life on an individual basis is another matter. Consequently, the selections reflect issues that affected the majority of Ohioans at the local level and reveal the most about the particular historical processes at work.

One of the striking themes that emerges from a survey of major documents in the state's history is the similarity of the economic, social, racial, educational, and political issues that faced each generation. The problem of financing education in Ohio was as poignant to the generations during the early 1800s as it was one hundred years later. The effects of industrialization and the exploitation of the state's natural resources on the environment were apparent one hundred years ago; in many instances the solution to these problems is no nearer now than it was then. The problems of intensive urbanization as it affected society are the same in the days of the Office for Economic Opportunity and revenue sharing as they were when George Barnsdale Cox fought for the passage of his own pet ripper bill through the Ohio General Assembly. It is often easy for pessimism to capture the spirit of the historian. The hope persists, however, that at some point an understanding of the past can help clear a path for a greater future.

AN
OHIO READER

1 Reconstruction

THE RECONSTRUCTION PERIOD—those years between the close of the Civil War and the disputed election of Rutherford B. Hayes—had a different meaning in Ohio than in the South. During this time the political scene witnessed a great deal of confusion: shifting party and personal loyalties, doctrinal contradiction, inflamed animosities, blatant racism, and above all the recognition of new issues to be considered by the public. At the same time, a new generation of politicians emerged from the Civil War. These men had served their country or parties well during the national strife, and they dominated politics in Ohio for the remainder of the century. To be sure, the issues during the state political campaigns were directly related to the issues of the Civil War. The dual issue of freedmen's rights—citizenship and suffrage—met opposition in Ohio and became a partisan matter. The Republicans supported citizenship for blacks; and while many of the party faithful—especially the radicals—were not social revolutionaries, they realized the political folly of enforcing suffrage for blacks on the South while denying it to them at home. On the other hand, the Democrats, not necessarily faced with such a dilemma, became the white man's party and opposed any extension of political privileges to blacks. Despite the Democrats' maneuverings, the Ohio General Assembly accepted the fourteenth amendment in 1867 and the fifteenth two years later.

Neither party faced the issues with unanimity. While the Democrats certainly had their share of intraparty strife, it was the Republicans who had the hardest time keeping their rank and file loyal. No longer equipped with their crusading antislavery, save-the-union fervor as a cohesive force, the Republicans factionalized not only over the social issues but also over both the Andrew Johnson and Ulysses S. Grant administrations. The divisions within the party ranks over Johnson's control of national Reconstruction policy and his subsequent impeachment were no less damaging than the Liberal Republicans' disenchantment with Grant's unsavory second administration. While weakened, the Republicans relied heavily on the partisan animosities resulting from the Civil War and waved the bloody shirt effectively during numerous state elections.

As noted above, one of the most controversial figures in Ohio's political history was Clement L. Vallandigham. A bright and energetic figure, Vallandigham continued his battle after the Civil War against Republicans, big business, and eastern supremacy of the Middle West. By 1871, however, Vallandigham recognized the political futility of beating the dead issues of the Civil War. He believed that new issues, reflective of a changed society, faced the nation. Consequently, the Democratic party, in an effort to capture the dissident voters in the state, accepted Vallandigham's "New Departure" platform, which declared the Civil War over and outlined fresh issues to the electorate.

Beneath the surface of American society lay a restlessness. Before the end of the Reconstruction period, the state witnessed the gathering of many discontented groups who were determined to organize in order to more clearly articulate their protests. Included among these were the suffragettes, the laborites, and the prohibitionists. Of greatest significance during this period was the convention of Liberal Republicans held in Cincinnati in 1872. Although many of those who attended were impractical reformers, they were dissatisfied with contemporary conditions and called for change within American society.

Reconstruction

JACOB D. COX

Oberlin, July 24, 1865.

Gen. J. D. Cox—Dear Sir: The people of this place, with entire unanimity, sought your nomination for Governor of Ohio. With equal unanimity we desire to promote your election. We rejoiced in your nomination because we had perfect confidence that your views and sympathies were in harmony with our own on the great issue before us—the equality of all men before the law. We still believe that we were not mistaken. But some of us have been startled by a report coming directly from Warren, to the effect that you are opposed to giving the elective franchise to colored people, and that you requested the editor of the *Chronicle* to publish your views on the subject, that you might not lose the support of Union men in the Southern part of the State. We do not credit the rumor, and yet it has so disturbed some of your warmest supporters, that the undersigned have been requested to address you on the subject.

We want to know directly from you your views on the following subjects: 1st. Are you in favor of modifying our Constitution so as to give the elective franchise to colored men? 2d. In the re-organization of the Southern States should the elective franchise be secured to the colored people?

Among us there is but one opinion on this subject, and we were never more in earnest on any political question. We believe that the distinction made by our Constitution between white and colored people was made in the interest of slavery, and is both wicked and absurd. And we believe that to re-construct the Southern States and admit them with constitutions excluding colored men from the polls would give the country and the negro into the power of the very men who have sought and still desire to ruin the one and enslave the other.

Deliver the four millions of freed people into the hands of their former oppressors, now embittered by their defeat, and they will make their condition worse than before. The Copperheads of the North, with the united South, would gain control of the General Government, and in various ways would harrass and oppress the negroes and their friends beyond endurance. A war of races would be likely to result. If as a nation we can be so wicked as to deliver our colored soldiers and the millions whose freedom we are pledged to maintain, into the power of the most cruel and vindictive people that

From *Ohio State Journal*, August 1, 1865.

ever laid claim to civilization, a terrible retribution will await us. We speak strongly that you may know how we feel on the subject.

If it be said that the negroes of the South are ignorant and unfit for the elective franchise, we answer, grant it; but this has nothing to do with the question. Our colored soldiers who have fought three years for the Union are not of this class, nor are those who have always been free, many of whom have amassed wealth. It is for these we ask the elective franchise. If it should take a year, or two or three to prepare the mass to vote, we would be content. Though we believe our free institutions would be safer in the hands of the colored people as they are, than in the hands of the best half of the white population of the South. The question is, Shall colored people be allowed to vote? The enemies of our country say no. The mass of the loyal say yes. So decided are our people on the subject, that they could by no means be persuaded to vote for a man known to be opposed to it. The Union party of this country, so far as we know, are unanimous on the subject, and we believe that throughout the country the party can be rallied on this platform with greater enthusiasm than on any other. All the prominent religious papers, and, with one or two exceptions, all the leading Republican papers are in favor of universal suffrage. We believe that nothing could be more suicidal to our party and the cause of freedom than to reject this doctrine.

Please let us hear from you soon. It is not our wish to publish your views, unless you desire it. But we wish to have our own minds relieved, and to be able to contradict any false reports that may be in circulation regarding your views on this subject.

Very truly and sincerely yours,
E. H. FAIRCHILD,
SAMUEL PLUMB,
Com.

General Cox's Response

Columbus, 25th July, 1865.

Gentlemen:—Your letter of yesterday, inquiring what are my opinions upon some of the phases of the question of the reconstruction of the Union, was received this morning. You sign yourselves as a "Committee," but have omitted to inform me what body or organization you represent, or to give me the instructions or resolutions committing the subject to you. This accidental omission would be of no consequence, since I know you both to be members of the Union Party of this State, and, though we have scarce seen each other for some years, have believed you to be personal friends of mine; but my relations to the Union men of Ohio are such that it may become of some importance to know who are those with whom you are acting and for whom you declare that a hearty and honest concurrence in the principles which you and the other loyal people of Ohio adopted in convention on the 21st ultimo expressly as the basis of united political action in the coming State election, shall not be sufficient to secure your votes.

Political organizations, like every other, are founded upon a mutual waiving of some articles of personal belief for the sake of securing united and effective action upon others which are avowed as the common creed; and the bond of union can hardly be said to be kept in good faith when individuals of a party propound as tests to a candidate questions which were not acted upon by the convention, especially when such questions were notoriously excluded from the list of those upon which community of belief was demanded, because the opinions of loyal and patriotic men had not yet fully ripened or taken definite form in regard to them, and the time had not come when, in the "logic of events," it was necessary to act upon them. In the political phase of the great conflict we have upon us, as in the military strife which has just ended, organization will be found to be of the first importance, and though guerilla warfare has its attractions, I am well convinced that results will be determined by the surer if slower march of the heavy columns.

I have always believed that adherence to a party platform does not exclude freedom of opinion or of discussion upon matters not included in it, though it does imply that such discussion should be a free and friendly interchange of views with the object of throwing all possible light upon subjects which may sooner or later become topics of importance, and upon which we may have to form a definite policy. When the time comes for action, all thoroughly loyal men should agree to support that policy which the wisdom of the majority may agree upon, unless it shall conflict with some principle conscientiously held; in which case those who so dissent have the undoubted right to withdraw their connection, not from a candidate simply, but from the party.—This view of political organization is the only one I have been able to find, which will secure proper unity and power of action, and at the same time afford full scope for true progress of opinion and that liberty of individual thought which, I beg you to remember, is as much the right of candidates as of those who nominate them.

Our Convention adopted a platform, of which the doctrinal part is substantially embodied in two propositions: 1st. "That slavery and its institutions are irreconcilably opposed to freedom and free institutions," and must be finally and completely eradicated; 2d. That President Johnson's policy of re-construction is "indorsed," with the proviso that the completed restoration of the rebel States "shall be at such time and upon such terms as will give unquestioned assurance of the peace and security not only of the loyal people of the rebel States, but also of the peace and prosperity of the Federal Union."

The spirit and disposition which should control us in determining the "time and terms" of reconstruction, and all other questions of policy accumulating upon us, were likewise stated in two resolutions, one, urging the example of our martyred President "in waiting for the solution of difficulties to be furnished by the progress of time and logic of events;" the other declaring the necessity "of keeping steadily in view the great principles of our government as set forth in the Declaration of Independence."

To condense still more, the essence of the position of the party may be said to be, the determination of the political results of the war by the united and harmonious action of truly loyal men, actuated by a spirit at once cautious and controlled by an earnest belief in the broadest doctrines of human rights.

To those principles I have given my public and sincere adhesion. You are the only members of the Union party of the State whom I have found impatient to commit your brethren in advance of the meeting of Congress to a definite policy upon a subject upon which the Convention had by strongest implication declared it premature to decide what course ought to be taken. The State election decides no such issues; the progress of events in the South will probably throw increased light upon all such questions; yet you insist that I shall give you my views, not for the purpose of mutual assistance in arriving at a solution of a difficulty, but under notice that the votes of your people will be determined for or against me by my answer. I think that in so doing you wrong both yourselves and the members of the whole political organization to which we belong, and to which you gave pledge of cordial co-operation upon the platform as adopted, through your delegates who were present at the Convention.

For myself, I have no secrets as to my opinions, and have never hesitated to declare them on proper occasions. So far have I been from desiring to conceal them, that I had sent, before the receipt of your letter, a private note to Professor Ellis, of your place, indicating my plan for the final solution of the problem of reconstruction, and seeking his criticisms upon it. No restrictions were placed upon him in making it known, except such as his own discretion and friendship might impose. You are misinformed as to my having requested my views to be published at my home or elsewhere. You must act upon your own responsibility in determining what publicity you shall give to this. The importance to our country of determining rightly the grave questions which must probably be settled within the coming year, is too great to make me willing to omit using whatever influence or information I may have in assisting at the solution. Whether in public or in private life, I shall freely give the results of my experience and observation in the South during the war, and the conclusions to which my study of both races has led me. I shall expect the facts that I have been an anti-slavery man from my youth up, that I assisted at the original organization of the Republican party, and acted with it and the Union party ever since, and that I have been a federal soldier from the surrender of Sumter to the surrender of the last armed rebel, will secure me a candid and even a friendly hearing from all who have loved the country and earnestly taken its part in the late terrible struggle. If other views than mine prevail, I shall hold it my duty to act cheerfully and promptly with the body of loyal men, believing that the best solution which they can give will be the best attainable, and that to divide from them will be to deliver the Government into the hands of its enemies.

I believe that the President is earnestly determined to seek the good of the whole country and of all the races in it: that he has full claim to that confidence which we declared that we reposed in him; and that what we as Union men cannot succeed in doing in harmony and co-operation with him and his administration, we shall fail of doing altogether. My support of him, therefore, will be no half-hearted support, but a zealous and thoroughly hearty co-operation, with no ulterior purpose or thought of separation on issues likely to arise. It is by the cordial harmony of Mr. Johnson and the Union members of Congress that the country is to be carried safely through its present perils; and division between them would place us in imminent danger of shipwreck. We may have diverse opinions as to the true solution of this knotty problem of reconstruction, and during the proper period for discussion we may and ought to discuss them with candor; with fullness, and with a tolerant spirit, but when this is done and the time for action arrives, it will be the business of Congress and the Executive *to agree* upon the plan to be adopted, and that which is in the manner honestly determined by devotedly Union men, I shall believe, as I have before said, to be the best attainable result, whether it agree with my views or not. In short, I believe that under no circumstances should we risk the transfer of the power of this Government to the hands of those who have been disloyal during the war, by any divisions among ourselves, until all the questions which grow out of the war are permanently and finally decided.

Having thus stated what I think is the true doctrine of political organization, and indicated the great danger of losing all for which we have been striving by such divisions as those at which you hint, I am now prepared to state my private views upon reconstruction, and the claim of the freedmen to political privileges in the Southern States, leaving to you the responsibility of your action in regard thereto.

I presume we shall agree in regarding the four general principles asserted in the "Faneuil Hall Address" as those which should guide the determination of our relations to both whites and blacks in the rebel States. That there may be no mistake in reference to this, I quote them:

"First. The principle must be put beyond all question, that the Republic has a direct claim upon the allegiance of every citizen, from which no State can absolve him, and to his obedience to the laws of the Republic, any thing in the constitution or laws of any State to the contrary notwithstanding.

"Second. The public faith is pledged to every person of color in the rebel States, to secure to them and to their posterity forever, a complete and veritable freedom. Having provided them this freedom, secured their aid on the faith of this promise, and by a successful war and actual military occupation of the country, having obtained the power to secure the result, we are dishonored, if we fail to make it good to them.

"Third. The system of slavery must be abolished and prohibited by paramount and irreversible law. Throughout the rebel States there must be, in the words of Webster, 'impressed upon the soil itself an inability to bear up any but free men.'

"Fourth. The systems of the States must be truly republican."

The application made of the last principle in the address, I do not regard as sound, but I shall perhaps agree more fully with you, than you do with the address, when I assert that in a republican community political privileges of any kind can never be rightly or safely based upon hereditary caste.

How then, it will naturally be asked, can there be any practical difference between us as to the mode of carrying out these principles? It is found in the views we take of the mutual relations of the two races in the South. You, judging from this distance, say "Deliver the four millions of freed people into the hands of their former oppressors, now embittered by their defeat, and they will make their condition worse than before." I, starting from the same principles, and after four years of close and thoughtful observation of the races where they are, say I am unwillingly forced to the conviction that the effect of the war has not been simply to "embitter" their relations, but to develop a rooted antagonism which makes their permanent fusion in one political community an absolute impossibility. The sole difference between us then is in the *degree* of hostility we find existing between the races, and its probable permanence. You assume that the extension of the right of suffrage to the blacks, *leaving them intermixed with the whites,* will cure all the trouble. I believe that it would rather be like the decisions in that outer darkness of which Milton speaks, where

> "Chaos umpire sits,
> And by decision more embroils the fray."

Yet, as I affirm with you, that the right to life and liberty are inalienable, and more than admit the danger of leaving a laboring class at the entire mercy of those who formerly owned them as slaves, you will say I am bound to furnish some solution of the problem which shall not deny the right or incur the peril. So I am, and the only real solution which I can see is the peaceable separation of the races. But, you will reply, foreign colonization will break down hopelessly under the very vastness of the labor, even if it were not tyrannical to expel these unfortunate people from the land of their birth. I grant the full weight of the objection, and therefore say the solution is thus narrowed down to a *peaceable separation of the races on the soil where they now are.*

The essential point in the discussion thus appears to be the actual relations of the two races in the Southern States as a question of fact, and the probable future consequences of those relations as a question of theory.

Upon the question of fact I think I may with all modesty claim that my antecedents and my opportunities of observation entitle my testimony to have some weight, even with the most radical anti-slavery men of the North.

The antagonism of which I have spoken is not entirely one-sided. On the part of the former master it takes the form of an indomitable pride, which utterly refuses to entertain the idea of political or social equality, mingled with a hatred intensified by the circumstances and the results of the war. This feeling is not confined to the slave-owners alone, but the poor whites share it fully, and often show it more passionately.

On the part of the freedmen, it is manifested in an utter distrust of the dominant race, and an enmity which, although made by circumstances more passive and less openly manifested, is as real and implacable as the other. They have the mutual attraction of race among themselves, and repulsion of the whites as another people, developed to a degree which surprised me. It is not as individuals of a nation common to us all, that they speak of themselves, but, to use the language of one of them, speaking to myself, they feel that they "have long been an oppressed and down-trodden *people.*"

Hildreth, in his *Despotism in America,* declared slavery to be in itself a state of war, and this character is indelibly impressed upon both races in the South. The captive learns duplicity toward his captor, and in the slave it has become a marked characteristic. It is a fair stratagem for which he feels no guilt. I have seen a master boasting of the fidelity of his servant, and discussing the subject of slavery in his presence, whilst the negro waited upon him, with an impassive humility which would make you believe no intelligent idea of freedom had ever penetrated his brain.—Yet I have seen that same negro afterward in camp, transformed into a clear-headed ally of our troops, leading them to his master's buried stores, or guiding them to the flanks of the enemy's lines, with an intelligence and steadiness of purpose which left no doubt as to his understanding of the conflict between himself and his master.

The daily and hourly repetition of proofs of this fact, many of them too subtle for description, but none the less convincing to the observer, has fully convinced me that never between Norman and Saxon, nor between Gaul and Frank, was there a more conscious hatred, or an antagonism more likely to prove inveterate, than between black and white on our Southern soil. The negroes will have no sense of security nor faith in their former masters, even if they offer them political rights; they will fear them as *Danaos dona ferentes.*

What does history teach us in regard to the permanence and durability of such prejudices and enmities of race? Speaking on this subject, Augustin Thierry, in his *History of the Norman Conquest,* says: "Whatever degree of territorial unity the great modern States of Europe may appear to have attained, whatever may be the community of manners, language, and public feeling which the habit of living under the same government and in the same stage of civilization has introduced among the inhabitants of each of those States, there is scarcely one of them which does not even now present living traces of the diversity of the races of men, which in course of time have come together in it. This variety shows itself under different aspects, with features more or less marked. Sometimes it is a complete separation of idioms, of local traditions, of political sentiments, and a sort of instinctive enmity distinguishing from the great national mass the population of a few small districts; and sometimes a mere difference of dialect or even of accent, marks, though more feebly, the limit of the settlements of races of men, once thoroughly distinct, and hostile to each other."

If fifteen centuries of common government and political union have not been able to obliterate the distinctions and even the "instinctive enmity" of races which were physiologically similar, what encouragement have we that success will attend a forced political fusion of bitterly hostile races from the antipodes of the human family?

The process by which even the comparative unity of the English people was achieved, is described by the same philosophic historian, whom I have quoted, near the close of his great work, as a "complete amalgamation" of the Norman and Saxon idioms, and a "mixture of the two races," which it took four centuries of sanguinary war to accomplish.

Just stepping as we are from the battlefield on which descendants of a common ancestry, so little removed from us that we can literally reach back our hands to grasp those of our common sires, have waged the most tremendous and terrible of modern wars, it does not become us to argue that peaceful discussion will quietly settle differences which in former times were settled by the sword; but the memory of the almost present as well as of the remote past calls upon us to build our polity solidly upon principles which experience as well as reason prove to be durable, and more than ever to avoid deluding ourselves with the cry of "peace, peace, when there is no peace!"

As, during these weary years of war, I have pondered this problem in the intervals of strife or by the camp fire at night, I have been more and more impelled to the belief that the only basis of permanent nationality is to be found in complete homogeneity of people, of manners, and of laws. The rapid fusion of the races of western Europe as they have met upon our shores has secured the former of these requisites, and the Yankee race (I adopt the epithet as an honorable one), marked as it is with salient characteristics, is so complete an amalgamation of all families from the eastern boundary of Germany to the western coast of Ireland, that there are few of us in whose veins are not mixed the blood of several. But this unhappy race of which we are speaking does not amalgamate with the rest. It is entirely immaterial to discuss why it is so; the fact no one can deny; nor can it be denied that its salvation or its destruction will surely be worked out in its family isolation.

Because there could be no real unity of people between the Southern whites and Southern blacks, it seems manifest to me that there could be no political unity, but rather a strife for the mastery, in which the one or the other would go to the wall.

The struggle for supremacy would be direct and immediate, and I see no hope whatever that the weaker race would not be reduced to hopeless subjection, or utterly destroyed. There is no reason to suppose that Missouri border-ruffianism could never be repeated on new fields, and the strife once inaugurated, the merciless war would continue as long as the obnoxious race had an existence. You have expressed your anticipation of such a result in one state of the case, how is it that you do not see that a direct struggle for power at the ballotbox would make the contest more deadly?

I hold that there is great philosophic truth in the words of

Guizot, in summing up the eight centuries of bloodshed out of which the French emerged into nationality from the strife of petty races and tribes. He says, "In the life of nations, that union which is exterior and visible, the unity of name and of government, although important, is by no means the first in importance, the most real, or that which makes indeed one nation. There is a unity which is deeper and more powerful: it is that which results not merely from identity of government and of destiny, but from the homogeneity of social elements, from the likeness of institutions, of manners, of ideas, of tastes, of tongues; the unity which resides in *the men themselves whom society assembles, and not in the forms of their associations;* in short, that moral unity (*l'unite morale*) which is far more important than political unity, and *which is the only solid foundation for the latter.*"

I have watched with deep interest the educational effect of the war upon our own army, and I assure you that while our white soldiers have uniformly and quickly learned to appreciate the fact that the existence of our free government could only be preserved by the destruction of the system of slavery, and so became radically and thoroughly anti-slavery, the tendency of battling for the old flag was almost equally uniform in increasing and deepening their pride of race. The fact is one which cannot safely be overlooked in any calculation involving their action upon the political problems before the country, and it is one in regard to which I think I can hardly be mistaken.

The details of any system of separation could only be determined by careful study and a wide comparison of views. Suppose, however, that without breaking up the organization of any State, you take contiguous territory in South Carolina, Georgia, Alabama, and Florida, and there, under the sovereignty of the United States, and with all the facilities which the power and wealth of the Government can give, we organize the freedmen in a dependency of the Union analogous to the western territories. Give them schools, laws facilitating the acquirement of homesteads to be paid for by their own labor, full and exclusive political privileges, aided at the start, should it seem necessary, by wise selection from the largest brains and most philanthropic hearts among anti-slavery men, to give them a judiciary or executive which would command their confidence in the first essays of political existence. There need be no coercive collection of the colored race in the designated region, the majority are there now, and the reward of political power would draw thither the remainder quite as rapidly as their place could be supplied by white immigration into other States. The forts and seaport cities could remain under the direct control of the Federal Government as the basis for that common trade and intercourse with other parts of the country and the world, which would be necessary. The fullest opportunity to develop the highest civilization they are capable of, would there be given. Colored men of talent and intelligence would not then make a vain struggle for the empty name of being lawyers without briefs, or merchants without trade, but would have what a leading journal at the East has frequently demanded for them, the opportunity, as well as the right, to take rank according to their real character and ability.

That there are difficulties in the realization of such a plan I shall be the first to admit, but there are difficulties in all plans. It is natural to men to struggle to avoid responsibility, and to drift upon the current trusting to fate; but drifting also leads to difficulties, as we who drifted into war which has cost half a million of lives and untold millions of money, should not need to be told; and I agree with you that drifting will probably decide this matter against the black race, and involve its destruction, while by leaving the labor of the South in the hands of a degraded caste, it entails upon the country the worst material effects of slavery, and prevents that homogeneity of institutions and manners, North and South, which I have said I believe to be the only sure foundation of permanent peace.

The Anglo-American and Africo-American races now stand face to face upon the Southern soil in irreconcilable hostility.—The few colored men whom we have amongst us, may be regarded as the waifs and strays of the great body which is a nation in numbers, and in its isolation by mental and physical characteristics. It is as a unit that we must deal with them, and no paltering with the edges of the difficulty will avert the doom which all history teaches us will follow a wrong solution.

The magnitude of the problem is immense, but the principles which must decide it one way or the other are simple. When we deal with a whole community, however closely related to ourselves, it is not by the application of the maxims of municipal law as applied to individuals that we must decide the case, but by a modified form of international law, which so far from ignoring our responsibility to God our common ruler, or the obligation to recognize the fundamental rights of men, necessarily implies them all. Religion, honor, humanity, republicanism, all call upon us to see well to it that we do not allow the seething and molten elements to crystalize into a new form of oppression, and I recognize as fully as you possibly can the burden of responsibility which this great epoch in the world's history rolls upon all who have even the humblest part in determining the shape of public policy.

I have approached the subject as an anti-slavery man. I have thought as deeply as I was capable of, and have carefully revised my opinions and tested them by all the fundamental principles of right and justice. If others do not agree with me, and it part me from any whose principles and motives are the same as my own, my deep regret that it should be so cannot change my convictions.

It has seemed to me that the solution I have offered rids us of most of the difficulties in our way. It gives to the black man political rights and franchises without onerous terms; it reduces the representation of the Southern whites in Congress to a proper basis, their own numbers; it secures the permanent peace of the Government and the allegiance of the people by the only sure guaranty, viz: that of common interest and identity of institutions. What more would you have?

It is worth while to consider that in such a plan as I have suggested there is that which is likely to attract co-operation on the part of reflecting men in the Southern States. There can be no question that some portion of the sectional bitterness which finally led them to secession and war, was caused by a more or less distinct perception of difficulties like these we are considering, from which they saw no reasonable outlet, and that any plan which recognizes the facts I have stated and endeavors to provide for them so as to secure harmony and prosperity in the South, will soon find advocates there. I do not mention this as an important argument, because I fully accept the responsibility which the military subjugation of the rebel territory has imposed upon us to determine the matter by the counsels and the action of those who have been truly loyal, and not by those of the disloyal of either section. We must, however, remember that the ultimate object we aim at must be to return the people of the South to their relations to the Federal Government as equal and full participators in its rights and blessings. Through what delays or intermediate steps, their own action under the experimental organization granted by the President must determine. But in the end, the genius of our institutions will tolerate no unequal or sectional laws. The homogeneity must be made perfect and complete, for neither subject provinces nor military pro-consulships can long co-exist with Republican Government.

Such are my personal opinions upon the subjects you have called to my attention. For them, I alone am responsible. The subjects themselves can in no sense be matter for executive action in this State, and whether I am elected or defeated, my opinions will have only such weight or influence as their own value will entitle them to. As they will not hinder me from giving cordial support to the action of a loyal Federal Government, if other views shall finally prevail, I have thought they ought not to be made a ground of opposition in the State canvass; but such as they are, they are the product of my honest thinking, and in view of the real importance of the subject, I would not conceal them to receive an election as unanimous as the nomination with which the Convention honored me.

Very Respectfully
Your obedient servant,
J. D. COX.

Messrs. E. H. Fairchild,
Samuel Plumb,
Committee, &c., Oberlin, Ohio.

Waving the Bloody Shirt

RUTHERFORD B. HAYES

The leaders of the peace Democracy were for a time over-whelmed by the popular uprising which followed the attack on Fort Sumter, and were not able during the year 1861 or the early part of 1862 to mark out definitely the course to be pursued. But, like the Union party, they gradually approached the position they were ultimately to occupy.

Their success in the autumn elections of 1862 encouraged them to enter upon the pathway in which they have plodded along consistently if not prosperously ever since. Opposition to the war measures of Mr. Lincoln's Administration, and in particular to every measure tending to the enfranchisement and elevation of the African race, became their settled policy. By this policy they were placed in harmony with their former associates, the Rebels of the South. The Rebels were fighting to destroy the Union. The peace party were opposing the only measures which could save it. The Rebels were fighting for slavery. The peace party were laboring in their way to

From a speech of Rutherford B. Hayes, in Charles Richard Williams, *The Life of Rutherford Birchard Hayes*, Vol. 1, (Boston, 1914), pp. 293-320.

keep alive and inflame the prejudice against race and color, on which slavery was based.

· ·

Now came the work of reconstruction. The leaders of the peace Democracy, who had failed in every measure, in every plan, in every opinion, and in every prediction relating to the war, were promptly on hand, and with unblushing cheek were prepared to take exclusive charge of the whole business of reorganization and reconstruction. They had a plan all prepared—a plan easily understood, easily executed, and which they averred would be satisfactory to all parties. Their plan was in perfect harmony with the conduct and history of its authors and friends during the war. They had been in very close sympathy with the men engaged in the Rebellion, while their sympathy for loyal white people at the South was not strong, and they were bitterly hostile to loyal colored people both North and South. Their plan was consistent with all this.

According to it, the Rebels were to be treated in the same manner as if they had remained loyal. All laws, state and national, all orders and regulations of the military, naval, and other departments of the Government, creating disabilities on account of participation in the Rebellion, were to be repealed, revoked, or abolished. The rebellious States were to be represented in Congress by the Rebels without hindrance from any test oath. All appointments in the army, in the navy, and in the civil service were to be made from men who were Rebels, on the same terms as from men who were loyal. The people and Governments in the rebellious States were to be subjected to no other interference or control from the military or other departments of the general Government than exists in the States which remained loyal. Loyal white men and loyal colored men were to be protected alone in those States by state laws, executed by state authorities, as if they were in the loyal States.

There were to be no amendments to the Constitution, not even an amendment abolishing slavery. In short, the great Rebellion was to be ignored or forgotten, or, in the words of one of their orators, "to be generously forgiven." The war, whose burdens, cost, and carnage they had been so fond of exaggerating, suddenly sank into what the Reverend Petroleum V. Nasby calls "the late unpleasantness," for which nobody *but the abolitionists were to blame.*

· ·

But the loyal people, who under the name of the Union party fought successfully through the War of the Rebellion, objected to this plan as wrong in principle, wrong in its details, and fatally wrong as an example for the future. It treats treason as no crime and loyalty as no virtue; it contains no guaranties, irreversible or otherwise, against another rebellion by the same parties and on the same grounds. It restores to political honor and power in the Government of the nation men who have spent the best part of their lives in plotting the overthrow of that Government, and who for more than four years levied public war against the United States; it allows Union men in the South, who have risked all,—and many of whom have lost all but life in upholding the Union cause,—to be excluded from every office, state and national, and in many instances to be banished from the States they so faithfully labored to save; it abandons the four millions of colored people to such treatment as the ruffian class of the South, educated in the barbarism of slavery and the atrocities of the Rebellion, may choose to give them; it leaves the obligation of the nation to her creditors and to the maimed soldiers and to the widows and orphans of the war, to be fulfilled by men who hate the cause in which those obligations were incurred; it claims to be a plan which restores the Union without requiring conditions; but, in conceding to the conquered Rebels the repeal of laws important to the nation's welfare, it grants conditions which they demand, while it denies to the loyal victors conditions which they deem of priceless value.

. . . .

Enough have been given to show how completely and how exactly the Reconstruction Acts have met the evil to be remedied in the South. My friend, Mr. Hassaurek, in his admirable speech at Columbus, did not estimate too highly the fruits of these measures. Said he:—

"And, sir, this remedy at once effected the desired cure. The poor contraband is no longer the persecuted outlaw whom incurable Rebels might kick and kill with impunity; but he at once became 'our colored fellow citizen,' in whose well-being his former master takes the liveliest interest. Thus, by bringing the negro under the American system, we have completed his emancipation. He has ceased to be a pariah. From an outcast he has been transformed into a human being, invested with the great national attribute of self-protection, and the reëstablishment of peace, and order, and security, the revival of business and trade, and the restoration of the Southern States on the basis of loyalty and equal justice to all, will be the happy results of this astonishing metamorphosis, provided the party which has inaugurated this policy remains in power to carry it out."

The peace Democracy generally throughout the North oppose this measure. In Ohio they oppose it especially because it commits the people of the nation in favor of manhood suffrage. They tell us that if it is wise and just to entrust the ballot to colored men in the District of Columbia, in the Territories, and in the Rebel States, it is also just and wise that they should have it in Ohio and in the other States of the North.

Union men do not question this reasoning, but if it is urged as an objection to the plan of Congress, we reply: "There are now within the limits of the United States about five millions of colored people. They are not aliens or strangers. They are here not by the choice of themselves or of their ancestors. They are here by the misfortune of their fathers and the crime of ours. Their labor, privations, and sufferings, unpaid and unrequited, have cleared and redeemed one third of the inhabited territory of the Union. Their toil has added to the resources and wealth of the nation untold millions. Whether we prefer it or not, they are our countrymen, and will remain so forever."

They are more than countrymen—they are citizens. Free colored people were citizens of the Colonies. The Constitution of the United States, formed by our fathers, created no disabilities on account of color. By the acts of our fathers and of ourselves, they bear equally the burdens and are required to discharge the highest duties of citizens. They are compelled to pay taxes and to bear arms. They fought side by side with their white countrymen in the great struggle for independence, and in the recent war for the Union.

. . . .

Slaves were never voters. It was bad enough that our fathers, for the sake of Union, were compelled to allow masters to reckon three fifths of their slaves for representation, without adding slave suffrage to the other privileges of the slaveholder. But free colored men were always voters in many of the Colonies, and in several of the States, North and South, after independence was achieved. They voted for members of the Congress which declared independence, and for members of every Congress prior to the adoption of the Federal Constitution; for the members of the convention which framed the Constitution; for the members of many of the state conventions which ratified it, and for every President from Washington to Lincoln.

Our government has been called the white man's government. Not so. It is not the government of any class, or sect, or nationality, or race. It is a government founded on the consent of the governed, and Mr. Broomall, of Pennsylvania, therefore properly calls it "the government of the governed." It is not the government of the native-born, or of the foreign-born, of the rich man, or of the poor man, of the white man, or of the colored man—it is the government of the freeman. And when colored men were made citizens, soldiers, and freemen, by our consent and votes, we were estopped from denying to them the right of suffrage.

In Ohio the leaders of the peace Democracy intend to carry on one more campaign on the old and rotten platform of prejudice against colored people. They seek in this way to divert attention from the record they made during the War of the Rebellion. But the great facts of our recent history are against them. The principles of the fathers, reason, religion, and the spirit of the age are against them.

The plain and monstrous inconsistency and injustice of excluding one seventh of our population from all participation in a Government founded on the consent of the governed in this land of free discussion is simply impossible. No such absurdity and wrong can be permanent. Impartial suffrage will carry the day. No low prejudice will long be able to induce American citizens to deny to a weak people their best means of self-protection for the unmanly reason that they are weak. Chief Justice Chase expressed the true sentiment when he said, "The American nation cannot afford to do the smallest injustice to the humblest and feeblest of her children."

Much has been said of the antagonism which exists between the different races of men. But difference of religion, difference of nationality, difference of language, and difference of rank and privileges are quite as fruitful causes of antagonism and war as difference of race. The bitter strifes between Christians and Jews, between Catholics and Protestants, between Englishmen and Irishmen, between aristocracy and the masses are only too familiar. What causes increase and aggravate these antagonisms, and what are the measures which diminish and prevent them, ought to be equally familiar. Under the partial and unjust laws of the nations of the Old World men of one nationality were allowed to oppress those of another; men of one faith had rights which were denied to men of a different faith; men of one rank or caste enjoyed special privileges which were not granted to men of another. Under these systems peace was impossible and strife perpetual. But under just and equal laws in the United States, Jews, Protestants, and Catholics, Englishmen and Irishmen, the former aristocrat and the masses of the people, dwell and mingle harmoniously together. The uniform lesson of history is that unjust and partial laws increase and create antagonism, while justice and equality are the sure foundation of prosperity and peace.

Impartial suffrage secures also popular education. Nothing has given the careful observer of events in the South more gratification than the progress which is there going on in the establishment of schools. The colored people, who as slaves were debarred from education, regard the right to learn as one of the highest privileges of freemen. The ballot gives them the power to secure that privilege. All parties and all public men in the South agree that, if colored men vote, ample provision must be made in the reorganization of every State for free schools. The ignorance of the masses, whites as well as blacks, is one of the most discouraging features of Southern society. If congressional reconstruction succeeds, there will be free schools for all. The colored people will see that their children attend them. We need indulge in no fears that the white people will be left behind. Impartial suffrage, then, means popular intelligence; it means progress; it means loyalty; it means harmony between the North and the South, and between the whites and the colored people.

Against Radical Reconstruction

DEMOCRATIC PARTY

Resolutions

The nominations having been completed, the report of the Committee on Resolutions was called for.

Mr. Vallandigham came forward as Chairman of that Committee, to report, and was received with tremendous shouts and yells, showing, as remarked by a bystander, "which way the wind blows." It was some time before Mr. V. was allowed to proceed, by reason of the clamor. At length, order was restored, and Mr. V. remarked that the resolutions he was instructed to report, were somewhat lengthy, but he could say they were truly Democratic, and contained good reading. (Applause) He then read the resolutions, as follows:

The Platform

Resolved, That the Democracy of Ohio steadfastly adheres to the principles of the party as expounded by the Fathers and approved by experience. That, in accordance with these principles, we declare, that the Federal Government is a Government of limited powers;

From *Ohio State Journal,* **January 9, 1867.**

that it possesses no powers but such as are expressly, or by necessary implication, delegated to it in the Federal Constitution; that all other powers are reserved to the States or the people respectively; that a strict construction of the Constitution is indispensable to the preservation of the reserved rights of the States and the people; that all grants of power to governments, whether State or Federal, should be strictly construed, because all such grants abridge the natural rights of men; that the preservation of the equality and rights of the States and the rights of the people is necessary to the preservation of the Union; that the Federal Government is unfitted to legislate for or administer the local concerns of the States; that it would be monstrous that the local affairs of Ohio should be regulated by a Federal Congress in which she has but two Senators, and the New England States with but a little greater population, have twelve; that the tendency of Federal administration is to usurp the reserved rights of the States and of the people, and that, therefore, a centralization of power in its hands is an ever impending danger; that such an absorption of power would, while it lasted, be destructive of the liberties and interests of the people, and would end either in despotism or a disruption of the Union; that a national debt, besides impoverishing the people, fosters an undue increase of the powers of the Federal Government; that high protective tariffs have a like effect, sacrificing the interests of the many for the emolument of the few, and plainly violating the equity and spirit of the Constitution; that the collection and disbursement of enormous revenues by the Federal Government have the same tendency, besides corrupting the government, and that therefore economy is essential, not only to the prosperity, but also to the liberties of the people; that unequal taxation is a plain violation of justice, of which no government can safely be guilty; that to each State belongs the right to determine the qualifications of its electors, and all attempts to impair this right, either by congressional legislation or constitutional amendments, are unwise and despotic; that the tendency of power is to steal from the many to the few and that, therefore, eternal vigilance is the price of liberty; that the tendency of government is to enlarge its authority by usurpation, and therefore government needs to be watched; that another of its tendencies is to govern too much, unnecessarily and vexatiously interfering with the business and habits of the people; that freedom of speech and of the press are essential to the existence of liberty; that no person not in the military or naval service, or where the civil courts are prevented by war or insurrection from exercising their functions, can lawfully be deprived of life, liberty or property without due process of civil law; that the courts should always be open for the redress of grievances; that no *ex post facto* law should ever be made; that in the language of the Supreme Court "the

Constitution of the United States is a law for rulers and people equally in war and in peace, and covers with the shield of its protection all classes of men at all times and under all circumstances. No doctrine involving more pernicious consequences was ever invented by the wit of man than that any of its provisions can be suspended during any of the great exigencies of Governments; such a doctrine leads directly to anarchy or despotism; "that the right of the people to peaceably assemble and consult upon public affairs is inviolable; that the military should be held in due subjection to the civil power; that while the majority, as prescribed by the Constitution, have the right to govern, the minority have indefeasible rights; and that a frequent recurrence to first principles is essential to the safety and welfare of the States and the people.

2. *Resolved,* That the States which lately attempted to secede are still States in the Union, and have been recognized as such by every department of the Government. By President Lincoln who, in the midst of the war, invited them to elect members of Congress. By President Johnson in various proclamations and official acts. By Congress, which permitted Andrew Johnson to set in the Senate as a Senator from Tennessee, by his inauguration as Vice President and President of the Senate, and by the admission of members from Virginia, Tennessee and Louisiana to set in the House of Representatives, after those States had passed their ordinances of secession and while the war was being carried on, and which further recognized them as States in the Union by the Congressional Appointment Act providing for their due representation in Congress; by various tax laws and especially the Direct Tax Act; by the resolutions submitting Amendments to the Constitution for their approval—and by various other acts and resolutions importing the same recognition, all which were passed since the attempted secession of these States. . . . That being thus in the Union, they stand in an equal footing with their sister States—States with unequal rights—a thing unknown to the Constitution. That by the express terms of the Constitution, each State is entitled to have two Senators and a due proportion of Representatives in the Congress and to vote at all elections of President and Vice President. That though these rights are subject to interruption by a state of civil war, they cannot by civil war be extinguished, or in time of peace, be so much even as suspended, without a plain violation of the Constitution! That the assent of three-fourths of all the States, whether represented in Congress or not, is essential to the validity of the Constitutional Amendment. That Congress has no power to deprive a State of its reserved rights and reduce it to a territorial condition. That therefore, the exclusion by the so-called Congress of all representation from ten States, the proposed exclusion of those States from all voice in the next Presi-

dential election, the threatened overthrow of their State Governments, and reduction of those States to the condition of territories, are each and every one of them, unconstitutional, revolutionary and despotic measures, destructive not merely to the rights of those States, but also of the rights of every other State in the Union. That those measures are parts of a plan to nullify the Constitution, virtually overthrow the State Governments, to erect a consolidated despotism on their ruins, and to establish and perpetuate a tyrannical rule of a minority over a majority of the American people. That the people cannot, without a loss of their liberties, posterity and honor, submit to such a result; and we, therefore, in the hope that the warning will be heeded, and the danger to our institutions be peaceably averted, do solemnly warn the advocates of the plan, that it will not be submitted to.

3. *Resolved,* That Congress is not an omnipotent law-making power. That the Constitution provides that no bill shall become a law without the approval of the President, unless it be passed by two-thirds of each House of Congress. That one of the objects of the present so-called Congress in excluding ten States from representation, is to pass bills by a two-thirds vote which, were all the States represented, could not so pass; and thus to virtually abolish the constitutional provision aforesaid. That if this precedent be acquiesced in, there will be nothing to prevent a bare majority of Congress, at any time in the future, from nullifying the constitutional veto of the President and usurping uncontrolled legislative power, by an exclusion of the minority from their seats. That the exclusion of even a single State might give the control, and a pretext for such an exclusion would not be wanting to an unscrupulous and revolutionary party.

4. *Resolved,* That the people, and especially those of the agricultural states, have suffered too long the exactions of high protective tariffs, and, as the representatives of an agricultural and laboring population, we demand that their substance shall no longer be extorted from them in order to fill the pockets of Eastern monopolists.

5. *Resolved,* That unequal taxation is contrary to the first principles of justice and sound policy; and we call upon all Governments, Federal and State, to use all necessary Constitutional means to remedy this evil.

6. *Resolved,* That the Radical majority in the so-called Congress have proved themselves to be in favor of Negro suffrage by forcing it upon the people of the District of Columbia against their almost unanimous wish solemnly expressed at the polls; by forcing it upon the people of all the territories in violation of the Constitution, and by their various devices to coerce the people of the South to adopt

it. That we are opposed to Negro Suffrage, believing that it would be productive of evil to both whites and blacks, and tend to produce a disastrous conflict of races.

7. Resolved, That for all their efforts to uphold the Constitution, we tender to the President and the majority of the judges of the Supreme Court of the United States, our hearty thanks.

8. Resolved, That we are in favor of a Democratic Convention of delegates from all the States, to be held at such time and place as may hereafter be agreed upon. And that the State Central Committee be authorized to concur with other proper committees in fixing the time and place.

New Departure

CLEMENT L. VALLANDIGHAM

After the appointment of delegates to the State Convention, and the transaction of some other business, Mr. Vallandigham, from the Committee on Resolutions, reported the following:—

"Whereas, The Democratic party of 1871 is made up of men who previous to and during the late war, as also for a time since, entertained totally different opinions and supported totally opposite measures as to the questions and issues of those times, and whereas it is reasonable to assume that these same men still entertain, to a large extent, their several opinions, and would, if in like circumstances, support again substantially the same measures; and whereas a rational toleration among men resolved to unite in a present common purpose, does not require a surrender in any particular of former opinions, or any acknowledgment of error as to measures heretofore supported:

"Resolved, BY THE DEMOCRACY OF MONTGOMERY COUNTY,

"1. That agreeing to disagree in all respects as to the past, we cordially unite upon the living issues of the day, and hereby invite all

From James L. Vallandigham, *A Life of Clement L. Vallandigham,* (Baltimore, 1872), pp. 438-442.

men of the Republican party who believe now upon present issues as we believe, to co-operate fully and actively with us upon the basis of perfect equality with every member of the Democratic party.

"2. That waiving all differences of opinion as to the extraordinary means by which they were brought about, we accept the natural and legitimate results of the war so far as waged for its ostensible purpose to maintain the Union and the Constitutional rights and powers of the Federal Government, including the three several amendments *de facto* to the Constitution recently declared adopted, as a settlement in fact of all the issues of the war, and acquiesce in the same as no longer issues before the country.

"3. That thus burying out of sight all that is of the dead past, namely, the right of secession, slavery, inequality before the law, and political inequality; and further, now that reconstruction is complete, and representation within the Union restored to all the States, waiving all question as to the means by which it was accomplished, we demand that the vital and long established rule of *Strict Construction,* as proclaimed by the Democratic fathers, accepted by the statesmen of all parties previous to the war, and embodied in the Tenth Amendment to the Constitution, be vigorously applied now to the Constitution as it is, including the three recent amendments above referred to, and insist that these amendments shall not be held to have in any respect altered or modified the original theory and character of the Federal Government as designed and taught by its founders, and repeatedly in early times, in later times, and at all times, affirmed by the Supreme Court of the United States; but only to have enlarged the powers delegated to it, and to that extent, and no more, to have abridged the reserved rights of the States; and that as thus construed according to these ancient and well established rules, the Democratic party pledges itself to the full, faithful, and absolute execution and enforcement of the Constitution as it now is, so as to secure equal rights to all persons under it, without distinction of race, color, or condition.

"4. That the absolute equality of each and every State, within the Union, is a fundamental principle of the Federal Government, and that no department of that Government has power to expel a State from the Union, or to deprive it, under any pretext whatever, of its equal rights therein, including especially the right of full and complete representation in Congress and in the Electoral colleges.

"5. That we will always cherish and uphold the American system of State and Local Self-Government, for State and local purposes, and a General Government for general purposes only; and are unalterably opposed to all attempts at centralisation and consolidation of power in the hands of the General Government; and the more especially when such attempts are in the form of usurpation by any department of that Government. And further, that we adhere firmly to the principle of maintaining a perfect independence between the co-ordinate departments of that Government, the Legislative, the Executive, and the Judicial; condemning all encroachments by one upon the functions of the others.

"6. That outside of fundamental law, all legislation is in its nature and purposes temporary, and subject to change, modification, or repeal at the will of a majority of the people, expressed through the law-making power; and that the pretence that any Act of Congress, not executed and spent, or any legislative policy of a party, is an absolute finality, is totally inconsistent with the whole theory of republican government; and that it is the unquestionable right of the people of themselves and through their representatives, at each successive election, and in each successive Congress, to judge of what legislation is necessary and proper or appropriate to carry into execution or enforce the constitutional powers, rights, and duties of the Federal Government.

"7. That as an instance of eminently appropriate legislation under the Fourteenth Amendment, in the name of wisdom, justice and republican government, and to secure universal political rights and equality among both the white and the colored people of the United States, to the end that we may have peace at last, we call now, as well on behalf of the North as of the South, upon Congress for a universal amnesty.

"8. That we are in favor of the payment of the public debt at the earliest practicable moment consistent with moderate taxation; and the more effectually to secure and hasten the payment, we demand the strictest honesty and economy in every part of the administration of the Government.

"9. That we are in favor of such revenue reform as will greatly simplify the manner of and reduce the number of officers engaged in collecting and disbursing revenue, and largely diminish the now enormous expense to the Government and annoyance and vexation to the people attending the same; and further, will make the burdens of taxation equal, uniform, and just, and no greater than the necessities of the Government economically administered shall require.

"10. That we are in favor of a searching and adequate reform in the civil service of the Government so as to secure faithfulness, honesty and efficiency in all its branches, and in every officer and appointee connected with it.

"11. That we are in favor of a strictly revenue tariff conformed to the theory and principles of all other just and wise tax laws.

"12. That all taxation ought to be based on wealth instead of population; and that every person should be required to contribute to the support of the Government in proportion to the amount and not with reference to the character of his property.

"13. That specie is the basis of all sound currency, and that true policy requires as speedy a return to that basis as is practicable without distress to the debtor-class of the people.

"14. That there is no necessary or irrepressible conflict between labor and capital; that without capital or consolidated wealth no country can flourish; that capital is entitled to the just and equal protection of the laws, and that all men, whether acting individually or in a corporate capacity, have the right by fair and honest means, and not for the purposes of wrong or oppression, to so use their property as to increase and consolidate it to the utmost extent within their power. But conceding all this, we declare our cordial sympathy and co-operation with the producers and working men of the country who make and move all capital, and who only seek by just and necessary means to protect themselves against the oppressive exactions of capital, and to ameliorate their condition and dignify their calling.

"15. That we are totally and resolutely opposed to the grant of any more of the public lands, the common property of the people of the States, to corporations for railroad or other purposes; holding that these lands ought to be devoted as homesteads to actual settlers, or sold in small quantities to individuals at a price so low as to induce speedy occupation and settlement.

"16. That, holding still to the good old Democratic doctrine of annexation or acquisition of territory, we are yet totally opposed to the scheme of President Grant to acquire San Domingo as a 'job,' and by the means and for the purposes evidently intended, and accept the issue he has tendered in his late message submitting the subject to the decision of the people.

"17. That the Act commonly called the 'Bayonet Bill,' recently passed by Congress, amendatory to the Act of May 31, 1870, and a supplement to the Act of July 14, 1870, each and all intended and so contrived as to interfere with and practically subvert free popular elections in all the States, subjecting them to the absolute control, through the military power whenever called forth, of the President and Commander-in-chief for the time being of the land and naval forces of the United States; and the more recent Act of Congress commonly called the 'Ku-Klux Bill,' extending by its terms to every State, intermeddling with the exclusively local concerns of every State, authorising the President upon the existence of a condition of things to be ascertained and determined by himself and in the exercise of his sole judgment, to suspend the writ of *habeas corpus* in time of peace, and to march the standing army into any State and declare martial law therein at his own mere will and pleasure, thus subverting the entire civil power, legislative, executive, and judicial, of such State, destroying freedom of speech and of the press and the peaceable assembling of the people, and subjecting every person therein to military arrest, trial and execution, were enacted for no other purpose than to complete the centralisation of all power in the hands of the General Government, establish a military despotism, and thus perpetuate the present Administration without regard to the will of the people, and are not only utterly inconsistent with the whole theory and character of the Federal Government and revolutionary and dangerous in their nature, but in direct conflict with the spirit and letter of the Constitution, including the amendments which they pretend to enforce.

"18. That the Radical party of 1871 as now constituted is not the Republican party of the period previous to the war, nor the so-called 'Union party' during the war, and is in no respect entitled to beg the public confidence as such; that it is now only an 'Administration' or 'Grant party,' dating back to March 4, 1869, and to be judged by its record since; and that upon that record, totally hostile to the doctrines and policies herein maintained, and wholly committed to the policies and doctrines herein denounced, it deserves the emphatic condemnation of the people."

Liberal Republicans

J. R. STALLO

At this hour Judge Wm. B. Caldwell, president of the Cincinnati Reunion and Reform association, called the Convention to order, and nominated J. R. Stallo, of Cincinnati, temporary President. Judge Stallo on appearing on the stage, was received with considerable applause. He then delivered the following address:

"While I am profoundly sensible of the honor you have conferred upon me by selecting me as the temporary Chairman of this Convention, I approach the attempt to discharge the duties thus devolved upon me with great diffidence. I very much fear that as reformers who propose to inaugurate the practice of selecting men for the discharge of public trusts with a single regard to their merits, you have made a somewhat unauspicious beginning, for I am sadly deficient in all qualifications, including great physical vigor and thorough familiarity with parliamentary usage and rules, without which it is impossible satisfactorily to preside over your deliberations, even for a brief hour. But I bow to your decision, trusting that there is some promise of success in the honesty of my endeavors. With the purposes for which this Convention has been called, and the circumstances under which we have met, you are all familiar. We are here as independent citizens of the American republic. We have emerged from a conflict which involved the very life of the nation. That conflict is now ended. The nation lives, the old home of our fathers is still the home of the whole American family—of all its children, native and adopted. That home has been beautified and enlarged, but it has not been divided. The Union is unbroken. Wherever, in all the land, an American freeman turns his eye heavenward, he beholds its sacred emblem, the old flag, and there are none but freemen now to behold it. The old aspirations which always arise from the heart to the lips whenever the Union is thought of, *'Esto perpetua,'* is no longer a trembling prayer, but the spirited utterance of an imperishable faith. And now you who have come here from all parts, no longer sections, of our common country, stand here side by side, united in spirit as you are united in interest. There is but one throb now to all your hearts, and but one purpose to all your endeavors. That purpose is to make our country prosperous and great; to secure the freedom, happiness and equal rights of all its citizens; to reform the abuses which have sprung from the long prevalence of mere party sway and from the lawlessness and turbulence involved in the recent semi-revolutionary condition of our civil affairs, and to restore the

---

From *Ohio State Journal*, May 2, 1872.

foundations of constitutional liberty wherever they have been impaired or destroyed. You meet here with a firm resolve to preserve a recollection of so much only of the past as is necessary in order wisely to profit by its lessons, and to consign to oblivion whatever, though it originated in honest impulses, ended in bitterness and anger. You have been arrayed against each other upon questions which the voice of history has answered. You have been divided as by a cloud, which has not only ceased to be fiery, but which has been wholly dispelled. You have been engaged in the trial of issues which have been settled irrevocably and forever. In the clear light of dispassionate reflection you see that the issues left to be decided are issues of to-day, and not of yesterday; that all the problems which present themselves to the American people for present solution, are problems of peace, and that the questions of the future find expression not in the watchwords of camps that have long since been abandoned, or in the slogans of parties that have degenerated into clans, but in the articulate demands resulting from the practical necessities of the hour. Having met here in this spirit and with these convictions, you would not permit me to address you by any old party names. You are no longer Republicans or Democrats. [Great cheering.] You are no longer divided by a diversity of interest or feeling, and you are no longer separated by mutual distrust. The visors are up. The old party masks are off, and you stand face to face, and your faces exhibit the common lineaments of patriotism. The old Democrat, as he looks into the eye of his Republican brother, finds there an inextinguishable love of liberty and an imperishable affection for Union—and these he recognizes as good old Democratic virtues, though things may have been done and may be done now in their name which the true love of liberty and the Union reprobates. The Republican, as he meets the glance of the Democrat, finds there stern resistance to all arbitrary rule, the inflexible purpose stoutly to uphold not only the Constitution, but also its proper limits; and these are good Republican virtues as well, though like all virtues they may degenerate into vices by excess. But we mean now to guard against all excess by tempering the sterner virtues of the old Democrat with the milder virtues of the old Republican. There may be much to regret and something to atone for, but there is nothing now in the soul of any man who has come to this city to attend this Convention, to be distrusted. [Cheers.]

"You are all aware that in another and larger hall in this city there is now, or soon will be, a gathering of other men, who have come here substantially for the same purpose which has brought you to this hall. Like us, they are intent upon restoring the Government to its constitutional foundation. Like us, they propose not only to reform abuses, but to remove the conditions from which these abuses have sprung. Like us, they are about to protest against the perversion of public instrumentalities to private ends. [Cheers] Like us, they propose to search for the natural, immutable laws which govern the growth of industry and the production of wealth, and as far as may be, to see to it that our statutes shall be a simple expression of these laws. Like us, they love the Union and insist upon the preservation of the equal rights of all the citizens of the Republic. But, unlike us, while they concede that there is both community of interest and identity of purpose between Liberal Democrats and Liberal Republicans, and while they themselves harbor no distrust against any one because he chooses to call himself by another name, they fear that there might still be lurking disquietude among them whose sons or brothers lately bore arms in defense of the Union, because of the proposed open fraternity of Republicans with those who do not choose to assume the Republican name. I believe that in this they are mistaken—[Cheers]—that the generous trust of the people is even larger, if possible, than ours. We had hoped to stand by their side on the platform at Industrial Hall, as we already stand on the same platform of principles. But they deem it wiser for the moment not to admit us. While we regret to differ from their judgment in this one matter, we acquiesce in their determination. But we know that as we travel towards the same goal we will very soon find ourselves on the same broad road, [Cheers]; and I hope that before this Convention adjourns you will send them your greeting and inform them that your arms are open, and that we are ready at all times to receive them, whether it be in the inclosure selected by them or on the open ground chosen by us. [Prolonged cheering.] The Liberal Republicans and Liberal Democrats look up to the same stars in the same sky above them, and in these stars is written that as there is now truth there must also be open union between them. [Cheers.]

"And now, thanking you sincerely for the patience with which you have listened to me, I await the further pleasure of this Convention." [Prolonged cheering.]

2 Social Growing Pains

THE PATTERNS OF life changed quickly in Ohio following the Civil War. The agrarian economy no longer dominated: the frontier environment, with its isolated simplicity, vanished with improved transportation, and a rural society reluctantly gave way to urbanization. Inherent in these changes were the problems of the exploitation of both human and natural resources, and critics filled with social consciousness, no matter how unsuccessful at the time, promoted solutions to end human misery and environmental destruction. At the same time, state government took on new aspects as specially appointed boards and commissions researched social ills in order to gather data to assist an often sluggish legislature.

In an age impressed with science and technology, social and political reformers speedily turned to the scientific method to help solve problems that faced people in Ohio and across the nation. James A. Garfield, for example, while no spokesman for the scientific community, was a well-educated man of the nineteenth century. As a member of the national House of Representatives he recognized the need to identify problems facing society and to gather data for solutions. "A striking analogy exists between the laws that govern the development of societies and masses of men," Garfield suggested, "and those that govern the inorganic world." The future president was not afraid to ask penetrating questions and had faith that science would be used for social predictability. Other concerned persons rebelled against the exploitation of natural resources and began to articulate the relationship between the natural world, man's institutions, and man himself. For example, Edward Orton, a professor at Antioch College and later president of Ohio State University, defined the interrelationship between the natural resources and the quality of man's life as early as 1871. He called for positive legislative action to save the environment and to protect man against himself. In 1887, T. Clarke Miller, president of the state board of health, pleaded for "greater vigilance and energy in protecting our streams from pollution." Although an antipollution measure to protect the state's rivers passed the lower house of the general assembly in 1886, it was not until April 1908 that the first antipollution bill was accepted by the state legislature.

While conservationists chipped away at the continued destruction of the natural world, civil reformers lashed out at the exploitation of their fellow man. A particular target was the state's penal system, which, as urbanization and industrialization grew, was strained beyond its useful limits. Conditions in the state, county, and municipal jails were primitive and harsh, and the system's procedural methods were crude. The penal system was basically paid for by the prisoners themselves and was used more to provide revenue for the state than to rehabilitate wayward citizens. Prison labor was contracted to the highest bidder: in Columbus, for example, state prisoners labored for saddlemakers, agriculture implement manufacturers, stonecutters, and carpenters for forty to sixty cents a day.

Along with the move toward penal reform, there was a concern for the less fortunate in the state, those who were not only considered paupers but also thousands who were orphaned, blind, deaf, or suffered from any of a myriad of mental disorders. Following the example set in Massachusetts, Ohio in 1867 became the second state to establish a board of public charities with the responsibility of examining the conditions of individuals who were the wards of local government. Through unselfish labor and a persistent dedication to learning the truth, the members of this board described conditions in state-run institutions at all levels. Although nineteenth-century Ohioans apparently were more concerned with personal rather than societal improvements, the evidence was gathered and the foundation established for reform legislation in the next century.

Government in a newly industrialized and urbanized society encountered problems that were almost inconceivable to the politicians of an earlier generation. Because of the magnitude of these problems, the politicians turned to special boards or commissions to gather information and to suggest corrective or regulatory legislation. During the second half of the nineteenth century, for example, the legislature created the Bureau of Labor Statistics, the Ohio State Board of Health, the Forestry Bureau, the Commissioners of Fisheries, and the Ohio Inspector of Workshops and Factories. The work of these agencies, while not always fruitful, certainly propagandized the need for reform to an unconvinced public. Thus, while the generations following the Civil War were concerned with industrial development based on the exploitation of natural and human resources, the period was not without its critics. Faith in the age of science and all the miracles it brought to relieve human suffering was used to find solutions to the problems inherent in the new age. State government was to play a positive role. Yet, while the groundwork for reform was laid during the second half of the nineteenth century, the fruits were reserved for another time.

Population Growth

JAMES A. GARFIELD

Washington, D. C., December 25th, 1871.
Gen. Isaac R. Sherwood, Secretary of State:
Dear Sir:—

I rejoice that Ohio has had done so much in the past, and is still doing so much to ascertain those statistical facts which exhibit the material and social prosperity of her people. The information which your office collects, under the provisions of State laws, and the additional information which the late National Census affords, in regard to Ohio, will throw new and important light upon many subjects of the deepest interest to our people.

. . . .

It should constantly be borne in mind that the increase of population in the United States is exceptional, and stands almost alone in the history of the growth of modern nations. The normal law doubtless is, that all populations tend to become stationary. There are conditions which limit a continual increase, on the one hand, or a continual decrease on the other, and, though in the same country, oscillations are frequently observed, above and below the point of stability, yet there are forces which constantly resist any long continued movement in either direction.

. . . .

In striking contrast with the condition of all the populations of Europe is the development of population in the United States. Hitherto the vast spaces of our unoccupied territory have been opening ever new and varied fields for the expansion and support of our people. Our soil, enriched by the decayed vegetation of unnumbered centuries, has hitherto afforded an almost inexhaustible supply of the means of subsistence. Our population has grown thus far with such marvellous rapidity, because it has not reached those limits where the obstacles to growth are so numerous and formidable as seriously to diminish the ratio of increase.

The number that represents the population of 1870 is nearly 1,000 per cent. of the number that represented that of 1790. During the period from 1790 to 1860 the population three times doubled upon itself. During the five decades preceding the last the increase was very uniform, at about 35 per cent. each decade. The last decade shows a decline in the rate of increase, which was about 22¼ per

From Letter, James A. Garfield to Isaac R. Sherwood, December 25, 1871 in *Statistical Report of the Secretary of State, 1871, Ohio Executive Documents*, (1872), pp. 272-280.

cent. This decrease is, no doubt, due mainly to the direct and indirect effects of the late war; but there are many evidences that the general obstacles to an increase are beginning to be felt. The rich, unoccupied lands of the West are every year becoming less abundant, and the occupied lands are beginning to require from the husbandman a restoration of that first gift of fertility which he can never again enjoy without paying for it in advance. We have no right, therefore, to expect a much longer continuation of the rate of increase which has so long been maintained.

In the older States there is a marked tendency towards a stationary population, and this tendency is not due to emigration alone, but to an actual decrease in the average fecundity of marriages—in the falling off of the birth-rate as compared with the death-rate.

The same tendency, as I will show further on, is manifesting itself in many of the older counties of Ohio, and, indeed, in all of them except those in which some special enterprise has aided to keep up the old rate of increase.

· ·

The Population of Ohio

The rank that Ohio has taken among the States and Territories, in respect to population, may be seen in the following table:

Year.	Rank.	Population.
1800	18	45,365
1810	13	230,760
1820	5	581,295
1830	4	937,903
1840	3	1,519,467
1850	3	1,980,329
1860	3	2,339,511
1870	3	2,665,260

This table exhibits, in a striking manner, the general law according to which population increases. While there has been a marked increase, in each decade, the ratio of increase has been less at each period. The result is manifestly a tendency towards a stationary population.

· ·

Legoyt, the leading statistician of France says:

That "the three great facts of civil life upon which the existence of society rests, are marriages, births and deaths; and the relations which these three bear to each other determine what statisticians call the movement of population." These are, of course, the primary elements of vital statistics; but in the more popular acceptance of the term, "movement of population," immigration and emigration play a most important part.

In all the States of this Union, one or both of these movements constantly appear. In the new States immigration is the chief movement. In the older States the chief movement is emigration.

Ohio has reached a period of development in which these two forces, are almost exactly equal. That is the number of her native population, that Ohio has given to other States and nations, is nearly equal to the number which she has received from other States and nations.

The account may thus be stated in tabular form: Of her present population Ohio has received—

From other States of the Union	450,454
From foreign countries	372,493
	822,947
She has given to other States of their present population	806,983

We have no means of knowing what number of her native population Ohio has given to foreign countries; but probably the number, added to what she has given to other States of the Union, would make the sum of her vital gifts fully equal to those she has received.

From the Census returns, which show the birth-place of the present native population of the United States by States, I have compiled a table, that exhibits the items of Ohio's population account with the States and Territories, as follows:

States and Territories.	Ohio has received—	Ohio has given—	States and Territories.	Ohio has received—	Ohio has given—
Alabama	680	682	North Carolina	4,891	140
Arkansas	323	2,199	Oregon	32	4,031
California	297	12,735	Pennsylvania	149,784	19,295
Connecticut	12,408	928	Rhode Island	1,127	202
Delaware	2,632	152	South Carolina	1,135	95
Florida	76	128	Tennessee	3,703	4,420
Georgia	867	366	Texas	244	2,052
Illinois	6,274	163,012	Vermont	9,055	310
Indiana	17,382	189,359	Virginia and West Virginia	72,950	12,705
Iowa	2,837	126,285			

Kansas	277	38,205	Wisconsin	1,868	23,164
Kentucky	26,230	19,533			
Louisiana	1,137	1,499	Arizona	3	235
Maine	2,686	160	Colorado	13	2,057
Maryland	23,392	1,163	Dacota	5	635
Massachusetts	13,390	1,427	Dist. of Columbia	676	1,042
Michigan	6,348	62,207	Idaho	2	550
Minnesota	372	12,651	Indian Territory	10	—
Mississippi	890	1,171	Montana	6	1,127
Missouri	2,103	76,162	New Mexico	13	274
Nebraska	76	10,729	Utah	3	1,133
Nevada	9	1,858	Washington Ter.	3	866
New Hampshire	3,329	212	Wyoming	2	547
New Jersey	13,229	1,868			
New York	67,594	7,512	Totals	450,454	806,983

. . . .

Having found the state of our population account, with States and Nations, beyond our own borders, it remains to consider the growth of population within the State itself. Here we are confronted with facts of great significance. We have already seen that the total increase of the population of Ohio during the last decade was 13.92 per cent. Was this growth uniform throughout the State? If not, what portions gave the increase? What portions remained stationary? What suffered a decrease?

The total increase, during the past decade, was 323,749. By examining the progress of the population, in the different counties, it will be seen that this increase is produced, almost exclusively, in thirty-seven counties. In eighteen counties there has been a positive decrease of population; and in the remaining thirty-three counties it has remained nearly stationary.

The increase, in the thirty-seven counties referred to, may be traced to three causes. The settlement of unoccupied lands, the development of mining and manufacturing interests, and the growth of cities.

And, first, in the block of seventeen counties, extending from the southern line of Darke and Miami to Michigan and the lake, the increase has been 89,288.

Second. In the two groups of mining and manufacturing counties the increase is also marked. In the Mahoning Valley Group, which consists of Trumbull, Mahoning, Columbiana and Stark, the increase has been 28,111; and in the Hanging Rock Group, which fills the bend of the river, from Pomeroy to Portsmouth, viz: Meigs, Gallia, Jackson, Lawrence and Scioto, the increase has been 25,387.

Third. But much the largest item of increase is found in the growth of our cities. I append a table which exhibits the increase of each of the cities having a population of more than ten thousand inhabitants. The table also shows the total increase of the counties in which these cities are located:

Increase since 1860.

1.	Cincinnati	79,612	Hamilton county	43,960
2.	Cleveland	38,815	Cuyahoga county	53,977
3.	Toledo	11,999	Lucas county	20,891
4.	Columbus	7,611	Franklin county	12,658
5.	Dayton	7,423	Montgomery county	11,776
6.	Sandusky	4,604	Erie county	3,714
7.	Springfield	2,169	Clark county	6,770
8.	Hamilton	3,062	Butler county	4,070
9.	Portsmouth	2,062	Scioto county	5,005
10.	Zanesville	1,563	Muskingum county	470
11.	Akron	2,594	Summit county	7,330
	Total	160,614		170,621

It will be seen that, subtracting the growth of the cities, the population of these eleven counties has remained nearly stationary. Indeed, in several of them there has been an actual decrease. Summing up the result, it will be seen that the main increase of the State was as follows:

In 17 new counties in the northwest	89,288
In 9 mining and manufacturing counties	53,498
In 11 city counties	170,621
Total	313,307

Outside of these three groups, the total increase of the State was but 12,442.

The rapid growth of cities is one of the most striking features of modern civilization, and its bearings on the development of industry, and the well-being of society and of individuals, are worthy the most thoughtful study.

. . . .

I may add, as a further illustration of the same tendency, that the aggregate increase of population, during the last decade, in the ten incorporated villages, of Chillicothe, Steubenville, Mansfield, Newark, Xenia, Delaware, Fremont, Wooster and Marietta, amounted to 11,034; while the whole increase in the ten counties in which these villages are situated, has but 11,565. Outside of these principal villages, the population of these ten counties has remained stationary.

All the merely agricultural districts are suffering a constant drain of population, to supply the growth of cities and villages. I have, as yet, seen but a few of the advance sheets of the forthcoming Census Report, and cannot, therefore, draw from that rich mine of social statistics, which will exhibit the number, and average value of our American home, and the progress of our people in education and wealth.

At the end of another year, we shall hope to have many additional facts of the deepest interest to our people. In the meantime, I hope that the General Assembly of Ohio will enlarge the scope of your duties, in the matter of statistics, so that our citizens may be able to note the progress of our noble State, and to guide, with a still greater wisdom, her future development.

I am dear sir,
Very respectfully yours,
JAS. A. GARFIELD.

Farm Lands in Ohio

EDWARD ORTON

Gen. I. R. Sherwood, Secretary of State:

My own time has been devoted for the last year, as heretofore, to an extended examination of the geological structure of Southwestern Ohio. Its great limestone formations, which have principally occupied my time, are surprisingly rich in geological interest; and though by no means destitute of economic values, still it must be acknowledged that their supplies of lime, cement and building stone, seem of but small account, when compared with the coal seams and ore beds of the district on which they border—lying east of the

From Letter, Edward Orton to Isaac R. Sherwood, December 9, 1871, in *Statistical Report of the Secretary of State, 1871, Ohio Executive Documents,* (1872), pp. 160-162.

Scioto. There is, however, one source of wealth in South-western Ohio, which though not generally classed among its geological formations, indisputably belongs in this category, and the products of which, may safely challenge comparison with those of any other geological horizon of the State—whether the horizon of salt springs or oil wells—of iron ore or block coal. I refer to the *soil* of South-western Ohio, and I deem it proper to call attention through your Report, to certain points connected with it, which have seemed to me worthy of general consideration.

A fertile soil is in many points of view the most valuable and desirable geological formation that a country can contain. Such a soil gives to the regions that possess it, some signal advantages over those whose value lies in any of the forms of mineral wealth. The state of society that it renders possible, is safer and more in harmony with republican institutions than any other. There is a greater diffusion of wealth and comfort in a productive agricultural region, than is generally possible in a mining district. The investments required for working land, are but moderate in amount, as compared with those that are required in mining operations, so that in an agricultural community, a much larger number reap the advantages, in character and fortune, of carrying on business for themselves. In a mineral district, though large fortunes are possible to the few, the majority of the population remains permanently poor. The pursuit of agriculture is counted unsuccessful in America, if the second generation does not attain to comfort and independence, even though the first generation came bare-handed upon the soil.

The durability of a good soil, is another of its striking and peculiar advantages. The richest mineral veins find at last their limit—coal seams run out, oil crevices are exhausted, and silence and decay follow in the footsteps of the most successful industry. But where a fertile soil comes under the control of intelligent husbandry, its tribute is rendered perennially. Generation after generation is enriched by the rewards which it returns to industry and skill.

. . . .

There are no topics, indeed, that concern the material interest of the country more directly than those which relate to the amelioration of its soils, and the preservation of their original fertility. It is to questions of this character, in their relations to South-western Ohio, that attention is now directed.

There is no question that this portion of the State, may be said to have originally possessed a fruitful soil. Its wide alluvial valleys were early recognized as among the richest and most desirable lands of the newly opened West, and neither subsequent discovery nor purchase, has made us acquainted with anything to change this estimate. The valleys of South-western Ohio, are pronounced by Hon. Luther Tucker, of New York, an eminent authority, in matters pertaining to agriculture, to be as desirable lands for general farming, as any in the United States, or indeed in the world.

. . . .

If, now, the question should be asked—Have these soils been so treated since their present occupation began, as to increase or to maintain their fertility?—the answer that we are obliged to make is as unwelcome as it is unequivocal. The truth is, that the agriculture of South-western Ohio is in an unpromising condition, and suggests grave questions to every one who seriously considers it. It is not to be understood, however, that there is any thing exceptionally bad in the system of tillage pursued in this section of the State. The system that is here in force is the same that is impoverishing the soil of the country at large, and the only peculiarity is, that in a limited district, and one of great original fertility, the process and rate of exhaustion can be more readily marked.

While the signs of progressive deterioration are to be found in all varieties of soil in the district under consideration, it is still true that they are much more obvious in the thinner and less tractable soils of the uplands than elsewhere. The most evident proof of this deterioration is found in the lessening average of production of the two main grain crops of the country, viz: wheat and corn.

. . . .

Another indication of this deterioration is to be seen in the growing uncertainty of the harvests—in the frequent recurrence of failures, more or less complete, in the raising of ordinary crops. It is the fashion to refer these failures mainly to climatic changes, which the clearing of the country has induced, and there can be no question but that this element is to be regarded in the explanation; but a weightier element will certainly be found in a worn and depleted soil, upon which all unfavorable climatic agencies act with intensified powers of mischief.

The dilapidation of farm buildings and equipments, that is to be marked in some districts, must also be referred to this same deterioration of soil as its cause. The comfortable dwellings and ample barns that a more profitable agriculture raised, the present shrunken income does not serve to keep in repair.

. . . .

The cause of this deterioration and incipient exhaustion is not far to seek. It lies in the system of farming to which these lands have been subjected from the date of their occupation—a system which was, naturally enough, adopted in the outset, and which worked, without apparent disadvantage, for a score of years, and sometimes even for twice that time—but which long ago passed the limit within which it can be safely tolerated, and the maintenance of which is certain to inflict irreparable loss upon the country.

. . . .

The farming of south-western Ohio would be immeasurably improved by a careful and thorough use of the fertilizers now easily within reach. Most prominent among them is stable manure or the excrements of the live stock of the farm. The very general failure to appreciate its importance and value can be seen from such facts as the following:

1. A large proportion of the barn-yards of the country—in some districts as many as seven out of ten—are traversed or drained by water-courses in such a way that all of the wash of the yards is entirely lost to the land. The object of this arrangement is to provide a convenient supply of stock-water or to keep the yards dry.

2. The straw of the grain crops, instead of being turned to proper account in the barn-yard, is often burned in the heaps in which it was left after threshing.

3. The highways are often used as feeding grounds for stock, and especially for fattening swine, and thus all the value to be derived from the feeding of thousands of bushels of corn is wantonly lost to the land.

4. A large item in the present farming of several counties adjacent to Cincinnati is the production of hay for the city market. The only possible compensation for so heavy a drain upon a farm as the selling of a hay crop involves would be a generous return of fertilizers, so easy to be secured in a great city; but the hay wagons, without exception, return empty to the farms which they are despoiling.

Another of the fertilizers within easy reach, and in very considerable quantity, is wood-ashes. Containing, as they do, the mineral matter that was sufficient for a forest growth, they furnish these substances to vegetation again in the most easily appropriated form. The towns and villages that still depend on wood for fuel could furnish to the adjacent country thousands of bushels of this invaluable fertilizer, if only the demand were made. Even after the ashes have subserved the purposes of the soap-factory, by giving up their pot-ash and soda, they still contain the phosphates, the sulphates and the lime—substances pre-eminently serviceable to agriculture. The farmers of Connecticut and Long Island find it to their interest to buy leached ashes at 25 cents per bushel.

In Springfield and its immediate vicinity at least 10,000 cords of wood are burned annually in the manufacture of its famous lime. Very large quantities of wood are also used at Yellow Springs, at Cedarville, and elsewhere, for similar purposes. All the ashes derived from this source, mingled with lime-waste, have always been accessible to the farmers of these regions, and could generally be had for the hauling; but it is of the rarest occurrence to find them applied in any way to the land. They are used to fill up waste ground, to make into road-beds, or are carted to the streams; but not one bushel in a thousand has ever found its way to the only proper destination—the soil.

If there is one substance more than another that deserves to be considered the fine gold of the soil, it is the phosphate of lime that it contains. It exists in the soil in minute proportions, frequently constituting not more than 1-1000 part, and seldom exceeding 1-200 part, of its weight. It is absolutely indispensable to the growth of our most valued crops, and doubtless the loss of fertility in soils depends more upon the abstraction of this substance than of any other. Its ultimate office is to supply the material from which the bones of animals are composed. The demand, therefore, for this substance by all cultivated lands must be immense and imperative. No fertilizer could be more grateful to the soil, and none would show more immediate and satisfactory results. But, though thousands of tons of bones are annually available in south-western Ohio, there is not a single establishment in this portion of the State for their preparation.

But, after all, the great and fatal drain upon the vitality of our soils remains to be mentioned. It is found in our privy vaults, and in our systems of town and city sewerage. So long as the present mode of dealing with these subjects remains in force, so long the country must suffer a steady and rapid exhaustion, no matter how thorough and complete all the instruments and appliances of our farming may be. The great equation of agriculture is more wantonly violated here than in any other direction, and with more ruinous results. This whole question is quite as worthy the attention of our political economists and legislators as that of tariffs or taxes, or any other which occupies their time, for it concerns the perpetuity of our national patrimony itself.

. . . .

Though the country has already suffered an irremedial loss from the reckless mismanagement of its soil, the greatest source of its wealth, enough remains to make it still the most valuable heritage of the nations of the world. Its agricultural capabilities, if wisely husbanded even now, will suffice for an unlimited career. Motives of patriotism and self-interest combine to urge us to begin the work of putting American agriculture on a true and rational basis.

I have the honor to remain

Very truly yours,
EDWARD ORTON,
Ass't State Geologist.

Ohio's Forests

ADOLPH LEUE

When, a few decades ago, the subject of forestry began to be agitated on this western hemisphere, and the attention of the people of this country was directed to the wasteful destruction of our forests and to the probable consequences of such destruction, and, when at the same time, a more economic management of existing woodlands was advised, people, who had become tree destroyers by necessity and who were accustomed to look upon those very woods as so many impediments to progress, as something to be got rid of at any cost, were very much disposed to consider such an advice as an outgrowth of an ill-balanced mind and paid little or no attention to such warnings. But the advocates of forestry persisted in their endeavors to change the general apathy of our people toward our woodlands into a more friendly relation, by showing them that "Trees are the best friends of man, and forests of nations;" that "Not *gold* but *wood* is the true basis of national wealth;" and that "An animal flayed or a tree stripped of its bark does not perish more surely than a land deprived of its trees."

In consequence of these labors many of the most eager tree-destroyers of by-gone days are now numbered among the most zealous advocates of a reaction; and many a hand which, in its younger years lifted up the ax upon trees and set fire to the

From Adolph Leue, "The Forestry Question in Ohio," *Second Annual Report of the Forestry Bureau, 1886, Ohio Executive Documents,* (1887), pp. 6-15.

woodland, is now planting forest-trees and cultivates them; men who but a few years ago looked with either scorn or pity upon the promoters of the forestry movement, and upon forestry as a subject that might well be discussed upon the prairies of the great west, or in the backwoods of Michigan and Wisconsin, are now seeking information on forestal topics. Forestry has, moreover, received the attention of legislative bodies, both State and National. The National Government has its *Forestry Division,* New York, New Hampshire, California and Colorado have Forest Commissions, and Ohio has its State Forestry Bureau. These institutions, it is true, are still in their infancy and labor under many disadvantages. The attainments of the efforts made to bring forestry into proper recognition are encouraging, and indicate a satisfactory solution of the great forestry problem.

This problem, briefly stated, is:

To perpetually keep a certain percentage of the superficial area of our country in forests, properly distributed, and to use and husband this in a manner that its usefulness be unimpaired.

Among all the questions which the people of this country, and especially the farmers, are called upon to decide, the perpetuation of our forests, is certainly one of the most important. "For," as Dr. F. L. Oswald well said, "in an agricultural country the preservation or destruction of forests must determine the decision of Hamlet's alternative."

This very ("to be or not to be") solemn truth will come home to us when we remember that forests, as has repeatedly been shown, serve—

1. To ameliorate the climate by sheltering the ground, keeping it warm in winter and cool in summer.

2. To regulate, in a certain degree, the water-supply of our streams.

3. To shelter our fields, our farm animals, and our homes against the trying winds of the winter.

4. To furnish material for our various industries.

. . . .

As to the rapid removal of our forests in almost all parts of the country, let us see what part we, the people of Ohio, have taken in this great work.

At the time of the first settlement by white people, Ohio was one of the most densely wooded States of the Union. With the exception of the wet prairies found on the great water-shed extending through the State in a northeasterly direction, and in the western portion, the whole State was one continuous tract of woodland, stocked with forest-trees of many different varieties, mostly of the deciduous kind.

From statistics we learn that in 1853 the woodlands of Ohio occupied 13,991,426 acres, or 50.19 per cent. of the superficial area of the State. The latest agricultural statistics show that there are only 4,258,767 acres of woodland in Ohio, or 16.69 per cent. of the entire area of the State. Thus, within the thirty-two years immediately following 1853, the woodland cleared in Ohio amounted to 9,732,659 acres, or 33.50 per cent. of the superficial area of the State, or an annual decrease of more than one per cent.

In addition to this absolute clearing of thousands of acres annually, there is another, a sort of intermediate clearing, known in some parts of the State as "logging," by which many thousands of the best trees are removed from the remaining woodlands every year, so that, in many parts of our State, none but inferior trees of inferior varieties are met with.

. . . .

This growing scarcity of wood in Ohio and in the neighboring States necessitates the importation from greater distances, whereby the cost of transportation is added to the original price. The manufacturer, in order to balance his expense, raises the price of his manufactures, and the consumer of these articles is made to pay the penalty of the ruthless destruction of our home woodlands.

While all of these industries are more or less affected by this growing scarcity of timber, there are certain, and very important industries at that, which for want of material, indispensable to their existence, have been discontinued. As for example, several furnaces of Southern Ohio, at which formerly a very high grade of charcoal-iron was manufactured, have already been abandoned, and the abandonment of others is but a question of time.

Last year one of the largest tanneries of Cincinnati was discontinued because of the growing scarcity of tanbark. Kentucky, West Virginia, Indiana, and even Tennessee have, since Ohio ceased to furnish this valuable forest-product, supplied the Queen City of the West with tanbark, and so great has been the drain upon these States that they, too, are nearly stripped of their oak trees, especially along the railroads. The days of the tanning industry of Ohio, there can be no doubt, are numbered, unless by a wise foresight immediate action be taken to grow oak-coppices for the production of tanbark. Chattanooga now competes with our home tanneries in the Cincinnati market, and it is thought will ere long ruin some tanners there.

The decline of this industry will to some extent affect the cattle market; for, if the skins of animals bought and slaughtered in

Cincinnati cannot be manufactured into leather in that city, but must be shipped to a southern or eastern place of manufacture, the price of animals furnishing these skins will depreciate, and the farmer, who raises and fattens cattle for the Cincinnati market, will receive for his product the full price, less the decline in the price of the skin, which will be the cost of transportation to the distant tanneries.

This destruction of our woodlands also prevents the development of new industries.

. . . .

Neither let us allure ourselves into a momentary sense of safety, and into a prolonged inaction, by supposing that we are now suffering the worst forms of the consequence of forest destruction. The pernicious effects are only beginning to show themselves. If we continue in this damnable work of forest annihilation, and make no decided efforts to raise forests where they are needed, the time will surely come which, about fifty years ago, Will. Cull. Bryant predicted, when he represented an Indian as saying:

> "The realms our tribes were crushed to get,
> May be a barren desert yet."

Indeed, the time has fully come, when the people of this great and blessed State should adopt very decided measures, not only to prevent an increase of the evils, the effects we now so sorely feel, but even also, by changing present conditions, remove those evils.

. . . .

Owing to the former abundance of woods in this and other States of the Union, we have become rather extravagant in the use of wood, so that, unless we acquire a more economic habit, at least a like proportion of the total area of our State will be needed for forestal purposes to supply the home demand upon timber.

Now, I do by no means expect or desire that Ohio should produce all the timber needed to supply the home demand. The greater portion of our State can be used to greater advantage for agricultural purposes than for the production of timber.

The hilly parts of eastern, southeastern and southern Ohio, which by nature are not well adapted for tillage, should be, and, in the course of time, unquestionably will be the great forest region of the State. There should also be a broad belt of forests along the great water-shed, dividing the waters of the Ohio from those of Lake Erie, for the protection of the head waters of our streams.

Besides these mentioned sites for our forests of the future, there are in all parts of the State, at greater or less intervals, larger or smaller tracts of land, which should be devoted to forest culture.

These are the ravines, the barren hillsides and such other pieces of land, which, if cultivated, produce poor crops, and if left uncultivated, a bad pasture. On these weak spots of the farm, the farmer should raise timber for his own use, and if these so-called waste lands be sufficiently large, there is no reason why he should not raise timber for the market.

About four years ago, exemption of taxes on lands devoted to systematic forest culture was proposed. But such exemption was found to be unconstitutional, and to meet this, a rebate of taxes actually paid on such lands for the first ten years of forest cultivation was suggested, consequently a bill was introduced in our Legislature, but failed to become a law. That a rebate of taxes on lands devoted to forestry would become a very strong incentive to engage in forest culture can hardly be doubted, and yet the passage of a bill to this effect is undesirable, because it would be unpopular among the people, as it would throw the burden of taxes on other property. Practical forestry, moreover, will undoubtedly prove to be a paying investment. Let this become thoroughly understood, and forestry will take care of itself. What we need is: *Information in every branch of practical and scientific forestry.*

For every other branch of human knowledge and industry, schools have been founded in various parts of the country and State, at which the needed information may be obtained. For many industries there are even special laboratories at which to test the attainments of experience, and to devise new methods of performing certain work, or of obtaining certain results. For agriculture this great need is covered by our Agricultural College, and by the Agricultural Experiment Station. But in regard to forestry, which as to importance is second to none, no provision of any kind has been made.

. . . .

While we are laboring for the development of an Ohio system of forestry, or a system that shall be adopted to the wants and conditions of our State, let us bear in mind that a knowledge of other systems will be of the greatest advantage to us in this great work. We can not afford to ignore the attainments of our brethren in the sister States. Let us, therefore, gather facts, wheresoever we can get them, and while doing this, let us diffuse whatever knowledge we may have in matters pertaining to forestry. The more we do in the work of spreading forestal knowledge among our own fellow-citizens of Ohio, the more able co-laborers we shall win.

To accomplish this great work, more means are needed. To get these, we must apply to the centre of our State Government. This centre is the people. Let the people of Ohio understand the importance of forestry, and we shall not need to beg for an appropriation.

Ohio's Polluted Waters

H. J. SHARP

The Pollution of Darby Creek

Upon receipt of the following letters, I visited the scenes of complaints on September 17, 1886, for the purpose of investigating the alleged causes of complaint and to subserve a duty as a member of the board:

Extract from letter from Dr. F. N. Mattoon:

Plain City, Ohio, September 10, 1886.

Dr. H. J. Sharp—Dear Sir: * * * * The washings from the paper mill in our town are conducted into Darby creek, and so pollute the water that vegetation that grows in the edges of the stream, and the fish, for two or three miles below the mill, cannot live; hence if you were here now you would observe the water in the creek as black as ink and offensive in odor, dying the vegetation and killing the fish for miles down the stream. * * * In the family of Mr. James Boyd, living one mile south of town, I have been and am treating four cases of typho-malarial or continued fever, viz., Mr. Boyd, daughter and two sons. * * * * At Mr. Huff's, the next family below Mr. Boyd's, I understand there have been three cases of similar fever, and there are several other cases in the neighborhood. In my opinion, the miasm from the creek is the cause of so many cases in the two families, for their houses are favorably situated to receive it, being only a few yards distant from the creek. * *

Respectfully yours,
F. N. MATTOON.

Letters from Mrs. Ann E. Boyd and Mr. L. Y. Huff, Plain City, Ohio:

Plain City, Ohio, September 14, 1886.

Dr. H. J. Sharp, London, Ohio—Dear Doctor: Having learned recently that you are a member of the State Board of Health, I feel it my duty to enter a complaint against the paper mill located at Plain City. The drainage from said mill has polluted the water in the creek, killed the fish and vegetation in the creek, and is causing malaria. We have been sorely afflicted; our house has been a hospital. Mr. Boyd is very low with typho-malarial fever; has been sick over forty days.

From H. J. Sharp, "Report on the Pollution of Water-Courses by Straw-Board Factories," *Report of the State Board of Health, Ohio Executive Documents*, (1887), pp. 1899-1902.

Our children, who have been sick are improving. The doctor says it is the condition of the water in the creek that causes our sickness. Our neighbors are sick. I send this message praying that something be done to relieve us. We will be obliged to leave our home if this continues.

This is a second attack. That of one year ago was not so severe. To be convinced of the fact, come and see.

Respectfully yours,
ANN E. BOYD.
Wife of James Boyd.

P.S.—Wish to say that we have lived here on the farm for twenty years without any sickness whatever.

A. E. B.

Plain City, Ohio, Sept. 15, 1886.

Dr. H. J. Sharp, Member State Board of Health—Dear Sir: I write to you concerning a matter of great importance to me, that is, the health of my family. I reside about one and a half miles south of Plain City, Madison county, on the west bank of Big Darby creek. At Plain City there is a paper mill which empties its waste-pipes into this stream and so pollutes it as to kill the fish and poison the atmosphere to such an extent as to cause serious malarial troubles. My family have nearly all been down with it, and our neighbor, Mr. James Boyd, has a family of five, four of whom have been very sick. Mr. Boyd, himself, at this writing, is lying very low of typho-malarial fever. Dead fish are to be seen all along the creek; the water is black, and the odor arising from it during the evenings is almost unbearable. Our live-stock have to drink this bad water, (as our creek lands are almost invariably in pasture,) and we fear bad results from this source, also. Now, we do hope you will take an interest in this matter, and, therefore, we pray you to see that a committee be appointed, as soon as possible, to investigate it. We certainly are entitled to protection from some source, and we appeal to you hoping that you will give this your earliest attention.

I am very truly your obedient servant,
L. Y. HUFF.

The mill referred to is situated in Plain City, near Darby creek, from which it pumps a large amount of water used in washing and preparing the straw-pulp. Large quantities of lime are used in macerating this straw, which is then passed through large revolving vats filled with water, the lime being thoroughly washed out, and this water, saturated with lime, and containing a large amount of organic matter, washed out of the pulp, and a small amount of log-wood and sulphate of iron, which is used in the process, is carried through a sewer-pipe and emptied into Darby creek, at a distance of about forty rods from the mill.

The amount of waste water thus constantly drained into the stream is enough to nearly flush a four inch sewer-pipe.

As this water flows from the pipe it is of a dirty straw color, and has little odor and can not be very objectionable to the taste, as cattle drink it where it escapes and before it reaches the creek. After it reaches and mixes with the water in the stream, the whole becomes darker in color, and, at times, offensive in odor, and proves destructive to the fish. At the time of my visit the water in the creek was at a low stage, and was very dark colored, and in places might be seen numbers of dead fish. I could not, however, distinguish any odor, which, perhaps, might have been due to the time of day and heat of the sun's rays. I would expect any odor to be much more perceptible in the evening or at night, and such, upon the testimony of persons living near the stream, is the case, the odor becoming, according to some, almost intolerable at times in the evening.

I visited the families of Messrs. Boyd and Huff, and found the conditions corresponding to those enumerated in the letter above. Mr. James Boyd was very sick and died the day succeeding my visit. His residence was situated on a beautiful elevation overlooking the creek, and everything surrounding it seemed well kept, and would not lead one to suppose that the sickness of the family was due to any local causes affecting the premises. At a point opposite the house the creek makes a bend, and the breezes sweeping over the creek for some distance would carry its vapors toward the house, thus favoring any deleterious conditions that might arise from this source. Mr. Huff's residence is situated near the stream, and the location would favor the same condition affecting that of Mr. Boyd, and I have no doubt but that the sickness in these families was caused by miasmatic poisons, emanating from the creek. I found that the color, during the low stage of the river, affected the water for four or five miles below the mill, and that the fish were killed, and the water seemed very objectionable for the use of live stock.

In the following letter addressed to the president of the company operating this mill, I called attention to the conditions complained of, and to the statute referring to the case:

London, Ohio, September 28, 1886.

Mr. Dudly, President, Plain City Paper Mill Co., Plain City, Ohio—

Dear Sir: Complaints having been filed with the State Board of

Health, charging that the washings and refuse from the Plain City Paper Mill, are a cause of pollution of the Big Darby creek, rendering the water unfit for live stock to drink, killing the fish in the stream, and causing sickness of persons living near it.

To learn the facts in the premises, I visited the scenes of complaint on Friday, the 17th inst., and am convinced that some of the charges are well-founded—there being no doubt but that pollution of said creek exists, and that said pollution is caused by said paper mill, and I adopt this medium of asking your attention to this matter, and beg that you, at your earliest convenience, will inform me as to what action the company of which you are a representative and president, may have to propose to remedy the evils complained of.

I would respectfully refer you to sections 2921 and 2923 of the Revised Statutes providing against pollution of water courses, and would add, that we will be compelled to instruct the prosecuting attorney to bring action under the sections of the statutes referred to, if some steps are not soon taken to avoid and remedy the evils referred to. Hoping for a reply at an early date,

I am, most respectfully, yours,
H. J. SHARP, M. D.,
Member State Board of Health.

No reply having been received, the prosecuting attorney of Madison county, was instructed to bring the matter before the grand jury in proper manner, and the names of parties having knowledge of the evils complained of, were given him to be summoned before this body at its session in November.

At this session of the grand jury a few of the witnesses subpœned appeared, but others whose testimony was considered more important did not appear, and so far as I could learn no effort was made to compel their attendance. I have been informed that the grand jury did not deem the evidence of sufficient weight to find an indictment, and thus the case rests.

That there was pollution of the stream seemed clear enough; but to get those parties who were loudest in their complaints to appear and testify before the grand jury was the difficulty encountered, and this same difficulty is encountered in other similar cases of complaint, so that it is doubtful if we will be able to reach these cases, and remedy the evils complained of, except by persistently fighting in the cause of right and the people and, perhaps, without any grateful recognition on the part of those whom we attempt to benefit.

The Farmers' Plight

F. B. McNEAL

The beauties of farm life, the independence of the farmer's calling, his communion with nature and the healthfulness of his occupation, have been sung in the ears of the American farmer, until they have well nigh lulled him to sleep, whilst others have outstripped him in the race of life, and much of the result of his industry has been appropriated by others without compensation or reward. Since 1840 the wealth of this country has increased more than a thousand fold, while our agricultural wealth, has increased less than three hundred fold. In the discussion of the cause, result and relief of these conditions we should, as much as possible, divest ourselves of all prejudice and without bias discuss the different environments surrounding our industrial life.

For more than a score of years there has been an almost continual shrinkage in all agricultural values. Our lands are less valuable, our prices have been declining and our taxes are higher. While these conditions have existed with the farmer, let us inquire whether the same conditions have surrounded the other industrial and monetary interests of our country, or whether they have borne equally with us the burdens of state, for we should ask only an equal chance with them in life's battle; we can ask for nothing more, we should be satisfied with nothing less. The vast accumulations of wealth in the hands of individuals in later years in this country has been the wonder of the world. Many can remember when the millionaires of this country could be counted on one's fingers, today their numbers can scarcely be ascertained; the multi-millionaire only is accounted the very rich individual and some have reached hundreds of millions. Among these not a single farmer stands today a millionaire made such by the operations of agriculture. The capital invested in farm lands, especially in the older states, is worth less by 40 per cent. than it was twenty years ago. The capital invested in many other pursuits has increased a hundred fold and in some cases a thousand fold. The representatives of values bartered in a single city in a single year are greater than all the agricultural land values in the United States. The average net profits of our lands have been less than 4 per cent. for ten years, while the net profits on manufactured goods in 1890 were more than 20 per cent. The net profits of a single railway in Ohio, in a single year, were a million and a quarter of dollars.

. . . .

From F. B. McNeal, "The Farmer in Relation to Other Industrial Citizens," *Ohio Agricultural Report, 1897, Ohio Executive Documents*, (1898), pp. 455-460.

While receiving less return for our labor, and less profit for our investment than other classes of our citizens, our rates of taxation have been increasing, and the difference between the valuation of real and personal property in Ohio has been constantly increasing since 1826, when personal property was first placed on the tax duplicate. In 1826 the rate was seven mills, in 1895 it was twenty mills. In 1826 the difference between the value of real and personal property was thirty-four million dollars, in 1895 this difference had increased to six hundred and eighty-seven million dollars. As the greatest part of agricultural valuation must always be in real estate, and the greatest part of other industrial valuation must be in personal values, it follows that this increasing discrepancy must result in detriment to the farmer.

. . . .

The increase in the products of the labor of the American farmer in the last generation is unparalleled in the history of the world, and does not admit of comparison with any other nation. In 1845 we produced fifteen million tons of grain; in 1895 this was increased to eighty-nine million tons. Our meat, dairy products, hides and poultry were valued in 1840 at two hundred and seventy-five million dollars; in 1895 they were valued at one billion, six hundred and thirty-five million dollars. This makes the increase in our products about seven fold. Let us see if our earnings have kept pace with this increase in our products, or if the increase in our earnings has kept pace with the earnings of those engaged in other industrial pursuits. Mulhall, in his "Wealth of Nations," gives the increase in earnings from all sources from 1840 to 1894 at a ratio of three hundred and thirty-one to three thousand one hundred and sixteen, while the increase in agricultural earnings were as one hundred and eight to four hundred and eighty-eight. Thus it will be seen that while our products increased seven fold, our earnings increased only a little more than four fold, and during the same period the increase in the earnings of other industries was more than a thousand fold.

From 1850 to 1890, the wealth in the cities and towns of this country increased from three billion dollars to fifty-one billion dollars; during the same time the agricultural wealth of the country increased from four billions to sixteen billions. While agricultural wealth increased four fold, urban wealth increased nearly seventeen fold, or more than four times as great an increase. Why is this vast difference in the returns we receive for our industries? Why this great inequality in the burdens we bear in common with our fellow countrymen? Is it because the farmer is less industrious than others? No, none work more hours or harder than he; the average amount of produce per hand is four times greater in the United States than in

Europe. (In the United States it is eight tons per year per hand, in Europe it is two tons.) Is it because the farmer is more extravagant in living? No, perhaps no other class is as economical as the farmer, certainly his living costs as little as any other class of our citizens. Can it be that he has less ability than others? Certainly not; were we to acknowledge this to be true we would become the inferior class, fit only to be the slaves of those whom we would declare superior to us in intellect. The history of this country demonstrates that more than a proportionate number of our greatest statesmen, wisest philosophers, and truest patriots, have come from among the followers of the plow. Is the farmer's integrity of a lower grade than that of his fellows? No, it is not egotism for the farmer to assert that as a class he stands at the top of the moral standards of his country. These four cardinal virtues, industry, economy, capability and integrity, coupled with the inalienable rights of man to "life, liberty and the pursuit of happiness," form the God given bases of success to human energy. With the proper exercise of these there can be no failure, except through accident, natural calamity, or some dereliction of the government under which we live. Of the accidents affecting our depressed agriculture, there are none to be mentioned, save, perhaps, that of over production in our own country, or under production in the countries dependent upon us for their supplies. These cannot explain our difficulties, for if the prices of our commodities depended upon our export trade it would follow that, as our exports increased, our prices would increase as a natural result; never in the history of our country have our exports increased more rapidly than in the last two decades, yet with a few slight exceptions, prices have continually decreased throughout the same period.

No natural calamity, of fire, flood or pestilence, has befallen us to account for our disaster, hence we are forced to the third source of our trouble, namely, the evils that have crept into our government. Though we have the best form of government that ever existed among men we believe its functions have not always been exercised in the interests of the people. Vicious legislation may exist from no legislation or from the enactment of bad laws. Examples of the former are when the United States Congress, regardless of the petitions of thousands of her citizens, neglected to pass a law to prohibit speculation in futures, in the prices of farm products; or when it failed to enact laws to effectually check *quasi* public corporations from exercising their corporate powers in the interest of those having them in charge, regardless of the rights of the people whose domain they have appropriated.

Speculation in the agricultural products of the country has reached such a pitch that scarcely a food product has escaped the gambler's touch, even the bread we eat, is controlled by the same baneful influence. Scarcely a baking establishment in the country can run except by the sufferance of certain baking companies. Immense fortunes are accumulated, and thousands of men live in princely style on the profits thus accruing, every dollar of which comes off the price of your produce, or out of the pockets of those who consume them.

. . . .

Of the bad laws that have been enacted there has been no class more pernicious than the subsidizing of public improvements. The United States has granted to railways more than two million of acres of the public domain, to aid in the construction of more than fifteen thousand miles of road, requiring actual settlers to pay for every acre thus donated, in order to obtain the right to settle on adjoining sections; add to this the subsidy bonds given to the same roads, and you will find that more than a billion of dollars have been given to corporations of this kind, with almost no check to the corporate powers thus granted. The pernicious system thus inaugurated has been followed up through National and State Legislatures, through county, city and town governments until there is scarcely a hamlet in the country that can get a creamery within its limits without a subsidy, and often the subsidy is the only real money invested in the enterprise. But it is needless to enumerate, incidents might be multiplied without number.

Out of all this want of legislation and bad legislation, has arisen the almost innumerable corporate bodies of the country, granted special franchises and powers by the government, with very little responsibility to the power that gave them life and with very little respect for the people from whom their patronage must come, their management has become corrupt, their stock the plaything of stock boards and individual speculators, their special privileges and franchises looked upon as the individual plunder of those who have them in control; thus vast amounts of capital centering in the hands of a few individuals, the combining of operations, the pooling of interests, and formation of trusts, have made the United States the grandest gambling place of the world today, for Wall street is no less a gambling center than the pool rooms of our race courses, whose jockeys are better paid than the professors of our colleges; nor are the grain pits and stock exchanges any less so than the prize rings, whose participants are better paid than the best preachers of our land. Speculation and transfer of representatives of value without production, is the incubus that sits upon our body politic and upon our citizenship today. The millionaire, made such in a day without adding to the wealth of the community, is made such at the expense of so many additions to the pauper element of the country.

．．．．．．．．．．．．．．．．．．．．．．．．．．

These evils are neither self limiting nor self correcting; like a loosened train on a down grade, the farther they run the greater will be their momentum, and the harder it will be to change direction. The ballot in the hands of honest citizens is the only peaceful avenue to success.

Let the farmer then arise in his might, join hands with every honest son of toil, uniting with the good and true from city, town and country, and declare that this is not the kingdom of caucus, the empire of corporations, or the realm of money kings, neither is it the mobocracy of communism. Show to the world that America is still the government of the people, the nursery of equal rights and the home of liberty, drawing our inspiration from Him whose coming was heralded from Judea's mountain with "Peace and good will to men," believing that "all men were born free and equal," standing up in the conscious rectitude of our purposes, looking squarely into the eyes of all men, demand that the legislation of the country shall be such that the money invested in agriculture shall return an average profit equal to the average profit of other investments; that the time, talent and energy expended in tilling the soil shall be equally rewarded with the other pursuits of life; that we shall be required to bear only an equal share of the burdens of our government; that official emoluments shall be only a fair remuneration for the service rendered; that in the distribution of official position and patronage the industrial classes shall receive the recognition their numbers and importance entitle them to; that integrity and capability shall be the only passports to political preferment, and that every officer be required to rigidly enforce the laws given him in charge to execute.

Crime

BOARD OF STATE CHARITIES

To His Excellency, Governor J. D. Cox:

Sir—In presenting this, their first Annual Report, the Board owe it to themselves to state that they have been organized less than four months, and that they have been greatly embarrassed from the fact that the Legislature failed to provide for even a Secretary to preserve and arrange the results of their observations and study. We would take occasion here to say, however, that we were partially relieved from this embarrassment by the kindness and liberality of the Directors of the Penitentiary who placed at our disposal for a short time the valuable services of Chaplain Byers, who has given us a hearty co-operation in our work, whose report we hand you herewith.

. . . .

It did not take us long to discover that the condition of our County Infirmaries and Jails were in many cases not only deplorable but a disgrace to the State and a sin against humanity. We think some of the results of our investigations, given in this report, will warrant the use of this strong language.

We have visited the large and noble Benevolent Institutions of the State, and with the time and means at our control for investigation and comparison we can only report very generally in terms of high praise. What may be their comparative merits as to economy and successful treatment we have been entirely unable to investigate.

. . . .

Startling and humiliating as the fact may be we must accept it, that crime is on the increase among us. Does it not follow, that our present prison system is lacking in the great essential principle of deterring men from crime by its terrors, or shielding them from it by its moral influence? We must then either admit that it is impossible to hinder the increase of crime, or that we are not treating crime in the best way practicable, and that our method should be changed. Let us not blindly accept the one truth, that "Offenses must needs come," and forget the other: "Woe to that man by whom the offense cometh."

The cardinal principles in the treatment of crime with us are essentially but two: We aim to protect society, and to punish the offender. This is well as far as it goes. Society must be protected;

From "Report of Board of State Charities," *First Annual Report of the Board of State Charities, 1867, Ohio Executive Documents,* (1868), pp. 220-234.

crime should be punished. But this is not enough; self-interest would prompt us to restore the guilty one to society in the best moral condition possible. The criminal, too, has a claim of this at our hands. He may have forfeited every other right, but this one he has not forfeited. For our own sakes, then, for the criminal's sake, ought we not to consider the question of his reform?

In reaching the best method of treating criminals for reform, the first step in advance of our present system must be *Classification,* made indispensably necessary from this fact, that among all criminals the inevitable tendency is for the worse man to drag the better down to his level, instead of the worse rising to the plain of the better. Taking the men now in our Penitentiary, we could safely range them under one or the other of these two classes, viz: Those who have a desire to be better men, and who would be under favorable circumstances; and men who have no such desire, but are incorrigibly, willfully bad. But as it is not for man to look into the heart of man, probably the best basis of classification as a beginning would be age, antecedents, kind and degree of crime, and number of convictions—scrupulously keeping young men, and those susceptible of good influence, from those more hardened in crime.

In this respect ought we not, at least, to be as careful of the moral health of those whom we have assumed the care of as we are of our flocks and herds, when we separate our well stock from those that are diseased, or when we endeavor to keep contagion from our common hospitals? As a rule, men first arrested for crime would not be diagnosed in Ethics as incurable, under proper treatment; and this *indispensable* condition, that their disease be not further aggravated by contamination with the hardened and hopeless.

In the treatment of the one class, the State cannot do too much. Every good influence, consistent with her other interests, should be thrown around them. All such influences upon the other class are as "pearls before swine;" hence we say, *classification* is indispensable to reform. Every principle of justice and humanity; yea, even the narrow one of self-interest, demand the separation of the young offender from the hardened villain, and all due influences lent him to lead him back to honest ways.

. . . .

County Jails

The report of the Secretary, in relation to our county jails, is commended to the especial consideration of the General Assembly, as involving many abuses for which some remedy ought to be speedily devised.

Every offender, or even one accused of crime, (excepting the comparatively few that are sent to the Reform Farm), are necessarily consigned to the common jail, surrounded by its filth, and the depressing influence of a first exposure, and usually furnished by the State, in some old convict, with the teachings of an expert in crime and debauchery—often captivating—always debasing. A combination of influences most perfectly adapted to destroy self-respect—the basis of all manly character—and to educate and perfect the younger and less hardened, to the full capacity of their teachers.

Our jails and prisons, as now arranged, are little better than seminaries of crime. One fact will sustain this terrible statement: There is not a single jail or city prison in the State where anything even under the name of *separation of prisoners* is attempted, or even practicable. All ages, classes, grades and degrees, are huddled together in idleness, and generally in filth, and from the present arrangement of the buildings are necessarily so. We have found the boy of twelve years "in for fighting," or some boyish offense, the young man "in for drunkenness," a crowd "in" on a great variety of accusations, with the hardened convict on his way to his third term in the penitentiary.

A large number of young men are now found in the jails, many of them with honorable discharges from the army, who, under the excitement of drink, committed some offense against the peace of society, and are confined, month after month, under the debasing influence of old and confirmed criminals. This is surely, in the end, an expensive school to the State.

Your prisons for males are bad, and call for immediate remedy. The condition of *the prisons for females* is more deplorable. In these prisons may be found the servant girl accused of theft, the young girl caught in the beginning of her downward course, the insane, (the old as well as the recent case just waiting for the action of the probate court), along with the hardened street walker and the keeper of a house of prostitution.

A young woman, once confined for any cause in our public jail, is well nigh consigned to go from bad to worse in a career of crime.

It may well be asked, can the cause of these sweeping denunciations of our jail system be remedied. Your committee is confident it can be done, but only by a radical change in the internal arrangement of the buildings themselves—an arrangement such as is proposed is now found with more or less perfection in the jail buildings in our Eastern cities. This arrangement would allow of the introduction into the jail system the first and most important bases of the improvement.

1st. *A thorough classification of the criminals.*

To this then may be added

2d. A religious, moral and encouraging influence especially for the young.

3d. A cleanly and healthy condition of the jail.

4th. Employment for the time, either in labor or improvement in education.

The County Infirmaries,

as is shown by the accompanying reports of their various Superintendents, are found to vary very widely as to condition and management. Some are as well planned and kept as can reasonably be expected, and some are in a condition alike disgraceful and loathsome.

The condition of the insane in some of the county infirmaries is simply brutal. But, thanks to the enlightened policy of the State, their condition will soon be remedied by the proposed new asylum and the enlargement of the old. One need not leave the Capitol of the State to find revolting arguments for haste in these projects for the relief of the insane now cared for by counties.

There is, however, one portion of this pitiable class still unprovided for, which should no longer be neglected—we refer to the *colored insane*. Humanity and economy alike implore the attention of the Legislature to this strangely neglected class. All the Superintendents of our Insane Asylums agree that separate apartments are essential for their treatment. The insane asylum is not the place to break down, but rather to gratify every possible whim or prejudice; and while no good would come to them from the disregard of color in their treatment, a great injury would result to many of the whites. There are in our infirmaries some most pitiable colored insane, now hopeless and furious, who were in the early stages of their disease as hopeful as the most yielding, yet who were deprived of proper treatment as no provision has ever been made for them by the State, and they gradually became a permanent burden and a revolting spectacle. We implore the immediate attention of the Legislature for the benefit of this class of insane.

The Counties' Poor

BOARD OF STATE CHARITIES

Champaign County

The Infirmary in this county has evidently received more than the ordinary care bestowed upon such institutions.

The buildings are well arranged and in good condition. The inmates are classified, and apartments so arranged that a general separation of classes is maintained.

The ventilation is more than ordinarily good. Cleanliness is observed throughout the building, but, unfortunately, from appearances, there was no adequate drainage, too much being left to such drainage as the surface of the grounds would naturally afford. This could, and, doubtless, will soon be remedied.

The children, at proper age, are sent to the district school. Religious services on the Sabbath, for reasons deemed sufficient, had been recently suspended. But for the very pitiable condition of the insane and idiotic, for which, apparently, the management is in nowise responsible, the whole establishment would wear a home-like aspect. General cheerfulness seemed to characterize the inmates.

. . . .

This county, it is sad to state, seems to have very largely expended, if not wholly exhausted, its benevolent sympathies upon its infirmary, or, at least, it has been exceedingly chary of its charitable feelings toward its vicious and criminal classes. Its jail is indescribably mean; and apart from a cleanliness which was highly creditable to the jailer, not one word can be said in toleration of such a place. It is very old; is dark, and unavoidably infested with vermin.

There are two (upper and lower) apartments, allowing—possibly designed—for the separation of sexes. At the time of my visit there were but two prisoners—girls—one 14, the other, perhaps, 16 years of age. They were, at this early age, common prostitutes, and were occupying the same apartment, where, by association, while separated from other, but scarcely less pernicious forms of evil, they were being mutually confirmed in a life of utter shamelessness.

This jail had been condemned, as I understood, by grand juries, time after time, and, recently, the question of a "New Jail" had been submitted to a vote of the people, and defeated.

. . . .

From "Secretary's Report," *First Annual Report of the Board of State Charities, 1867, Ohio Executive Documents*, (1868), pp. 250-268.

Franklin County

This Infirmary, likewise, came under the observation of the Board, and, beyond the horrors attaching to the condition of the insane, nothing additional, perhaps, need be said.

In an upper room of a small outer building there are a class of insane inmates for whom any conceivable change of horrors would be a relief. Certainly nothing more wretched than their present condition could be well conceived. The cells are necessarily strong, heavy plank and studding being used in their construction. These cells are but little larger than ordinary stalls for oxen or horses. The violence of the inmates precludes the use of windows to the cells, and the apartment is lighted by small windows at either end of the building. Through one of these windows the strong light of an August sun was barely sufficient to discover the interior and reveal the condition of the inmates of one of these cells. In it were confined a maniac and an idiot. The latter, entirely nude, was crouching, amid his own filth, in one corner of the cell, while the mad-man stood grasping the strong timbers of the door—now raving wildly, and anon entreating mildly, for deliverance from his terrible thraldom.

In an opposite cell, furious in his madness, which literally "no man could tame," was another inmate, who, seven years ago, had been transferred from the Ohio Penitentiary.

Further on, in another cell, was still another. He, too, had been a crazy convict, transferred at the expiration of his sentence from the lunatic department of the Penitentiary to this horrible place. He, however, represented a different type of insanity. He was in a state of nudity, sitting upon the bare floor, having scraped, with apparent care, the straw, which constituted his only bedding, from beneath him. He was lean and haggard, and sat with a vacant, but quiet and seemingly harmless stare upon objects around him. Recognizing the Secretary as his former Chaplain, he remembered the misnomer which, while he had been in prison, the Chaplain had often inadvertently applied to him, and he said: "You used to call me Michael." (His name was Matthew.) When asked if he would not prefer his old quarters at the prison, he said: "No; they tell me I'll go from here to the grave, but I won't if I can help it." Poor "Michael" has since then "gone to the grave, but we will not deplore *him;*" but may we not ask, in the name of our poor, fallen, helpless humanity, is there not much in these sad, pitiable facts that all must deplore, and which, while we deplore, seek, if possible, to remedy?

. . . .

Scioto County Infirmary

The buildings consist of an old, poorly arranged and sadly dilapidated one, which constitutes the main or infirmary building proper, and a new building for the insane separate from the other.

The latter building is so arranged as to render not only the building itself inconvenient and altogether uncomfortable, but is a nuisance to the other parts of the institution.

The insane are kept up stairs, and when, as is often the case, their rooms require scrubbing, all the filth must be washed down the stairway, the landing of which is in the centre of the main hall above, and the foot in the centre of the main hall below, and just inside of the main entrance, which opens so as to connect conveniently with the other buildings. There are no pipes or sewers, no escape for filth save as carried or washed out, so that the bad odor of one filthy cell is of necessity diffused throughout the premises. This county "lets" its infirmary premises, with its paupers, to the "lowest bidder." The premises are rent free as an inducement to board the paupers at low figures. The present rates are as follows:

Ordinary paupers—adults, $1.35 per week; children under 4 years of age, half price; insane inmates, confined in rooms, $2.50 per week.

The present Superintendent and his wife seem to be very kind people. And certainly under such a system kindness must be a desirable quality.

. . . .

Infirmary Children

In no less than three different infirmaries, we found little boys confined, for constraint or punishment, with the insane. In one instance, a little deaf and dumb boy was locked in a cell, in the insane department, opposite a cell in which a violently insane woman was confined. This woman had been casting her own filth, through the shattered panels of her door, at this little boy, the door of whose cell was all bespattered. He was crying bitterly, and, on being released, made signs indicating that he was very hungry. He was locked here to prevent him from running off.

This little boy is something over 10 years of age. His father was killed in the war of the rebellion; his mother is an inmate of a lunatic asylum. He (the boy) is of sound body and mind. A gentleman to whom a letter from this office (directed to the Superintendent of the Infirmary) had been referred, in his answer to certain inquiries concerning the boy, says: "If there is a possibility of getting him (the boy) into the Deaf and Dumb Asylum, please use your best endeavors to do so, as the place where he now is is far from being what it should be."

In another infirmary we found quite an interesting little girl, said by the Superintendent to be "remarkably smart," entirely blind. This child is probably 7 or 8 years old; but as we have failed to get answers to letters inquiring into her history, we cannot state more in regard to her, than that she seemed to have won for herself an unusual degree of affection from those who had her in charge, and that they earnestly entreated that some better provision should be made for her than they could possibly make.

In another infirmary we found another blind child. Its parents had sinned; its blindness was the effect of congenital syphilis. As we stood by the rude cradle of this sightless child, in a bare room where it was sole occupant, and where it sat swaying to and fro in its darkness, shrinking from our voice, with its thumbs pressed with nervous twitchings beneath its senseless eyeballs, a half-witted pauper woman thrust her head through the open window of the apartment, and with her finger giving dreadful emphasis, pointing to that little helpless, abandoned waif, demanded to know, of an officer of the institution, whether or not she, in addition to the "milking of four cows," was to "take care of that thing!"

These are sad details, but there are other children, to whom God has given all their senses, and who are fully endowed with the social instincts and mental faculties of our nature, whose condition is not less deplorable than those already mentioned.

Let those who appreciate the importance of early impressions, who acknowledge childhood as the seed-time of life—let such estimate, if they may, what it must be to have these impressions formed by association with the idiotic, the insane, and amid the loathsome moral corruption so common to our poor-houses. Let them calculate the harvest not only to the future individual life of the child, but to the State, which must be gathered sooner or later from such sowing.

May I not, therefore, commend these "little ones"—the destitute, neglected, afflicted children of "Our Father," thus, in His providence, cast into the lap of the State? May I not in this closing line, consummating as it does a most painful task, commend with earnest entreaty to your honorable Board these "little ones," who, in the midst of the many for whom the State has provided so nobly, have hitherto been so greatly overlooked and neglected?

Conditions in the Infirmary

ROSS COUNTY

Poverty's Penalty—How Our Poor Are Cared For—Paupers, Idiots and Lunatics—Manacles and Chains

"Am I my brother's keeper?" was the response of one of old, on an occasion which will be readily recalled. Though in its corporate capacity the county of Ross does not exactly murder those whom adverse fate has thrown upon its charity, yet it dooms them to a condition of life—say rather a lingering death—to which we are not sure but the "happy dispatch" of the barbarous Japanese is preferable.

If any one doubts the truth of this statement, let him go, as we did one day last week, to the institution known as the Ross County Infirmary—a den which is a disgrace to the county, a shame to humanity, and a standing refutation of our claims to Christianity. Let him go through this libel upon the name of charity as we did, from cellar to garret, and note the bountiful (!) provision which this magnificent county has made for those upon whom poverty and affliction have laid their pitiless hand, and let him bless God that he was born in this land of Bibles and churches and missionary enterprises, but let him be still more thankful that fate has dealt more kindly with him, and not made him a pensioner upon the public bounty.

It may be that in bringing this subject before the people we are repeating an oft-told tale. We care not. It is one of which they should be constantly reminded, and the agitation of which should never cease until a thorough and complete reform is secured. We wish it distinctly understood that in this matter we are actuated by no political feeling, and desire to make no party capital. This is something with which politics has nothing whatever to do. We place it upon a higher plane and a broader ground—the common instincts of humanity.

In the first place, then, we state it as a fact patent and self-evident to every man of common sense, that the present infirmary is totally inadequate and unfit for the purposes to which it is applied. It is badly located, miserably ventilated, not half large enough, and has not a single redeeming feature. It is old and rapidly falling to decay, and has around it none of the conveniences which should

From "Poverty's Penalty—How Our Poor Are Cared For—Paupers, Idiots and Lunatics—Manacles and Chains," *Fourth Annual Report of the Board of State Charities, 1870, Ohio Executive Documents*, (1871), pp. 419-421.

distinguish a building of this kind. It has no drainage, no bathing facilities, no good outbuildings—nothing, in fact, which such an institution should have. When we state that this building is nothing more nor less than an old fashioned farm house, which was standing on the place when the county became the owner of the farm, *more than fifty years ago,* our readers can form some idea of its adaptability to its present purposes. True, some changes have been made in the original structure, but it can never be made what it should be.

In this old rookery, last winter, were *imprisoned* one hundred and five people. At the present time there are seventy eight inmates, eighteen of whom are insane, and twenty-three children. Aside from these, the county is furnishing outside aid to seventy-five poor, sixteen of whom now hold orders for admission to the institution. The Superintendent anticipates not less than one hundred and twenty-five inmates the coming winter, and, to use his own words, "how in the name of God I am to care for them, is more than I can tell." Even now, in rooms of ten by twelve, there are six, eight and nine persons; and the atmosphere which they inhale continually in these ill-ventilated rooms—laden as it is with the foul exhalations from their filthy bodies—is sickening and poisonous in the extreme. We say filthy bodies, for they can not be otherwise when to bathe their persons is an impossibility. And here the miserable wretches lie from year to year, festering in their own filth and corruption, a constantly accumulating mass of vermin, dirt, disease and death. In one room, *under ground,* with two small windows which are *never opened,* four men slowly rot away. In others eight persons vainly seek repose on four rickety old bedsteads covered with ancient army blankets, for the possession of which they are obliged to wage a constant warfare with veteran bedbugs who have seen fifty years of service, and their annual reinforcements of tens of thousands.

And the children who are here receiving their first lessons of life—what of them? They are growing up in utter ignorance, rags, squalor, filth and wretchedness. Familiarized as they are from infancy with dirt, disease and vice, what can be expected of them than that they will inevitably continue the course so inauspiciously begun, reinforce the ranks of crime, and eventually ornament the penitentiary and the gallows. An effort was once made to hold a Sunday school here, but for lack of a suitable room it was discontinued. Now they are sent to a Sunday school in the neighborhood, but what will one hour's instruction avail against the influence and example of a whole week?

But the saddest spectacle of all is the insane—whose disordered minds, "like sweet bells jangled out of tune," ring the sad changes of dethroned reason. For want of any other security, five of these poor wretches are kept in irons—actually *chained to the floor!* And here, from year to year, like chafing beasts or convicted murderers, they tread the weary circle described by the length of their chains, wearing their miserable lives away in gibbering, helpless, hopeless lunacy. One woman has thus dragged her manacles for *twenty-two years!* And in the same room are *six other persons*—women and children! What a life, or rather living death is this! We have read of a living man chained to the decaying dead, but this seems humane when compared with chaining in effect a living woman and helpless children to a howling lunatic.

In addition to all these things, there is no effectual bar to an unrestrained intercourse of the sexes; and not a year passes that there is not one or more illegitimate accessions to this motley crowd of helpless paupers, driveling idiots and raving lunatics.

And here from year to year—on pleasant days droning in the sunlight, in winter shut up in narrow, illventilated rooms, shivering over the coals, breathing the mephitic vapors which arise on every hand, patiently waiting for "Death, the poor man's kindest friend"—these poor people exist. All ages and conditions are here, from the palsied octogenarian to the prattling child, the able bodied lunatic and the tottering old woman, the mumbling idiot and the blear-eyed debauchee—all mingling in one common herd like swine in a common pen, inhaling and exhaling a common atmosphere of most sickening odor and rank corruption.

Do our people know what a horrible cess-pool we are fostering in our midst? Do those good people who are so much interested in the spiritual welfare of the heathen of foreign lands, know what a body of heathen are at our doors? We raise immense contributions to build fine churches, to send missionaries and Bibles to Borroboola Gha, and shall our own poor, whom we have always with us, hunger and thirst and die? A few Christian ladies and gentlemen of this city have visited the institution, but there has been no organized effort to better the condition of the inmates. And the ministry—they who break the bread of life to a dying world—how have they met the case? We are informed that they refuse to minister to these poor people unless they are paid by the county! We hope this is not true, and shall be glad to be able to publish a contradiction. At any rate, during the past summer, but one minister has visited the institution, and he but once. Is this as it should be?

We do not wish any remarks we have made to be applied to the Superintendent, Mr. John Kelley. We believe he does everything in his power for the comfort of his unfortunate charges. But it is simply impossible for one man to manage such an institution, and at the same time work a large farm with no help but pauper labor; and of this labor, he informs us, all that is available is that of the mildly insane, requiring constant watching, of course. The only thing, he says, that can be said in favor of the institution is, that the paupers have enough to eat. He does his best—the fault is not with him, but in the system itself, which is radically wrong, and in the building.

3 The Developing Urban Crisis— 19th Century

NOTHING EMPHASIZED the impact of industrialization in post-Civil War Ohio more than the growth of urban areas. As industries developed at key locations within the state, people from the farm-lands, blacks from the South, and newly arrived immigrants from Europe streamed into the cities seeking employment. As the cities became overcrowded, local governments were faced with multiple problems of both service and safety. Services that had been poor at best prior to 1860 were burdened beyond usefulness. Water systems, solid waste plants, sewer lines, and paved streets had to be developed. For safety, full-time and professional fire and police departments, as well as health agencies, had to be created and maintained. In order to care for the unemployed, the poor, and the handicapped, workable relief mechanisms had to be organized. Of course, threatening all of these services was the specter of insufficient funding, a cumbersome state government apparatus, public apathy, and political bossism. As Frederick Jackson Turner prophetically suggested in 1901, by the end of the century the task of an American society that had embraced urbanization was "to reconcile popular government and culture with the huge industrial society of the modern world. The democracies of the past have been small communities under simple and primitive economic conditions." He concluded: "At the bottom is how to reconcile real greatness with bigness."

Within a fifty-year period (1850 to 1900) Ohio was transformed from a rural into an urban-directed state. Across the state, municipalities expanded in response to the demands placed on them by the economic race towards industrialization. Cleveland, at the head of the Cuyahoga Valley, as well as Youngstown and other cities in the important Mahoning Valley, changed quickly in character and style. From a small city of 17,034 in 1850, Cleveland grew to 261,353 by 1890 and 381,768 by the end of the century, surpassing Cincinnati as the largest city in the state. Youngstown, which had a population of only 2,759 in 1860, expanded to a city of 44,885 by 1900. In the other corner of the state, Toledo, comfortably situated at the mouth of the Maumee River, developed from a sleepy village of 3,829 in

1850 to the third largest city in the state by 1900, with a population of 131,822. Cincinnati, the Queen City and formerly the great city of the West, though boasting a population of over 100,000 at midcentury, did not experience the explosive growth of her sister cities. Although ignored by newly constructed railroads and outbid for industry and commerce by urban centers outside the Ohio Valley, Cincinnati's population reached 325,902 by 1900; but it could no longer claim to be the greatest city in Ohio. Akron, Canton, Lorain, Findlay, Dayton, Lima, Marion, Springfield, and many others also witnessed growth during the latter half of the century—growth based on local economic expansion.

The urban crisis in Ohio at the end of the century represented a social, economic, and political mess of great magnitude. Reformers found it difficult to seek specific improvements in the quality of municipal life without first being struck by the enormity of the task and the realization that the interrelated problems formed a structural house of cards. To illustrate the point: cities were invaded by epidemics that were directly related to the poor quality of fresh drinking water. These epidemics, which affected both the rich and the poor, placed a burden on the city to provide adequate medical facilities. At the same time, fresh sources of water were sought and new water systems built to alleviate the causes of epidemics. However, diseases also emanated from sources other than drinking water: poor drainage and the absence of sewers led to the stagnation of water. Consequently, to improve health conditions, it became necessary to lay sewers; to build hard-surfaced streets with curbs; to eliminate cesspools; to encourage indoor plumbing; to connect plumbing facilities to sewers; to establish municipal plumbing standards; to license plumbers in order to insure satisfactory work; and to hire plumbing and building inspectors to enforce the standards.

Providing city-dwellers with drinking water in sufficient quantity was also a concern of local government. The relationship between impure drinking water and communicable diseases had been established by scientific research, and the medical profession, increasingly concerned with public health, pursued the development of modern clean water systems. Cities, of course, tapped local available water sources for their needs. For instance, Cleveland in 1856 drew its water from Lake Erie through a pipe extending 300 feet into the lake at a depth of twelve feet. By 1865, however, this system was no longer able to provide an adequate supply of water; in 1867 a tunnel system that would allow a greater pumping capacity was begun. This new system was in use by 1874 and enlarged in 1885 and 1895. As industry also used local water sources, clean, fresh water became increasingly difficult to find. Public health officials worried about the ramifications of industrialization and urbanization on local fresh-water sources and began to warn of the dangers of waste and wanton misuse of local supplies. With increasing regularity they called for government action to preserve the environment by protecting a vital natural resource.

The need to develop efficient and adequate police and fire departments to keep pace with the population and physical growth of the cities became apparent in both the public and private sector of local communities. Begun on a voluntary basis, the protective agencies soon faced demands that surpassed their capabilities. Unfortunately, it usually took some major disaster—a rash of murders, a riot, or a major fire in the tenement area or at an industrial site—before local indignation could be aroused. While attempts were made during the 1870s and 1880s to organize adequate police and fire departments, it was not until the end of the century that most major cities in the state could boast professional protective agencies equipped with the latest scientific apparatuses.

Blame for the inefficiency in local government cannot be laid entirely at the municipal doorstep. The state government, before the home rule amendment was adopted in 1912, controlled local government through inefficient city charters, which were basically unaltered despite urban growth, and through the imposition of ripper bills, that is, special interest legislation, which changed local government for partisan advantages. Within municipal government, antiquated city charters allowed for the division of legislative and executive authority, creating confusion and inefficient government. This system fostered the political bossism that too often typified Ohio municipal government in the nineteenth century. Most famous of the bosses were Toledo's Guy Major, George P. Waldorf, and Walter F. Brown; Dayton's Joseph E. Lowes; and Cincinnati's George Barnsdale Cox. Hand in hand with bossism went the corrupting influences of business interests that were quick with the bribe and kickback to get special contracts and privileges; along with them came the smothering effect of the private utility companies, which supped too freely at the public trough. It certainly was no accident that by the turn of the century reformers were making demands and were struggling at both the state and local level to break the hold of special privilege and influence peddlers.

Thus, while a great deal of lip service and rhetoric was paid to the individualistic qualities of American society during the nineteenth century, it was soon apparent to those who were earnest urban watchers, that positive government action was needed to check the detrimental effects of industrial growth.

Tenement Housing in Cincinnati

LABOR STATISTICS

Outside of the two principal cities of the State, each family, as a rule, occupies a whole house and has plenty of breathing room, and to a very great extent is responsible for the sanitary condition of its home; but in the two cities of Cincinnati and Cleveland, the tendency appears to be to crowd families together under one roof, until health, decency, and morality must each and all suffer. No adequate idea of the condition of the homes of workingmen in the two cities named can be had by correspondence; it will require a thorough personal investigation by parties fully empowered to make such investigation. This Bureau has been unable to make such an investigation during the year, but, fortunately, is in possession of data collected by the Board of Health of Cincinnati, which must convince every unprejudiced mind that legislation on the tenement-house system has become an absolute necessity, before its proportions become so great as to become another "social evil," which no laws seem to be able to reach.

In 1868, there were, in the city of Cincinnati, 1,410 tenement houses, containing six or more families to each house.

. . . .

The total number of rooms in these 1,410 houses, was 16,197, an average of over eleven and one-half rooms to each house. These rooms were occupied by 9,894 families, comprising a population of 38,721 persons, an average of a fraction over seven families to each house, and a fraction over twenty-seven persons to each house. *Four thousand two hundred and eighteen* (4,218) families, numbering 15,604 persons, had but one room to a family, in which to cook, eat, sleep, etc. Three thousand five hundred and seventy-one of these rooms thus occupied, had but one window to each room; 4,469 families had two rooms each.

A very considerable portion of these tenement-houses have only one stairway or means of entrance and exit; the number of stories varies from two to six; so that in case of fire it would be almost impossible for many of the inmates to escape alive. These figures present the strongest reasons that could be adduced in favor of a law to regulate the construction of dwelling-houses, and the uses to which property should be devoted. It is in such crowded tenement-

From "Sanitary," *Second Annual Report of the Bureau of Labor Statistics, 1878*, (Columbus, 1879), pp. 287-292.

houses where diseases of every name and character are most prevalent and fatal, and these are the foci from which pestilential and contagious diseases spread over the whole city.

In 1869, Cincinnati was the most densely populated city in the United States, and was more densely populated than the city of London. New York city has twenty-two square miles, or 32,068 inhabitants to each square mile; Philadelphia has 129 square miles, or 6,200 inhabitants to each square mile; Brooklyn, twenty-five, or 17,388 persons to the square mile; Chicago, twenty-nine and three-fourths; Buffalo, thirty-seven; Pittsburgh, twenty-four; Louisville, twelve and three-tenths; while Cincinnati had an area of only seven square miles, or 37,142⁶/₇ persons to the mile, or fifty-eight and one-twenty-eighth to the acre.

Since that date, considerable of the surrounding country has been added to Cincinnati, and the average would not, perhaps, be so great; but tenement-houses and their teeming population yet remain; and that population is composed entirely of workingmen and their families.

"There are localities in Cincinnati so compactly built up with high buildings front and rear of lots both covered, that there is no means for the admission of air and light, only that afforded by a narrow passage way, which, too, in the majority of instances extends only as high as the second story. These buildings are almost always in a bad sanitary condition, due to two causes, viz.: those due to faults in the original construction of the building, and, second, those due to over-crowding and neglect.

"There are many large tenement-houses in this city without one square yard of air space, excepting that used as an entrance. A single privy is provided, in most instances, for the occupants of the building, and it is commonly placed at one end of the entrance way, so that it is almost impossible to prevent the *gasseous* exhalations arising from it from being disseminated through the entire building, poisoning the atmosphere, and causing discomfort, disease, and death.

"A stringent law is needed to regulate the construction of dwellings designed for the poor. Crowding human beings together is fraught with the most terrible physical and moral results; the practice is certain to cause sickness, and the forced companionship of the old and young of both sexes is demoralizing and pernicious in the extreme."

In 1871, there were, in the city of Cincinnati, 306 dwellings without water, 862 without yard space, 251 without privies, and 480 cellars used as dwelling places, and, in addition, 1,116 were found to be in bad sanitary condition.

In 1873, that dread plague, cholera, visited Cincinnati, and from

June 14, to October 18, 207 persons died of the disease, of which number 142 were residents of tenement-houses and boarding houses, while but thirty-four died in private residences, the balance dying in the hospitals or their residences not ascertained.

An average of over 70 per cent. of the deaths in the city occur in tenement houses and either of two things must be apparent: 1, that a vast majority of the people of the city live in tenement houses, or 2d, the number of deaths in tenement houses are out of all proportion to their population. In either case every power of the law should be exerted to compel the owners of such property to keep it in the best possible sanitary condition, to prevent over a given number of persons being permitted to each tenement according to its size and surroundings, and above all to prevent the erection of such buildings, except upon plans approved by the board of health or other police authority, who should have full power to enforce obedience to their rules. The facts herein given must convince the most skeptical, that from a sanitary point of view, these tenement houses are a standing menace to the health of the city, and no considerations of private property should be permitted to interfere with the strictest police regulations.

Two rooms, front or back, in the second, third, fourth, and even fifth story of a barracks, hemmed in on all sides but one, is the average home of the workingman in the Queen City of the West, and for these two rooms he pays an average rent in excess of the rent of four-roomed tenements in most of the towns and smaller cities of that State.

Slums in Cleveland

NEWSPAPER REPORT

A Chapter on Cleveland's Uncleanliness—A Visit to Back Yards and Tenement Houses—A Few Facts Worthy of Consideration.

In the interests of the public health and for the purpose of showing what slums and moral sink holes are hidden away behind the walls of the city and under the cover of night, and also to give an idea of how our city, in some parts, is not yet ready for the coming of cholera, a *Leader* reporter has made a tour in some parts of the city, and is now prepared to call the attention of the proper authorities to a number of places and cases which demand instant attention.

A visit under the care of Officer Farrell was made yesterday afternoon to a number of dwellings and streets on the West Side but more particularly on and near Main street. Along said street, in many places, are low dwellings which are occupied by people whose nature and standard of cleanliness matches well with their buildings. In front of a number of these houses the gullies are filled with almost stagnant wash water which has been poured into the street. The water is heavy with filth and deposits a sediment which the sun strikes and causes to smell in a short time. This lies there and pollutes the air until a rain happens to come along and wash it away.

In the sunken railroad track running from Main street to Spruce street a slimy, crawling stream of water passes by one of the tracks and runs over a bed of foul filth a foot or so deep. The ditch is full of all the nastiness man's ingenuity and nature's decay can produce. Half-rotten straw, the refuse of pig pens, old bottles, rotten clothes, garbage and almost everything else can be mentioned.

At the corner of Spruce street and these tracks the catch-basin is choked up entirely, and the water when it reaches that point either lies there stagnant or goes meandering down Spruce street. The water at that point is spread clear across the track and is quite deep. It cannot strike the sewer, and so lies there and gives forth a sickening odor. The apparatus which is there for watering locomotives does not help matters a particle.

On that corner, a day or two since, Officer Farrell's attention was called to the condition of the back yard. Entering, he found a heap of garbage which was literally alive. He ordered the parties to remove it, and they would only do so when threatened with arrest.

On Mulberry street the yards behind the houses run back to the track. In one was dry garbage full of a deathly smell. In another the water and slops lay scattered about. Farther down a loathsome pig-pen sent its sweet scents out on the air, which wended its way about the city for the furtherance of health and the public good.

At the corner of Center and Spruce streets is a grocery and tenement house. The house is occupied by four families, which mix together in infinite confusion and live in universal filth. From under a corner of the house oozes a stream of foul, green water, which leads to the supposition that the house is over a pool of water. The people living there had never given any thought to the water and were surprised that any one should notice it.

From Cleveland *Leader,* July 10, 1873.

Near the corner of Elm and Main streets, a box gutter discharges a mass of dirty water and garbage from a boarding house into the street. The water crawls along, leaving deposits all the way, until it reaches a sewer a couple of hundred feet below.

At the Willow street bridge a garbage boat is anchored. On it was a barrel half full of soap-grease and bones. A million flies were circling around or feasting upon it. A dozen empty barrels near by, loudly proclaimed to the sense of smell that they were a part of the arrangement. On the ground near by an active young man, who had just brought a load of refuse stuff, was engaged in distributing a few fish heads upon the highway. The boat, it is said, is left there for hours, and although no one lives near there is a constant stream of travel passing over the bridge. When the boat is full the load is dumped into the lake—and Cleveland drinks it.

. . . .

In Hazard's block, on Detroit street near the West Side station, a number of families inhabit the upper floors. They are mostly emigrants just arrived, and have brought old country filth with them.

Last night, under charge of another officer, a visit was made to several establishments on Canal street and in other places. On Canal street near Seneca street are a number of small shanties which are worthy of notice. The first one is foul in the extreme. On an old bed a woman and girl were lying in filthy bed-clothes. A man and boy in the same room were spread out on a couple of chairs. A young woman rocked a babe in a rickety cradle, while two dogs made up the happy family. All was filth and wretchedness. Outside were two little boys who had crawled into an express wagon and lay asleep. Being awakened, they said they had come out "because it smelt so" inside.

The next shanty was approached by a pair of old stairs, and the gauntlet of three or four dogs had to be run. Inside the house it was as bad. A man and woman, three children and a boy were all in a room about eight by nine feet in size. In a small room to the rear were three or four others. All the windows were closed, and the same damp, sickly smell prevailed. The hole in the wall was next visited. It is a boarding house under the basement of the New England Block on Broadway and looks out upon Canal street and has a commanding view of a couple of soap factories and the Cuyahoga river. Climbing up a stretch of broken, filthy stairs, covered thick with dirt and cumbered with garbage, the party reached the place and knocked at the door. The room which is spoken of opens from a low, damp and dark hall or cellar, which is lighted only by the few straggling rays of sun or moonlight which are able to penetrate the gloom. A deathly odor, sickening and heavy, strikes the nostrils when one enters the passage.

The magic word of "police" being whispered through the keyhole, there was a harried shuffling of feet and a few whispers and the door was thrown back, and suddenly a whiff of the foulest air came out. It was thick enough to be cut with a knife.

The place is well known to the police as the "Hole in the Wall," and is kept by a negro woman known as Mother Bell. She is one of the lowest creatures in this city, and boards both white and black.

The scene which was presented on entering beggars description. The room was small and low, a swarm of flies hung on the dirty, filthy ceiling, a small amount of light was admitted through the window, while all of heaven's air was completely barred out. Rags, filth, squalor and wretchedness were everywhere. On a narrow bunk, with a bundle of rags for a pillow and an old blanket for a mattress, lay a white man with his clothes on, near him on an old bed were two other men with their clothes on. In a small adjoining room which had no door, the keeper of the place, a dirty, ragged colored woman lay on a narrow bed with a little child, while at the foot of the bed a white man lay stretched on a bunk. The police claimed that this was only about one-half of the usual lodgers.

In the inner room the stench was awful. To think that human beings could exist thus for any length of time seems almost impossible. And to sleep there through a hot summer night with the doors closed and with several dogs lying about—it is almost beyond imagination. Three minutes in these apartments was sufficient. Out into the hall and up a short flight of stairs brought the explorers to another nest as foul as the former but not as thickly populated except by bugs. A man and his wife lay on one of the filthiest beds ever spread and a dog lay beneath it. The floor was crusted with dirt, the same heavy odor hung in the air and indolent poverty and idle wretchedness were marked everywhere. An old cook stove was in one corner of the room covered with grease and bits of cabbage, the walls were discolored and damp. Vermin was everywhere and the place was litterly alive. The man and woman lay with their clothes on as if even the work of dressing and undressing was not thought of from year to year. The police say that when one of their class manages to get a shirt on it is his thenceforth until it falls to pieces and no washerwoman ever gets a hold of it.

In an inner room smaller and nastier one little girl and two small boys lay on a bundle of rags. They were almost entirely naked and looked thin and pale. All the air they could receive was that which came through the basement, up the stair and by the other and outer room. By the time it reached the children it had lost every particle of health giving power and purity.

The next visit was to an old square house on Canal street west of Seneca. The place is a double fronted house, and is said to belong to the city, having been taken in default of tax payments. If this is so let the city pull it down immediately. The same old tale was told in every feature of the place—rags, wretchedness, filth, distress and drunkenness. In one room on the upper floor was a woman who said she was sick and that her husband had deserted her. A fire burned in the stove and the windows were closed. The walls were bare and broken. The table was covered with dirty dishes. The floor was broken and foul, and the woman lay on a ragged bed. In the next room a family lives in as bad a condition. A bleared eyed woman with black and blue marks on her face put her head through the door in response to the knock, and said her husband was sick. The explorers were also nearly sick with the smell, and departed.

On Spring street below Water are from forty to fifty shanties perched up on the hill-side and filled to their utmost capacity with men, women and children whose existence in such quarters seems almost an impossibility. The houses are small, dirty and wretched. Most of them are mere sheds boarded up and provided with a floor. The woodwork is rotten, the real estate lies thick on the floor and the windows are stuffed with rags. The houses are ranged so that the floor of one on the hill-side is on a level with the roof of another and so the refuse water and filth from those above finds its way upon the tables and into the beds of those beneath. Narrow spaces run between them up the hill side and in these the steps are slippery and slimy. In these old shanties there ranges from one to three familes each, and to each one is accorded space sufficient only for a bed. There is no ventilation, the stench is only what might be expected, and all the habits of the inmates are directly opposed to the rules of cleanliness and health. The buildings, by their mere existence, are a perpetual violation of the health ordinance and ought to be torn down.

Into this sweet-scented and highly classical region the party ventured. On the upper bank of the street is an old establishment kept by one whose nickname is Saxt. Clambering over the usual foul steps and knocking at the door, entrance was demanded and granted. The family was asleep, but as that portion of our population are always expecting the police, no surprise was shown at the late call. Entering, the usual sight was presented. The same old tale of indolence, filth, and consequent wretchedness. The family had all retired with their clothes on, and the remnants of the last meal smeared the floor and lay scattered over the greasy table. In an outer room Saxt and his wife slept, while in a little dark hole in the rear seven children were crammed, crowded and huddled. They were divided into two parties, four in one bed and three in the other.

· ·

Not a quilt or sheet was to be seen. The whole affair was a mass of rags and the children lay sleeping as calmly and unconscious of their filthy condition as if they were reposing on down. The air was beyond imagination and needs to be breathed to be appreciated.

A dwelling occupied by three families on the other side of the street was next visited. When the door was opened it is an actual fact which can be proven by four witnesses, that when the stench from the room came out it smote a stalwart policeman so suddenly that he was fain to depart to a retired place and perform an important part of sea sickness. An old man opened the door and in an inner room five children were asleep in one bed. The same wretchedness prevailed and the only distinguished difference was the greater strength and power of the smell.

These two places are but samples of the rest. A number of others were visited and to describe them would be but a repetition of the foregoing. If cholera seeds were even sown with willing and open hand in the streets and dwellings of our city, the residents of Spring street can carry off the medal for being the most liberal handed and generous of all the husbandmen.

On Third Street, above the hay market several places were visited. One boarding house kept by an old colored woman named Ross was found packed full of white and colored boarders. Clambering over a roof into another house, a white man and a colored woman were found in a small and unsightly room. Further up the street was found a number of colored men sprawled out on the floor, either asleep or drunk.

In this locality it is unnecessary to enumerate. There are dozens of places which are vile and foul. To describe one describes them all, and any disease which thrives on filth could, in this part of our beautiful city, find ample food for its growth. These places mentioned are but few compared to those which exist.

Some action on the part of some one is absolutely needed. In mercy to the people who inhabit these holes as well as for the safety of the rest of the city, it is necessary that they be cleaned out. Better that the little children who dwell herein should sleep in wagons or open boxes, for then they could breathe pure air, than to be housed in pens worse than those made for cattle, and where health is ruined and decency unknown.

These few examples of Cleveland's filth are respectfully presented to the authorities, with the suggestion that as they have been pointed out plainly and exactly, there can be no excuse for their being longer in existence.

Poverty and Crime in Cleveland

NEWSPAPER REPORT

Chapter Third—More Unsavory Odors—Low Life Under the Crust—About the New England Block—Gutters and Catch-Basins Needed—Another Batch of Italians—A Tour with Health Officer Kitchen.

It is fair to suppose that the Leader reporters have unveiled enough of the nauseating and disgusting characteristics of certain localities in Cleveland to more than satisfy our readers that we possess all the filth, scum, slime and putridity that should be allotted to any one city of one hundred and forty thousand inhabitants. It is equally supposable that enough has been related to satisfy the taste for such kind of literature, but there is more to come, and those who wish to know where the filth is and how whole families live in it, are respectfully invited to accompany our reporter in a day's rambles through the lower grades of society and see what is transacted under the crust.

Starting in the New England block, under the guidance of the health officer, Dr. H. W. Kitchen, we entered the basement under the sidewalk. Here are a number of small rooms, fourteen feet below the street, having no ventilation, and all occupied by numerous families, who pay six dollars per month for two rooms. A narrow stairway leads us down into a cellar, below these rooms, occupied as a general receptacle for everything that seems to be unfit for any earthly use. There are old rotten boards, broken wheels, stove pipes, rags, pieces of carpets, old shoes and heaps of straw, all pitched together in a confusion natural to the locality. Emerging from this cellar the rear of the building is reached, and the most prominent feature of the disease-breeding nuisance here meets the eye. The rear is about three stories higher than the front, and the whole long block looks as if it were ready to slide down the hillside upon the smaller hovels fringing the canal. As the eye glances up the sides of the block, a variagated display of old clothing, dish-cloths, pails and brooms are seen, with long blackened ridges left by trickling streams of dish-water and slops thrown from the windows. A wooden pipe, destined to convey water from the apartments to a cess pool, runs down the side of the wall; but the cess pool is stopped up, and the offal consequently runs down the hill, filling the air with unhealthy odors. Every step taken reveals one or more pools of water, constantly forming from the offal thrown down from above, and interspersed with heaps of ashes, potato parings, onion tops and almost every thing comprehended in the word rubbish. Every thing is thrown from the upper windows down this hill, and the whole neighborhood is pervaded by an insupportable stench. The vaults, cess pools and water pipes are out of order, and the interior of the building is swarming with human beings.

A Colored Physician

After examining the rear of these buildings, we entered a room in the basement occupied by a colored woman named Rachel Turner. The room was about nine feet by nine in dimensions, and near it was a closet about four feet wide and nine feet long, dark as midnight and void of any ventilation. Hearing some one in the closet, our reporter entered and saw a white woman bending over a miserable bed, in which lay a little girl emaciated by sickness. The mother said she had brought her child there to be treated by Mrs. Turner, who was a doctor, and while she was relating how long her little one had been ill, our attention was attracted by a noise to a spot where a young white man lay on squalid rags, sleeping off the effects of a spree.

"What are you doing here?" we asked, as he turned and rubbed his eyes at the sound of strange voices.

"I board here" was the reply, as he took in the situation and feigned to be asleep again.

"How many boarders have you in these two rooms?"

"It depends upon circumstances, sir, sometimes we have eight, but now we have only five," was the answer.

"Aunt Rachel, they tell us you are a doctor, is it so?" asked we.

"Yes, sir, I'se a doctor, and a good one."

"Where did you learn medicine?"

"Oh, I always knowed it."

"What do you give that little girl?"

"Catnip tea, sir, dat'll cure anyting."

Our conversation would have been prolonged with this learned physician, were it not for taking too much of Dr. Kitchen's time, so we moved on into another story, where several rooms were visited, each being occupied by four or five persons. They were all dirty and had no possible means of ventilation. Each room served for a coal house, kitchen, dining and bed room. Up stairs, in another portion of the building, a large family was packed into a small room, into which came deleterious odors from door and window. A little girl was sick, and her mother, ignorant of the existence of a city physician, had no means of obtaining medical advice or treatment. During the day the whole family, except the men, work and sit about in this room, and during the sultriest nights of summer they sleep scattered about on the floor, no breath of air reaching their nostrils until it has become unwholesome by passing through the fetid atmosphere of the surroundings.

Halt, There!

Dr. Kitchen next conducted our reporter down a few steps in front of the house, and as we were walking through a passage a man rushed angrily towards us, crying "Halt, there! you youst go somewhere else mit your nuisance, and don't come here some more." On explaining to him the object of our visit, he explained his conduct by saying that the spot had become a public vault for the market people and all the habitues of the neighboring saloons. It was directly under the sidewalk, and the stench that arose from it penetrated the homes of several families.

More of 'em

Just beyond the New England block and in the rear of No. 53, is a building similar to the one above described to which Dr. Kitchen directed our attention. All the sweepings and house offal are thrown behind the building, where they generate an odor that seems indigenous to the neighborhood. Our reporter meandered pensively down the rickety stairs that led to this *omnium gatherum* of filth and had just began meditating on the scene around him, when down came a pail full of highly flavored liquids and vegetable debris close to his feet. Retreating a few steps the explorer of this region of infected zephyrs betook himself again to contemplating the scene, and was a second time interrupted by a similar onslaught. He then made up his mind to withdraw and had taken a few steps when his attention was arrested by several shrill cries and on looking around . . . [saw a] boy, dressed only in a dirty polonaise, and a pair of short socks, going head over heels down a flight of stairs. This brought out the occupants of all the rooms, boarders, children and all. There were thirty to forty little white heads and nearly half as many grown persons. A few minutes were consumed in enquiring into the cause of the accident which was traced to a rotten step that gave way as soon as the child's foot touched it. This question settled our perambulations were continued through the dim and ill-ventilated apartments around us. The rooms were all occupied by different families and kept in as good a condition as was possible with the surroundings. There was no way of emptying swill and waste water except by throwing it out the window upon the hillside, and the place is consequently reeking with the foulest odors.

An earthen pipe, leading from the top of the building down to a catch basin, empties out on the ground, within a few feet of several windows, infecting the atmosphere of the whole neighborhood. Every rain washes the ground sending the filth down the hill around a score of shanties, forcing the inmates to close every aperture communicating with the outer world. "Please attend to that nuisance from the earthen pipe there gentleman," was the request made by all the occupants of the shanties. Dr. Kitchen has already attended to it to a certain degree. He has reported it to the Board of Health, but that body cannot abate the nuisance without tearing down the building. First class sewer connections would perhaps remedy the evil, but Dr. Kitchen cannot procure them.

In several buildings in this neighborhood many changes must be made to remove the unwholesome influences. They are all surrounded by stagnant water, which daily increases in offensiveness and in quantity. At the window of one room stands an out-house through which passes every breath of air entering the apartment. Within a few feet of another room is a stable tenanted by a horse, a cow, several chickens and dogs. On every side there are objects of filth which are all the more deleterious in their effects as the neighborhood is thickly peopled with unclean, half-fed, ignorant men, women and children who are also lacking in habits of sobriety and industry.

Other Plague-spots

Leaving this uninviting neighborhood we strolled through several quarters of the city to which Dr. Kitchen has called the attention of the Board of Health. On the corner of Huron and Middle streets the catch basin is choked up and full of water. The gutters here are in a bad condition. On Wood, Hamilton, Bond, Muirson, Bolivar, Third and Canal streets the gutters are in such a state as to prevent the water from flowing into the catch basins. In some of these places the water is putrid from decaying vegetables and animal matter, emitting a poisonous taint through the whole atmosphere. On Third street the gutters are filled with filth, notwithstanding the fact that they were cleaned a few weeks ago. Water trickles down into them from the neighboring hill sides, passing through heaps of rubbish which impart their deleterious odors to every drop. Along Hamilton and a few other streets, the nature of the soil is such as to permit water to readily soak through, and there are consequently no stagnant pools in these localities. Here and there, however, in these quiet streets, the sides of the roadway show a green, crusty surface, where water has lain until it reached a condition almost like that on Third street. This is injurious to the health of the community and although it may not be of great importance it nevertheless suggests the propriety of better sewer connections.

A Nest of Italians

At No. 332 St. Clair street, Dr. Kitchen conducted our reporter into a nest of Italians, as *recherche* and refined, in their filth, as the far-famed, ear-torturing brigands of Wood street. The room opening into the street is a bar room and in this we found about fifteen Italian bandits and two French conspirators, all talking at once, their beautiful language ringing in discordant tones, like sweet bells jingling out of tune. In the rear of this bar room were the headquarters consisting of one large room, used as a dining room, kitchen, sitting room and store room. A long calico curtain was stretched across the room, separating the store room from the other apartments, and above it was suspended the word "Welcome" in large letters. Beyond this curtain were ten bedsteads, ranged on either side of the room, leaving a passage between them, in which several lazzeroni were lounging or playing cards. An old man sat in a rocking chair asleep, a woman leaned against a bed post, another bent over a hot stove on which was a large pot filled with last year's potatoes, onions and dried beans, and the Impressario of the troupe held a hurried *tete-a-tete* with the maestros to the probable business of the two intruders. In one end of the room several instruments of torture were piled upon each other ready to be paraded and set in motion on our street corners, and at the other end, just outside the door, lay a chubby little vagabond asleep in the sun covered with flies. In close proximity to him was a heap of manure and a dead kitten, then there was a stable and a horse.

The Occupants

The head vagabond of the troupe found his tongue after we had fully inspected the premises, and gave us the particulars as to his boarders. The house contains generally from twenty to forty individuals who, contrary to the ghost of Hamlet, make the day hideous, and at night huddle together in their purgatorial abode. The house is not so filthy as the well known den on Wood street, but its condition is such that Dr. Kitchen has ordered its inmates to vacate the premises.

The sight of all the miserable people seen in the various low haunts of the city excites in the visitor not only feelings of disgust but pity. They suffer in these hovels from every loathsome disease engendered by vice and filth, but equally as much from lack of ventilation and poor diet. The health officer may visit them and order them to change their style of living, but it is not sufficient to say: "Be thou clean" and then go your way without providing any means for carrying out the order. Their quarters are so small and crowded that an improved condition in their habits is almost impossible. The rent many of them pay for even the little room they now occupy taxes them severely. How, then, can their condition be alleviated? Certainly it cannot be done in their present location. They should be provided with small houses and cheap rent in the outskirts of the city, where they are not crowded together in one-fifth the space they ought to occupy, and when this is done there will be less danger of disease in our midst.

Sanitation in Cleveland

G. C. ASHMUN

The territory now embraced in the city of Cleveland comprises about thirty square miles or twenty thousand acres. This tract lies mainly inclining toward the north and Lake Erie, above which it rises from sixty to two hundred and fifty feet. About two-thirds of the surface has a sandy soil, some of which is clear lake sand, resting upon clay or shale at the depth of from five to twenty feet. The other third of the surface is a moderately firm clay. This tract of land is traversed from south to north by the Cuyahoga river, a small stream about eighty-five miles in length, capable of being and now is used for docks and large vessels for about three miles from its mouth. The city is thus divided, with about three-fourths of its population and business on the eastern side of the river, with the natural watershed for both portions of the city into the river. Following the

From G. C. Ashmun, "Sanitary History of Cleveland," *First Annual Report of the State Board of Health, 1886, Ohio Executive Documents*, (1887), pp. 1907-1911.

natural flow of storm water, the citizens drained their streets, cellars and, later, their sewers, chiefly into the river and creeks within the city. In 1853 a system of public water supply was established by taking the water from Lake Erie within a few hundred feet of the shore at a point about half a mile to the west or above the mouth of the river. But about 1860, when oil refining began to be a large element in the city's productions, the refuse from that source being drained into the river and thence to the lake, it became apparent that the river water and some of its burden was at times reaching the intake point of the water supply. On this account, and to assure a supply of pure water for the future, a tunnel was constructed out from the shore into the lake about one mile. And it may be stated in passing, that except when the surface of the lake is covered with heavy ice, no taste of oil or other sign of contamination of water supply from the river, has been since shown.

From its village days to 1873, when its population had reached about 135,000, the city had health organizations and health officers as emergencies or fears prompted. In the year mentioned, under a new State law, a board of health was organized, and either as a separate board or as the Board of Police Commissioners acting as a board of health, has existed and exercised functions ever since. Soon after its first organization the board secured the adoption of a rule excluding children from the public schools unless they had been vaccinated. And in order to secure a fair basis for estimate as to protection, free vaccination was furnished all scholars then in the schools. Since that time no child has been permitted to attend the public schools without furnishing satisfactory evidence of recent successful vaccination.

. . . .

In 1876 the Board of Health was legislated out of existence and its functions assigned to the Board of Police Commissioners. During the following four years very little aggressive sanitary work was attempted or accomplished. Some instructions in regard to contagious diseases; some improvements as to gathering statistics were made, but none of the Commissioners had the interest or knowledge to press forward the work begun.

In 1880 the Board of Health was re-established with an intelligent and interested membership. A vigorous policy was adopted and put into effect. One of the first general measures was to stop the construction of wooden privy vaults. An order was made and issued that such vaults should be built of hard brick or stone laid in the best Portland cement, the wall coated on both surfaces with the same material, and the bottom filled to the depth of eight inches with concrete. This rule has been enforced ever since that time, while at

the same time where sewers could be reached, new vaults uncon-
nected with sewers have been prevented. In addition to a corps of
sanitary patrolmen, a sewer inspector was appointed, whose duties
included the inspection of plumbing, both as to new work and
defective old work.

District physicians were employed to furnish medical care to the
sick poor in their own homes, and to furnish free vaccination to
those unable to pay for it. New contracts were entered into for the
removal of night soil and house garbage, and the offensive trades
were made to respect the comfort and well-being of their neighbors.
Some of them, such as bone boiling, drying and grinding were
ordered and forced out of the city, and as yet are kept out; while
slaughter houses and rendering establishments were either improved
and made endurable, or compelled to suspend.

. . . .

There are now about five hundred miles of public streets and
alleys, only about sixty miles of which are paved, mainly with stone.
The Nicholson wooden block pavement has nearly all disappeared,
although a few half rotten fragments remain. The same can be said of
all forms of asphaltum pavement. There are one hundred and twenty-
five miles of "main" and "branch" sewers built, with about seven
thousand "house connections," and twenty-five hundred "catch
basins." Of public parks there are seven, varying in size from one and
a half to sixty four acres each, with a total area of about ninety-three
acres. There are about two hundred and twenty miles of main and
branch water pipes laid, with eleven thousand house connections. All
the main and branch sewers are laid for both storm water and house
sewage, and all discharge into Cuyahoga river within the city, or
along the lake frontage of the city. About three-fifths of the city area
is unprovided with sewers or ground drainage, and about two-fifths
of the population dependent upon wells for their water supply.

Privy vaults are cleaned by contract at $2.25 per cubic yard; the
measurement determined by the sanitary patrolmen before the vault
is cleaned, and corrected afterward. The citizens deposit the money
with the secretary, where it remains until the patrolman certifies that
the amount paid for has been removed. The contents of privy vaults
and also all house garbage is put into a scow and taken out into the
lake, eight miles, an officer of the board accompanying and directing
each trip.

During the spring, summer and autumn the sanitary force is
largely occupied in keeping yards and vaults clean. The city ordinance requires all vaults to be cleaned whenever the contents are
especially offensive, or when the vault is filled to within two feet of
the surrounding surface of the earth. In the winter the patrolmen are

employed largely with the workshops, tenements, lodging houses, and all places likely to be poorly ventilated and overcrowded. The Board of Health has exclusive charge of all sewering in private grounds, and all plumbing.

. . . .

The sanitary problems now demanding attention in the city of Cleveland, are those suggested at the outset as pertaining to nearly all of our lake cities: How to obtain and maintain a pure water supply from the source so abundant and so near, and still use Lake Erie as a receptacle for all the excreta and waste substances from a large city. Can these two demands upon the lake be rendered and kept compatible with the health of people so using it?

During the last six years, whenever the rainfall along the watershed of the Cuyahoga River was small for a few weeks, the force of its current has been insufficient to clear it of the impurities drained into it. This deficiency in force of current is not all due to the small rainfall, but results in part from the large amount of water pumped from the river by the Standard Oil Co. and others for business purposes. The amount thus removed is at times greater than the entire inflow from above, and thus at such times there is a positive current up stream from the lake. From this condition there results a stagnation and deposit, with decomposition and effluvia, causing the boatmen and others engaged in business along the river nausea and often vomiting. People crossing the bridges, especially at night (in the summer), pass through a vapor loaded with the gases from the substances decomposing in the river below. These substances come from oil works, slaughter houses, soap works, tanneries, breweries, sewers and other drains. When large rainfalls occur the river is flushed and the deposit of weeks or months is carried into the lake. The problem presented for the relief of this condition is simply one of engineering, and must be met and solved very soon or dire results to life and health may follow. A plan was suggested some years ago by Rudolph Herring, by which all sewage and other offensive drainage should be collected into one large sewer and carried so far down the lake as to keep the river pure and protect the water supply. Another plan has been proposed, i.e., to pump river water out and convey it by tunnel to the lake below the city, and thus invite lake water in to take its place. But as yet neither has been done. The great resources of nature toward purification in such large bodies of water as Lake Erie are not forgotten or underestimated, but even in these nature must have something like an adequate opportunity. But for these great agencies in this respect, the citizens of Cleveland and other lake cities must have perished long ago from their own carelessness.

As time passes not only are individual cities and towns involved in these questions, but collectively, the entire territory depending upon the chain of great lakes for drinking water, is interested in their solution.

Analyses of water taken from Lake Michigan at Chicago, Lake Erie at Cleveland, and the Niagara River near Buffalo, made about two years ago, show that at that time the main bulk of water in these lakes was not injuriously contaminated by sewage. Neither the free ammonia, albumenoid ammonia, organic matters or other substances, showed any marked degree of change from analyses of several years before, or material difference in the samples obtained from the different points named. Of course the part of wisdom is to not reach the danger limit, but all will admit such a limit in this matter. It may be that national and international measures will be required for both rivers and lakes, where a joint use by States imperils the health of people depending upon them. Such legislation should anticipate the necessity for it.

Inspection of Food

J. STRONG

Inspection of Food

The report of the Inspector of Food, and the tables connected therewith, furnish information of much interest and are worthy of careful attention, especially those portions of the report which refer to the inspection of milk; the standard which should be adopted for cream; and the recommendation that additional legislation is needed governing the inspection and sale of milk, and requiring parties selling mixed articles of food—a process always of questionable safety—to publish the exact composition of such compounds.

Cleveland is fortunately located in point of convenience so far as obtaining an abundant milk supply is concerned for the use of its inhabitants; in fact, it is doubtful whether there is another city in the

From "Report of the Health Officer," in Department of Police, Annual Reports, Cleveland, 1891, (Cleveland, 1891), pp. 633-636.

whole country which possesses equal facilities in this respect. The milk product of Northeastern Ohio is exceptionally large, and this city is its natural and chief market, is easily accessible and speedily reached through the numerous railways which centre here.

As milk contains all the constituents of normal nutrition, an article of food so universally desired, its abundant supply to a large community is an advantage which cannot well be overestimated, and that it should be pure in quality is a matter of still greater importance.

The daily average quantity of milk consumed in this city will exceed 24,000 gallons. To uniformly secure a pure and reliable quality of milk, in view of the large quantity sold and consumed by the citizens of this city, and in view of the possible temptation to indulge in its adulteration by dishonest dealers, the necessity of subjecting it to frequent and reliable tests by those thoroughly competent to perform that work, must be apparent to all. In order to meet satisfactorily all the requirements of a pure food supply, especially so far as both meat and milk are concerned, the animals producing each should be examined by those who are competent to judge of their condition, and whenever any doubt regarding the purity of the former or healthfulness of the latter is entertained by the examiner, it should be deemed a sufficient cause for condemnation and rejection.

Admitting that milk is the product of a perfectly healthy animal, which has been previously ascertained by those competent to judge, the business of repeated testings should follow it from the time it leaves the hands of the producer until it reaches its final destination and is delivered to the consumer. The present method of milk and food inspection, like many other kinds of sanitary work, is in point of efficiency only a feeble approximation of the kind and amount of service actually required. Of course a method of food examination like the one here indicated would require a largely increased addition to the present force, and consequently a larger expenditure of money, but in reality these considerations are insignificant, indeed, when compared to the paramount claims involved in the more weighty matters which pertain to the welfare of the public health. A very small part of the time, attention and money expended in many business enterprises devoted to the interests of the public health would impart an impetus to sanitary work which would soon result in greatly reducing the number of persons now usually found on the sick list, sick from causes which are manifestly avoidable, with the still further effect of largely diminishing the death rate of the community.

Under these circumstances, and in view of what is actually needed to secure the best sanitary results, and more especially when we take into consideration our present imperfect and limping sanitary methods, we can but regard the science relating to this work as being in its infancy, as having made simply a beginning, and for more beneficent results than any yet attained there must doubtless be a patient waiting. A consideration of this character, however, will not excuse us if we fail to put forth and employ with vigor and efficiency the means already at our command.

Garbage

The collection and disposal of garbage appears to be one of the most perplexing questions connected with the sanitary work of this city. The necessity of vaccination, the importance of providing facilities for the removal of sewage and night-soil are universally conceded to be absolutely essential to the prevention of disease, and the protection of the public health, but by a strange sort of inconsistency no provision is made for the proper disposal of garbage. If the removal of sewage and night-soil be considered vital to the welfare of health—a matter which none will dispute—so much so that the removal of the latter is made compulsory by ordinance, why should we not take steps to prevent the accumulation and decomposition of the refuse vegetable and animal material of the kitchen and kindred places, which may also become a source of infection? The waste products of the human body must be eliminated through the various channels of excretion or disease will inevitably follow. It is equally true that the waste material of a city which, under certain conditions abounds in germs of disease, should find a speedy, safe and systematic outlet. If this be not done, it will surely return, sooner or later "to plague the inventor."

Suppose, for instance, that the city had, up to date, taken no steps whatever to prevent the spread of small pox, had made no provision for the disposal of sewage, or the removal of night-soil; in brief, suppose we were without any sanitary protection whatever, what would be our condition? As a place of residence and business it would and should be shunned as a pest house, and it would know no such thing as prosperity in the broader sense of the term. So we see that strictly speaking there is no wealth like health, and whatever means or measures which are calculated to promote the health of the community should be adopted and rigidly enforced by those in authority. These are matters which will not take care of themselves.

The government of a city, like a large business enterprise, will not take care of itself, does not run automatically, is not an affair free from responsibility on the part of those to whom its control is entrusted, but on the other hand, a sacred trust confided to certain authorities legally constituted, having in charge the protection of the property and welfare of its citizens, and it cannot be denied that the health and lives of our citizens are essential to their welfare, and if this be conceded, the duty of those in authority becomes clearly apparent.

We already have some laws and regulations in force, having for their object the protection of the public health against some of the evils which are sources of infection, and which favor the spread of contagious diseases, but much more is required at our hands before the circle of our sanitary work is completed. Included in the neglected work here referred to is the garbage nuisance, which will continue to haunt us until measures are adopted providing for its effectual and permanent disposal. How is this to be accomplished? By a frequent and systematic collection of all garbage which may accumulate in the streets, in or about buildings or premises of the same, either public or private, and its prompt removal to a building, suitably located, and there subjected to the Merz Process, which is highly approved by those sanitarians who have thoroughly investigated its merits.

The method here suggested has already been adopted in several cities, namely, Pittsburg, Buffalo and Milwaukee; is receiving the sanction of many sanitarians, and is constantly growing in public favor. The cost of this plan of disposing of the garbage nuisance will doubtless be regarded by some as an objection, but in reality will be slight compared with its beneficial results to the public health. The doctrine of the ounce of prevention instead of the pound of cure, applies with more force to the community than the individual. It has already been demonstrated that the recent advance and triumph of modern surgery are chiefly attributable to the scrupulous care observed in protecting the patient from every possible source of infection. Here is a hint which, if heeded and insisted upon as a public health regulation, can but prove of priceless benefit.

Cleveland Police

JOHN W. GIBBONS

To the Honorable Wm. G. Rose, Mayor:

. . . .

Your attention is respectfully called to several needed improvements:

The Central Police Station on Champlain street, with its unclean, cramped and limited quarters, is a disgrace to this city. The police business of the entire city, to a great extent, centers in this building, the Police Court is held here, and all prisoners are brought here for trial.

The prisons are connected with the main building, and the foul odors of the former are the cause of much sickness to the officers who are compelled to inhale the unbearable stench.

The whole building is infested with vermin, coming from the prisoners as they are escorted through the main building. All efforts to disinfect, clean and otherwise keep these prisons in decent condition have failed.

Common decency demands that the whole building should be razed to the ground, and a new one erected in its place.

The rooms and houses of the Fourth, Fifth and Eleventh Precincts are leased by the city, but neither of them are suitable for Police Stations, requiring constant repairs, and as a matter of economy it is to be hoped that the city will soon build its own houses in these precincts, when the necessary funds are provided for that purpose.

Being fully convinced of the great utility of the Patrol System, I would earnestly recommend that it be extended over the most populated districts of the city.

According to the estimates of the City Auditor, there will be a surplus of resources over the expenditures for the first six months of 1892. I would, therefore, urge the passage of an ordinance appropriating sufficient amounts for the sites and erection of a new station house in the Eleventh Precinct, and the building and equipment of a Patrol Station in the vicinity of Woodland and Wilson avenues, so that the work may be commenced early this spring.

. . . .

After mature reflection, I am fully convinced that the present

From "Report of the Director of the Department of Police," *Annual Reports, Cleveland, 1891*, (Cleveland, 1891), pp. 505-511.

force is inadequate for the protection of persons and property of our city, and more men are required to give certain portions of the city the protection to which the residents are entitled.

Having a population of 261,353 (according to the last Federal Census) there is one patrolman to every 1,037 of population.

At night two thirds of the force is on duty, leaving but one patrolman to every 1,555 of population, and in day time only one-third of the force being on duty, would leave but one patrolman for the protection of every 3,111 of population.

The city contains within its limits 453.3 miles of streets, giving an average of each patrolman 5.60 miles to patrol in the day time and 2.80 miles at night.

The city, in accordance with law, is entitled to one patrolman for each 750 inhabitants, which would give us 348 patrolmen, an increase of 96 over our present force, when all vacancies are filled.

I would, therefore, recommend that the force be increased to at least 350 members, when sufficient funds are provided for that purpose. This number is conservative in comparison with other cities of the size and population, importance and wealth of Cleveland.

I would also recommend the necessary legislation to abolish the detailing of patrolmen to act as sergeants, and to increase the number of regular sergeants, thereby bringing them into a position so as to perform their duties in a more fearless and better manner.

The police force has been improved and brought to a high standard of discipline, and in the diligent discharge of its duty, fully merits the confidence of the people of this city. A number of persons who added no strength to the force and some of whom brought great discredit upon it, have been weeded out and their places will be filled by those who will consider it an honor to serve in the Cleveland Police Force.

The police business, from its nature, is liable to make enemies, for the officer, who, in performance of his duty, conscientiously shows no favors, is liable to run against the sharp corners of men and test the peculiarities of human nature, for seldom is a man arrested who has not sympathizing friends, who are ready to believe that the officer has exceeded his authority. So long as it is necessary to arrest annually several thousands of persons, so long will there be a considerable number of people who are not friendly towards the police, and who will criticise it and magnify its shortcomings whenever an opportunity offers.

This holds true in every city and in this or any other country.

W. M. Bracket, Superintendent of Police, Minneapolis, in his report of 1889, among other things says:

"The officer who is 'a good fellow' is liable to be a bad officer. The duties of the police are of such a character that it is absolutely impossible for a conscientious officer to pander in the smallest degree to the wishes of the disorderly element.

"The fireman, in response to an alarm, bravely rushes to a place of peril and bravely fights against the elements. All honor to his manly calling; but he does not war with the passions, wants and desires of vicious men and women, as do the police. When the contest of the fireman is done all classes unite in doing honor to the noble efforts of the fireman. The police force respond to the same alarm with the firemen, form a cordon around the premises so that the firemen will not be interfered with in their work, look after the property that may be removed from the burning building, force back the idle, curious crowd that always congregates, and after hours of hard labor return to their regular beats followed by abuse and curses—often too, of reputable citizens. Again, respectable business men fail to comply with, or willfully violate certain ordinances. It is the sworn duty of the officer to bring this good citizen into court. He discharges that duty promptly, and gets the lasting enmity of not only the respectable business man, but of all the large circle of friends of the said business man.

"The public at large have but little conception of the difficult and often preplexing position in which officers are daily placed. At best, the lot of an honest policeman is not a happy one."

JNO. W. GIBBONS,
Director of Police.

Epidemic in an Ohio City

MARTIN FRIEDRICH, M.D.

Dear Sir:—

I have the honor to present to you the report for the year 1902 of this division of your department.

It was a strenuous year. After having extirpated smallpox in 1901, it was brought back to us in 1902 and this time in its severest form. It was no longer the mild, slightly contagious disease of the previous years which left no marks and seldom proved fatal. It was the smallpox "we read about," that terrible scourge that struck so much terror into the former generations. Its contagious nature showed itself everywhere. One case, if not promptly reported to the health office and removed to the hospital, would invariably infect the whole neighborhood. Its severity manifested itself even in the milder cases, whilst confluent cases, almost without an exception, developed hemorrhages during the pustular stage. (Variola hemorrhagica pustulosa). We had some 30 cases of black smallpox (purpura hemorrhagica variolosa), all of which were fatal. Of the 1,248 cases, 224 died, a death rate of 17.95 per cent. Of these, 1,142 were treated in the hospital and 200 of them died, or a death rate of 17.51 per cent. The remaining 106 were cared for at their homes and 24 of these died, or a death rate of 22.64 per cent, which shows a 5.13 per cent lower death rate for the hospital.

The disease was brought here from Hoboken, N. J., by a man by the name of Arnold Schwink, who was broken out when he arrived, but not discovered until four days later in a lodging house on Michigan street, called "The Light and Hope Mission." The men who patronized this place were mostly tramps. Some escaped to other lodging houses and during April we took 16 cases away from these places. The first patient I asked if he had been in a saloon told me that he did not know of any down-town in which he had not been. A good many men, whose business brought them down town, had also frequented these saloons and I presume that this is the cause why the disease appeared in so many places all at once.

During the month of May 82 cases developed. It was not so much the number of cases as the severity of the disease that made me afraid of a general outbreak, and I asked the Mayor for more help. I intended then to start vaccination and employed 12 physicians during the month of June to go from house to house to vaccinate whomsoever they could.

. . . .

At the Mayor's request, a meeting of physicians was held in Director Lapp's office, August 30th, to consider the smallpox situation. They passed a resolution that the "Committee on Public Health of the Academy of Medicine" be added as an advisory committee to the health office. As it happened that I was a member of this committee, the gentlemen were not strangers to me. We held many meetings. I received variable suggestions but mostly appreciated the moral support of the committee. Vaccination was recommended

From "Annual Report of the Health Office," *Department of Police, Annual Report, Cleveland, 1902,* (Cleveland, 1902), pp. 937-942.

from all sides, but people were not prone to get vaccinated. Up to September 1st the demand on the health office for points did not exceed 30,000. Wholesale vaccination was finally effected by the action of the school council and the help of the Chamber of Commerce. The school council amended the vaccination clause making vaccination a conditio sine qua non for attending school and giving the health officer the whole control of the matter. Without this amendment the schools could not have been opened last fall. The situation was too critical. With it the opening of the schools helped greatly to extirpate smallpox. Every school, private or public, was put in charge of a physician. It took 106 of them. The doctors worked with a will and if anything was done thoroughly and conscientiously in this city it was the vaccination of all teachers and pupils last fall.

Of no less importance than the action of the school council was the timely and effective aid I received from the Chamber of Commerce. Through their influence the employers prevailed upon their employes to get vaccinated. Also to have every one of their family vaccinated. The consequence was that the people got vaccinated by tens of thousands. Men who formerly spurned the vaccinator from their door, came now to his office. Only one who has been through the trying ordeal of fighting a smallpox epidemic can fully appreciate the help that the Chamber of Commerce gave us in time of need. The city owes the gentlemen a vote of thanks, and I feel grateful to them indeed. The city paid for 195,000 vaccinations. Physicians were paid for successful vaccinations only.

. . . .

If this report would be read only in this city, it would not be necessary to say that we did not rely upon vaccination alone in our fight with smallpox. Since the middle of August every case without exception was removed to the hospital, with force where necessary. Every person directly exposed to a case was put under strict quarantine, if not immune from the disease by a recent successful vaccination or a former attack. Cats and dogs were included in the quarantine or sacrificed where they could not be controlled. Exposures were traced as far as possible. Every suspicious case was investigated, even if the informer was a layman or did not give his name. Every infected ward in the city was disinfected house after house, and every nook and corner of the house. Doctors, preachers and undertakers who had to do with smallpox were obliged to wear a long gown with a hood, during the performance of their duties. These gowns were donned on entering and shed on leaving the house or hospital and then immediately disinfected in a strong bi-chloride solution by the guard of the place. The health department furnished the gowns.

. . . .

I earnestly advise the administration to hasten the sewering and paving of all streets as much as possible. The city's health is in jeopardy as long as we have 234.5 miles of streets which have no sewers and 363.5 without pavement. In some sections of the city the water stands in the basement of the houses the whole year around. People who have to live there are doomed to sickness. Dirt streets cannot be cleaned. The dust which rises from them is laden with germs. In time of an epidemic they become an actual danger. As soon as the sewer in the street is finished, the best interest of the neighborhood demands that connections be made as rapidly as possible. I am sorry to say that some house owners are so hard to convince of their own welfare and the welfare of their tenants. The continual digging up of streets and the tearing up of pavements as soon as laid is not conducive to health. All kinds of germs which have been washed into the roadbed and buried there are brought again to the surface. The winds and rain distribute them and an increased sick and death list shows their work.

Another menace to health is the many dumps and pools of stagnant water. Both are breeders of germ life. Flies and mosquitoes, who make these their favorite habitat, are germ carriers, so are dogs and cats.

Cleveland is a manufacturing center. The smoke that annoys us has made the city what it is, the metropolis of Ohio. Nevertheless this smoke is injurious to the lungs. But by far more injurious is the dust that flies through the air. The thorough cleaning of streets is a sanitary necessity.

Riot in Cincinnati, 1884

E. B. FINLEY

Adjutant-General's Office,
Columbus, Ohio, June 21, 1884.

General Thomas Moonlight, Adjutant-General, Topeka, Kansas—

My Dear Sir: I have your letter of May 2, 1884, asking for an accurate statement concerning the late Riot in the city of Cincinnati, and the action and conduct of the Ohio National Guard in suppressing it. Public and official duties are numerous and pressing, but I purpose to suspend them long enough to comply with your request and answer your inquiries—for I recognize the fact, which you so pertinently state, that the press has done great injustice to the military force engaged in that conflict, and is chiefly responsible for the misapprehension that exists respecting the action and conduct of the citizen-soldiers during the Riot. I also recognize the justice and propriety of your strictures concerning the action and conduct of some of the better class of citizens of Cincinnati; and I agree with you fully as to the duty of good citizens at a time like that.

. . . .

On Friday evening, March 28, 1884, pursuant to a call that had been published, there was held in Music Hall, in the city of Cincinnati, the largest in-door meeting ever assembled in the city. It was made up mostly of solid men of the city, with a large sprinkling of spectacled and gray-haired men. It was characterized as being remarkable for its respectability. While there seemed to be an absence of the elements known as "toughs" and "roughs," there were yet many there (among so many thousands) who constitute and make up mobs. Its object was to give expression to the public judgment respecting the punishment of crime and the administration of the criminal law, and to denounce the action and verdict of the jury in the case of the State against William Berner, who had been indicted for murder in the first degree, and convicted of manslaughter only.

. . . .

The trouble was inaugurated when the meeting adjourned and the enraged and excited thousands left Music Hall and reached the street. As the people poured out of the great Hall their attention was attracted by a shout. It came from a young man not over twenty-one

From Letter, Major General E. B. Finley to General Thomas Moonlight, June 21, 1884, in "The Great Riot in Cincinnati," *Annual Report of the Adjutant General in Ohio, Ohio Executive Documents,* (1885), pp. 237-246.

years of age. Rushing wildly into the street he yelled, "To the jail! Come on! Follow me, and hang Berner!"

Whatever intention there may have been on the part of others to organize a mob, this was the first time it found vent in a decided expression. The cry acted as an incentive, and was soon taken up by many others. Down Elm street and out Twelfth went a crowd of ten thousand people. There were in the lead about two hundred men more determined than their followers, taking the initiative at every step, and saying but little. They made their way to the entrance of the jail, on Sycamore street, and in a very short time broke down the doors and were in the office. Then they battered down the double iron door leading to the cell-room, and immediately the stairways leading up to the tier of cells and the landings were thronged with an excited crowd.

The riot-alarm was sounded at 9:55, being the first time since the great railroad riot of 1877; and the greatest excitement prevailed all over the city. Other thousands hurried to the scene to swell the mob, which had now assumed immense proportions. The shouts of the multitude and the firing of shots by the mob created a veritable pandemonium.

. . . .

Shortly after 11 o'clock, when matters began to look exceedingly desperate, and the battering-rams of the mob were getting nearer and nearer, Sheriff Hawkins decided to call out the militia. He sent an order to Col. C. B. Hunt, commanding the 1st regiment, Ohio National Guard, requesting him to send all the men possible. Two companies of his command had been on duty at the Armory, for several days, guarding their ammunition. As I am advised, less than forty soldiers were present when the order was received. They immediately repaired to the jail, under command of Col. Hunt. That officer also sent messengers abroad to hunt up all the members of his regiment they could find. He issued an order for the entire regiment to report for duty at the Armory the next morning. He and his men entered the jail, on Friday night, by passing through the tunnel. There was some shooting by the soldiers at and about the jail, off and on, for several hours; but it was all done in obedience to the command of officers, and not until it was actually necessary for the protection of life and property. The casualties of that dreadful night were mostly the result of the violence of the mob. The casualties resulting from the firing by the soldiers and the action of the police, were inflicted in the discharge of a public duty, and by order of proper officers.

All of Saturday, March 29, changing crowds filled the streets as near the jail as they were allowed to go.

The jail and Court House occupy a square, bounded on the West by Main street, East by Sycamore, and North and South by narrow streets called North and South Court. The Court House fronts West on Main, and reaches from North Court to South Court. The jail is a circular building with two wings, extending North and South, and faces East on Sycamore street, and the yard is inclosed with a high stone wall, surmounted by an iron fence. The East front has doors leading into the residence of the jail, or which open on the sidewalk. The entrance proper to the jail is reached by a stone winding stairway leading down to an area twelve feet below the sidewalk. Here was the beginning of the attack Friday night, March 28. The crowd surged up to the very doors of the jailer's residence, and filled the front of the lower door, which they battered open with a heavy sawed beam, obtained from a new building near by. The jail office and jailer's residence had scarcely an unbroken article of furniture left. Even the large heating stove was wrecked.

General Ryan, Sheriff Hawkins, Col. Hunt, and the other officers who were present, held a conference, on Saturday afternoon, when it was decided to erect three barricades—one at Sycamore and South Court streets, another at Sycamore and North Court, and a third at East Court and Canal. The police and two companies of the First Regiment were detailed for this work, and all the old drays, wagons, carts, boxes, barrels, stones, lumber, and the like, to be found in the neighborhood, were brought into use for this purpose; and the barricades so constructed proved to be exceedingly effective defenses against the mob, and obstructions to its progress toward the objective point—the jail. But, unfortunately, the rear of the position, which was the Court House front, on Main street, was left exposed. To supply this omission, additional barricades were constructed, after the arrival of the Fourteenth Regiment, on Saturday night and Sunday, as follows: On West Court street, on Main at Ninth, and on Main at Canal.

Col. Hawkins, the Sheriff, believed all day Saturday that the mob would renew the attack on the jail at night. Col. Hunt and the other military officers who were with him concurred in this belief, and requested the Sheriff to telegraph the Governor for troops from outside the city. They saw that the press and people of Cincinnati had so terrorized a portion of the home troops that they would not respond to the call of their officers to aid in quelling the Riot; and that help would have to come from abroad. Sheriff Hawkins thereupon wired the Governor for troops. This was about noon on Saturday.

. . . .

Immediately after Sheriff Hawkins had telegraphed for troops, he ordered Colonel George D. Freeman, of the Fourteenth Regiment, Ohio National Guard, Head-quarters at Columbus, to assemble the companies composing it, at their armories, equipped for duty, and to be in readiness to go to Cincinnati the moment the order should be given to move. He wired a similar order to Colonel Frank B. Mott, of the Fourth Regiment, Ohio National Guard, Head-quarters at Dayton. So when the Governor received telegrams from his Cincinnati advisers, concurring in the request of Sheriff Hawkins for troops, he immediately ordered the Fourteenth and Fourth Regiments to Cincinnati, together with several outside companies—special trains having been provided, and being in readiness to take them to the scene of the Riot.

It was almost 9 o'clock, Saturday evening, when Col. Mott, with his command, reached the Cincinnati, Hamilton & Dayton Railway Depot, in the city of Cincinnati. It was not long till they were on their way to the jail, where they had been ordered to report to Sheriff Hawkins for duty. Col. Hunt was there with 117 men of his regiment, and 20 men of Capt. Joyce's 2d Battery, who, having no ammunition for their guns, were armed with rifles. About 9:45, Col. Mott, with his command, arrived within three squares of Col. Hunt's lines, when the command was halted and remained for some time, the mob mingling with the soldiers and assaulting them with violent epithets, if not with missiles. After enduring this treatment for some time, the command marched back to the depot whence it came.

. . . .

Soon after dark, Saturday evening, the mob filled Main street in front of the Court House, North and South Court streets, and extended North and South on Main from the canal to Ninth street, and West to Walnut street—thus completely filling and blocking these streets for more than seven squares.

Col. Hunt distributed his little force so judiciously for the protection and defense of the several barricades and the keeping back the mob, that each assault by the rioters was successfully repelled, and the barricades were all held intact. The repeated assaults of the mob were met by the soldiers on duty with a cool and steady bearing and an heroic courage never surpassed by veterans of long service; and not a shot was fired by them, except when ordered by officers in command, after all the means to repel the assaults of the rioters, without bloodshed, had been tried in vain.

Between 9 and 10 o'clock the Court House was fired by the mob. At first there were stones thrown through the windows from Main street. This soon grew general, and many of the rioters fired revolvers and shot-guns through the windows. The militia took no notice of this, and the mob was emboldened to go on. The rioters broke into the Treasurer's office, piled up the furniture, and set it on fire. The incendiary fever grew, and one after another of the offices and rooms was treated in the same way. As office after office in the magnificent structure was inwrapped in the seething flames, the mob grew denser and denser, and was packed solidly in the adjacent streets up to a point where the heat was unendurable.

Capt. John J. Desmond, with his company, was ordered to pass through the tunnel, from the jail to the Main street front of the Court House, and drive back the mob, which would not permit the fire department of the city to arrest the spread of the flames and save the Temple of Justice, and the accumulated books and records of an hundred years. At the head of his command, while carrying out the order of his superior officer, to protect the firemen in the discharge of their duty, the brave and gallant Desmond was instantly killed, in the angle outside the rotunda, by a gun-shot wound, which crushed the upper part of the skull, from the frontal to the occipital bones —as the Surgeon of the regiment reports. He was shot in the forehead by one of the rioters, and not by a soldier. There never was any ground for the assertion that he was shot by one of his own men.

. . . .

It was nearly 11 o'clock, Saturday night, when Colonel George D. Freeman, with his command—embracing his own Regiment (the 14th), two unattached companies, and two companies of Colonel Picard's 13th Regiment—arrived at the Little Miami Depot, in the city of Cincinnati. Colonel S. H. Church, of the Governor's Staff, accompanied Col. Freeman and his command to Cincinnati, and remained there until the trouble was over.

. . . .

The command was immediately formed, and, before leaving the Depot, each company was directed to keep cool, and to be especially careful not to fire unless absolutely necessary, and then only when ordered to do so by an officer commanding. The Colonel directed that there must be no tapping of drums, nor demonstrations of any kind whatsoever, on the march to the jail. "Silently the soldiers marched up the quiet streets. Some of the curious population, who are ready for excitement almost at any hour, followed on the sidewalks, and some among them were very profuse in heaping epithets on the soldiers, and firing pistol shots from alleys and windows at them, while they seemed to pay not the slightest attention, nor take the least notice of what was said. Many windows along the line of march were thrown open, and people aroused from their beds gazed in awe and wonder at the solemn procession, and, in truth, it was a solemn sight—a regiment of soldiers marching through the streets of a metropolitan city with muffled tread and in profound silence to the scene of a great Riot, on what promised to be a mission of death."

On reaching Ninth and Sycamore streets, the mob blocked the way of the troops, and threatened an attack at every point; but the soldiers remained cool and declined to be provoked into making retort. The shouts of the mob rose above the cracking of the burning Court House and the noise of its falling walls. After reporting to Sheriff Hawkins at the jail, Colonel Freeman quickly formed his command into two bodies—one to march down North Court street, and the other down Ninth, to disperse the mob on Main, between Ninth and the Canal. Both bodies pushed forward, driving the crowd before them at the point of the bayonet. Near South Court the mob made a stand to resist the onward progress of the troops. It then pressed forward, throwing stones and firing guns and revolvers, and repeating the wild demonstrations of the preceding few hours. Col. Freeman and officers under him, again and again, warned the mob that if it failed to fall back, the soldiers would be ordered to fire into it. But not until six men had fallen at its hands, was that order given. There was no other alternative, when the first platoon was ordered to fire. The order was instantly obeyed, with good effect. This checked the rioters, and they fell back. Their leader was killed, and several of them were wounded. The square was then soon cleared by the soldiers, and the Fire Department resumed its work. The jail and its surrounding streets, at all points, were now in complete possession of the troops; and the rioters retreated to the Market House, below the Armory, on Court street, where, under cover of the buildings, they pelted the soldiers with stones and fired on them, wounding Lieut.-Col. Liggitt, of the 14th, Capt. Slack, of the same regiment, and eight others. A platoon of soldiers was now, again, ordered to fire into the mob; and it was done effectively. From this time on until after 2 o'clock that night, the rioters made frequent attacks upon the soldiers, and were promptly repulsed, with more or,less loss—while a number of the soldiers were wounded.

. . . .

The mob reassembled on Sunday, the 30th, and continued to get larger and larger, as the hours went on. By night, it had assumed immense proportions once more. It pressed up to the several barricades on all sides, which were resolutely held by the troops. During the afternoon, threats were uttered, many of the rioters became unruly, and numerous arrests were made by the police, under cover of the soldiers, at or near the barricades. Repeated assaults by the mob were repelled by the troops, with as little injury as possible. Between 10 and 11 o'clock at night, the section of the mob that had gathered at the Market House, at Court and Walnut, commenced firing, protecting themselves by the stands at the Market House and the buildings on the corner. No response was made by the soldiers for some time. When the aim of the mob became too accurate for endurance, it was deemed best to give the rioters the benefit of one case of cartridges from the Battery Gun, by firing it into the Market House. But before this was done, due warning was given by the officers in command. The rioters responded by oaths and a volley of balls from their guns. Then, the twenty shots were fired from the Battery Gun. A number of casualties was the result. The mob then scattered, and, with the exception of random shots from the rioters, there was comparative quiet till after midnight. Near one o'clock, a fusillade was opened by the mob from its position at the corner of Walnut and Court. No response having been made by the soldiers for some time, the rioters became bold, and decided to charge, and, as they expressed it (interlarded with oaths), "clean out those blue coats." The soldiers, obeying orders, remained quiet, and not until the rioters came forward, firing and yelling, was the order given to fire. Two volleys, by company, in quick succession, were then fired. Five of the rioters were known to be hurt. This was the last shooting that was done; and gradually all became quiet.

. . . .

Very truly yours,

E. B. FINLEY,
Adjutant-General of Ohio.

Bossism in Toledo

WILLIAM S. COUCH

Staff Special. Toledo, O., Aug. 30.—

A machine administration, approving Coxism, early lent a helping hand to its development in Toledo. All the turmoil that Cleveland suffered through legislative efforts to cripple Mayor Johnson was repeated in Toledo where Walter Brown seems to have thought that his antagonist could be legislated out of public confidence. The present state administration recognizes Toledo Coxism by taking care of Sam Cohn, Walter Brown's chief lieutenant. Cohn has the state free employment bureau in his hands, and a shrewd politician can do much with a free employment bureau, maintained by a state appropriation. Moreover there is a comfortable salary attached for Sam Cohn.

Toledo's Little Czar

The "old Fift' " ward in Toledo corresponds to the "old sixteenth" in Cleveland. Canton avenue is its highway, Toledo's Bowery. In the days of turbulent Major rule, prior to the Jones regime, a character known as "Moxie" was "king of Canton avenue." He voted the male adults of its variegated foreign and colored population as "Czar" Bernstein votes the population in his bailiwick. It was Moxie's cheerful wont to award these votes to the highest bidder. Like other machine men politics did not spell principle to Moxie. It was a struggle in which the most fit survived. It was profitable for men higher up, wherefore should he bear the burden and heat of the day without value received?

Moxie was the machine politician developed to his logical end.

Now Mayor Major was irritated the more at Moxie as time went on. He needed those Canton avenue votes and as his need increased, so did the price. Moreover even Mayor Major still held that notion, long since discarded by all machine politicians, that a man should have his side and stick to it. He would perhaps have paid Moxie more willingly the price demanded had Moxie claimed steadfast Republican faith and explained his demands for money with the time-honored excuse of "getting out the vote."

Sam Cohn Dethrones a Monarch

Sam Cohn, running a little saloon in this district, has shown an aptitude for politics as a Major cadet. Mayor Major called in Sam Cohn, placed in his hands a campaign fund of $200 and ordered him to go forth and capture Moxie's stronghold. And Sam Cohn did it. That was his real entrance into Toledo municipal politics. He had been a Democrat. Subsequently he became a Jones man and was made market master. Another change of heart and he denounced

From *Cleveland Plain Dealer*, August 31, 1905.

Jones, who laughed—and retained him as market master. Today Sam Cohn, as chairman of the Republican county committee, is the official head of that proud party organization in Toledo and Lucas county. He continues to be "King of Canton avenue," vice Moxie, dethroned and now passed to his fathers. It suits the purpose of Walter Brown, boss, that Sam Cohn should appear to be the real political czar of Toledo, as well as of Canton avenue. Cohn is a bearded, shifty eyed man of middle age, of slight build and rather below medium height. Some time ago he collected damages from a corporation for an accident. Since that time he has clung to crutches. He is a shrewd, evasive fellow, this chief lieutenant of Walter Brown, and unlikely ever to challenge for himself the young corporation lawyer's title to supreme power. He was more backward than the rest in countenancing the opera bouffe revolution aimed to secure Brown's abdication after the failure of the franchise fight. But quite a number of Republicans, proud of their party, its traditions, its principles, are not enthusiastic at the spectacle of Canton avenue's king for its local leader.

John Bolan, Who Helps

After Sam Cohn the most important factor in keeping Toledo under the control of Coxism is John Bolan, Democratic leader. With him is associated John O'Dwyer, appointed by Secretary of State Laylin to be the representative of Toledo Democrats on the board of elections. John Bolan is a character. "Honest John Bolan" they call him. He controlled the Lucas county delegation in the recent state convention, as he has in many others during recent years. He has been a delegate to many national conventions. He is a fine, upstanding man in physique, with a firm, grim jaw and steady blue eyes. His saloon is headquarters for sporting men and for many actors. You can find prize fighters, horse trainers, the hero of melodrama and politicians elbowing each other at his bar. John Bolan's notion of playing practical politics is the Cox notion, and the Brown notion, the Tammany notion, and the machine notion generally. He has an honestly expressed disgust of "indipindints" in politics. While he has power in his elbow he means that a "Dimmycratic" ticket, sor, shall go into the field at every election.

Valuable Democratic Ally

Now see the value of this to Brown, which is as the value of Lewie Bernard's consistent effort in Hamilton county to Cox. For this city and county are normally Republican. A Republican machine must be beaten here, as it has so often been beaten, by Republican

votes. Much of this support is not for any attempt to substitute a
Democratic machine for the Republican one. But a union of local
Democrats and independents, with Republicans hostile to machine
rule, would be ever invincible. Remember, too, that it is municipal
government at stake, not the tariff, coinage, or whatever other
national policies the Democratic principles which John Bolan so
eloquently maintains can affect at all. The advantage to Coxism in
Toledo of a Democratic ticket in the field in every municipal fight is
that it tends to split the strength of machine opposition. Many
people credit John Bolan with perfect sincerity in his obstinate
efforts to keep a Democratic ticket in the field of every municipal
fight.

But whether John Bolan is sincere or not,—and his son Mike
Bolan has a good job in the city engineer's office, where Republican
machine politicians dispose of the patronage—his efforts are of great
assistance to Walter Brown. Wittingly or unwittingly, willingly or
unwillingly, he is Brown's lieutenant. John O'Dwyer, associated with
him, a keen, active, stocky little fellow of about thirty-five, labors
under no delusions, whatever may be the case with John Bolan.
Toledo Democrats protested his selection to represent them on the
board of elections. Other members of this Democratic city machine
have found soft places, Billy Malone on the board of review, Dan
Donovan on the board of public safety, and so on. Men they
recommend are quite likely to secure city jobs. And as for the rigid
party loyalty they profess their devotion to the ticket when nominated, they cheerfully knifed Mayor Johnson when he was their
party's candidate and they show little more enthusiasm for John M.
Pattison.

Democrats Not All in Bonds

Police Judge Wackenheimer, who commands a large Democratic
following and who is an ardent member of this party, recently
announced that no man was a good Democrat who would permit his
opposition to boss government to be diverted to any ticket the local
Democratic machine put in the field in any municipal fight. Brand
Whitlock, to whom these machine Democrats have offered their
mayorality nomination, and whom they supported for the guberna-
torial nomination in the recent state convention, is intimately associated with the independent movement.

The efforts of Bolan and O'Dwyer to keep their tickets in the
field during municipal fights have failed, however, to save Toledo
Coxism from defeat by the independent voter. Jones swept triumphantly into office through the gantlet of two party tickets. Last fall
the independents polled the strength to beat the machine and franchise candidate for councilman at large, in spite of the presence of

Bolan's candidate in the race. In this respect Walter Brown has been less successful than George B. Cox, who has pretty well discouraged opposition by controlling the Hamilton county organization of the Democracy.

Walter Brown even went to the extreme of putting independent candidates for council in the race under his own auspices, in order to confuse the voters. This was a step in advance of Coxism, but not an original idea at that, since Chairman Dick of the Republican organization has sustained with solid and substantial sympathy many a third party movement in Ohio that was on the verge of extinction on the principle that these might prove an effective safety valve for discontent that would otherwise be felt in opposition to the Republican ticket.

Brown Encourages Delusion

George P. Waldorf, collector of internal revenue for this district, would like to be persuaded that he is the local Republican boss. He was brought out of Lima, some years ago, by President McKinley, who entrusted him with national party interests in this vicinity. While he held that position he was a force. Brown, whose policy is to keep himself in the background behind a screen of figureheads, has encouraged Waldorf to believe that his power is still at its full, to be exerted when the collector likes. And Waldorf and Frank Baird, with Sam Cohn, are permitted to parade at the head of Lucas county delegations to the state conventions. While they patronizingly tell delegates in the hotel lobbies what they intend to do Walter Brown slips in at a side door and takes the elevator to the rooms occupied by Dick and Cox and Herrick for the real conference that counts.

Frank Baird, protege of Noah H. Swayne, a wealthy dabbler in politics, draws his splendid income as oil inspector for the northern district of the state, one of the two jobs that pay best of all those included in state administration patronage, and cuts but a small figure in any other field of political activity. These men have their wards to keep in line, under the Cox system, and they sometimes have their hands full with that. Mike Mullen, entrusted with the Cincinnati council by Cox and Herrmann, is a stronger man than either. Baird has retained his oil inspectorship under Gov. Herrick because Noah Swayne demanded that as the reward for effective work he did in the Hanna-Herrick campaign.

Voters Not Represented

As it has been said, the state machine politicians have recognized the development of machine politics in Toledo with legislation and patronage. Now notice Coxism's return for that support. It is the theory of party government that the rank and file of the party nominates its state candidates through its representatives in state conventions. The Toledo machine is represented in the state Republican conventions by Sam Cohn, and Waldorf, and Baird, and Nauts and other men of similar type sent there by Walter Brown. It is represented in Democratic state conventions by delegations selected by John O'Dwyer and John Bolan. The Republicans and Democrats of Toledo are not represented at all. Machine politicians cry out against the crime of "bolting the ticket." All objections should be registered in the state convention of the party, say they. A fine chance have the Republicans of Toledo and Lucas county for a voice in selecting state candidates! Similarly Hamilton county and Cincinnati Republicans have as much to say there as a policyholder in the Equitable society had at a directors' meeting of that institution before the reorganization. It is Cox of Cincinnati and Brown of Toledo, who are represented. So do the local machines control state conventions in the interest of the state machine that, in turn, sustains the local machine through patronage and the legislature. So Gov. Herrick was renominated. Unless this combination is broken by defeat at the polls in one election its effectiveness will be sure to increase. With the Hamilton county and Lucas county delegations to start with, the machine candidates will enjoy an always increasing handicap over other candidates. But if machine candidates find election increasingly difficult a reaction is sure. This is the condition confronting honest Republicans of the rank and file in this campaign.

And yet Chairman Dick insists that Coxism and bossism in localities can not be a state issue, and Gov. Herrick explains that no one man can be a state issue. Wherefor they solemnly advise the voter to "talk of other things." Now the tariff, for instance, and the national administration. How about the schedules on "ships—and shoes—and sealing wax, and cabbages—and kings?" After which the Columbus Glee club will sing and the band will play "Marching Through Georgia."

W. S. COUCH

Canton, A Lurid City

WILLIAM S. COUCH

Canton, O., Sept. 11.—

For a lurid little city, commend me to Canton. Here will be erected that splendid memorial to the dead McKinley, who reflected the greatest glory upon Ohio politics. The shadow of that shaft will fall athwart another memorial, a monument to present day Ohio politics built by the present day Ohio politicians, who have piled gambling hells and Parisian music halls on a foundation of other iniquities in their effort to attain such immortality of memory as may be derived from public office and political power.

The chaste marble and rigid bronze of one memorial will tell achievements in the field of national government and international diplomacy: of prosperity at home and a war waged abroad for the rescue of an oppressed race; of public greatness and the beauty of a private character, of world admiration and a people's love.

Fluttering, tawdry rags, faded tinsel, leering faces and satyrs' figures, a frieze of poker decks and roulette wheels, these predominate in the design and decoration of the other memorial, the flimsy whole lit with red lights by night and covered from sight by day. To show what they thought of this handiwork the Republicans of Stark county recently seized upon a congressional fight for excuse to smash the machine and pitch the scrap iron on top of the grotesque pile. The memorial became in very truth a monument.

But the city machine is uninjured and the experts of the political repair shop are busy with the pieces of the damaged county machine. And rebellion within the party is as intermittent and ineffective as the efforts of farmers and urban citizens to stop the speeding of automobiles. The machine politician pays his penalty and the chauffeur pays his fine and both are off again, at a mile a minute.

Cincinnati Out-Coxed

Every outlawed amusement offered by Cincinnati is duplicated in Canton, and the smaller city has added a few frills. One section of a narrow street, not a block long, appropriately known as Whisky alley, is lined with gambling dens, each located above a saloon. During a moment's quiet, when the music machines are still, the rattle of ivory chips reaches the ear on the street. In Cincinnati the

---

From *Cleveland Plain Dealer*, September 12, 1905.

gambling dens are scattered, but it is more conveniently arranged in Canton.

Chicago boasts that Custom House place is the most wicked thing this side of Paris. A certain theater of Canton has all the characteristics of Custom House place. Cincinnati has nothing to equal it; Cleveland never had.

Safe Haven for Crooks

Canton has followed the Toledo example of not molesting crooks who care to take refuge there, on condition that these valued citizens "don't pull off anything in Canton." There is no observance to indicate the existence of Sunday closing laws and ordinances. Canton's habit of improving on imported giddiness is shown when there is a race meet. Not only are posts sold, but every other gambling device is operated in this connection at the track.

These proceedings characterize the administration of Mayor W. H. Smith, Republican, who has the reputation of being personally a clean man. He is a candidate for re-election.

Nothing Better in Sight

But the candidacy of Arthur Turnbull, Democrat, a contractor, is no promise of any improvement in case he is elected. In fact, there is talk, apparently accepted as serious, of the Canton gamblers being opposed to Smith. One wonders what can be their grievance. One or two of them have had some trouble. The administration conducted one general raid, in which much valuable paraphernalia was destroyed. Elsewhere, where it is permitted to operate at all, the gambling fraternity accepts that sort of thing philosophically at its periodical recurrence, knowing that the wool must now and then be readjusted over the public's eye. But these Canton members of the tribe evidently are impatient of the slightest interference with their business.

Canton papers have recently contained accounts of suits brought against local gamblers by their victims. There is one pending over money lost at the race track during the last meet. A young man of good prospects who holds a position of trust was found short in his accounts by his employers, who compelled him to sue for the return of their money from the gamblers who had taken it away from him. This difficulty was finally settled with a purse raised among all the dens.

But while Democratic and Republican machine politicians unite in their decision that these conditions are best for Canton the people will have no opportunity to reform them in a mayoralty election, unless an independent movement develops. There is some vague talk of that, but it has come to no head as yet. Canton mayoralty elections have been close; Mayor Smith was elected by a plurality of twenty-one votes, but offices and not decent government have been the issues of these battles.

Dominant Democracy

As a matter of fact, neither in city nor county have the people been championed by the Canton Democratic organization since the days of McKinley. There is some excuse in the condition that made support of everything Republican a principle of local loyalty while McKinley lived. Almost the same applied while Senator Hanna governed the party in Ohio. During these lean years the once dominant Democratic party of Canton and Stark county degenerated into a patient, passive, plodding outfit that loved its ease. Leading Democrats were not badly treated. John C. Welty, legal representative of the Tucker-Anthony syndicate of Boston, or whatever name by which the local street railway company is known, found it not difficult to smooth the way for his clients through any difficulty that arose. Smaller fry were remembered with little bites of the patronage pie. The rank and file went to the polls on election day, or stayed at home. Either way they were not bothered by any strenuous attempts made to get out the vote. Today Republican politicians in Stark county do not know who is chairman of the Democratic county committee. A Democrat volunteered his opinion that the chairman was "some fellow named Kaufman, or something like that; works out at the Diebold safe concern, I think." It is not difficult, from that starting point, to estimate the activity of the minority in Stark at present. Remember, too, that under the theory of party government an active, insistent, aggressive minority is the only safeguard for the public; the only restraint upon deterioration in administration or the conduct of the dominant party's affairs. Stark county Democratic leaders have done little in the line of this duty during recent years. And their chief, the king pin of this amiable Democratic organization, John C. Welty, was the choice of the machine Democrats of the state for a candidate with whom to fight Gov. Herrick on the issue of bossism and machine politics! Although politicians are prone to take themselves very seriously, some of them must have laughed in their sleeves. Ostensibly, Welty was considered eligible because of his connection with local horse racing interests. As has been said, the horse racing game in Canton has a gambling attachment quite independent of pool selling. So the Democratic leaders of Canton do not call to account a Republican city administration for taking the lid off this little city and then losing the lid. And yet Mr. Welty was the choice of Lewie Bernard and John Bolan and Jimmie Ross and Hanley as the champion to fight Coxism. Mr. Welty is a man of fine presence. And he is an able lawyer.

Graft Not Well Organized

From the municipal standpoint Canton stands at the parting of the ways. If present conditions continue there is promise of a development in grafting that will be on the Cincinnati pattern. Finding such a wide open town it was the natural inference to suppose that the gamblers were paying heavily for their protection. Of course the "sporting element," where it has its way, will cheerfully put up campaign funds to keep men in office who will continue to leave the pasture gates open. But from collecting campaign contributions from these clients such easy going officials and politicians who work hand in hand with this element soon come regularly to hold up the concessionaries for something on the side. Not only are campaign funds collected, but private fortunes are made. The sporting element of Canton could be exploited for dividends that would make a gold mine look like a poor investment. It is, of course, possible that this is being done but there is no evidence of it. And generally it is one of the hardest things to hide in the whole gamut of graft, this holding up a sporting element. Undoubtedly there is already petty grafting from this gambling source. But the Cincinnati plan has not been installed, or else it is operated through a subway unique enough to patent. There is no "man higher up" who can be identified. But if that step has not been taken it is the next one. Sooner or later the temptation will be irresistable to some official or politician. That is Canton's danger. For, once systematic grafting of gambling is put in operation other features of the exploitation business will follow.

Meanwhile, since no man higher up can be located, municipal grafting in Canton becomes a question of the individual politician and official. Individual sinners can be safely left to the inevitable punishment that follows the inevitable exposure. It is when graft is developed into a system and a municipality is exploited as scientifically as the earth is mined for gold that the real danger develops. If any city in Ohio has an interest in checking a spread of this system before it gets further that city is Canton.

W. S. COUCH

A Baseball Game

NEWSPAPER REPORT

The Base Ball Match

The match between the Forest City Club, of Cleveland, and the Penfield Club, of Oberlin, took place yesterday afternoon, upon the old State Fair Grounds. The ground was dry and hard, the sun shone out brilliantly, the immense common furnished ample "sea room" for the players, and nothing was lacking to render every accessory perfect for such an occasion, but the fierce gale, that prevailed all day.

As it was, however, the game went on finely from first to last, and was keenly enjoyed by both players and spectators. Of the latter there was a large number on the ground.

The match commenced at a few moments past one o'clock, and was concluded at half past five. Seven innings were played. The rules of the game, fix nine innings as the full game; but contain a proviso, that, if foul weather, or any other unforseen impediment should occur, seven innings may constitute a game. Oberlin scored sixty-seven; Cleveland twenty-eight. Thus it will be seen that the Forest City Club was pretty roundly beaten. The Club, however, has only been organized six weeks, and has had but little practice.

The Penfield Club is an older organization, and is in much better practice. The Cleveland players are not discouraged, however, but hope to do better next time.

. . . .

INNINGS

	1st	2d	3d	4th	5th	6th	7th	
Forest City	2	2	2	5	15	0	6	28
Penfield	11	22	10	8	4	5	7	67

Two of the Cleveland players—Messrs. Leffingwell and Smith—were quite unfortunate. The former suffered a severe sprain of the arm, and the latter had three front teeth knocked out. The latter casualty occurred through a collision with a brother player. Both were rushing forward to catch the ball, that had been knocked high

From Cleveland *Herald*, October 21, 1865.

in the air, when they came together in such a manner, that Smith received the other's elbow against his teeth, with great force.

We hear it hinted that our local cricket club is to challenge the Forest City club to a game of base ball. We hope the match will take place. Such contests are healthful, spirited and interesting.

4 Labor

EVEN TO THE MOST OPTIMISTIC, nothing illustrated the agonies created in the new industrial age more poignantly than the plight of the American laborer during the last half of the nineteenth century. The laboring class faced low wages, long hours, unsafe working conditions, no job security, and untold dehumanizing experiences. While on the edge of existence, American labor had remained dedicated to the principles of capitalism, had rejected revolution, and had toiled for reform within the system. Almost reluctantly and with little hope of improving conditions, labor turned to unionism to secure a share of the wealth that it had helped to create. Although advances were made by the end of the century, labor had to wait another generation before it reached what it called the "promised land."

In response to the demands of labor reformers, the Ohio legislature created the Bureau of Labor Statistics in 1877. The bureau was to gather data and report on the condition of labor to both the legislature and the general public, to suggest labor legislation, to influence capital investments in economic fields scarcely touched, and to encourage laborers in overcrowded cities to try their luck in the underdeveloped areas of the West and the South. Consistently critical of the traditional concepts of political economy, the annual reports painted pictures of gloom and despair suffered by Ohio laborers. "The labor question is becoming, if it is not now, the leading question before the people," warned Harry J. Walls, the first commissioner of the bureau, "and upon its solution depend the peace and prosperity not only of the people of Ohio, or the nation, but the whole world."

Perhaps no segment of the laboring class suffered more from the companies' exploitative abuses than the coal and iron miners. Paid on a piece basis, miners were charged by the company for every tool they used, forced to live in company houses, badgered to buy in company stores, and paid in company script, not national currency. Though they were free citizens in the abstract, miners were scarcely free as long as any prospects of economic independence and security were denied. They truly owed their souls to the company store. The abuses of miners were also applied to other groups of laborers. Consequently, labor turned to trade unionism for self-protection. After 1859, many local trade unions became affiliated with national unions, and in trades where no national unions existed local unions were organized. Many cities and counties in Ohio had trade assemblies of which membership represented the local unions. By 1870, according to the report of the Bureau of Labor Statistics, "the workingmen of Ohio were as thoroughly organized in unions as were workingmen in any other of the United States." By 1900, 956 trade unions, representing 123 occupations, with a membership of 79,884, had been organized in the state.

Ohio witnessed the creation of numerous national unions, each of which called for united action in order to help remedy the poor conditions of labor. For example, in 1873 the National Industrial Congress was organized in Cleveland and, among many proposals, sought an eight-hour day, an end to convict labor, arbitration rather than strikes, and the end to open immigration. That same year the state's miners met in Youngstown and formed the Miners' National Association of the United States. Aside from promoting miners "morally, socially, and financially," the new union called for miners to become citizens, to use the ballot to elect politicians who were friendly to labor, and to remove the causes of strikes. In December 1886, after a bitter struggle against the leadership of Terence V. Powderly and his Knights of Labor, a group of laborites met in Columbus and formed the American Federation of Labor. Four years later, the United Mine Workers was also founded in the state's capital city.

The early struggles of labor toward organization and improved conditions were directed by men of talent. One of the most notably talented was John Fehrenbatch who, as a member of the Ohio House of Representatives, sponsored the bill that created the Bureau of Labor Statistics. Representing the reform spirit of the nineteenth century, he also worked against the use of convict labor in the market place. Harry J. Walls, who learned his trade unionism from William H. Sylvis, became the first commissioner of the Ohio Bureau of Labor Statistics, and through detailed and descriptive reports he sketched the harsh conditions of labor for Ohioans. Alonzo D. Fassett, eventually elected to the Ohio Senate, owned and edited the *Miner's Journal,* and in its pages lobbied for labor reform. Also in the *Miner's Journal,* under the nom de plume Jock Pittbreeks, Andrew Roy called for improved working conditions for the state's coal and iron miners; because of his work, he was appointed state mine inspector in 1874.

The work of the unions and their leaders was not in vain. Modest improvements in the condition of labor were made by the turn of the century either as the result of strikes or through positive government action. The reports of the Bureau of Labor Statistics educated the legislators and the public—no matter how slowly. Legislation was passed to restrict the use of child labor, to reduce the number of hours worked, to improve working conditions for women, and to provide for the inspection of factories, workshops, and mines. While none of the acts produced sweeping reforms with immediate results, at least the state was taking positive steps to aid labor. More importantly, labor's voice was being heard.

The Mines in Ohio

ANDREW ROY

The Ohio coal fields form part of the great Appalachian basin which extends through portions of nine different States, to wit: Pennsylvania, Maryland, West Virginia, Virginia, Kentucky, Ohio, Tennessee, Georgia and Alabama, and cover an area variously estimated at from 50,000 to 55,000 square miles. The coal measures of our State occupy from 10,000 to 12,000 square miles of this great coal field, or about one-fourth of the area of the State. The western margin of the Ohio coal measures runs through the counties of Trumbull, Geauga, Portage, Summit, Medina, Wayne, Holmes, Jackson, Pike and Scioto. All the territory lying west and north of this line of outcrop is occupied by the older formations—the sub-carboniferous Devonian and Sulurian strata. All the territory east and south of the outcrop is occupied by the coal bearing works. The line of dip of the coal measures of the State is south 60° to 80° east, and from 25 to 30 feet to the mile. On the margin of the coal field in the counties named above, only one bed of coal is due, the lower bed of the series, while along the Ohio river in the counties of Harrison and Belmont, the measures are fully 1,500 to 1,600 feet thick, and enclose no less than 40 to 50 different beds of coal, many of them too thin, however, to be of any commercial value.

The seams of coal in course of development range in thickness from 28 inches to 11 feet; the thickest seam found in the State is 14 feet, the thinnest bed of any commercial value is reckoned at 1 foot in height, though midway beds are met as low as 2 to 6 inches, but no seam of one foot or less will ever be mined for centuries to come. The maximum thickness of all the beds of coal would exceed a column 80 feet in height, were all the seams found in place where they are due, but owing to the numerous wants and thinning down of every bed all over the coal area, 30 feet will be about the aggregate thickness, and 9 feet the average thickness. After due allowance is made for slack and waste in mining, there are no less than 60,900,000,000 tons of merchantable coal in the State, which at the present rate of consumption would keep up the coal supply for 12,500 years.

The important mining districts are the Mahoning Valley district, the Tuscarawas Valley district, the Hocking Valley district (including the Straitsville and Shawnee mines), the Steubenville district, the

From Andrew Roy, "Sketch of the Mines and Miners of the State," *Third Annual Report of the Bureau of Labor Statistics, 1879,* (Columbus, 1880), pp. 100-106.

Bellaire district, the Pomeroy district, the Jackson county district, the Salineville district, the Coshocton district, the Leetonia district, and the Ironton district.

. . . .

There are three hundred mines in the state which work more than ten men at once, and nearly three hundred small mines which work from two to eight men during winter and are mainly idle during summer. The largest establishments have an underground force employed of from 200 to 250 men and boys, 150 to 175 of whom, according to the varying conditions, will be engaged in digging and loading coal, 10 to 15 driving mules or horses, 4 to 6 laying track, and if the seam is less than four feet thick, 6 to 10 will be engaged blasting roof and taking up bottom to make hauling roads for the mules; 2 to 6 are often required pumping and bailing water; 4 to 8 boys are employed tending trap doors. In the thick coals of the Hocking Valley, and where the mines are accessible by drift mining, not more than 12 per cent. of the miners are engaged on dead work, and most of this force is employed as drivers, hauling the coal from the working faces to the chutes outside.

There are 18,000 people employed in and about the coal mines of the State. The annual coal production or output is 5,225,000 tons, valued at the present selling price of coal at $8,000,000 at the pits' mouth. The first coal mined in Ohio was got by "stripping," near the village of Talmadge, in Summitt county, in the year 1810. In 1828 the first shipments were made to Cleveland from the mines of this county. The mines on the Ohio river at Pomeroy were opened in the year 1833. In 1840 the late Governor David Todd commenced shipping his famous Brier Hill coal to Cleveland.

The annual output will double itself every ten years until the close of the present century. In the year 1900, only 22 years hence, we will have in the State of Ohio a force of 70,000 subterranean workers hewing coal, and an annual coal production of 22,000,000 tons.

. . . .

The number of men and boys employed in and around the coal mines of the State, as I have already stated, is 18,000, of whom 14,000 work underground. Since the passage of the mining law boys under twelve years of age are prohibited from working under ground. As, however, there is no penalty attached for any violation of this provision of the statute, it is optional with the miners whether they obey it or not. To their credit it must be stated, that they have very generally complied with the requirements of the act in this regard.

The number of boys between the ages of 12 and 21 at work in the mines, is about 15 per cent. of the whole underground force of the State.

During the past 10 or 12 years the coal miners, not of Ohio alone but all over the United States, have attracted a good deal of public attention, owing to two causes: First, the numerous, bitter, and protracted strikes, growing out of wages disputes with their employers; and, second, the perilous nature of their employment, resulting in accident to life, health, and limb. The first of these troubles have been sought to be remedied by the enactment of conspiracy laws, and the last by the enactment of mining codes for the better protection of the lives and safety of miners.

. . . .

The mining law of Ohio, which was enacted in 1874 after the burning of the Atwater slope in Portage county, is a bungling piece of legislation. Several of the most important sections of the law have no penalties attached for the due enforcement of their provisions.

The enactment of proper and necessary mining codes for the protection of the lives and safety of miners, and the appointment of properly qualified mining experts to see the laws enforced and obeyed, I regard as not only an act of justice and mercy to our fellow-citizens who daily imperil health, life, and limb in the gloomy chambers of the coal mine, but as tending to elevate the status of the miner and make conspiracy laws neither necessary nor desirable.

The miner is peculiarly surrounded. Deprivation of solar light, the awful gloom of the mine, the inhalation of an atmosphere contaminated by the noxious and poisonous gases of the mine, blanches the human face and impoverishes the human blood like vegetable products similarly deprived of solar light and a life-sustaining atmosphere. Moreover, the danger to life and limb, to which there is no parallel on earth, and which the miner often can not see to guard against, added to the awful hardness and gloom of the coal mine, affect the minds and emotions of our subterranean workmen, and not conspiracy laws are required to make them better citizens, but good, efficient laws for the proper protection of their lives, and health, and safety—laws made to be enforced and obeyed.

. . . .

There are other causes tending to produce discontent among miners, such as the irregularity of work and the manner in which the work of mining and loading the coal is done. Few of the mines run steady all the year round. Most of the coal is shipped by rail, or river, or lake, to the coalless regions lying north and west of the coal field. During summer the river is too low for shipments, and in winter it is usually frozen up; in winter, also, lake navigation closes. The miner hews and loads the coal at the wall faces at so much per ton—usually fifty cents for coal four feet thick and upward. He is thus in a sense his own boss, and when cars are scarce and work slack during working hours, he spends much of his idle time with his fellows in the mine. At these social gatherings the question of wages and every possible grievance of the miner is discussed from one standpoint only, and he has become in consequence the best special pleader in the world. When he makes up his mind that he is entitled to an advance of wages, or that a proposed reduction is unnecessary and unjust, no power on earth can convince him to the contrary. Every person who fails to view the matter in the same light that he does, is regarded as an enemy of workingmen—as a mere tool of the mine operator.

The rules of the honor which miners have established among themselves are as hard and exacting as the laws established by Lycurgus. A simple notice published in a labor paper that, at a certain mine or district, there is a strike in progress, or any other misunderstanding, and all miners are requested to stay away until the difficulties are settled, is sufficient to keep every one of the one hundred coal miners of the Union away from the mines in question, no matter if they could double or treble their wages by accepting employment. The general American idea of manhood and duty is for every individual working man to make contracts, and to work for his employer on any terms he may choose. The sense of propriety and duty on the part of the coal miner is the very reverse of this. No single workman, according to his view, has a right, or at least ought, as an honorable man, to do anything affecting the price of labor against the will of the majority of his fellow-workmen. During a strike it is held to be an act of measureless infamy to work (black-leg), and, no matter how pressing the necessities of the true miner may be—his wife and children starving and in rags—he will endure all rather than disgrace himself by accepting work while his fellows are battling for their rights. (?) But when one suffers all suffer, for, with a self-sacrifice rarely met with elsewhere, those who have a dollar divide with those who have none—even the last crust of bread is divided and shared. The daring spirit which, amidst miphitic and explosive vapors, the falling of overhanging rocks, and the rushing of many waters, ventures far into the bowels of the earth to wrest its hidden mineral treasures for the use and comfort of man, is not surpassed nor equaled in devotion to what is regarded as the duty of one workingman to another on the occasion of a strike, growing out of a misunderstanding with the operators of a mine. Similar acts of devotion are occasionally found in other trades during the prevalence of a strike; but what is regarded as remarkable among workingmen in other situations of life, is a common occurrence among miners. Whatever the miner does, he does with all his might. When he works, he works with all his might; when he strikes, he strikes with all his might. On the occasion of accident in the mines, imperiling the lives of his brother miners, acts of heroism and self-sacrifice, never, perhaps, surpassed on any field of battle, are performed by the miner. He rushes through miphitic air or burning fire-damp, or will face any danger to rescue an imperiled comrade. The public have seen and heard a good deal of the imperfections of the miner—of his fondness for strong drink, and his love of striking; but of the noble traits of his character little or nothing seems to be known.

The Payment of Wages

LABOR STATISTICS

The question as to when and how the laborer shall receive his wages is of equal importance with the question of what the wages shall be. As a rule, in the cities of the State wages are paid weekly, in cash, many firms paying even the fractions of the dollar, but the majority paying the even dollars, retaining the fractions until they amount to one dollar, when it also is paid. Some few establishments in the cities, and almost every one outside the cities, pay wages but once in each month. This is noticeably the case in large establishments and many coal mines and iron works. The reason usually assigned for a failure to pay weekly is that it would require extra office help—perhaps in the largest establishment one clerk extra would be necessary. To save this five or six hundred dollars per year the workmen are compelled to suffer losses that in the aggregate would pay half a dozen clerks.

The rule is to pay on or about the fifteenth of each month the wages due on the last day of the previous month, and even that rule is too often stretched a week or even two weeks, or, as in the case of some of the railroads, two or three months. The system of paying on

From "The Payment of Wages," *First Annual Report of the Bureau of Labor Statistics, 1877*, (Columbus, 1878), pp. 672-678.

the fifteenth of the month for the month previous works a double injustice—it is unjust to the workman, and it is unjust to the employer who pays his employés weekly. To the workman the withholding of his wages for thirty days, with a forced deposit, so long as he continues in employment, of two weeks' wages in the hands of his employer, is a practical reduction of the wages of the workman of not less than ten per cent. as compared with similar wages when paid weekly.

. . . .

The payment of wages in cash, once in each month, is far preferable to the system growing in this State, by which wages are paid without cash. The Bureau had but commenced operations, when it was urgently requested to investigate what is known as the "Truck system," by those who suffer under it. Under the system, the largest percentage of wages is not paid in cash, but in merchandise. "Truck" stores are of two kinds. First, the "company store," a general merchandise store, owned by the firm or company, which has a large number of employés, said employés being directly or indirectly compelled to trade at such store. Second, the firm or company employing a large number of men, and paying the men in orders or "checks" upon particular stores.

Considerable attention has been given to the investigation of the subject, but some difficulty was experienced in getting at the facts, as those who had most reason to complain, feared to give publicity to their grievances, because, if it were known who gave the information, their discharge from employment would follow, and such discharge, too often, meant banishment from the locality in which perhaps they were born, or had for years resided.

. . . .

Taking into consideration the very small wages earned by workingmen, the very few of the common necessaries of life that such wages would purchase, even if work was constant and wages paid weekly in cash, the fact that such wages are not paid in cash, but are paid in groceries, dry goods, boots and shoes, at prices fixed by the employer, and when such prices, as will hereafter be shown, are fully twenty per cent., on the average, above the prices charged for similar goods, when purchased for cash, surely the greatness of the wrong done to workingmen, compelled to take their hard-earned wages in that way, cannot be over-estimated.

. . . .

Before 1861, the system of paying in store orders, or in "checks" payable in merchandise at a company store, had obtained consider-able of a foothold, especially in some of the eastern States, but with the issue of legal-tender money, and the great demand for labor incident to the war, workingmen everywhere were enabled to de-mand cash for labor performed, and were also able to enforce the demand, resulting in the destruction of hundreds of company stores as such, the destruction of the order system, and the system of checks.

. . . .

Truck originally meant barter, by which the laborer took his pay in a portion of what his labor produced, which he could dispose of to the best advantage if not suitable to his wants. Under our truck system the laborer does not receive pay in what he consumes.

. . . .

The system of paying wages in "orders" upon stores not owned by the person issuing the orders, is equally as shameful an imposition and deserving of as severe condemnation. It is purely an American method of defrauding the laborer, as is also the system of "checks" issued by the proprietor of a store and loaned to the employer of labor, to be by him paid to his employés instead of cash, thus compelling the employé to purchase his necessaries at the store of him who originally issued the checks. The wages of the employé are made the subject of barter and sale before they are earned, by parties who have no claim, legal or moral, upon such earnings. The trade of the employé is sold to the highest bidder by the employer—not the highest bidder in the interest of the employé, not to him who will bid to furnish first class goods at the lowest cash prices—but the highest and best bidder is he who will pay the employer or his agent, for his own private use, the largest per centage on the sales made to such employés.

The system of "company stores" is confined almost entirely to the coal, iron, and salt regions of the State. The order system is gradually extending to all sections of the State, while the "store checks" are also confined to the coal, iron, and salt regions.

Hocking Valley Strike, 1884

H. B. BRILEY

March 11, 1885, 9 A. M.

Q. Please state your name, age, residence and occupation.

A. My name is H. B. Briley, 50 years of age, and reside within the vicinity of Carbon Hill. My occupation—well, I have spent a large portion of my life in the ministry. For four years and a half I was check-weighman for the miners at Carbon Hill, Ohio.

. . . .

Q. Now, you may state as briefly as you can, what, in your judgment and opinion, was the cause or causes which led to the strike in the Hocking Valley.

A. Like every other conflict in the world's history, I believe it to have been a combination of causes. The manner of transacting business had created a conflict between capital and labor that might have been called an unnatural one, but as far as I could judge, from being present there a number of years, there seemed to be an effort upon the one part to resist the other, and in all organizations which partake of an organic form, there is always danger of extremes, and in all organic bodies there are possibilities of mistakes of persons or bodies overreaching their real intentions. In view of this fact, when it was in the power of the miners and they were subjected to a majority vote, there is no doubt that many of them overreached what was really their rights. I believe most of the miners will confess that at present, while on the other hand there appeared to be among the operators a constant effort to resist the power of this organic body, namely, the miners' association or union. I recognize the existence from common report. There was a conflict between capital and labor, like a tendency to revolution among nations.

No one thing causes a revolution or a conflict among nations, but a combination of things, such as caused this conflict or strike, as it is called; in addition to that, there was, in connection with the relations between the miners and the operators, as I have observed, another matter which had a tendency to bring about the strike, viz.: the difficulty in procuring the commodities of life. Then the issuing of checks was one of the causes which led to the trouble, or in other words, compelling them to trade at the company's store, and pay a much higher percentage for some articles than they could have been

From Testimony of H. B. Briley, Carbon Hill, Ohio, March 11, 1885, *Proceedings of the Hocking Valley Investigation Committee*, (Columbus, 1885), pp. 64-68.

purchased for at other places. This was usually the case, though not always; some articles indeed have been sold at an ordinary price, but others again at an extraordinary price. Usually, however, we may say that the percentage was higher for goods at the company's store than that retailed at other places. There was another thing that took place at the mine where I worked, and that was, that after the organization of the Columbus & Hocking Coal & Iron Co., an increase was made in the number of men above and beyond the capacity of the bank; it is a fact that only a certain amount of coal can be shipped with certain kinds of machinery, or loaded and handled, and the number was increased the following year from 82½ turns to 135, while the amount of work was rapidly diminished. And in advance of this a reduction of 10 per cent. was first put up; the miners had accepted a spring reduction of 10 per cent., because this had been the contract previous to the organization of this company. It was stipulated that during a certain time in the fall season they would pay 80 cents, and then during a certain time in the spring, they would pay 70 cents. The miners accepted the 70 cents, but in a short time after another reduction was ordered of 10 cents on a ton, and they concluded that the limited amount of work at that price would not support them or give them a respectable living. Consequently they refused to accept the reduction. This appears to me to be one of the chief causes which led to the trouble, but back of this, as another cause, came the contract system, which seemed to require every operative to surrender the liberties enjoyed by every citizen of the United States, or which ought to be enjoyed, at least, by them. If I understand that contract system, it simply required all the demands of the employer to be complied with, without any advantages being given to the miner, and he could accept just such pay as they would give, and just such work as they would allow. The only privilege he had was to quit, and I think if he quit inside of the contract, he was not to have any money.

Q. Suppose at the time of the commencement of this strike, a miner in the Carbon Hill mine had all the work he could do, laboring ten hours a day regularly and right along, what amount per week could he have earned at the price of 70 cents per ton—I mean a man of average capacity as a miner?

A. The average miner, I should suppose, had from fifteen to twenty dollars per week. His expenses for powder, oil and pick sharpening would come out of that, of course, which is sometimes a considerable amount. I would like to add in reference to this, that under favorable circumstances, a good miner may do twice as much work; but I have observed that banks are subject to accidents, though I am not acquainted with the business and I cannot fully explain what they are; sometimes the best miners would be two or three weeks when they could do but little—turning a room, as they call it, and cleaning up a room, and other occurrences which frequently happen in mining. But a good miner, well acquainted with his business and with a good place to work at, could do considerable more than this. Probably there are men that could do twice that amount of labor and earn twice that amount of money under favorable circumstances. But these drawbacks coming on as they did for 4½ years that I was check-weighman, bring down the price which the men receive so that they do not make such extraordinary wages after all. I have told young men (single men) that I believed they could do better to leave the mines and work in the Scioto Valley at eighteen dollars per month and board, than they do at working in the mines. A large portion of my life has been spent west of here a few miles, and I was sincere in giving this advice to young men. I believe that eighteen dollars a month on the farm, and board, is better than the mining of coal at 80 cents per ton, taking all things into consideration.

Utopia in the Valley

JOHN R. BUCHTEL

March 21, 1885—9 o'clock A.M.

The Committee met pursuant to adjournment, all the members being present.
John R. Buchtel, recalled, testified as follows:

(Examined by Mr. Kohler.)

Q. You may state, Mr. Buchtel, what acquaintance you have with the business of carrying on stores at the mines, what connection you have had with such stores, and what knowledge you have of prices charged to miners for goods at such stores, and how these prices compare with the same class of goods in the Columbus markets.

From Testimony of John R. Buchtel, Akron, Ohio, March 21, 1885, *Proceedings of the Hocking Valley Investigation Committee,* (Columbus, 1885), pp. 237-240.

A. Well, when we first went into the Valley, we decided that we would do nothing but a cash business; that we would have no connection—I am now speaking of the Akron Iron Company—that we would have no store connected with our business. We commenced operations and we found it almost impossible to conduct our business without having a store. For this reason—there were not any stores in the neighborhood nearer at that time than Nelsonville, and many men that were working for us had to draw their wages almost from day to day, and they had to have the necessaries to life to live on, and it took a good portion of their time to go and get these necessaries of life; so I finally made arrangments with a man by the name of Jackson, who came there and started a store; but it created a good deal of dissatisfaction, as I thought, because most of our men, or nearly all of them, were very anxious that we should have a store of our own; so I finally bought Jackson out, and we then, since that time, had a store of our own.

Q. At Buchtel?

A. Yes, sir; we have been carrying there, for the last three years, about sixty thousand dollars' worth of goods; I found it necessary, in connection with our store, to try to supply everything that was necessary for the family comforts of the miner; so I connected a meat market with the store, so as to furnish them with everything that was needed. I used to say to them, "Here, if there is any complaint or any over-charge in any way, shape or manner, let me know it and I will see that it is rectified." I didn't know but possibly the man in charge of the store might try to take advantage of the miners. I have always enjoined upon him to sell the goods as cheap as they could be afforded. I have frequently gone to the stores in Nelsonville—of course there would be some complaints, and I wanted to see if there was anything in a complaint—I have frequently gone to the stores in Nelsonville and priced goods, and if I found that there was any article sold cheaper than we were selling the same, I at once made them come down, because I determined that no goods should be sold to the miners for more money than they would have to pay elsewhere; my object was to try to create a home-like feeling for the miners; I built the store, which your Committee probably saw; I arranged my cellar with a view to laying in a large stock of potatoes and other necessaries of life, when they could be bought at a very low price; now, for instance, a year ago last fall—I had a cellar 130x60—I bought, I think, 15 or 16 car-loads of potatoes; I sold potatoes all along as cheap as they could be bought at wholesale a year ago this last spring.

Again, when I first went down there, there was no school-house. I tried the Board of Education, and they claimed that they were too poor to build a school-house; so I went to Akron, to an architect there, and got up plans and went and built a school-house, without reference to the Board of Education at all, that cost me three thousand dollars. The Board of Education did finally pay one thousand dollars, but we paid the two thousand dollars; we made it as comfortable as we could. Then we had a hall and let them have it for religious purposes and social gatherings, free of charge; also for Sabbath-school. I tried to make it as comfortable as I could for the miners. Now, I also let them have a piece of ground to erect a hall for the meetings of their Union, and I did everything I could to be in harmony with them, and to have everything possible harmonious. Now, they had made demands upon me, wanting me to pay them twice a month. Well, I said, "If I can do it I will try," and I did do it for two months, but I had to work my men day and night, and Sundays as well, so as to get up the pay roll so as to pay twice a month. You see, where we have five or eight hundred miners, there are a great many things which make up complicated accounts; for instance, here is the blacksmithing and the powder question and the drivers, and matters of that description, and it makes a great deal of work to keep their accounts. I tried it, as I stated, for two months, and at the end of the two months with almost—well, they agreed that we should abandon it, which we did; many men who could have had their pay on the middle of the month never drew it at all; they never called for it, and we had a great many men in our employ that didn't draw a dollar or ask for any credit at all; they got their money at the end of the month.

Q. One part of the question I don't believe you have answered, Mr. Buchtel; I refer to the comparison of prices.

A. I stated that I had gone to different stores and have always tried to sell as cheap as the markets—cheaper, in fact, than they could be sold elsewhere; and we could afford to do it, because we buy our goods by the wholesale, as you would call it. Now, in the last week, I happened to be down here, at a grocery down here (indicating)—I don't know whether I can name it now—oh, yes, Hayden's, I think it is—and I asked the price of potatoes. He said 90 cents. We are selling the same potatoes at 70 cents—Burbanks, per bushel, and meat—we have been selling better beefsteak than they have at 20 cents, and we have never asked more than 15 cents for; and, furthermore, I never allowed them to kill anything but the best beef. I says, "I don't want to give the miners anything that I would not eat myself," and in justice to us I must say, that there never has been a complaint of our treatment of our men in that regard.

Q. Taking your stock, Mr. Buchtel, comprising dry goods, groceries, drugs, medicines, provisions, and all things that you keep in that extensive store, were your prices above or below the prices charged in the Columbus markets for the same quality of goods?

A. I can only speak of one grocery, and that is down here at Scott's grocery, where I have some property and am boarding. They ask more for their goods than we asked at our store.

Q. Did you give your superintendent at your store any instruction as to any prices that he should charge the consumers?

A. Yes, sir; we have always enjoined upon him not to ask any more than a reasonable profit on the goods, and not sell goods any higher than the same goods could be bought for in any other markets. I was going to say—you were speaking about the miners and their condition—but the facts are that many of them—a great many of them, get the worse for liquor; in this regard, that with a store they do not have so much money, while without a store, of course, they have all money, and the drink which they consume will last longer with a great deal of money than with a small amount; and for that reason I had my men go to the railroad office, and I knew there was a great deal of liquor sold in our place, and I wanted, for my own satisfaction, to see what amount of beer and liquor was sold in Buchtel, and I had him go to the books of the railroad company, and told him to be very careful and make a correct examination of them, and get the amount of beer and whisky and gin that was shipped into Buchtel and consumed there largely by the miners, and see whether that would not account for some of the distress claimed among the miners. It seemed to me that this liquor question had a good deal to do with the cause of the strike.

Q. Well, Have you any other suggestions to give to the Committee as to the cause of the strike further than what you have already given?

A. I believe, as I have just remarked, that the liquor consumed in Buchtel has had as much to do with it as any other one cause that I know of, and my reason for it is this: I have frequently been on the train when delegates were going to conventions, and have seen them so drunk that they would have fights and trouble on the train. Now, I claim that when they go to conventions in that condition, in that desperate state of drunkenness, of course they will pass resolutions that they would not do if they were sober; I don't wish to be understood that this is the entire cause, but in my judgment and opinion it is one, and has a good deal to do with it.

Cigar Making

LABOR STATISTICS

It is doubtful if the employés of any trade or calling in the State, or in the United States, have been reduced to greater extremities than have been the cigar makers.

Previous to the year 1861, no class of employés were more absolutely independent of employers than were the cigar makers. Large manufactories were the exception, the retailer of cigars was, as a rule, the manufacturer.

. . . .

Every town and village, with a consuming population large enough to consume the product of the labor of one cigar maker, had that cigar maker in their midst.

Since 1861, however, the whole system has changed, not by the introduction of machinery or a division of labor that has caused such radical changes in other occupations, but the entire change has been brought about by the action of the general government, in devising a system of taxation that drove the business into large manufactories, and compelled the cigar maker to become an employé working for wages, or a mere retailer without the privilege of making his own stock.

. . . .

The center of this industry in Ohio is located in Cincinnati, where there are over four hundred establishments employing a capital, in cash and real estate, of one and a half million dollars, and nearly twenty-five hundred men, women and children. In 1876, 79,815,625 cigars were made, of the value of $1,955,390.

. . . .

In 1870, a cigar machine was introduced into the trade in Cincinnati. The men claimed that it did not save labor, but, instead, added thereto. One firm purchased fifty of the machines, and their employés refused to use them, and the result was that the men were discharged to the number of seventy-five, and girls and boys were hired in their places, and this was the commencement of the female cigar makers in Cincinnati. A cigar machine company then came into operation, hiring men at first, but as there was no extra profit in their labor, they were discharged, and women and girls were taught

From "Cigar Making," *First Annual Report of the Bureau of Labor Statistics, 1877,* (Columbus, 1878), pp. 715-719.

to make cigars, they, in turn, being discharged to make way for other learners—learners receiving but little, if any, wages. By this means a large number of so-called female cigar makers were competing with the men for the privilege of work. Wages rapidly fell, until a week's wages were not sufficient to pay the board of a single man; and yet men with families, who had served years of an apprenticeship, and supposed their mastery of a trade was a sure source of revenue, found themselves working for from five to seven dollars per week, and even that pittance liable to be reduced at any time, without the power on their part to resist.

In 1869, the cigar makers were on strike for eighteen weeks against a reduction of wages, and it was at the close of this strike when the molds were first introduced. The men, instead of being governed by all past experience in other trades—instead of taking hold of the machines and getting full control of them—foolishly struck against them, permitting the molds or machines to fall into the hands of boys and girls; their defeat was a foregone conclusion, and they have never recovered from the blow.

. . . .

It is charged against the smaller manufacturers, that instead of paying their employés in cash, they pay them in cigars. This charge is made both in Cincinnati and Cleveland, and the employés thus paid are compelled to carry the cigars around beer shops and other drinking places, and dispose of them as best they may—the result, as a rule, being that half the agreed upon price is at once spent in beer, etc., and a half week's wages is wasted in dissipation that the employer is altogether responsible for. Not only are the men thus robbed, but the manufacturer who tries to act fairly with his employés is thus forced out of the market by this certainly unjust competition. The men who thus take their wages in cigars and peddle them, are liable to arrest and punishment, under the laws of the United States, for peddling or selling without a license.

The wages paid to cigar makers have never been very large, especially in Ohio. The chief of the Statistical Bureau at Washington (Edward Young), in his work, "Cost of Labor and Subsistence in the United States," published in 1870, gave the wages of cigar makers in seven States, including Ohio, in 1867, at $11.59 per week, and in 1869, in the same States, at $12.35 per week, while the average wages in Ohio were, in 1867, $10.00 per week, and, in 1869, $11.00 per week. In both years the cigar makers in Ohio were earning below the average. In 1874, in another work on the same subject, he gives the average wages of cigar makers in Ohio at $9.50 per week.

. . . .

When the tax upon cigars was increased from $5 to $6 per thousand, instead of the consumer or manufacturer paying the tax, it was at once taken from the wages of the cigar makers. In one factory in Cincinnati in which the workmen were paid in cigars that were sold at wholesale at $13 per thousand, the men were forced to take them at $18 per thousand. Fortunately this concern was short lived. At the other factories that pay wages in cigars, no complaint is made as to the prices at which they are charged, but the outrage is none the less great, and the results just as pernicious.

As a set-off to the very low wages paid cigar makers, they are allowed a certain number of cigars per week. The rule in the large factories is as follows: On the Saturday of each week the cigar maker makes forty cigars, for which he receives no pay, and twenty out of the forty are presented to him for his own use; the other twenty are divided among the other employes, who also do some extra work for them.

The Sweated Industries

LABOR STATISTICS

There are thousands of women throughout the State who have families dependent upon them, and the instances are few where they are enabled to earn anything near the average of men's wages.

There are thousands of females employed who are in no way dependent on their earnings for the necessaries of life. Their earnings help to swell the family income and its comfort or savings, and those not seeking below the surface are apt to class all female labor under this head.

Those entirely dependent on their earnings for board, clothing, and other necessaries of life, have much to contend against. Small wages and unsteady employment mean far more to the struggling woman than the average man.

. . . .

From "Women's Work," *Third Annual Report of the Bureau of Labor Statistics, 1879,* (Columbus, 1880), pp. 267-270.

The following statements, clipped from the Cleveland Herald, were prepared by a woman who apparently gave considerable time and attention to the investigation of woman's labor in Cleveland:

"Should a reader of the Herald have the time or disposition to stand some Saturday afternoon either on the corner of Water and Superior, or Bank and St. Clair streets, he would see a large number of women and young girls passing and repassing those points, and if he chanced to be stationed there between six and seven in the evening, would find the throng had increased into a small army, this time all going one way. Those who have noticed these women, and have been curious to know whence they came and whither they were going, will find their curiosity satisfied in this and other articles that may follow, in which we shall endeavor to interest the public in a class of persons who receive too little attention at their hands. They are working women, and their occupations, which are numerous, widely differ in many respects, but there is one feature common to all—the wages are uniformly small."

. . . .

Many carry large bundles, and as they seem to be in the majority, we will, as a good starting point, peep into some of these packages and acquaint ourselves with their contents. Were we to take that liberty, we would find that they contained men's clothing—coats, pants, vests, overalls, blouses and shirts—obtained from the wholesale and retail clothing stores on Superior and Water streets, and that these women are carrying them home to make up, or bringing them back finished and ready for sale, even to the ticket upon them giving their dimensions and cost prices.

Uncomplaining Suffering

A Herald reporter visited the homes of over fifty of these women, living in widely different portions of the city, and by so doing learned all that can be told of this kind of work, and the average earnings of those who do it.

. . . .

Out of the mouths of these many witnesses there was no conflicting testimony, but from each and all was the truth confirmed that there are men in our midst who grind the faces of the poor, and grow rich out of the very life-blood of those whose necessities give them no alternative but submission. It was astonishing to find how many women are now, and for many months have been, supporting families, the husbands and fathers of which have been out of employment for some time. Another class found doing this shop work are those who are for the first time in their lives experiencing the pangs of poverty; who have never before known what it was to feel the anxiety and mental suffering attendant upon an empty purse and larder. The community would be surprised if it really knew how many of those who, by bravely keeping up appearances, are never suspected of straitened circumstances, yet, nevertheless, are fighting desperately to keep the wolf from the door. It is not the very poor who have been suffering this winter.

. . . .

A Widow's Story

In a small room of a tenement house on an alley we found a widow who was trying to support herself and little boy by making vests. Everything about her spoke of better days, and when we stated our business she flushed and seemed unwilling to discuss the subject, but before leaving we gained her confidence, and was volunteered much information that we at first despaired of receiving. A pile of woolen vests lay on a table, and we were allowed to examine them. They were corded all around the edges, and contained four pockets each. Although of inferior material, they were made as neatly, and as much pains taken with them, as the finest broadcloth.

"If I work steadily all day, and quite late at night," she said, "I can make fourteen of these a week, but I hardly ever go to bed at all Friday night, as I must have them done by Saturday noon in order to get my pay, for it sometimes takes all the afternoon of that day to deliver them, as I always find a crowd of women before me, and must wait my turn to have my work examined. When the time arrives I tremble from head to foot with nervousness, for the fellow who does it is invariably overbearing and insolent. If he cannot find a flaw in the work, he will say, 'Can't you make more than a dozen vests a week? If you don't do better than this, we won't give you any more to do.' If I were alone in the store I would not care, but there is always such a crowd around to overhear it, and it humiliates me so to take abuse from a person so utterly beneath me in every way."

"And what," we asked, "do you get for these vests?"

"Only fourteen cents each," was the answer.

"Then you make, with all this toil, $1.96 a week?"

"Yes, and sometimes even less, and the rent of this room is $2 a month."

"Then," we suggested, "you have only about $5.50 a month to live on?"

"Not even that, for my machine is not yet paid for, and I ought to have $3.00 a month for payments on that. This I have been unable to do lately, for my child has been sick, and I have had to buy dainties for him. I am ashamed," she continued, "to tell you how little we spend for food. I have all my life heretofore been accustomed to a bountiful table, and I would never then have believed that any one could exist on what I have had to this winter."

· ·

A Shocking Story

Another widow, whose husband died but a few months since, leaving her with a young babe, has been sewing all winter on heavy woolen pants, at ten cents each. These, besides the work on them, required a great deal of pressing with hot irons, and if she made one pair a day, besides attending to the wants of her child, she did well. Now she is at work on overalls—stiff, ugly, cinnamon-colored affairs that felt like pasteboard. There were two pockets in each, and these were stayed at the top and bottom by three-cornered pieces of leather, which were stitched on by machine. These leathers are very destructive to machine needles, and one or more are frequently bent or broken in a day. There are buttons, buckles, and tickets to be sewed on each pair, and the woman who completes a dozen of these ungainly over garments has the satisfaction of realizing that she has earned just fifty cents. Now, no one, unless possessed of more than ordinary endurance, can make more than four dozen a week. This poor woman falls far short of it.

"The firm I work for," she told us, "only pay on Saturday. I finished three dozen of these last Monday, and carried them back, but of course, as it was not pay-day, received no money. They gave me three dozen more, and oh! how hard I worked to get them done before Saturday afternoon, but it was impossible, and as I had not a cent nor a morsel in the house to eat, I took a dozen that were finished and started down with them. I waited three hours for my turn at the desk, and then the man wouldn't pay me either for those I had just brought in or for the three dozen the previous week. 'Wait until your work is all done, then come in next Saturday, and we will pay you.' 'But I have not a cent,' I urged, 'to carry me over the Sabbath.' 'We can't help that; these are our rules, and we won't break them.' So I crept back home, faint from want of food, and sick at heart. A neighbor, who had cared for my babe while I was gone, lent me some change, or I do not know where I would have been now." This woman is also trying to pay for a machine.

The Workingwomen

NEWS REPORT

The Enquirer this morning presents some vitally interesting facts about working-women. The information is secured in advance from the annual report of the State Labor Commissioner. It relates particularly to the work of women in Cincinnati, and gives a gloomy picture of the condition right at home. The facts are official, the result of very careful investigation, and are therefore authentic. They present an exhibit that is startling, and should command the most earnest consideration. Here they are:

The Lines of Work. Principally investigated were tailoring, shoe-fitting, laundry work, housework, cloak and vest making, sewing of different kinds and restaurant work.

General conditions of women at work, and also home conditions, were particularly investigated; and, in many cases, a most pitiable state of affairs was disclosed. It was no unusual thing to find families of from four to seven living in one small room, where light could seldom penetrate, and pure air never; where infancy and old age, sickness and health, all huddled together, were living on an income less than it takes to keep the average business man in cigars.

The destitution thus unearthed. Among the working people of Cincinnati, if caused by some sudden catastrophe such as swept over Louisville or Linn, would call forth the sympathy of the world, but, coming as it has, gradually, year by year, through the natural operation of business systems, it has been systematically ignored and its existence even denied.

Investigation has shown that the number of people in desperate circumstances was greater at the taking of statistics for 1889 than at any year previous, and that more people were out of employment, the number in Cincinnati alone being estimated at from 8,000 to 10,000.

Wages have been steadily on the decrease in some trades for twenty years.

Of the people who are the victims of these adverse circumstances, there are just two classes: those who have come down from better positions—a class which seems to be increasing—and those in the same condition in life into which they were born. But those to whom poverty has been a heritage do not feel its iron heel, as a rule, more keenly than do those of the other class, and thousands of both classes are at all times within a week of starvation. With both the battle of life is fierce and unremitting.

From *Cincinnati Enquirer,* April 13, 1890.

Children are crying for bread; old people, too old and infirm to work steadily, are slowly starving to death, and hundreds of girls are being driven into the vortex of sin *by the gaunt specter of want.*

But, with all this, there is still a large element of good citizenship among them, and a degree of moral integrity that is surprising. Particularly is this true of the women, who choose lives of bitter privation rather than gilded paths of vice, and bravely live their chosen lives to the bitter end.

Among the many pitiful cases brought to light was one that may serve to illustrate the true condition of the homes of many unfortunate working people, and also to show under what terrible privations a woman must sometimes live and labor.

She was young, not more than 24 or 25. Her husband was an invalid and she had two children, a little boy of 3 or 4 years and an infant daughter. She was a tailoress, and was doing what is called shop tailoring—the cheapest work in the market. She went to the shop and got the work and took it home with her.

Her "home" was one small room about 12 by 14 on the ground floor of a queer, rambling old tenement house in the West End. The street in front gave no indication of a tenement house, and the only means of entrance was through an arched passage-way just large enough to admit a small wagon or dray, and through which undoubtedly the people moved their small belongings. This passage-way led back and opened into a sort of court-yard, around which the building rose four stories on every side. A row of windows and doors marked the entrance to perhaps twenty-five "homes" on (or in) the ground floor, while outside stairs led to the floors above, and a sort of outside corridor, somewhat on the plan of the Ohio Penitentiary, ran along the building just above the lower windows.

Her room was one of the first, and was even more cheerless within than it *was prisonlike without.*

The bare floor, the blank and dingy walls, the few old wooden chairs, the unmade bed, the almost fireless stove around which the family were huddled, all spoke a mute language of privation and toil.

She ate by a bare wooden table near the one window, through which the struggling rays of the wintry day shone feebly from under the corridor without, and lighted up with a sort of chill and ghastly light the miserable home within.

By her side lay a pile of unfinished pants, and as her thin fingers moved deftly and swiftly over her work, making button-holes, sewing on buttons and doing all the numberless little things that go to make up "finishing," one foot was busily engaged rocking the little wooden chair upon which the baby daughter had her tiny bed.

A loaf of black rye bread, a little molasses in a bowl and a cup of water sat upon the table, and a little boy of some 3 or 4 years of age sat up in a high chair vainly striving to satisfy the *craving hunger of childhood* with this meager and doubtless oft-repeated diet. As though any thing had been lacking to prove to the investigator how great a luxury in that poor home were the things called common necessities in others, the little fellow lisped in a guileless baby way:

"Mamma, we's dot some suddar in de tubbard, ain't we, mamma?"

"Yes," answered the mother, flushing with embarrassment, and anxious to dismiss the subject.

"Mamma," continued the little one, not to be silenced upon a matter of such importance, "we has to teep that for baby, don't we, mamma? Mamma, some time when papa dits well we'll dit some more suddar, won't we, mamma, and den I tin have some too, tant I, mamma?"

The father, who sat by helpless with rheumatism, sighed deeply, but said not a word.

Here the little one woke from her uneasy slumbers with a frightened cry. The mother laid down her work and took up the babe, and as she nursed the child at her famished breast told the investigator *something of her life.*

For nearly two years her husband had been out of work, part of the time on account of sickness, but oftener because work could not be found. He used to be a teamster and owned his own team, but for a long time had been only a common laborer.

When misfortune first came she went into a tailor shop to work, thinking it would only be for a little while, but times grew harder and harder, until now they had nothing at all but her small earnings, which usually ranged from $1.50 to $2 per week. Before baby came she used to go to the shop, and then she made more money. Now she must work at home, and it was no unusual thing to put in eighteen, sometimes twenty, hours a day over her work.

But rent had to be paid, and though it was only $4 per month, yet it was sometimes hard to pay, with husband and baby both sick and needing food and medicine.

Labor's Competitors

ALONZO D. FASSETT

My attention has been frequently called to the alarming growth of women and child labor in the gainful occupations. Good girls to do kitchen work are hard to find in the cities at three and four dollars a week and board, but girls can be found in the factories, and in the planing-mills running planers, and in the potteries doing men's work, receiving from 50 to 75 cents a day, while men working beside them get from $1.50 to $2.00 for the same kind and quantity of work.

Children are crowded into workshops at twelve years, and at fifteen they are able to do a man's work, but their wages are fixed at thirty, forty and fifty cents a day. They are given work at meagre wages until they reach the years of manhood, when they are thrown out of employment to make room for some other boys who will work cheaper, and who have been crowded into the works behind them. I have found boys twelve and fourteen years old, struggling for a livelihood in a room heated 120 degrees, Fahrenheit.

. . . .

The statistics compiled in this report furnish some idea as to the number of people who are suffering because of enforced idleness. It is evident that nearly all the trades are depressed largely because of over crowding. The poorest paid trades are the ones most crowded. Three agencies, in my judgment, have combined in producing this result, viz.: Foreign immigration, foreign goods competing in our home markets, and invention. The latter agency is what opened the doors of the workshop to child and women labor. In the old days before machinery supplanted the mechanic, it took a man to drive the jack plane, shape the iron, and construct the vehicle; now a delicate child guiding a machine can do most of this work. The spoke of a buggy is made by machinery in one place, the hub in another, the axle in another. One person learns to make a spoke, another the hub, another the axle, but no one learns to make them all. Invention has centralized the industry, and the effect makes it more difficult for labor to find remunerative employment. It has not only made the productive power of each person intensely greater, but it has brought new productive forces as competitors in the gainful occupations.

. . . .

From Alonzo D. Fassett, "Labor's Competitors," *Eleventh Annual Report of the Bureau of Labor Statistics, 1887, Ohio Executive Documents,* (Columbus, 1888), pp. 1105-1109.

The three causes above enumerated have united in producing this result. Some localities and some trades view invention with apprehension and alarm, but more is to be feared from ignorance. The machine is a blessing that would lighten the toil of all, that would serve all alike, if labor was sufficiently intelligent to meet it with an organization that would reduce the hours of labor to correspond with the increased facilities it affords. The right to labor is being denied. Thousands of able and willing men and women who do not recognize the fact that they are deprived of a right and not simply debarred a privilege. They stupidly believe the assertion that there has been over-production, or that as a nation we have been living beyond our means. They are prone to believe that their misfortunes have been increased by, or are wholly due to political troubles, and they foolishly undertake to remedy the evil by the ballot, where organization is destroyed and education impeded; instead of by organization, which promotes education, now more than ever needed by workingmen. There is not an idle workingman in this country who, in his own person, is not a living witness of the over-production lie. No matter what his trade or calling, he would produce something that would be gladly taken by another; providing, that other could also produce and thus have something to give in exchange. The machine and the mechanic will produce 6 times the amount that the mechanic alone could produce, but the mechanic gets none of the increase. The owner of the machinery takes that, and when with the machine he has filled his warehouse, the machine and the mechanic are stopped, and the mechanic can starve because there has been over-production—that is, more than people who want have the means to purchase.

. . . .

What the workingmen want and what they should have is regular employment for all who are willing and able to work at eight hours a day. A reduction of the hours of labor would not diminish the amount of the national wealth, as some political economists assume, but it would spread the employment for its creation over a larger area, and slightly alter its distribution in favor of the poor. If ten hours a day sufficed in the dark ages to make some people rich, and feed, clothe, and shelter the poor, one would think that a little less would suffice for the same purposes now when the productive power of the machinery of the United States is more than equal to the labor of 500,000,000 human beings.

The workingmen of this country must learn that shorter hours bring good wages just as short crops bring high prices for potatoes. They must also learn that when the fathers crowd their little boys and girls into the factories, they place therein the agencies for dragging themselves down in their wages.

Again, workingmen must learn the difference between political questions and party politics. They must come to view the questions of labor from the workingmen's standpoint, and not the politician's. The labor question is a question of labor, of life—of opportunity for the poor. Workingmen must learn to oppose all who oppose labor measures, and to never oppose labor measures just because their party concludes to. They should move in one solid body to secure legislation that will restrict immigration. The United States can no longer advertise itself as the home of the oppressed of all nations. India's 250,000,000, working for $2.00 a month, may conclude to come. Egypt's seven cents a day labor may accept the invitation. As there is no room in this country for the pauper labor of the world, there is no room for the manufactured product of foreign countries.

The reports of the treasury department show that $38,000,000 worth of iron alone was brought into this country the first eight months of the present year. That manufactured product has a more injurious effect upon workingmen's wages than the landing upon our shores of as many poorly paid laborers from foreign countries as would be required to manufacture it here. A conservative estimate places this number at 200,000. Here is enough iron manufactured in foreign countries coming to this country during the first eight months of this year, to have employed 200,000 iron workers, coal miners, ore miners, and limestone workers, eight months. This vast product—this product of 200,000 foreign laborers, is allowed to enter our markets and strike down to idleness 200,000 of our own people, as fully that many are idle in the coal and iron, the ore and limestone interests of the United States.

Trusts and their Relation to Labor

ALONZO D. FASSETT

The most potent factor in the disturbance of the industrial conditions of the country, and causing such wide-spread discontent and uneasiness among the mass of the people, are the "trusts" and

"syndicates" that have, within the past few years, become so numerous, powerful, and merciless. They not only control the prices of the
necessaries of life, but diminish or not, as it may suit their interests,
the production of these necessaries, thereby lessening the ability of
laborers to buy what they need for the support of themselves and
families; first, by reducing the quantity of labor, and secondly, as
necessarily resulting from the first, cutting down the amount of
wages received for the labor actually performed.

These "trusts" and "syndicates" were almost, if not entirely,
unknown until within the last fifteen or twenty years, and the
disastrous "strikes," those unnatural disturbances that are now almost "always with us," were, until the advent of the "trusts," so
"few and far between," and withal so trifling in character, as scarcely
to attract attention outside the parties immediately interested. One
has followed the other as naturally as effect follows cause, and the
trouble will certainly continue, becoming more intense and bitter
with time, until the government, as an act necessary to self-preservation, finds some means to curb the power of these combinations,
which seem to seek nothing less than the subjugation of the whole
world to their arbitrary and merciless control.

What is a "trust?" It is, in plain terms, a combination of capital
for the purpose of controlling a particular business, regulating the
production and price of an article of general consumption, and, as a
natural incident thereof, fixing the price of labor in connection therewith. It is a double-edged sword, cutting both ways. It limits production that the price of the product may be increased and the cost of
labor lessened. The ability of the wage-worker to consume is lessened
to the extent that his earnings are diminished; but this apparent loss
is far more than compensated by the enhanced price exacted of those
who are able to stand the extortion. It is, in short, a huge boa
constrictor. It crushes the life out of every one caught within its coils
effectually and with as little remorse of conscience as can be supposed to trouble that of the reptile as it beslimes its helpless victim
preparatory to the act of swallowing. And what makes the matter
worse, the trusts necessarily deal almost exclusively in articles of
prime necessity, or, otherwise, they would not possess such resistless
power.

To enumerate these trusts, "these man-eaters," is to name almost
every business that is essential to the sustenance and comfort of man.
The one, perhaps, deserving of the first place in the list, as it is, in
fact, the parent of the whole progeny, is the famous, or rather
infamous, Standard Coal Oil Trust. This huge corporation hesitates at

From Alonzo D. Fassett, "Trusts, and their Relation to Labor," *Twelfth Annual Report of the Bureau of Labor, 1888,* (Columbus, 1889), pp. 199-204.

nothing that stands in the way of its complete absorption of the coal oil business of the country. It buys up transportation companies as a merchant buys goods, seeming to consider such transactions as legitimate as the purchase of any other "raw material." During the investigation last summer into the "ways that are dark" of this concern, it was developed that it had drawn in seventeen months from four railroad companies, as rebates, the enormous sum of $10,151,218, viz., from the Baltimore and Ohio Railroad Company, $1,116,633.98; from the Erie, $2,131,755.78; from the New York Central, $2,131,755.78; and from the Pennsylvania Central, $4,771,072.76. This vast sum represents the amount of discrimination by these four roads in seventeen months in favor of the Standard Oil Trust. That is to say, for the transportation of an equal amount of oil other refiners had to pay these four railroad companies over *ten millions of dollars* more than was paid by the Standard Oil. The effect of such discrimination is not difficult to see. All competition, or nearly all, has been crushed out, and the huge boa constrictor remains the undisputed master of the situation. Last year (1887), as was learned in the course of the investigation referred to, this overgrown "trust" declared a dividend of nine per cent. on a capital stock of $90,000,000; or, in other words, a profit of more then *eight millions of dollars* on a capital stock two-thirds of which was water.

. . . .

Every advance in the necessaries of life causes the wage-worker to make an effort to correspondingly increase the price of his labor. This generally results in a strike, and a consequent loss to all concerned, and leads frequently to riot, bloodshed, and a demoralization of trade. The "striker," in most of the States, soon learns to his sorrow that there is a law to prevent and punish combinations of laboring men, even though the strikes be unattended by any acts of violence; but the courts know of no law that will prevent a combination in the form of trusts and other corporations from producing a condition of things that entail suffering and hardship upon millions of men, women and children.

Strikes, with their attendant evils, were almost unknown previous to the appearance of trusts and other collossal corporations. When one did occur, it was small and insignificant in results. It was local in character and effect, and not infrequently had no other foundation than personal feeling or a misunderstanding. But they are now so frequent in their recurrence, and of such alarming proportion as to challenge the attention and most serious consideration of all classes of community. Men speak learnedly, or think they do, from the platform, the rostrum, and even the pulpit, of the evils of trades unions and the strikes they produce, and declaim in the most approved style of the horrors of the imaginary "commune," they see looming up in the near future, when all property rights will be destroyed, and when anarchy and indiscriminate rapine and slaughter will reign supreme. All these evils, present and to come, are generally charged to the toiling millions. Other men, who have examined into the remote, as well as the immediate cause of these manifestations of popular feeling, take a much less gloomy, as well as a far more correct view of the situation. They see, and tell their hearers that these working men have a greater interest in the preservation of the government and of law and order, than have any other class, and say that it is a sad commentary on the intelligence of any man for him to say that he fears the destruction of all we hold most dear, by the very men relied upon by the country, in the hour of peril and threatened ruin, to defend its integrity and the lives and property of its citizens. And never yet has the country relied in vain on this great army of workers. Their stalwart army, responding to the noble and patriotic impulses of their hearts, have always beaten back all who would in the least injure or mar our social fabric or our grand political structure. How many of the two million soldiers who carried muskets on their shoulders during the war of the rebellion, how many of those who suffered martyrdom in rebel prisons, or died like American patriots and heroes on the battle-field, that others, both the born and the unborn, might possess a government under whose flag no man, woman or child could be sold from the auction block? How many of these men, I ask, were from any other class than that which tills the soil, delves in the mines within the bowels of the earth, fills the factories and workshops of the land, or is otherwise engaged in creating wealth or ministering to the comfort of our people? It sounds strange to hear such men denounced. Their only offense is their determined opposition to wrong, whether it appear in the shape of trusts or human slavery. They are not always correct, it is true, either as to the cause of the wrong or the remedy therefor; but they will continue their opposition to that which plunders them of so much of their hard earnings, no matter who or where it may strike. They have read the Declaration of Independence, and become imbued with its teachings, and it will not be their fault should these revolutionary lessons bear fruit of a kind, very different from that which the beneficiaries of trusts and syndicates would like to see.

. . . .

Believing that trusts and all kindred devices to plunder the people are radically wrong in their inception, in their management, and pernicious and ruinous in their effects, it is to be hoped that some adequate remedy will be discovered and promptly applied. In a government like ours, of constitutional limitations (and without limitation in the organic law, the people would be at the mercy of the powerful and unscrupulous), it is difficult to restrict the freedom of the individual so as to prevent his committing a great wrong without, at the same time, arbitrarily and seriously hampering him in the pursuit of legitimate and honest trade. Some of our ablest statesmen contend that the legislative power cannot interfere in such matters, while others, equally as able and learned, claim that the subject is clearly within the constitutional power of the national congress. The question is now fairly before the people, as well as before congress, both the Republican and Democratic parties having, at their last national conventions, inserted clauses in their respective platforms, denouncing trusts of all kinds, and demanding of congress their suppression, and a bill with that end in view has been introduced into the United States Senate and is now pending before that body. "Where there is a will there is a way" is an old adage, and as true as it is old. It would indeed be strange if no power resided anywhere in our government to suppress a great wrong. The argument of want of constitutional power to "coerce" a state was relied upon by those who, in 1861, sympathized with the cause of the rebellion to protect the seceding states from invasion by the armies of the government; but we had a man in the executive chair at that time who believed in the common-sense principle that a government, like an individual, possessed all the necessary constitutional power to protect itself. That power was exercised, states "coerced," and the rebellion suppressed, yet the breaches of the constitution incurred thereby are not alarmingly visible. If the constitution does not possess sufficient vitality to protect the people who made it, then it is time that that instrument was reconstructed in such manner as to meet the requirements of the times, and be made an effectual barrier between the people and those who care neither for justice, constitutions, or the pleadings of humanity.

5 Progressivism

BY THE END of the century, demands for social and political reform arose in many sections of the state, particularly in the large urban centers. Having lost patience with political corruption, economic favoritism, and bossism, reform-minded politicians, intellectuals, and professionals who called themselves "progressives," began to strike at the governmental structure that permitted those abuses and thus threatened both the concept of competitive economics and the democratic process. These progressives were influenced by Henry George's *Progress and Poverty* and later by the work of Edward Bellamy in *Looking Backward,* and they declared that industrialization had not provided the material benefits to the masses that had been promised but had rather created unprecedented economic and social problems in modern society. Anchored to the principles of a competitive economic system and a democratic form of government, they labored to reform the system in order to provide an equal share of the benefits of industrialization and to provide for an even form of social and political justice. Individually divergent in method, yet reaching a broad consensus of purpose, these social reformers joined together in what was called the "progressive movement." This movement first entered the Ohio political arena at the municipal level during the closing decades of the nineteenth century, and subsequently moved to the state government during the first twenty years of the new century. Fighting against entrenched special interests and political corruption, the movement took on the dimension of a crusade, with faith that through human wisdom, common sense, and planning, institutions could be perfected that in turn could create a more perfect society. The Ohio pioneers of the progressive movement helped to give direction and meaning to the national reform movement.

Evidences of corruption were plentiful. Numerous muckrakers began to expose to the public the machinations of special interests at the state and municipal level. Lincoln Steffens, one of the best known of the political muckrakers, aimed his poignant pen at bossism and illustrated to the nation the corruption of Cincinnati, the city he called the most poorly governed in the United States. However, political corruption was not reserved for municipal use. In Adams county, deep in picturesque southern Ohio, it was discovered that politicians in rural areas were as vicious as their urban counterparts. To the skeptical Ohioan, not even Jefferson's dream of a rural gentry, jealously guarding the virtues of American democracy, was safe from the strains of avarice and corruption.

The progressives in Ohio were found among the successful middle-class and professional people, such as journalists, lawyers, and ministers, as well as a particular breed of wealthy businessmen who had acquired a social consciousness. The effects of monopolies threatened what they considered to be the virtues of both economic individualism and the democratic system. Trade unionism threatened their principles of American life no less than the large corporations, and, while willing to pass legislation that protected and benefited the laboring class, it was never their intention to give the power of monopoly to labor.

One of the most influential Ohio progressives was Samuel M. "Golden Rule" Jones. Jones, a successful manufacturer and owner of the Acme Sucker Rod Company, a firm that made parts for oil pumps, entered politics in 1897, when he won the mayoral race in Toledo as a Republican. Following an unsuccessful bid for governor in 1899, he left the Republican party and won three successive terms as mayor of that city as an independent. While Jones' style was not always orthodox, his colorful antics and boldness of leadership left lasting impressions on those who followed his career. Jones' first principle was to practice what he preached. In his factories he instituted reforms that were years ahead of their time—insuring that his workers labored only eight hours a day and received paid vacations. As mayor of Toledo, he pushed for municipally owned public utilities, public parks, city beautifying programs, free concerts, public bathhouses and swimming pools, and advocated that the city guarantee job security for its citizens through public works.

In Cleveland, Tom L. Johnson, former congressman and four-term mayor of the Forest City between 1901 and 1909, carried the torch for reform. Like Jones, Johnson was wealthy, and as a professed single-taxer devoted his energy and fortune to reform. During his administrations he pressed for control over public utilities and railway lines, solicited support for control of gambling and drinking, and maneuvered to achieve fair bidding for public contracts. Johnson carried the spirit of reform to the state level during his unsuccessful bid for governor in 1903. He became convinced that only through the success of home rule could the state's municipalities become reformed. Johnson has been judged one of the best administrators produced by the progressive movement. Symbolically, he was buried alongside Henry George, his philosophical idol, in Brooklyn, New York.

From the pulpit of the First Congregational Church in Columbus, Washington Gladden, who was heralded along with Walter Rauschenbusch as the author of the social gospel in American Protestantism, preached for social justice in American society. Through his sermons, speeches, and novels, he called for the protection of labor, espoused the application of biblical principles to modern industrial society, and argued for the end to discrimination against blacks, Catholics, and Jews. He served on the Columbus city council for two years and during that time fought for reduced streetcar fares, public ownership of utilities, and control over pollution. Gladden's cry for social justice on the basis of Christian ethics was a major contribution to the progressive movement—not only in Ohio but nationwide.

Without doubt, the highlight of the progressive movement in Ohio was the famous progressive constitutional convention of 1912 and the James M. Cox administration, which wrote the will of the people into law. Drawing national attention, the Ohio Constitutional Convention of 1912 listened to the principal figures in the progressive movement, including William Jennings Bryan and Theodore Roosevelt. After openly debating the tenets of progressivism, the convention drafted forty-two reform amendments and submitted them to the people. Although not all were approved, the amended state constitution of 1912 was the most progressive in the country.

Between 1913 and 1921 the Ohio General Assembly accomplished an unprecedented amount of reform work. Included among the reforms for a more efficient municipal government was a home rule provision—the authority for cities to operate public utilities and to extend greater power over many aspects of local government. At the state level, a budget system was established, the civil service system reformed and a general governmental reorganization took place. In the field of labor, compulsory workman's compensation was established, an eight-hour day fixed for public works, and a limit placed on the hours of labor for minors. Of course, the list of legislative accomplishments was longer. However, it had become evident that, through the work of the progressives, Ohio had become a state destined for reform. It recognized that, between the promises of industrialization and their realization, government had to take positive steps in order to insure a better quality of life for its citizens.

Cincinnati, Ohio

LINCOLN STEFFENS

The story of the latter-day politics of Ohio, as I understand the state, can best be told as a tale of two of her cities: Cleveland and Cincinnati; Cleveland, the metropolis of her North-east, Cincinnati, the metropolis of her South-west; Cleveland, the best-governed city in the United States, Cincinnati, the worst.

Going to Cincinnati

I shall never forget my first visit. Cities and city bosses were my subject then, and I thought I knew something about such things. I didn't know the worst. The train ran through the early morning sunshine up to a bank of mist and smoke, paused, as every train since has done, then slowly tunneled its way into the *cul de sac*, where the Queen City broods in gloom. I wanted to see Cox. The etiquette of my work seems to me to require that I shall call first everywhere on the ruler of the people; if he is the mayor, I call first on him; if the mayor is a figurehead, I call first on the boss. Some times one is in doubt. In Cincinnati, immediately after breakfast, I sought out the sign of the "Mecca" saloon, went up one flight to a mean, little, front hall-room. A great hulk of a man sat there alone, poring over a newspaper, with his back to the door. He did not look up.

"Mr. Cox?" I said.

There was a grunt; that was all.

"Mr. Cox," I said, "I understand that you are the boss of Cincinnati."

His feet slowly moved his chair about, and a stolid face turned to mine. Two dark, sharp eyes studied me, and while they measured, I explained that I was a student of "politics, corrupt politics, and bosses." I repeated that I had heard he was the boss of Cincinnati. "Are you?" I concluded.

"I am," he grumbled in his hoarse, throaty voice.

"Of course, you have a mayor, and a council, and judges?"

"Yes," he admitted; "but—" he pointed with his thumb back over his shoulder to the desk—"I have a telephone, too."

"And you have citizens, too? American men and women?"

He stared a moment, silent, then turned heavily around back to his paper. Well, I feel the same way now about the citizenship of this city; Cox, their ruler, and I have had several talks since; he doesn't

From Lincoln Steffens, "Ohio: A Tale of Two Cities," *McClures Magazine*, XXV (1905), 293-311.

say much, but I am sure he and I agree perfectly about them. But this, also, I never forgot, and let no one else forget it: Cincinnati is an American city, and her citizens are American citizens. Therefore, what has happened in Cincinnati can happen in American cities. What had happened there?

Tweed Days in Cincinnati

We need not go into details. We know Philadelphia, and that is to know most of the truth about Cincinnati. An aristocracy once, the best people were decent about the graft, but selfish, and the criminal classes took over the government. Tom Campbell, a criminal lawyer, led the Republicans, and John R. McLean, the son of "Wash" McLean, also a sort of boss, led the Democrats; but there was no politics. The good people knew parties, not the party politicians. John R. McLean and Tom Campbell were great friends, and they ruled by buying votes and indulging vice and crime. Campbell controlled the criminal bench. He defended criminals, out of the ring and in it; there was brawling, robbery, murder, and, in open court, over evidence which the public was reading in McLean's newspaper, *The Enquirer*—over evidence which convinced all but the corrupt judges and the "fixed" juries, this politician-lawyer got his clients off, till, in 1884, upon the acquittal of two murderers who killed a man for a very small sum of money, the town revolted. A mob burned the criminal court-house. The McLean-Campbell regime of Cincinnati, which corresponded to the Tweed days of New York and the McManes-Gas-Ring rule of Philadelphia, closed with the famous Cincinnati riots of 1881.

Tom Campbell moved to New York, and McLean soon took up a residence in Washington, D. C., but "better citizens" did not step into their places. The "best citizens" who led the "better citizens," were in gas and other public utilities; they were "apathetic," so other Republican grafters held down the Republican Party while McLean, the Democrat, with his "independent" *Enquirer* and his contributions, kept a paralyzing hand on the Democratic machine. Since McLean was "active" only when he wanted something himself or when he wanted to keep anybody else from getting anything, this dog-in-the-manger weakened the Democracy, even as a graft organization; and gradually the "grand old party" established itself. Among the Republican leaders of this period the only one we need to know is Joseph B. Foraker. He is the senior U. S. Senator from Ohio now, and we are asking what "our" senators represent at home. Mr. Foraker represented the Young Republicans of his day. Enthusiastic over his party, passionate in the defense of the Union soldier, eloquent upon the rights of the people, this young orator was dubbed the "Fire Alarm," because of the courage with which he fought corporate greed and corruption. The people of this country need, and they are forever looking for a leader who is not a boss, and Foraker is no boss. He is a politician; he must have been almost a demagogue once; certainly he raised the hopes and won the hearts of a majority of Ohioans, for they elected him governor of their state, twice. What did he do for these, his own people?

Another U. S. Senator Accounted For

Governor Foraker "discovered" Cox. A saloon-keeper and councilman, at the time, Cox ruled his own ward and was distinguished in his corrupt city as an honest politician; if there was boodle to divide Cox divided it "on the square," and if he gave his word, he kept it. Wherefore the world of graft trusted Cox. Governor Foraker, needing a boss for Cincinnati, made Cox an oil inspector and the dispensor of patronage in Hamilton County (Cincinnati). An oil inspectorship in Ohio is "good money" and, better still, brings a man into confidential relations with one of the deep sources of corruption in the state, Standard Oil. Foraker and Cox soon got in touch with other such interests. There are several instances to cite; one will do.

A while ago, we spoke of the Rogers Law. Cox and Foraker managed that. The Cincinnati Traction interests wanted a fifty-year five-cent-fare franchise in Cincinnati. Foraker wanted to go to the U. S. Senate. Public opinion out west is against long franchises, but the "Fire Alarm" expressed public opinion. It was charged in the public prints of Chicago and Ohio that Foraker was paid an enormous "fee" (ranging from $100,000 to $250,000) for his services—as a lawyer. He did not sue for libel, but he denied the charge; he said all he got was a present of $5,000 from an officer of the company. I say it doesn't matter whether Foraker took a bribe, or a fee, or a present, or nothing at all. His firm has been ever since counsel for the Traction Company and his son became an officer thereof, but that doesn't matter. And it doesn't matter whether the legislature that made Foraker a senator belonged to the Company, or whether the legislature that passed the Rogers Traction bill belonged to Foraker. The plain, undeniable, open facts are that that legislature of 1896 which elected Foraker to the U. S. Senate was led by the Senator, a popular leader, to pass in the interest of the Traction Company, a bill which granted privileges so unpopular that public opinion required a repeal in the next legislature of 1898. In other words this man who by his eloquence won the faith of his people, betrayed them for some reason, to those interests which were corrupting the government in order to get privileges from it. That's all any electors need to know about Joseph B. Foraker, that and the report that he hopes some day to be President of the United States.

Let's turn to an honest grafter. Cox made the councils of Cincinnati act for the Traction Company under the Rogers Law, but he doesn't pretend to represent the people. That isn't his business. Cox's business is to rule the people, and he does it. Cincinnati was enraged, and Cincinnati rose against Cox for this act. Cox was for licking them into obedience, but Hanna was back in Cincinnati again. Hanna had to be elected, in 1898, to the seat he had been appointed to. He wanted "harmony" in Cincinnati. He wanted Cox to hide and let some business men, such as used to rule Cleveland, run the 1897 campaign which was to elect his (Hanna's) legislature. It was selfish of Hanna, but Cox was willing. He told me about it.

"Wanted good men nominated," he said. "Wanted business men. Wanted business men to name the tickets and run the machine. Come to me, a committee of them, bankers and all like that. Said they'd name twelve men, and I was to name twelve. I was to pick six off their list, and they were to pick six off mine. Showed me their twelve and I took 'em all, all twelve, all business men, good people. Called 'em the dozen raw. Let 'em name the ticket and lent 'em the machine to run." He paused. "Who do you think they nominated?" he asked, and he answered: "They nominated fellers they met at lunch."

Cox's scorn of "good business men" reminds me of Croker. Croker has never been able to understand just how "bad" he was; he really was puzzled as to himself. "But" he said one day with assurance, "I know I'm better than them;" and he pointed off downtown toward Wall Street where his business backers and clients were. And it is so with Cox. He doesn't understand the standards of his critics, but he knows he is better than "them."

"Them," in Cincinnati, were beaten. The "dozen raw" who, largely for Hanna's sake, tried to give "front" to the Republican party, and save it with a respectable business man's ticket, failed. McLean wanted to go to the U. S. Senate, so he lent the Democratic machine to the Democrats, who combined with the independents and together they elected an anti-machine ticket. It looked so bad for Cox that he announced his retirement from politics, but the amiable old gentleman who was mayor, proved so weak and the "Democrats" and "independents" such poor stuff, that Cox recovered his courage. He bought some members of the administration, fooled others, and, with the help of these, set the rest to fighting among themselves. Cox so disgusted the town with "reform" that it came back to him, laid itself at his feet and he proceeded at his leisure to, what a judge called, the "Russianization" of Cincinnati.

Going to Cincinnati Again

But "they" were not through, not yet. Having torn down, they—and by "they," I mean the Hannas, the public service corporations and their political machinery, their banks and their courts—they had to build up something in the place of the ruin. They had to pass a general act giving one and the same city charters to all the cities in Ohio. Where did they go for a model? They went to Cincinnati.

Let's run down there again to see what Cox has done since 1898 to make Cincinnati the model Ohio city. He has "Russianized" it. His voting subjects are all down on a card catalogue, they and their children and all their business, and he lets them know it. The Democratic Party is gone. Cox has all the patronage, city, county, state and Federal, so the Democratic grafters are in Cox's Republican Club. That club contains so many former Democrats that "Lewie" Bernard, John R. McLean's political agent, says happily, that he is waiting for a majority, to turn it into a Democratic club. And "Lewie" Bernard's machine remnant is in touch with Cox when "John," as Cox calls McLean, doesn't want anything, either office or revenge. Conventions are held, and Cox plans them in detail. If he has been hearing mutterings among his people about the boss, he is very ostentatious in dictation; otherwise he sits in his favorite beer hall, and sends in to those of his delegates whom he wishes to honor, slips containing the motions and nominations each is to make. But there must be no nominating speeches. "Takes time; all foolishness; obey orders and get done." He picks ward leaders, and they deliver the votes. The citizens have no choice of parties, but they must get out and vote. Cox is good to some of them. If they knuckle under, he puts respectable men up for the school board. He has little use for schools; not much graft in them; except to cut down their appropriations in favor of fatter departments, and as a place to try respectable men. If they take orders on the school board, Cox tries them higher up, and he has a-plenty. The press is not free. The *Post* and the *Citizens' Bulletin,* the last a weekly organ of the smallest but one of the most enduring groups of reformers in America—these are the only papers that ever speak out honestly for the public interest. Official advertising, offices for the editors, public service stock and political prospects for the owners, hold down the rest. It is terrible. The city is all one great graft; Cox's System is the most perfect thing of the kind in this country, and he is proud of it.

"What you think of it?" he asked, when I had finished and was taking leave.

"Pretty good," I said.

"Pretty—!" He was too disgusted to finish. "Best you ever saw," he retorted, firmly.

"Well, I can't tell," I said. "My criterion for a graft organization is, How few divide the graft. How many divide it here?"

"Ain't no graft," he grumbled.

"Then it's a mighty poor thing."

He pondered a moment. Then, "How many do you say divides up here?"

"Three at least," I said. "You and Garry Herman and Rud Hynicka."

"Ugh!" he grunted, scornfully, and wagging one finger slowly before my face, he said: "There's only one divides up here."

Of course, that isn't true. He must mean only political graft, the campaign fund, police blackmail, contracts, etc., etc., and even that goes partly to others. Cox admits owning two millions, but some of his followers are very rich also. Cox wouldn't lie about a point like that; but he is growing vain and hates to see other men stand up like men and to hear them admired. They tell how once, in a beer hall when Herman and Hynicka, his two chief lieutenants, and some others were talking to some outsiders quite like free independent men, Cox who had been poring over his beer, broke in hoarsely, "But when I whistle you dogs come out of your holes, don't you?" They were still. "Don't you, Garry?" the master repeated. "That's right," said Garry.

But there is lots of graft besides political graft in Cincinnati, bankers' and business men's graft. Cox is reaching for that, too. Some Cleveland and Cincinnati financiers organized a trust company in Cincinnati, and they took Cox in for his pull and the public moneys he could have deposited there. A quarrel arose and Cox, taking one side, told the others to buy or sell. They sold, of course, and Cox, becoming president, wrote a letter to office-holders inviting them to use his bank; the letter to school teachers was published. Certain financiers of Cleveland and Cincinnati got up a scheme to take over the Miami and Erie Canal. They gave Cox stock for Cox's pull on the legislature, and his letter to the legislators was published. The bill was beaten; business men all along the canal were grafting the water for power, and they fought for *their* graft. The company had floated its stock and bonds, and the failure of the legislature threw the "canal scandal" into a receivership. Some of the financiers are in trouble but Cox is safe, and the scheme is to go through next year. Cox was in the scheme to sell or "lease" the Cincinnati Southern, the only steam railroad under municipal ownership. Leading citizens of Cincinnati concocted this grab, but the Germans beat it; and, though it went through later, the city got much better terms.

So, when Cox says only one divides the graft in Cincinnati, he probably means that one man can dispose as he will of all of it, police, political, and financial, as the examples cited indicate, but he has to let all sorts of men in on it. And he does. And that is his best hold on the graft. They talk in Cincinnati, as they do in Philadelphia, of apathy. Apathy! Apathy is corruption. Cincinnati and Philadelphia are not asleep; they are awake, alive. The life is like that of a dead horse, but it is busy and it is contented. If the commanding men, of all the natural groupings of society, were not interested in graft, no city would put up with what satisfies Cincinnati. For Cincinnati is not unhappy. Men like Elliot H. Pendleton, Rufus B. Smith, and a dozen others are eating their hearts out with impotent rage, but as for the rest—

The rest are in it for profit or—fear. The bums get free soup; the petty criminals "get off" in court; the plain people or their relatives get jobs or a picnic or a friendly greeting; the Germans get their beer whenever they want it; the neighborhood and ward leaders get offices and graft; "good" Democrats get their share of both; shopkeepers sell to the city or to politicians or they break petty ordinances; the lawyers get cases, and they tell me that the reputation of the bench is such that clients seek lawyers for their standing, not at the bar, but with the ring; the banks get public deposits and license to do business; the public utility companies get franchises and "no regulation;" financiers get canals, etc., they "get blackmailed," too, but they can do "business" by "dividing up"; property owners get low assessments, or high; anybody can get anything in reason, by standing in. And anybody who doesn't "stand in", or "stand by", gets "nothing but trouble." And there is the point that pricks deepest in Cincinnati. Cox can punish; he does punish, not with physical cruelty, as a Czar may, but by petty annoyances and "trouble", and political and business ostracism. The reign of Cox is a reign of fear. The experience that made my visits there a personal humiliation was the spectacle I saw of men who were being punished; who wanted to cry out; who sent for me to tell me facts that they knew and suffered and hated; and these men, after leading me into their back offices and closing the door, dared not speak. They had heard that I was shadowed, and they were afraid. Afraid of what? They were afraid of their government, of their Czar, of George Cox, who is not afraid of them, or of you or of me. Cox is a man, we are American citizens, and Cincinnati has proved to Cox that Americans can be reduced to craven cowards.

Rural Bossism

A. Z. BLAIR

The writer has just completed, in his court, the conviction and disfranchisement of one quarter of the electors of Adams County, Ohio, for selling their votes at the last election. This matter has excited much attention throughout the nation. Now that the work is finished, the writer, as presiding judge, is for the first time at liberty to describe it. In justice to the county where he has spent most of his active life, and to the nation at large, he should do so. If, as he has been credibly informed, conditions similar to those in Adams County exist in other sections of the country, his narrative may be of value.

Our county in southern Ohio is populated by as old and excellent American stock as any in the United States. Whatever the case may be concerning the venality of the foreign-born population in great cities, no such condition enters into the discussion of her case. In Adams County but one person out of twenty-five is of foreign parentage, against one out of three in the country at large; and but one man in a hundred is a negro, against one in eight in the United States as a whole.

There was no purchasing of votes, however, previous to the Civil War; there was no need of it; the county itself was too strongly Democratic. But the Civil War made a great change. Although the population of Adams County was Democratic, it was intensely loyal to the Union. It has been said that it furnished more volunteer soldiers in this war, in proportion to its population, than any other county in the North. Its largest town, Manchester, with at that time eight hundred and forty-one people, by actual records, furnished one hundred and fourteen soldiers. These young men, after associating with the other soldiers of the Union army, came back Republicans. The parties were now closely divided in Adams County; and the same old bitterness remained and was intensified. The buying and selling of votes began at that time. I have been familiar with this condition since I was a boy, and, as I shall speak of how other people were connected with the wholesale vote-buying, it is but just that I should bare to public gaze the part I myself have taken in it. Whatever the humiliation may be in the eyes of my countrymen, it is only right that I should do this.

Vote-buying on a large scale in Adams County began in the election of 1867—the year when Rutherford B. Hayes and Allen G. Thurman ran for the governorship of Ohio. This was a time when

From A. Z. Blair, "Seventeen Hundred Rural Vote-Sellers," *McClures Magazine*, XXXVIII (1911), 28-40.

feeling ran very high. On one side, the Democrats fought for their inherited political faith, with an intensity heightened by the fear that they would lose control of the county. On the other hand, the Republicans, with a ticket of Union war veterans, fought with much of the feeling aroused by the recent war. Votes were bought on a considerable scale then. But it was done quietly. In 1871 there was a bitter local fight over the location of the county-seat, between Manchester, the largest town, and West Union, which had been the county-seat for sixty years before. The buying of votes in that year was an open and accepted fact. From that time on it became established as a common-place practice.

From the time when I entered politics, in my boyhood, the voting inhabitants of Adams County were divided into two classes— buyers and sellers of votes. The guilt of these classes is the same, both morally and before the law; but it is a fact, well established by the court proceedings we have just gone through, that the buyers and sellers of votes have come from very different classes of the population.

The vote-buying class included, from the time of my first knowledge, many of the otherwise most reputable and trustworthy members of the population. They were men of sound metal—men who would stick by you and whom you could rely on. Church members, merchants, county and school officials were in this class. The intense feeling which started with the foundation of the republic, and which was intensified by the Civil War, drove the men who had genuine interest in government to make party politics a continual bitter warfare. So bitter was the partizanship in this class that it was not an uncommon thing to see a young man with a family, and with no property or means of his own on earth, take the last cent out of his pocket, when the funds in his election precinct were low, or even go to the bank and borrow money and give it to his party to buy the vote of some vote-seller which was still for sale.

The other class in the electorate, the sellers, were largely of the poorer people in the community. A few of them—like old Billy Grooms of West Union—were men with some property, generally land; but the majority of them were younger men, either unmarried or, if married, men who owned no property. Many of them were farm laborers. They were not foreigners, however, as has been wrongly stated; most of them were of the same native stock as their neighbors. They were the more careless members of the community— the men who had not much interest in government.

Selling a Voter at Auction

In the late '80's, when I began to take a more influential part in county politics, "money fights" were at their height. The "bloody shirt" issue of the Civil War still added especial bitterness to the local feeling, and the lack of an Australian ballot made the practice of vote-buying as much a matter-of-fact transaction as the trade in any merchandise. I remember, about 1889, standing before the courthouse in West Union, the county-seat, and seeing a voter auctioned off to the highest bidder of the two precinct leaders, like a horse or a hog. The price finally bid was thirty-odd dollars. The successful bidder took his man to the polls, cast his vote, brought him back, and stood him up again on the auction-block. Then he peeled the money from his bank-roll and paid him.

"I want you all to see," he said to the crowd, "that when I promise to do a thing I do just what I promise."

There were about a hundred men around the auction-block—including the prosecuting attorney, the sheriff of the county, and the mayor and marshal of West Union. The practice was set so hard and fast in custom that men paid no attention to it. At every election, it was the commonest of sights to see men paid off after they voted. Some of them would take money only from their own party; some would linger about the polls all day, and get the party leaders to bid for their vote. And the introduction of the Australian ballot, in 1890, virtually made no change. Election officials about the ballot-box watched the vote-sellers to see that they delivered the votes they were paid for.

The Revolt of the Women

There was, though, one class of the population which rebelled against the practice. It was the womanhood of Adams County, which had never become reconciled to the custom, and whose continual hostility has resulted finally, I hope, in its abolishment. The women could see very clearly that the buying of votes was degrading their husbands and sons.

National Figures Concerned

In all this time the vote-buying in Adams County had been going on with the full knowledge of the party managers of the State. The names of men very high in the nation were connected with it. Through my position as chairman of the county executive committee for first one party and then the other, I knew of my own cognizance, or from credible information, of many concrete instances.

Marcus A. Hanna, the late senator from Ohio, and John M. Pattison, who was first a congressman and afterward governor of Ohio, both, to my own personal knowledge, contributed largely to the funds used for buying votes in Adams County, with full understanding of how money was used in the county.

In Calvin Brice's second campaign for the senatorship, an interesting example of political methods in Adams County took place. The campaign manager of the Republicans was a popular little merchant who kept a harness-shop and drug-store in West Union. At one time he had been county treasurer, and his handwriting was familiar to all the tax-payers of the county. The Democrats got some one to practise his writing till he got it perfectly; then, a day or two before election, some one went into his store and bought some of his stationery.

On the morning of the election, at every one of the twenty-odd voting precincts in the county, a man drove up, handed a letter to the head Republican worker, and, making some excuse, whipped up his horse and drove away before the worker could read the letter.

The letter read something like this:

> Brice has put $5,000 more into county; we can not meet it. Don't pay out any money for votes.

It was signed with the name of the Republican county manager, and apparently was in his handwriting. When the Republican workers got this message, they stopped buying votes. The vote-sellers were on hand, as usual, for offers. The Democrats were well supplied with money, and in a few hours they had bought a great share of the votes that were offered for sale. Later in the morning word of this letter reached the county headquarters, and the county managers started to notify their workers that it was a lie. Every telephone wire leading out into the county had been cut and every livery team hired by the Democrats. The county was swept by the Democrats for the Brice ticket. In the evening the Republican managers got together and threatened to arrest the Democrats under the law for forgery. They found, however, that such a charge would be of no avail in connection with vote-buying, and abandoned it.

Vote-Buyers or Vote-Sellers—Which?

The first practical question to be met was this: Which class should be prosecuted—the buyers or the sellers? The main purpose was, of course, to break up the custom of vote-buying in Adams County. The court prosecutor and jury debated at length whether they should undertake to indict the buyers or the sellers, or should proceed with whatever information they could get against either side. They decided to indict the vote-sellers, and to compel the vote-buyers to testify. This meant that the vote-buyers would not be punished, as the law provides that whichever party to bribery transactions is compelled to testify shall be immune from punishment for the offense concerning which he gives his testimony.

This step was taken for a number of reasons. It appeared, first of all, the only way to secure results. Each buyer of votes, naturally, had more information in his possession than any individual seller. To get any full understanding of the practice as a whole, it was absolutely essential to trace the funds with which the voters had been paid.

It was clear, too, that no jury either in Adams or in any of the surrounding counties would, under existing circumstances and on the testimony of vote-sellers, sentence vote-buyers to prison, as the law demanded. An attempt to do this had already been made in the federal court of the district, and a grand jury—although selected from other counties—had refused to return an indictment. It was further taken into consideration that the vote-buyers had tried to break up the habit, and had been defeated by the vote-sellers; and that, if there were any wholesale imprisonment of vote-buyers (which would be required by law if they were found guilty), the heads of most of the important industries of the county would be sent to prison, all the commercial activities of the county would be affected, and much labor would be thrown out of employment.

Tracing the Money to the Voter

So the prosecutor and the grand jury proceeded at once to trace the funds with which the voters were bribed. This was not difficult. The cashiers of the banks—who were always told at election time to get together large sums in small bills—testified as to who received the moneys from them. The party leaders—some willingly, some under threats of punishment for contempt of court—testified just how and to whom the money was distributed in every one of the thirty-odd voting precincts in the county. The fact that both the court and the prosecuting attorney were perfectly familiar with the local political methods and with the people was of advantage in handling the situation.

The leaders of the voting precincts were then taken, at first from two specimen precincts—one a strongly Republican precinct and one a Democratic stronghold. When these leaders were brought before the grand jury, the prosecuting attorney went at them at once with a question worded something like this:

"Now, Sam Smith, you had $415 to spend on the last election. What'd you do with it?"

As the man would not know how the prosecutor had got such exact information, he would naturally be astonished and scared. He would hesitate and balk; but, finally, under threats of commitment for contempt of court, he would give half a dozen names—generally of men in the opposite party whom he didn't like very well. He would be dismissed for the time; and the same process would be repeated with the other leader in the precinct.

We started this on Friday, and by Friday night we had a dozen names of men who had been bribed. We knew that as soon as each leader got back home, everybody in his own party would come to him and ask him if he had given them away. He would say that he had not—which would be true. So everybody would be reassured and happy. On Friday night we picked out half a dozen men we were sure of, in three different townships in the county, and at midnight sent the sheriffs to drag them out of bed and bring them to the lock-up.

An Avalanche of Confessions

On Monday morning I left Portsmouth on the early morning train, and got off at Peebles, a little station from which we drive to West Union, the county-seat. It was about five o'clock in the morning when I arrived there. Everything was snapping and cracking with the cold. There were thirty-one men waiting for me in the dark.

"Hello, Judge," said somebody. "You ain't goin' to be too hard on us, are you?"

We walked up the long walk from the station to the hotel in a silent procession; and at almost every window somebody poked out his head to see what was going on. All thirty-one of them pleaded guilty at the hotel.

When I got down to West Union, at about eight o'clock, the yard around the sheriff's office was full of teams and men. The courthouse had burned down a short time before, and I had to hear the pleas in a little room about ten feet square in the sheriff's house. Two hundred and forty-one pleaded guilty that first day. While we were trying to keep the vote-sellers from breaking down the doors to come in and confess, the precinct workers whom we had had on the stand the week before telephoned in and begged for the chance to tell everything they knew. They didn't know what the sellers might be telling about them. In the next few days, from a hundred to two hundred sellers pleaded guilty every day.

As soon as the sellers began to plead guilty, the court announced that there would be leniency for those who confessed, but that the law would be fully enforced against those who put the State to the trouble of prosecuting them. Every man who pleaded guilty was fined $25 and costs and given six months in the workhouse. The prison sentence and $20 of the fine were both suspended, leaving the charge of $10.92, of which $5.92 was for costs. Each man was also disfranchised for five years.

Threats Against My Life

While these hundreds of vote-sellers were coming into court to plead, there was still resistance among the lower class of vote-sellers.

In the first place, several letters were received by me threatening my life. A Republican newspaper of Manchester, the *Signal,* criticized the action of the court in electing to prosecute the sellers of votes. Its editor was promptly punished for contempt. In various places individuals went around advising the sellers not to plead guilty. The court was kept informed of this, and whenever the stream of men from any particular district stopped, the men who were doing this exhorting were indicted, arrested, and brought into court—for they were all vote-sellers themselves.

In this way, there were by February over 1,400 who had pleaded guilty of vote-selling and were fined. At that time a group of vote-sellers secured an attorney, who desired to appeal and test the constitutionality of the law. By special arrangement, the case was heard directly by the Supreme Court, and the law was decided to be entirely valid. Since then something over 200 more men have pleaded guilty and received their sentence. At the time of this writing (in August) the work is practically done. We have convicted 1,679 to date—twenty-six per cent of the 6,505 voting in the election. A few have left the county.

In addition to these, the proceedings showed that there were at least 500 men engaged in the work of vote-buying. These men handled about $20,000, which would be about $12 a vote, if distributed among the men convicted of selling. As a matter of fact, we found the prices paid averaged from $5 to $25. Practically all of this money was spent for buying votes; and our investigations showed that it was handled with scrupulous honesty. It was believed by some of the party managers that a few of the workers might have retained money for their own use. We checked up the amount of money distributed by the party leaders with the amount received by the vote-sellers, and in every instance they tallied. Before we were through, we accounted for practically every dollar spent in the county.

A County One Quarter Disfranchised

As we now stand, a quarter of our voters in Adams County have been disfranchised. In some of the voting precincts as many as fifty per cent can not vote; in others only ten or twelve per cent are ineligible. In a number of cases, whole families, containing as many as thirty voters in the various branches, have been disfranchised. In one instance, a lay preacher and practically all the members of his congregation lost their vote.

It was our main purpose to free the county of the vicious condition which has existed there virtually ever since the Civil War, and not to punish individuals for an offense which had become almost universal. Of all those found guilty, only one young man, who refused to pay his fine—a man who was living off the means furnished his invalid father and mother by charity—was sent to the workhouse. Only six, the first arrested, were put in jail, and they for but a few days, after which their sentence was suspended, as in the case of the rest.

For the next five years the offenders in the last election will not vote. This will give time for the growth of a public sentiment concerning the value and sanctity of the franchise. At the end of the five-year period, if these men should engage in vote-selling again, they will immediately become liable to a sentence of six months' imprisonment in the workhouse, with $20 fine. I do not believe that many of these men will repeat their offense. In most instances, out of the nearly 1,700, the man pleading guilty of vote-selling seemed to have been brought by his experience to some sense, at least, of the character of his act.

Just how far conditions like those in Adams County are prevalent throughout the country I do not know of my own knowledge. I do know that conditions very similar prevail in most of the counties in the southern part of Ohio, and in the counties of Kentucky across the river from them. Since our investigation I have received scores of letters from other parts of the United States, stating that votes are sold and bought at wholesale in the writers' own community. It was this information concerning conditions elsewhere that led me to put into writing the story of our experience in Adams County. It is my hope that in this way the people of our county, whose ancestors helped to give to the world the American democracy, may now serve as a helpful example to this country at large by their purification of themselves from the degradation into which they had fallen.

Progressive Municipal Government

SAMUEL M. JONES

To the Honorable, the Common Council of the City of Toledo.

Gentlemen:—In transmitting to you my fourth annual message, I desire to make due acknowledgement of the uniform courtesy and candor that have characterized our association together during the past year. The fact that we have not always seen "eye to eye" with respect to matters of legislation, or have not fully agreed as to the details of municipal government does not, in the least, detract from the feeling of cordial good-will that I entertain for every one of you, and the confidence that I have in the general integrity of your purposes. The average man or woman has but a slight conception of the sacrifice, from the ordinary point of view, that is imposed upon a member of the Toledo Common Council. Indeed, the "man about town" is quite apt to speak of a Councilman's position as one that, in some mysterious way, yields a large profit, rather than to consider it a place that really calls for and receives a larger degree of personal sacrifice annually for the good of the community than the ordinary layman has any adequate conception of. I am sure that in my experience I have seen no more genuine manifestations of real devotion to the cause of fellow man than I have found in the experience of the members of the Toledo Common Council. The fact that the results in our city government are not more satisfactory is due more to the hindrances and restraints that are imposed upon municipal officers by

A Cumbersome and Antiquated System of Municipal Government than to any inefficiency that can be charged to individual members. It is no new discovery that our system of government is not adapted to the needs of a city of the size of Toledo, and that it does not provide that the public servants shall have an opportunity for the exercise of the best service.

Hindrances of the Law

All in all, I think that any candid man, after looking into the situation and taking into account the prohibitions and inhibitions and various restraints of law that hamper the officials who are charged with the care of the business of the City of Toledo, will admit that the wonder is, not that we do not get better results, but that we get as good; for I feel certain that if you were to place the business of a large private corporation in the charge of the best set of men that could be secured by a vote of the stockholders and subjected them to the restraints in the management of the business that correspond to the restraints of the municipal government of the City of Toledo, the result would be bankruptcy for the best business in the country.

From Samuel M. Jones, *Fourth Annual Message to Toledo's Common Council, 1900,* (Toledo, 1900), n.p.

The Reasons for the Conditions

The reasons for the condition that confronts us are many and deepseated. The primary one is the prevailing distrust of our fellow men, and the improvement will not be material or marked to any very great extent, except as we overcome this fundamental cause. Until we shall know a patriotism that will teach us to trust one another and to be worthy to be trusted, we shall not see much in the way of improvement in municipal government. There is no substitute that will supply the place of confidence. "Like begets like." Distrust breeds distrust. Suspicion begets suspicion. The crying need of the hour in this municipality, in the state, in the nation, in the world, is a social faith, ability to believe in the good in our fellow men and in ourselves. The way to make men honest is to believe they are honest until they have proven otherwise. The way to breed a nation of thieves is to continually harbor distrust of one another and put our confidence in "systems," "bonds," "oaths," "checks," "balances," "indemnities," "securities" and the artificial paraphernalia that seeks to pass as a substitute for plain honesty. There is none.

Partyism the Enemy of Progress

Among the causes that hinder the development of a pure patriotism, none has been more prolific of evil than our system of partisan politics, and the most promising sign of a better future for American municipalities is found in the fact that each year the party machines find the struggle for existence growing harder. We can never be a free people until each soul is free; each soul can never be free until party bosses and party politics have disappeared. I have talked with many municipal officers of American cities from the Atlantic to the Pacific coast, and, almost without exception, they uniformly agree that the curse of American municipal politics is the party machine. These "organizations," the only purpose of whose existence is to group a small band of men together in each city in order that they may capture the offices and then adminster the city's business, not for the benefit of the people but for the benefit of the party, for the spoils of office, are one prolific source and mainspring of the absolute personal distrust of which I have spoken and upon which we are endeavoring to build a patriotic system. It cannot be done. The signs of disintegration of the party machine in American municipalities is the most promising thing in our politics today, for when the machines once lose their hold in the cities, the day of deliverance for the people will be near at hand; and while the rule of the machine continues, there can be little hope of improvement for the reason that it is always the purpose of the machine in power to make the largest profit possible out of the possession of the offices and to resist any innovation calculated to simplify and cheapen the cost of government to the people. Under the prevailing party system of government, I think it is true that in all of the holders of public office in the nation, the cities and the municipalities, not one in ten is chosen by any spontaneous selection of the outsiders, of the people; they are nominated and put there by little or large caucuses of the politicians; they are gotten in by electioneering and often by corrupt rings rather than by any capacity or desert.

Need a New Charter

My opinion as to the privileges that should be conferred on the people by the new charter has already been stated in former messages and is so well known that I need not repeat it at length. I am a thorough believer in the principle of Home Rule; that is, that the people of a city should have the privilege of governing themselves, of making their own laws, providing such limitations to the powers of government as they themselves believe will best serve them.

Home Rule—The American Idea

I believe this is the truly American idea, and that the principle of having our cities governed very largely from the state capital and by state politics is false in theory, pernicious in practice and demoralizing in effect. As I understand the American idea, it is that the people are the government; that they should be made to feel that there is no other place where responsibility can rest, and with such a system, if, for any reason, a municipal government is a failure the people will do as the individual does when he suffers loss or injury through his own mistake and carelessness; he will look within for the trouble. As matters stand today, if there is municipal mismanagement or failure, we can easily shift responsibility from ourselves and lay the blame to the state laws that hamper us with their many limitations.

I favor a system of municipal government that will grant to the officials much the same sort of freedom, and impose upon them the same kind of responsibility that rests upon officials in charge of our large private corporations. The analogy between the two is not perfect, I am aware, as one business is carried on for purely economic reasons, for profit getting, while profit getting, as such, is eliminated from the business of a city official; nevertheless, the analogy is close enough that the illustration will serve the purpose.

Chief Executive in Name Only

In looking over the reports of my predecessors in this office for the past twenty-five years, I notice that several of them have called attention to the fact that the "Mayor in Toledo is chief executive in name only." This is absolutely true, and must remain so until a new charter is obtained. It is true that the mayor is, in effect, the head of the police department during the vacations of the Board. There is little wherein it can be said that he has the initiative, by which he may introduce or direct improvements in our system of doing business. He may recommend to the Council from time to time such measures as he believes for the well-being of the city. He has a seat in the Council, and by courtesy is heard on any matter of public interest. He has not, as is generally supposed, the privilege of appointing the members of the various boards; he merely nominates and then, owing to the distrust of which I have already spoken, he must submit his nominations to the Council and they may approve or reject. As if to atone, in some measure, for the humiliation of this sort of supervision of the acts of the Mayor by the Council, the Mayor is then given the reactionary power of exercising the veto over any of the legislation of the Council where it is proposed to expend money or grant franchises. The veto is autocratic, un-American and repulsive to any just conception of democracy; it should be abolished, and if any supervision of the acts of the legislature is needed, it should be lodged in the people through a resort to the referendum.

Relief Must Come from the People

The people are the power. The people can have any kind of government in Toledo that they want—good government, bad government, indifferent government or excellent government; and it is probable that our government is all of the time just about as good as WE collectively, all of us, desire that it shall be. The failures, the miscarriage, the imperfections and the evils of our city government are but the outward expressions of our inward moral imperfections. As well may we expect water to run up hill naturally as to expect a city government to be better than the average of the people, for the reason that water cannot rise higher than its source and the people are the source of the government.

The law of cause and effect is everywhere present. In municipal government as in everything else, we reap exactly as we sow.

Police Court

In no department of our municipal life is there more crying need for reform than in our method of dealing with unfortunates who fall into the hands of the police and are charged with petty crimes. There is much reason for belief that with the prevailing methods today, our police courts actually perpetrate more crime than they prevent, and this I say in no manner reflecting upon any individual court or any individual man. I am condemning a system that is outgrown, antiquated and entirely out of keeping with the spirit of the age. I believe our whole system of pretended punishment of crime by imposing a fine with the prison alternative is a fraud so ghastly as to be a travesty on justice; yet it is a system that is carried on in most of the cities of our country today, and few questions are asked as to whether it might be improved or not. If a man is arrested, I infer that the reason for his arrest is found in the fact that his liberty is considered a menace to the public good; in short, that he is arrested for the same reason that we would arrest a man whom we saw in the street with a well developed case of small pox. Such a man we would send to the contagious diseases hospital so that his liberty might not be a menace to the public health; but our so-called criminals are hauled into our Police Courts, "charged with disturbance, disorderly conduct," or that most convenient of all devices for taking away a man's liberty, the charge of "suspicion." He is taken into a court where, of course, every criminal must have a "first appearance;" he knows nothing of the tricks of the law or the practices of the bar; the reputation of the officer who arrested him is at stake; he must make a case; and the state has a hired prosecutor to help the officer secure a conviction; the victim is without money, without friends and ignorant of the law, and the result is not hard to forecast; it is "$25 and costs," or "$5 and costs." Here is a most direct discrimination in favor of the rich and against the poor, and under the operation of this farcical system, the great city of Toledo has had washer women working over time in order to get money to pay into the city treasury for the husbands' fines. Children have gone barefooted in order that their savings might be paid into the insatiable maw of the Police Court treasury to release a father who had been unfortunate enough to be drunk on the street instead of getting drunk at the club and being taken home in a carriage. Poor wretched girls are hauled up for the crime of prostitution; fines are imposed upon them, failing to pay which, the workhouse is their doom. They simply send for their friends, and after mortgaging their bodies to these friends, secure the money with which to satisfy justice (Police Court justice); they go out and prostitute themselves to earn money for Toledo's treasury.

Money Atones for Crime

As a citizen, as one who loves his city, as your Mayor, as a lover of humanity, I protest against this ghastly farce, and I plead with you, men of the Toledo Council and citizens of Toledo, to protest against this crying injustice and wrong inflicted upon people simply because they are poor. Today there are 114 persons in the work-house; of this number 62 could walk out if they had money to pay their fines; practically they are there because they are poor. The balance could also, no doubt, walk out if they had money, for, notwithstanding the fact that they have a time sentence to serve, it is more than probable that a capable lawyer could be hired for suffi-cient cash, who would discover a trick of law, a writ of some kind, or something nobody knows what and nobody knows how, but it would be sufficient to release them, if they only had money.

An Unjust System

It ought to need no argument to convince one that our system of dispensing "justice" is as yet very elementary and very imperfect. The deadly obstacle in the way of improvement, spiritual, social or industrial is a settled belief that our plan or our machine is perfect, and our only hope of improvement lies in the awakening of the public conscience to the imperfections and evils of the present system. This is by no means a matter of mere sentiment. It is as true of municipalities, states and nations as it is of individuals that whatsoever is sown must be reaped, and if we sow the seeds of injustice, while deluding ourselves with the belief that we are admin-istering justice itself, it is an aggravation of the offense or sin of one who openly and knowingly violates the laws. It introduces inhar-mony into the body politic and in this way becomes the cause of the very conditions we seek to remedy.

Caste in Crime

Many well-meaning people are settled in the belief that all of the crime in our cities is lodged in the "lower classes," and the outcry on the part of the Pharisees of politics and religion is against these; and occasionally we are overtaken with a spasm for "cleaning up the town." This is followed by a little extra vigilance on the part of the police, the petty offenders are driven to ply their unholy traffic in nooks and corners, but all of the time the cause of the evil, the social injustice which is the tree that bears this poisoned fruit, is left undisturbed. Periodically the demand for reform goes a little further. There is a great outcry against "corrupt aldermen and councilmen," and the clamor is raised for a "business man's administration."

The most superficial thinker only needs to stop one moment to realize that there cannot be "corrupt councilmen or aldermen" without a corrupt business man at the other end of the deal; and it is generally necessary to the completion of all these corrupt transactions that there shall be a lawyer of "eminent respectability" to do the engineering and act as a go-between for the public and private thieves. I know of no cure for the evils, political and social, that afflict us that will give us a better city government except the panacea for all of these evils, and that is, good men and women. These alone can give us a good city and a good city government. If you want to help the city, there is no way in which you can do it so much as to be a good man or a good woman.

I am well aware that this philosophy is derided in business circles, deemed unworthy the consideration of "practical men," and that one who advocates such a policy is a "dreamer" and a "crank". Many such charges have been laid at my door since I have been in the Mayor's office, and in concluding this portion of my message, I make use of a quotation from one of the speeches of Edmund Burke that expresses my sentiments better than any words of mine can:

"The charges against me are all of one kind; that I have pushed the principles of general justice and benevolence too far, further than a cautious policy would warrant, and farther than the opinion of many would go along with me. In every accident which may happen through life, in pain, in sorrow, in depression and distress, I will call to mind this accusation and be comforted."

Home Rule

TOM L. JOHNSON

Cleveland, O., May 4, 1904.

To the Council, Gentlemen:—

Something vastly more important is involved in the simple ceremonies of this occasion than the reorganization of our own municipality. We really stand upon the threshold of a new era in the municipal government of every city in one of the most influential States of the American Union. Throughout the great Commonwealth of Ohio, all cities come today under the sway of one law, a law of uniform operation with reference not alone to what concerns them in their relations to the State at large, but also to what concerns each solely in respect of its own local affairs.

Our outlook, therefore, is the same as that of our sister cities. But our duties are more exacting and our responsibilities correspondingly greater. For Cleveland has become the largest city of the State, and for that reason alone her policies and her administration, her failures and her successes, her progress or her decline, will exert an influence elsewhere which no one can measure and nothing avert. Potent as is that reason, however, there is another more potent still. Need I remind you of what this further reason is? Not alone is Cleveland the largest city in Ohio, but she has successfully taken the lead—a claim she may make with all modesty in working out the world-wide problem of municipal home rule by the people themselves.

Of all civic problems this one is the most pressing. It is even more pressing in the United States than elsewhere. Our old questions of State sovereignty were set at rest by the logic of the Civil War. Let the mere theory of State rights linger as it may, the stern fact is that federation has given way to nationality. In national affairs the central government is now supreme. The only power the States can any longer hope to preserve is power over their internal affairs—the exclusive right of home rule in matters of State concern. That readjustment of the relations of the Nation to the States is suggestive and prophetic of a similar readjustment of the relations of the States to their respective municipalities. This is clear to all who reflect. Along with the decline in the political power once asserted by the States has arisen a necessity, if popular liberty is to be preserved, for an extension to municipalities of the same benign principle of home rule to which the States themselves may still lay claim. Municipalities must cease to be answerable to their States, except in matters of State concern, and become answerable in matters of home concern only to their own people. Such a policy is in line with the trend of the times.

This being so—and who can dispute it?—we could have wished for a more generous recognition of the principle of home rule for the cities of Ohio than the expiring legislature has seen fit to concede. We could wish for a more complete application of the principle than is possible perhaps, under the State constitution as it now exists. A municipal code under which every city could make its own laws, could design its own organization, could in every way govern itself by the ballots of its own people, absolutely untrammeled by outside

From Tom L. Johnson, "Mayor's Message," *Annual Reports, Cleveland, 1905,* (Cleveland, 1906), n.p.

dictation or interference except with reference to matters of outside concern—such a code would be the ideal of State legislation for municipal government.

Short of that ideal it is doubtful if a better general scheme could be devised than the "federal plan" with which Cleveland is experimentally familiar and under which she has developed a civic consciousness and conscience among her people of a higher order than any other large city in the country. Lodging legislative power in a council elected from wards, and administrative power in a mayor who could be held responsible by all the citizenship for the good conduct of his appointees, that "federal plan" operated to inspire the citizens themselves with a sense of responsibility for good local government. The power of "bosses" was thus held in check and a wholesome respect was fostered in Cleveland for government for the people by the people.

But we are forced to face the problems of municipal government, as are the people of our sister cities of Ohio, without the advantage either of the ideal system of local self-government, or of the "federal plan" which served our city so well for more than a decade. Our new municipal system is singularly defective. Not only does it rest on no fundamental principle, not only does it embody no consistent scheme of popular rule, not only does it revive the universally discredited devices of board rule and divided responsibility, but in many respects it is obscure in terms and confusing in detail.

Actuated by this determination we shall find it necessary to protect the people of Cleveland against the aggressions of certain so-called "business interests." I do not allude to competitive business, but to interests that are grounded in special privilege. These have no natural affinity for legitimate business interests; and their beneficiaries know no political party except to use its influence to serve personal ends of pecuniary profit.

All such spurious "business interests" are now served in greater or less degree by unfair apportionments of taxation. Efforts were made by the city administration which has just retired to correct this gross abuse, but its beneficiaries were able—through county auditors, through state officials, through the courts, and through the legislature—to obstruct and for a time to nullify those efforts. May it be our aim to renew them and make them fully effective. In this let us miss no lawful opportunity.

Complete success will be impossible, however, until the State Legislature establishes fair rules for the taxation of steam railroads and the like, and permits municipalities to adopt systems of local assessment admitting of fairness in local taxation. Our work, therefore, cannot be confined to the boundaries of our own city. So long as legislators are under the domination of privileged corporations and individuals, unjust taxation will prevail here in spite of all we can do. It will, consequently, be our duty as faithful representatives of the people of Cleveland, to awaken the people of the whole State, regardless of their party affiliations, to the iniquities of unjust taxation. They must be made to realize that national issues and senatorial ambitions are of less importance to the people of Ohio in State elections than the fitness of candidates for such offices as County Auditor, State Auditor, as Attorney General, as Supreme Court judgships, and as legislators.

Nor is taxation the only subject with which this new government of Cleveland must deal even to the extent of appealing to the civic conscience of the people of the whole State. Chief among the questions of prime concern to Cleveland are those relating to the common municipal services that are distinguished as "public utilities."

Already the states permit cities to engage in the business of gas and electric lighting, and of this privilege it is our duty to avail ourselves at once. Let us begin with an electric lighting plant of the most modern type, by which we can produce electricity cheaply for street lighting, and in addition can give to the people in their homes and places of business the benefit of electric light and power at the minimum of cost. As that experiment proves its value, the same system can be extended over the entire city.

So far as supplies of light, power and water are concerned we are, even now, as I have already observed, legally empowered to abolish this prolific source of corruption. But with reference to street railroads and some other kinds of public service our powers are extremely limited. Yet there is no good reason why the city should not own, and under merit rules of employment, operate its own street car system. It owns the tracks on the public viaducts, although there is no specific legislative authority for it. Originally the rails were paid for by the city on all the great viaducts and on some of the small ones. The companies were required to keep these tracks in repair, and now not an original rail remains, the companies having substituted new ones. Yet these new rails belong to the city and the tracks are absolutely under its ownership and control. There is no reason why this should not be done on the streets as well as on the viaducts. Were we to attempt it, however, we should doubtless meet bitter opposition from monopoly interests and probably be tied up with injunctions. With reference to street car service, therefore, as well as to taxation, we, of Cleveland, will be obliged to awaken the interest and obtain the co-operation of the people of the State at large. In no other way can we secure for Cleveland the unobstructed right to establish the kind of system we ought to have and which our constituents clearly demand.

Meanwhile, however, it is fully within our power to begin anew the important work in this connection of establishing a system of low fares. To prevent this consummation a revolution in the judicially-approved practice of half a century of municipal government in Ohio was precipitated. Cleveland was thus divested of its admirable charter and placed for nine months virtually under the government of the Supreme Court. But the day of our city's deliverance is at hand. All the legislative precautions of monopoly lobbyists and party "bosses" have been set at naught by popular vote. The people of Cleveland have spoken, and the duty of their officials is clear.

These are but suggestions of the larger and perhaps more difficult duties before us. Other duties and other problems will unite with these to make our labors arduous and the necessity of our vigilance constant. Doubtless we shall often meet with difficulties that will try our patience and encounter obstacles to tax our resources. Even in the most favorable circumstances it is no easy task to execute with intelligent fidelity the delicate trusts which the people of a modern city, with all its marvelous complexity of public and private interests, repose in their officials. The severity of such a task is intensified as new municipal problems naturally press forward for solution. It is greatly aggravated when in addition the whole structure of the municipal government is suddenly altered by hasty legislation, undigested and unconsidered by the law making body, and dictated by conflicting private interests having little or no regard for the public good. But I venture the prediction that the officials of Cleveland will prove equal to their peculiarly delicate and difficult task.

Working harmoniously together, without regard to party, with malice toward no man and injustice to no interest, but in response to a lively spirit of fair play to all, whether rich or poor, I believe that the members of this new city government will overcome every obstacle, those that are designedly thrown in their way as well as those that naturally arise, and so triumphantly achieve the beneficent results they have been elected to secure. Upon you, gentlemen of the City Council, I trust we may depend for a courageous and untarnished record and wholesome local legislation. From you, gentlemen of the various administrative departments, I am sure we may expect industrious, sensible and faithful service. For myself, I pledge again my best abilities and my sincere devotion to the work we have in common to do—to this great work of making our city a model municipality.

What greater honor could any of us desire? What object could there be more worthy of any man's ambition than to succeed in giving strength and tone and exalted character to the municipality of which he is a citizen? To succeed in effectively co-operating in the work of establishing in his own city municipal self-government upon the basis of equal justice, and thereby setting an example of practical democracy to the civilized world.

Perhaps we cannot wholly succeed. Be that as it may, let us firmly resolve, each for himself, in his own sphere of official duty, and all of us together, that at any rate we will deserve to succeed.

TOM L. JOHNSON.

Christian Socialism

WASHINGTON GLADDEN

There is, then, some justification for this phrase, Christian Socialism. I think Laveleye is rather enthusiastic when he cries, "Every Christian who understands and earnestly accepts the teachings of his Master is at heart a Socialist, and every Socialist, whatever may be his hatred against all religion, bears within himself an unconscious Christianity." I would rather say that every intelligent and consistent Christian approves of the end at which the Socialists are aiming; and that, in many of their ideas and methods, Socialists and Christians are in closest sympathy.

. . . .

Socialism, as we have seen, is simply a proposition to extend the functions of the state so that it shall include and control nearly all the interests of life. Now, I take it, we are agreed that, as Christians, we have a right to make use of the power of the state, both in protecting life and property, and in promoting, to some extent, the general welfare. Not only have we no scruples against availing ourselves of these political agencies for securing the general well-being, we believe that this is one of our most imperative and most religious duties. . . . We think it desirable that all men should be Christians; and we believe that if all men were Christians, the government of this country would be in the hands of Christians, and we cannot imagine

From Washington Gladden, *Tools and the Man*, (Boston: Houghton Mifflin Company, 1896), pp. 281-308. Reprinted by permission.

that it could be in better hands. The more there is of genuine Christian influence and Christian principle in the administration of government, the better the government will be. That is our claim. Our problem is to christianize all our governments as speedily and as thoroughly as we may. Following this purpose, how far ought we, as Christian citizens, to go in seeking to promote the public welfare through political action? Especially ought we to favor the attempt on the part of the state to improve the condition of its poorest and least fortunate classes? This is the real motive of Socialism. The promotion of the common good is always the end proposed; but those whom it chiefly seeks to benefit are those who are neediest. This is the very spirit and purpose of Christianity; why, then, should not we who are Christians, as fast as we get into our hands the power of the state, use that power for the benefit of the toiling and suffering classes? Why should not "All-of-us," acting through those organized methods which the state furnishes, extend help and encouragement to the weakest and humblest of us? All will admit that there is much that the state can do to improve the condition of its neediest classes, without any straining of its functions.

1. Protection the state does surely owe to all its citizens, rich and poor, capitalist and laborer; concerning this there is no controversy. We may all unite in insisting that the state shall make justice swift and sure. "To establish justice for all men, from the least to the greatest," is the first of its duties. It is doubtful whether there is in all parts of the country an equal law for rich and poor. The friendless poor man gets short shrift and summary vengeance; the rich rascal can secure delays and perversions of equity, and often goes scot free. The man who steals a ham from a freight car goes to jail; the man who steals the railroad goes to the United States Senate.

. . . .

2. We can also demand that the state shall cease to create and foster monopolies. If it cannot prevent the growth of monopolies, it can certainly refrain from planting and watering them. The state has done a great deal of this vicious husbandry. Its representatives have granted, for no consideration, the most valuable franchises to great companies and corporations, and the money of these great companies and corporations has shaped legislation and purchased judicial decisions by which their power has been confirmed, and by which the tribute they levy upon the industry of the country has been legalized and perpetuated. We have been furnishing these people rope wherewith to strangle us. We have suffered our national domain, by hundreds of millions of acres, to fall into the hands of monopolists. All this legislation, establishing and fostering monopolies, is especially burdensome to the poorer classes. We must all pay tribute to these

lords of our own creation, but it is harder for the poor than for the rich. The street railways in most of our cities ought to bring large revenues to the municipality, by which the burdens of taxation should be greatly lightened. Instead of this, every workingman with his dinner pail pays toll to a rich corporation. The monopoly of the public land is a special hardship. This has always been the poor man's refuge.

. . . .

So much as this we can all agree upon. That the state shall furnish to its humblest citizen perfect protection; that it shall establish equal and even-handed justice; that it shall refrain from licensing and fortifying monopolies; that it shall do what it can to give all its citizens an equal chance; all this the devotee of *laissez faire* asserts as strenuously as the scientific Socialist. But this, says the philosopher of *laissez faire,* is the place to stop. Protection is the legitimate function of the state; the promotion of welfare is not. It is not wise to enlarge the field of state action. Much of the work that the state now does is poorly done; it would be folly to put any more work into its hands. The Socialists' demand for extension of the functions of government is the extreme of folly.

This argument is familiar; I have used it myself, more than once; but it is not so conclusive to my mind now as once it was. It is by no means clear that our governments would not all be improved by putting heavier burdens on them. Satan finds *some* mischief still for the idle hands of public officials. In my own city the power of the mayor is almost all taken away and distributed amongst various boards; the office, as an executive, is as near a nullity as the Legislature could make it; and the consequence is that no man of high character wants to take it, and it is a source of scandal and public shame. The Legislatures of many of our States have tried this experiment of stripping the people of the cities of political power; the attempt has been made to take as many as possible of the functions of government away from the people and confer them upon outside commissions; and the result has been, in every case, disastrous. The weaker the municipal government is, the wickeder it is: is not this a universal rule? If much responsibility is concentrated upon one person, the people are much more likely to see to it that that person is fit to bear it. The heavier the duties resting upon the officials, the greater the care exercised by the voters. And I am not at all sure that a considerable extension of the functions of government would not arouse our people, as nothing else has done, to attend to their political duties. At any rate I am quite ready to see the experiment tried.

. . . .

In the most curt and comprehensive fashion, let me proceed to name a number of the points at which, according to my conception of the Christian ethics, the functions of the state might well be extended beyond the boundaries laid down by the advocates of *laissez faire.*

. . . .

1. The Christian state may furnish a certain amount of public instruction, and require its citizens to avail themselves of it. This is not, of course, an open question in this country, albeit the measure is utterly socialistic. So Mr. Herbert Spencer and his friends most strenuously declare. The provision of elementary instruction for the common people at the expense of the state is denounced by them as a most dangerous encroachment upon liberty. . . . When a free people submits to be taxed for the purpose of providing educational opportunities for all its children, it is taking a long stride, so Mr. Spencer and his friends cry out, in the downward way from freedom to bondage.

2. The sanitary supervision by which pure air and water are secured for all the people is another of the functions of the Christian state. Professor Walker thinks that this is fairly included within the police functions; that it is simply a measure of necessary protection; Mr. Spencer would scarcely agree with him; nevertheless, whether it be old or new theory, it is good sense and good Christian morality.

3. The Christian state can discourage, if it cannot extirpate, the parasites which are fattening upon our industries. (1.) The criminals are parasites of labor; all theories of the state agree that they must be repressed. But there are other parasites toward whom a wholesome severity is required. (2.) The pauper class is rapidly growing, and it is fostered, in large measure, by careless administration of poor relief. The question whether the state ought to undertake the support of the helpless poor is an open question; but there is no question concerning the attitude of the state toward that large class of persons who would rather beg than dig. . . .

. . . .

(3.) The gamblers, including the crowds of so-called speculators in the great cities who get their living by betting on margins, are also parasites; economically they belong to the same class as the beggars and the thieves; they live without rendering to society any service whatever. These classes absorb a large share of the wealth produced. Whatever they consume is so much subtracted from the aggregate product of industry, and it leaves just so much less to be distributed among the productive classes. The state must find some way of suppressing this economical parasitism.

4. The Christian state will find itself enlisted for the suppression of the saloon. Under the theory which limits the power of the state to the suppression of crime and the preservation of the liberty of the citizen, this might be logically admissible; under the theory which commits the state to the promotion of the general welfare it is easily justified. Whatever manifestly tends to the detriment of society at large may and must be suppressed. The liquor interest has become a gigantic, consolidated, unsocial force, directly and malignantly assailing the community, undermining its thrift, corrupting its political life, destroying its peace; and against it, not merely the teacher with his science, and the preacher with his Bible, and the philanthropist with his sympathy for the fallen, but "All-of-us," with all the power we possess, must arise and do battle.

In these instances which I have last named,—the destruction of the parasites of industry and the overthrow of the liquor power,—it is the *general* welfare that is sought, rather than the welfare of any particular class; yet the evils against which they seek to provide bear most heavily upon the poorest people; and it may, therefore, be claimed that through such measures the strength of the state is interposed to shelter or succor its weakest citizens. This is a socialistic motive. This is Christian Socialism.

5. A more express interference of this nature is the prohibition of Sunday labor. In this action the state puts forth its power for the benefit of a particular class, the laboring class. The suppression of Sunday labor in a plank in the platforms of many of the socialistic and labor organizations of Europe. It is a purely socialistic measure. And I, for one, am Socialist enough to be heartily in favor of it. The one priceless good of which the workingman ought never to be robbed is the weekly rest day.

. . . .

6. I have no doubt that the state will also be compelled to limit the hours of labor in some callings, if not in all. With respect to the wisdom of such restriction upon the labor of women and children there can be no question. The fact that the machinery now in use in the various manufacturing industries will produce vastly more than the people can possibly consume, if it is kept in operation through all the hours of the present working day, indicates the wisdom of reducing the number of those hours. The simplest method for the accomplishment of this purpose may be the direct interference of the state. When "All-of-us" see that it is best for "All-of-us," "All-of-us" can say so and have it so. It is very often said that all these matters will regulate themselves if they are let alone. But they do not regulate themselves; the tendency to the degradation of the weak is irresistible.

. . . .

8. The Christian state has a great service to perform in healing strife, in making and publishing peace. It ought to stand forth as the peacemaker in the quarrel between the employers and employed. When the employer is an individual or a private company, perhaps the best thing that the state can do is to tender its good offices to assist the parties in coming to an understanding. To this end it may wisely furnish models and suggestions in certain rules of permissive legislation for the arbitration of labor disputes.

. . . .

Such are some of the changes in their methods of administration which a Christian people, intent on promoting the general welfare, may seek to realize. It is needful, first, to see what ought to be done in this direction, and how to do it. Statesmanship is an art—the finest of the arts; Christian statesmanship ought to be the highest type of this finest art. The Christian people of this country are called to rule; a great curse will rest on them and on the land if they come short of their high calling. If they are to rule, they must know how to rule. Not only the office-holders, but the people also must know how to rule. There is a right way to rule a state as there is a right way to sail a ship or to plant a field, and the Christian people must learn that way, and practice it.

. . . .

If men were better, the social arrangements would soon improve; but while some social arrangements remain as they are, it is hard for men to become better. The best teaching, the holiest example, the most inspiring influence would avail but little for the reformation of a family packed into one of those horrible tenement houses of New York; you must get them out of those associations. Men need mending, and their circumstances too. The Individualist cares only for men and neglects the environment; he is a fool; for the environment, in a thousand ways, reacts upon the man and checks or distorts his development. The Socialist cares only for the environment, and neglects the man; he is a fool; for the springs of power are in the human personality. You cannot make men temperate by law; and if your teaching gives the impression that the evil of intemperance is wholly or mainly due to the presence of temptation, it will be very mischievous teaching. It is the men that most need reforming. Nevertheless, it is far easier to reform men when the temptations are lessened—remove them utterly we never can; and therefore we must labor steadily at both ends of the line—to save men and to banish temptation. A better society to live in, and better men to live in it,—this is what we are working for. And so we come back to the point from which we started, and listen once more to the voice of our great Leader and Captain, as he cries, "Repent, for the kingdom of heaven is at hand!" To help in the utterance of that message, in the fulfilling of that promise, is the high calling of every Christian man. It is the faith, also, of every Christian man that this is no quixotic undertaking, but that the increasing purpose which he discerns is leading to the goal of universal peace. He believes that this great realm of natural powers can be christianized; that its worst abuses can be corrected; that its mighty forces can be sanctified; that industry and trade can be so transformed by humane motives that they shall be serviceable to all the higher interests of men. There are evidences that this work is going on silently but effectually; that some of our captains of industry are beginning to understand something of their true vocation, and to see that it is not alone their individual advantage that they ought to seek, but the welfare and happiness of all whose labor they employ. Faint signs are even now visible in our sky of the dawning of a day when business shall be to many men the high calling of God and the medium through which unselfish spirits shall pour out their energies in ministries of help and friendship; when political office shall be regarded as a solemn trust held for the welfare of the whole people; when the creatures who live by corrupting and despoiling their fellows shall seem to men's thought almost as fabulous as the dragons and vampires of mythologic lore. I write these last words while the Christmas bells are ringing and the happy voices of little children, with their hearts full of the gladness of good-will, are borne to my ear upon the frosty air. Surely it is a happier world than that to which the heavens bowed that night in Bethlehem! And is there not good reason for hoping that

> "Love which is sunlight of peace
> Age by age [shall] increase,
> Till anger and hate are dead,
> And sorrow and death shall cease"?

It is not all a dream; the happy time draws nearer with every circling year. Speed it, all powers of earth and air and sea; run with its messages all men of good-will; let its morning star shine upon your banners all children of the light; to its glad music, now faintly heard, now clearer growing, march to the battle all soldiers of the cross; till its light shall shine on every land, and in its peace and plenteousness all the sons of men shall rest and be satisfied.

Women's Suffrage: No

ALLEN M. MARSHALL

MR. MARSHALL: Mr. President and Gentlemen of the Convention: I appear before you this afternoon I believe as the first man who ever stood before a body of this kind in the state of Ohio on the negative side of what is termed the woman suffrage, whether the woman shall have the right to the ballot or not, and while I am here taking this position this afternoon I want to say to the gentlemen and also to the ladies within the sound of my voice, I am not here this afternoon to tear woman down; I am here to hold her up with all the power and might I have. By divine law and natural law I expect to hold woman up today and stand by her in her behalf, where she was placed by the hand that placed her on the grand and noble pedestal of God Almighty's creation. I shall stand for that, though I am alone, first, last and all the time.

. . . .

The law libraries have been thrown open, all the libraries have been thrown open and every avenue has been open to us that would lead to the foundations of information so to speak, that we might do our work and do it well. Not during this Convention has there been one brother, and I don't say that in any way of chastisement, but I do say that not since the convening of the Convention has any man referred to God's library.

MR. DOTY: The member from Hamilton did.

. . . .

MR. BOWDLE: No, not yet.

MR. MARSHALL: I hold in my hand the grandest book that has ever been known in six thousand years, the grandest book that ever will be known if the world stands six thousand years more. It is God's gift to man, God's library to man. It contains sixty-six books. It covers all time from the dawn of creation down the western slope to the end of the world. That library will tell every member of this Convention that lives in the world today or will live hereafter just where he is, his latitude and longitude at all times and under all circumstances, whether it be during the bright sunshine of midday or dead hours of the midnight, whether in sunny fields or on life's tempestuous sea in the middle of the Atlantic ocean—that library will tell you just where you are and how you stand, and all our relations to God's divine or natural laws.

From Allen M. Marshall (Coshocton), debate on women's suffrage, Constitutional Convention of Ohio, *Proceedings and Debates*, I, (Columbus, 1913), pp. 605-607.

Now there are some things I want to mention in regard to my being here at this time. I called your attention to the fact a few moments ago that perhaps I was the first man that ever stood in this hall and took the position that I am taking today; notwithstanding the state of Ohio is over one hundred years old, I stand here the first man to do it—and, by the way, this is my birthday, the first day of my sixty-fourth year. Sixty-three years ago today down in Coshocton county, on the north hillside, among the red brush, in a little log cabin, I first saw the light. Now I am going to commence my speech on the first day of my sixty-fourth anniversary, from the very first word in the very first book, the first chapter and the first word, that was ever given to man as his guide from a Divine God. I will read to this Convention each day's work and I will comment a little at the close of each day's work:

"In the beginning God created the heaven and the earth."

If there is a man in this house who doesn't believe that let him hold up his hand. If there is a lady in this house who doesn't believe that let her hold up her hand.

MR. DOTY: It is unanimous.

. . . .

MR. MARSHALL: When the first day's work of creation was completed we have light, called day, and night, called darkness. Day opposite night, and night opposite day. And there could be nothing more unreasonable or more impossible than for me to conclude that day could take the place of night or night the place of day, without confusing the entire system of creation from beginning to end or from bottom to top. The functions and endowments of day could not be clothed in the functions and endowments of night, neither could the functions and endowments of night be clothed in the functions and endowments of day. First, because they would not fit, and second because the Creator never intended that they should. Do you believe it?

MR. DOTY: Take a vote on it.

. . . .

Thus, we see the fourth day's work of the Creator was spent in the light business.

Some small, some large, some for day and some for night. Some for signs and some for seasons.

We stand in the center of High street, Columbus, Ohio, opposite the state house at night, we look north and we look south, and we see the effects of man's skill in the light business, and we say, oh, how beautiful! Turning then to the heaven's constellations, we are lost in admiration and wonder of the starry dome of heaven's canopy.

Were I a star in one of those constellations and a jealousy should arise on the part of Mrs. Moon, that she should have equal rights or all the rights of Mr. Sun, it seems to me that I would ponder long and well before I should cast my vote to interrupt the beautiful and harmonious constellation in yonder dome. I certainly would reason with myself that the God, our Creator, knows best. He has created men. He has endowed them, He has given them a place in His divine economy of creation. And it is only wise on my part to not pluck them from their divine place and sphere.

. . . .

"And God saw everything that He had made; and behold, it was very good. And the evening and the morning were the sixth day."

We have but little comment to make on the sixth or last day of creation, more than this, that at its conclusion He pronounced it very good. Still carrying out His divine principle of giving to everything its opposite, especially His creation of man and man's opposite, woman.

Thus, we have recorded one of the most wonderful acts of surgical skill known or that will be known in the world's history. This rib, this woman, was the crowning work of God's creation, last but not least. He placed her on the highest pinnacle of the wonderful pedestal of His creation, almost in hand-shaking distance of the angelic host of heaven, and I want to say if John D. Rockefeller at this moment would step into the halls of this Convention and upon some member of this body bestow a billion dollars endowment, it would be as a grain of sand on the seashore compared with the endowment given to woman by the hand of the wise Creator when He bestowed on her the endowments of helpmate, wife and mother.

An undeniable fact which we find before we come to the close of the third chapter of the book of Genesis: No part or particle of all God's creation ever received exalted place or rich endowment that God gave to woman whom he endowed with (I was going to say with the immortal power, and I guess I will) the power of motherhood. Would to God that woman could see herself today as the queen star in the firmament of creation, as her Creator sees her. And why is it that a few women over the state of Ohio have become so masculine in their conceptions of their divine place and sphere in the divine economy of creation that they want to make a fatal leap from the highest pinnacle of the pedestal of creation down to its base, alighting in the seething cauldron of political corruption? And not satisfied with this descent on their own part, they want to take with them in this fatal leap your daughters and my daughters, beautiful daughters, daughters clothed in their white robes of virgin purity, down with them, alighting in the whirlpool of political corruption, and thus immersing their white robes of purity in the indelible stench of the political world, which time can never erase.

And yet they come to me asking my assistance in this, their fatal leap.

Should I conclude to cast my vote in behalf of this fatal leap, at that moment I should feel that heaven's recording angel had dotted down against me the equal of the—if not the—unpardonable sin. And again I would feel that I had committed treason against God and the government of High Heaven by my revolt against divine and natural law. And again, I should fully realize that I was casting my vote to blot out three of the most sacred words known in the world's vocabulary of six thousand years, namely, mother, home and heaven.

Women's Suffrage: Yes

A. ROSS READ

In the first place it would be hardly possible to get a correct expression of the women on that question in that way. In the second place, if we did, it would not be authoritative. Therefore, it would simply be getting an expression of some of the women in regard to that matter. We know that a number of women do not want the ballot, and, as said by the first speaker from Trumbull [Mr. Kilpatrick] if there is one woman in the state of Ohio who wants the ballot, we have no right to deny it to her. This is one of the cases in which the rights of the minority rise to the same magnitude as the rights of the majority, because it is a question of human right.

Again it is said that the women don't vote now when they have the opportunity. That is true to a certain extent. In the state of Ohio women are now permitted to vote upon school questions and some of them don't vote. And if I were a woman I wouldn't vote either. They have an inherent and natural right, a right that was coeval with self-government and coexistent with every right of American citizenship, and we permit them to exercise part of the right but not all. I would not exercise part of a right either. I would feel humiliated in doing it. I don't blame them for not voting for members of school

From A. Ross Read (Akron), debate on women's suffrage, Constitutional Convention of Ohio, *Proceedings and Debates*, I, (Columbus, 1913), p. 612.

boards. Their vote on school matters is less needed than on any other. You talk about woman's influence being so great she don't need to vote because she has more influence without it—there is no place where she has more influence than in our schools; in fact, the schools have been handed over to her and she has practically everything to do with our schools. Therefore, she doesn't need the ballot there. Where she needs the ballot is in dealing with the social and national problems of the world, and this is a national and a human right. We are not granting her any right. We are simply laying down the bars that she may enter into the political arena and there exercise those rights. We are simply granting her the privilege which we have no right to deny her.

Now, whether or not it would be of benefit to the country at large for women to vote, can not be a mooted question. Is she not of value in the home? Is not her judgment and her intuition, which supplements the reason and experience of her husband, valuable in raising the family and conducting domestic affairs? And would not she in the same way, in that larger field, be of some value to him? We find that where the boys and girls in our schools have the same advantages, the average intelligence and quickness and alertness and natural development of the girls fully equal that of the boys, and we also find that the intelligence of the women, where they have the same opportunities that men have in life, equals that of the men. It may be of a little different kind; he may have stronger reasoning faculties, but she will have the stronger intuition, and sometimes intuition leads us in the right path better than reason. But there can be no question about her mentality or ability to vote on these questions.

Now, I do not want to take longer on this question because I know—I feel at least—that nearly every person in this Convention is in favor of giving women this privilege. The question that confronts us now is not granting the franchise to women, but whether we will give to the electors of the state the right to decide the question. We do not need to discuss the merits of this question. It is only a question of whether we will give the electors of the state a thorough opportunity to decide whether women shall have the right of suffrage or not. That is the question before us. And I think when it comes to a vote it will be agreed almost unanimously. I can not see how any man could refuse to give the people an opportunity to decide on this question. How any one who believes in the initiative and referendum, and who believes in self-government, can deny them the right, recognizing, too, that it is a natural right, I can not see.

Women's Suffrage: Yes

F. M. MARRIOTT

Gentlemen of the Convention, one of the strongest arguments that I can make or that I think can be made in favor of granting the women of this state the small boon that they are asking, to wit, to submit to the people the question as to whether the people of this state will vote to give the women of this state equal suffrage with men, is that the people should rule. I say that I cannot understand how any delegate who believes that the people shall rule can refuse to let the people say whether our wives and mothers and sisters and daughters may be permitted to have a part in this government of ours.

. . . .

In my judgment it is a part of practical wisdom that we adapt ourselves to the times in which we live. If we do not we will find ourselves standing alone while other states are pressing forward and winning the battles of life.

If we are to be progressive in fact and not in theory only, we must keep abreast of the progressive states of the Union, and not let such states as California, Washington, Colorado, Idaho, Utah and Wyoming blaze the way in every progressive movement.

Ohio should lead more and follow less. Our motto should be: "Ohio Leads," and not "Ohio Follows."

. . . .

Are the women of Ohio less intelligent, deserving, brave and true? Will we stand and let Wisconsin, Kansas, Oregon and Nevada also show us the way? I say no, a thousand times no!

For more than sixty years the women of Ohio, our mothers and our wives, have been knocking at the door of equal rights, asking only for simple justice, and the doors have not been opened to let them in.

I say this is to the everlasting shame of the men of Ohio. Today that army of mothers and wives is joined by our sisters and our daughters, and they are now unitedly appealing to this Convention for simple justice, appealing to be emancipated from the slavery in which men have held them for all these years.

Will we longer close our ears to their appeal and refuse their prayer? I say emphatically no.

From F. M. Marriott (Delaware), debate on women's suffrage, Constitutional Convention of Ohio, *Proceedings and Debates*, I, (Columbus, 1913), pp. 616-618.

I have too much confidence in the gallantry, the manhood, and the patriotism of the men who compose this Convention to believe for one moment they will be so unjust to the noble women of Ohio.

If I had a heart so indifferent and cold, so destitute of human justice, as to say by my vote that the women of Ohio are at least not the equals of the colored man, I would feel ashamed to again meet the mother of my boys.

Universal suffrage is no longer a dream, but is a progressive fact, as is shown by the several states named which have broken the shackles of slavery and granted to women equal rights with man.

In Ohio we have been generous enough to make them equal with the men in the right to own and hold property and pay taxes to support the government, yet we have denied them the right to have a voice in that government.

Taxation without representation is and has always been odious to every true American.

Our forefathers, under the slogan "Rebellion against tyrants is obedience to God," gave us our independence; that is, gave the men their independence, but left our women slaves.

Is not one hundred and thirty-six years long enough to earn freedom? Have our American women not proven themselves worthy during these long years of probation? What more do we want? What additional sacrifice do we require? Is she not the equal of man, yea is she not his superior?

If we men of Ohio, we, "the lords of creation," will not admit that our wives and our mothers are our equals, we will at least admit that they are the equal of the black man.

. . . .

Our boasted claim of a popular government, a government of the people, by the people, and for the people, so long as one-half of the people are deprived of a voice in our government is a farce and a delusion.

With a citizenship of about ninety million people, outside of the states that have given the women the ballot one-half of our citizenship is disfranchised, and hence deprived of a voice in shaping the policies of government, and yet we boast of a republican form of government, a government by the people!

Section 4 of article IV of the federal constitution provides that: "The United States shall guarantee to every state in this Union a republican form of government."

Yet in the face of this guaranty no state of this Union has in fact a republican form of government which refuses equal rights and equal privileges to all its citizens.

A so-called popular government which deprives one-half of its citizens the privilege of citizenship is a false pretense and is not a popular government in fact but in name only, and every state which withholds from its women the right to have a voice in its government violates the spirit, if not the letter, of the federal constitution.

Women are citizens, so declared by the constitution of the United States, and the state constitution which deprives any portion of her citizens of equal privilege with all other citizens is conceived in unwisdom and born of injustice.

A constitution which fails to guard the integrity of American citizenship, and to give all its citizens equal protection of law and participation in government, is and always will be a failure, because it is lacking in inherent honesty.

A successful and permanent government must rest primarily on recognition of the right of its citizens and the absolute sovereignty of its people. Upon these principles is built the superstructure of our republic. Their maintenance and perpetuation measure the life of the republic. These principles stand for the rights and liberties of the people, and for the power and majesty of the government. A republic, therefore, which does not recognize justice and equal rights to all its citizens cannot and ought not longer endure.

The greatest boon of American citizenship is the right to participate in government. When one-half of the citizenship is deprived of this right our boasted claim of a government of the people, by the people and for the people is a false claim, and Lincoln might well have said that "ours is a government, only we are ruled by men and not by man."

More Reforms Necessary

SAMUEL A. HOSKINS

I am not going to discuss ancient or mediaeval civilization or times. I just want to discuss the condition now in the state of Ohio and the proposal before us as it bears upon those conditions. I think the discussion as to the civilizations and the conditions of Greece and Rome are beside the question for one reason only, that never in the history of civilization have we had such a broad, expanded and deep-seated general intelligence among the voters, the common citizenship, as we have in Ohio today. All comparisons fail and it is useless to make comparisons about the failures of ancient governments because they did not have in those days a civilization such as this, with books, newspapers, printing presses, and all things that go to disseminate knowledge among the common people of the commonwealth.

Let us come down to the point. Is it not a fact that the people of 1912 in the state of Ohio are better qualified for self-government, or better qualified to say by what rules, laws and conditions they should be governed, than any people of any time or any age in the past? I am willing to believe that that question should be answered in the affirmative. I believe that I and those with whom I am associated, my children, are better qualified to pass upon the laws that must govern us in the state of Ohio than our fathers were, and better than our grandfathers, and men are many fold better than in any generation or age that has passed. So those things are all out of the way, and it is a mere academic discussion to get them into this record.

There is only one fundamental fact to which I desire to call your attention. There is a reason for the wide-spread unrest that is over this country. There is a reason for this progressive movement that is on all over this land. If there were not some fundamental reasons for it, the unrest and agitation would not be here, as we all know. If conditions were satisfactory this agitation of 1912 and of the last eight or ten years would not be upon our people.

. . . .

There is one thing sure. If legislation has improved it is because of improvement in the body of the citizenship and because the body of the citizenship has demanded the improvement of laws, regulations, etc., referred to last night in the debate.

As I say, I am not a pessimist; I am an optimist. I believe the world is getting better. I believe the citizenship is getting better and the legislative body must be getting better, but let us address ourselves for a few minutes to this present unrest, this demand for changed conditions. I came here a pure initiative and referendum advocate. I do not know whether I knew what it was or not when I came. Up at home I am called a conservative. Some people think I am too conservative. Up there in our little business affairs we often get together and we get to discussing the unrest of the people and

From Samuel A. Hoskins (Auglaize), debate on initiative and referendum, Constitutional Convention of Ohio, *Proceedings and Debates*, I, (Columbus, 1913), pp. 900-901.

condemning that unrest. We little business people in the little towns often imagine ourselves a part of big business. We little fellows who happen to sit around the bank table, or as a board of directors of some little two-by-four corporation, are in the habit of imagining ourselves "big business." Sometimes we actually think that, and we have a great many people on this floor who seem to consider it their special prerogative to ally themselves with the big business interests of the country.

. . . .

I think not; but it does make a difference to the Convention as to what sort of influences undertake to control the action of the Convention. I want to say that there is an unrest in this country, and there is a cause for it. We started out a few decades ago in this new land to build up new homes and a new civilization. We started out as nearly equal as we could and as nearly equal as any people in the history of the world ever started out. I mean we were equal before the law. We were largely equal in the actual possession of this world's goods, and probably as nearly equal as ever known before in any civilization. What are the conditions now?

For the last thirty years the people of this country have been money mad. We have been crazy over the accumulation of wealth and the wonderful prosperity that has come upon the country. We have been busy building homes, tunneling mountains and clearing the farms and doing all the things that have brought this present civilization and present condition to our doors, but what is the effect of all that? While that has been going on, the people have been dormant to every sense in the world except the accumulation of the dollar. We have been taught in this country that prosperity must come by government favoritism. We have lost track of the true theories of government, and the people are waking up in this latter day to find out that the resources of the country, the wealth of the country, have been largely concentrated in the hands of a few people. I believe myself (I don't care to be catechised about it, because I have not time for these discussions) the present conditions have been brought about by government favoritism—not always state favoritism, but by governmental favoritism we have arrived at the present conditions—and it is the cause in a large measure of the present unsettled conditions of the public mind.

Now, gentlemen, you have to make up your minds to this: The people of this country have determined that they are going to have a larger share in their own government and they believe the initiative and referendum are the best methods of getting that larger share in their own government, and if we are going to do our duty we must give them the initiative in a workable form.

Initiative

STEPHEN S. STILWELL

Out of the labors and sorrows and deaths of the world's heroes have been born that degree of knowledge, that measure of religious liberty and of political freedom, which you and I now enjoy.

I say our proper text is found in the Declaration of Independence or in our own bill of rights. Strange as it may seem, that with the volumes upon volumes of encomiums which have been piled, mountain high, upon this great epitome of human liberty, with the flood of marvelous stories of devotion and self-sacrifice which are told of its attainment, we seem to differentiate between the spirit which rebelled against the series of oppressive acts and relentless usurpations which finally resulted in the overthrow of English sovereignty and the spirit which dominated the convention which drafted our national constitution, completing its work September 17, 1787.

. . . .

While yet that spirit which impelled them to separation was dominant, while yet the memories of Lexington, of Valley Forge and of Yorktown were still vivid, the formulation of the state charters began, our own being concluded November 29, 1802. What did the framers of the Declaration of Independence and of the state constitutions of that period, including our own, have in mind when they specifically declared that the people have the right to alter, reform or abolish the same whenever they deem it necessary? At the same time that they thus declared they vested the legislative power in a general assembly, establishing thereby our representative form of government, which, at that time, and as a matter of fact ever since, has been the most practical form of democracy.

In establishing the republican form of government, and at the same time declaring that when government becomes subversive of human liberty, of the absolute will of the people,—they have the right to reform or to abolish it, can it be possible that in any reformation of the form of government it was their thought to return to the form from which they had just been separated, or that succeeding generations might find the form which they were then establishing destructive of life, liberty and the pursuit of happiness when it became "their duty to throw off such government and to provide new guards for their future security?"

No man can surpass me in profound admiration for the patri-

From Stephen S. Stilwell (Cleveland), debate on initiative and referendum, Constitutional Convention of Ohio, *Proceedings and Debates*, I, (Columbus, 1913), pp. 932-933.

otism and statesmanship of our Revolutionary fathers, and that admiration is only quickened when I read that having just separated themselves from their fatherland they were not unmindful of the fact that the form of government which they did then establish might become inimical to the well being of succeeding generations, and with a forethought that is marvelous they preserved to the people of such succeeding generations the right to provide new guards for their own security.

I ask you if it is not possible that they had in mind the corrupting influences which have invaded our legislative bodies, and which have been the bane of American government for the last half century? Perhaps the thought expressed in Goldsmith's "Deserted Village" was in their minds as well:

> "Ill fares the land to hastening ills a prey,
> Where wealth accumulates and men decay.
> Princes and Lords may perish or may fade,
> A breath can make them as a breath has made,
> But, a bold peasantry, their country's pride,
> When once destroyed can never be supplied."

I contend that in establishing a republican form of government it was the purpose of our fathers, and our constitutions guarantee it, to establish that form only as against a less popular form of government and not as against a more popular form of government.

The Crosser proposal provides for both the direct and indirect form of initiative on both proposed laws and proposed amendments to the constitution. The delegate from Hamilton [Mr. Peck] has offered an amendment eliminating the direct initiative on proposed laws. Since coming to this Convention I have formed a high admiration for Judge Peck, and regret that upon this matter I cannot follow his counsel.

What is it that has created an almost universal demand for the initiative and referendum law? The corruption and irresponsibility of legislatures, their failure to respond to the will of the people and their habit of responding too freely to the will of special privilege, and now it is proposed by this amendment that before it is possible for the people of Ohio to enact legislation which they desire they must first submit it to the servant body whose mistakes have occasioned this great awakening of the public conscience, and from whose influence, when baneful, this very bill seeks to relieve us.

I confess that the lower percentages provided for the indirect initiative would in all probability influence our citizenship to its use in preference to the direct initiative with its higher percentages, but I warn this Convention that to eliminate the direct initiative from this proposal is a virtual renunciation of popular government.

No Home Rule

DAVID CUNNINGHAM

Proposal No. 272 has received less real general consideration in open convention than any other important proposal before this body, and I believe should have received the most careful attention. It is true that we were assured by members of the committee on Municipal Government that they had sweat blood over its consideration; that not a syllable of any word or even a preposition had been overlooked; that it was the best thing of the kind that had ever been framed by mortal man up to this time; that it embraced on this subject the garnered wisdom of a thousand years. Some of us think that it falls far short of what is claimed for it. In the first place, the amended title is misleading. The title has been changed by the committee on Phraseology to "Municipal Home Rule." We think that title does not describe it at all and that it will have the effect to mislead and deceive the people. The title to describe in short the object of this proposal should be changed to something like this: "To provide an easy way for universal municipal bankruptcy." If the people are not deceived as to the real scope of this measure it will never be adopted.

Let us examine it for a few moments. It provides for a deluge of these corporations. Under it more than two thousand different and distinct municipal corporations can be organized in the state. This looks to me to be home rule run mad. So far as I am personally concerned I am in favor of granting the right to any city to establish a commission form of government. A proposal of twenty-five lines is all that is needed to provide this constitutional right.

The proposal is a mongrel, a mixture of a little organic law and a great deal of pure legislation, and that legislation of the very worst and most vicious kind.

It embodies features in total disregard of the rights of the owners of private property. For example, if an owner is seized of the title to town lots adjacent to each other and one of them is taken on condemnation for some fancied public improvement the price of the lot so taken can be assessed against the owner's remaining lot.

I fully recognize the right of municipalities to condemn private property for purely public uses, but do not recognize the right to compel the owner to pay for his own land so taken. This wonderful proposal provides further that if a municipality, however small, thinks that it needs an eighth of an acre for public use in some

From David Cunningham (Cadiz), debate on home rule, Constitutional Convention of Ohio, *Proceedings and Debates*, I, (Columbus, 1913), pp. 1861-1862.

near-by farm it has the right to condemn and take it, not only the part that is needed, but the owner's whole farm of five hundred acres of which the one-eighth of an acre is part. What for? may be inquired. Why, to subdivide and sell out in lots for mere speculative purposes.

This proposal gives every little village and city in the state the right to buy in, or to condemn if it can not buy, any and all public utilities inside its limits and issue bonds to pay for the same. For example, they can buy or build street-car lines, electric-light plants, gas plants and any other public utility that can be thought of, and extend them out into the country beyond the corporate limits and operate them. We are to have "no pent-up Uticas" in this great state of Ohio, and if there shall be in ten years a single village or city in the state that will not be absolutely bankrupt it will be because it will not be able to sell the bonds.

If the committee who framed up this measure had set themselves deliberately to work to propose the worst and most vicious form of municipal government in the world they couldn't have succeeded better; and hence I insist that if this measure is to be submitted in its present form that the title at least should be changed so as not to deceive the people, but at least give them a gentle hint as to its true character.

When all the money in the state is invested in the bonds issued to buy all these public utilities we will then have single tax without mistake. The bonds will be exempt and the utilities themselves will no longer pay any taxes. The millions now paid by them into the public treasury will be no longer available; consequently there will be but little left except real estate to pay taxes on. We are launching our municipal bank on an unknown sea without the rudder of common sense to guide it, and for one I protest.

For Home Rule

GEORGE W. KNIGHT

Gentlemen of the Convention: In the absence of the chairman of the committee I desire to explain this proposal somewhat in detail.

The proposal undertakes to accomplish three things not now possible under the present constitution:

First, to make it possible for different cities in the state of Ohio to have, if they so desire, different forms and types of municipal organizations.

Under the present constitution it seems that it is not competent for the lawmaking body to classify municipalities, save in the two classes mentioned in the present constitution, namely, cities and villages; and the further provision which requires uniformity of laws for corporations makes it necessary that the legislature in enacting laws shall provide for one general uniform type of government for all cities and another general uniform type of government for all villages. With cities in the state varying in population from five thousand to half a million, it is obvious that either the large city must get along with crude machinery inadequate for its needs, or the small cities must have all the machinery of government adequate to a city of half a million. In either case the awkwardness is apparent and the burden of expense upon the smaller municipality is needlessly large. Therefore, the first thing that this proposal undertakes to do is to provide that municipalities shall—and I shall go into the details of that a little later—have the right, if they so desire, to frame charters for themselves, to provide each for itself such type or form of organization for municipal business as it desires.

The second thing, and the main thing, which the proposal undertakes to do is to get away from what is now the fixed rule of law, seemingly also required by the constitution, that municipal corporations, like all other corporations, shall be held strictly within the limit of the powers granted by the legislature to the corporation, and that no corporation, municipal or otherwise, may lawfully undertake to do anything which it has not been given specifically the power to do by the constitution or the lawmaking body. It has often been found under our present system, and undoubtedly would be found also in the future, that many things necessary from the standpoint of city life, which the city may need or urgently desire to do, can not be done because of the lack of power specifically conferred on the municipality itself. Therefore, this proposal undertakes pretty nearly to reverse that rule and to provide that municipalities shall have the power to do those things which are not prohibited, that is, those things with reference to local government, with reference to the affairs which concern the municipality, which are not forbidden by the lawmaking power of the state, or are not in conflict with the general laws of the state under the police power and the general state

From George W. Knight (Franklin County), debate on home rule, Constitutional Convention of Ohio, *Proceedings and Debates*, I, (Columbus, 1913), p. 1433.

regulation. So the presumption would now become a presumption in favor of the lawfulness of the municipalities' act, and that presumption would only be overcome by showing that the power had been denied to the municipalities or that it was against the general laws of the state.

In the third place the proposal expressly undertakes to make clearer or make broader the power of municipalities to control, either by leasing, constructing or acquiring from corporations now owning or operating the public utilities within the corporation and serving the corporation, the water supply, the lighting and heating supply and the other things—without specifying—which come within the purview of municipal public utilities, thus removing once and for all, all legitimate questions as to the authority of municipalities to undertake and carry on essential municipal activities.

These three things are the fundamental things which are undertaken by the proposal, and these three things taken together certainly constitute what may be termed, and rightly termed, municipal home rule.

For Home Rule

ROBERT CROSSER

Every amendment that has been offered here to this proposal is clearly intended to destroy the principle of home rule as involved in this measure. The struggle for municipal home rule which has gone on in this country for so many years is actuated by the same motive as that which has advanced the cause of direct legislation, direct primary, and every other democratic measure which has agitated this country for some time, namely, the desire to control the machinery of government by those who are subject to that government.

Direct legislation is an attempt to restore to the people control of their political destinies and welfare further than that of merely

From Robert Crosser (Cleveland), debate on home rule, Constitutional Convention of Ohio, *Proceedings and Debates*, I, (Columbus, 1913), pp. 1483-1485.

changing their rulers every year or two, as is the case at present, for after all that is the only democracy which they have had so far in this country.

The advocates of home rule merely insist that municipalities be allowed to solve their own problems and control their own affairs, independent of outside authority, whether that authority be a monarchy, or oligarchy or the people of a whole state. In short, the cities merely ask that the principle of self-government be extended to them. At the present time they find themselves in the predicament of the women, the only other beings in the state denied the right to self-government.

In order to have real self-government all those, and only those, who are appreciably affected by governmental activities should have a voice as to what that government should be. In other words, if there be a problem which affects the city of Cincinnati or Columbus or Toledo particularly, it is not home rule in any sense of the word if the people of the whole state of Ohio undertake to decide that question, merely because those outside of the cities have more people to vote upon it than the particular municipality.

It is difficult to understand by what reasoning the framers of our constitution and some other constitutions justified the taking away from municipalities the right of self-government, since this has been the principle of which the United States was supposed to be the best example. Such constitutions have reversed the natural order of things.

I contend that the natural and correct method proceeds upon the theory that municipalities exist first and provide for a government suited to themselves, and that for their own mutual welfare, and also for the welfare of the intervening territory, general governments should be established, but which should exercise authority only in regard to matters of a general nature. As the federal government in its relation to the states has only such powers as are specifically granted to it by the people of the states, so it should be with the state in relation to municipalities. The state should have only such powers as the people specifically grant to it.

. . . .

If you stop to consider a moment, you will realize that the municipalities, the village communities, as they are sometimes called, were the first forms of government in the history of any civilization. There was no need for a general or central government until there were a great many municipalities and cities. The villages and cities are simply aggregations of people who have congregated in some particular part of the earth. They found it necessary to have governmental machinery of some kind to regulate their affairs, and it was only natural that all powers of government should remain in them when they established a general government, except such as was necessary to discharge the government functions arising from the interrelations of the municipalities.

. . . .

So not only in theory but in fact that has been the natural growth of all governments. They grow from the smallest unit up to the community or village, and from that on to what is known as the state, and from the state to the nation, and at the present time it might be well to call attention to the fact that in our analogy we must remember that the United States government, the federal government, has not all the power of government over the states of the Union, which it may dole out to the states as it may see fit, but the converse is true, the theory which I am advocating here for municipalities in relation to the states is true, namely, that the United States only has such power as the people have specifically granted to it, and wherever problems can be handled by the people of any locality, where they affect the people of that locality more than some other locality, that locality should be allowed to do as it sees fit, not because of any sentimental feeling, but for the most practical reason imaginable, namely, that the people being on the ground and having the problem facing them every day, the people knowing their resources, wants, and the exigencies of the situation, are better able to control by governmental process the difficulty involved in that particular case. It is a practical proposition. It is real self-government, that those actually affected by any law shall have the right to enact and enforce that law. The state should have control over certain functions of government. For example, not even I would insist that cities and municipalities should regulate intrastate railroads or canals, for the very simple reason that the railroads enter a number of different municipalities and the canals pass through a great part of the state.

. . . .

Why, in the state of Ohio I find that a few years ago the city of Cincinnati made application to the legislature, through a member of the legislature, for the passage of a bill giving cities of the first grade of the first class a grant of power to open a street called Gilbert avenue, and the bill provided that the street should be of a certain width. Think of it, going to the legislature to get authority to open a street in Cincinnati or Cleveland!

I was talking the other day to a gentleman who was once a

senator from Cuyahoga county. He told me that when he was in the legislature a few years ago all he did when he wanted any legislation for Cleveland was to go to the Cincinnati crowd and say, "We have a bill that doesn't affect Cincinnati; I want you to help it through." And it would go through. They would each have bills providing for bonds for park purposes and all sorts of things, and they each helped the other through. This gentleman said that one day an old gentleman came to him and said, "Senator, don't you think you had better stop for a little while? I hear a good deal of growling that these bills are vicious and rotten in every particular." And he said, "Old man, do I bother you when you want something for Cincinnati? Don't I come to you with my delegation? Don't you think we had better handle this matter just as we have handled the rest of them?" And the old man went on and voted the rest of the session in the same way, and had all of his friends in Cincinnati do the same thing. What naturally results, therefore, is not only a great detriment to the cities, but also to the country, because it results in the system of trading votes. You vote for this bill which affects my city, and I will vote for something that you want. The result is you get a lot of confused laws on the statute books, obnoxious to the whole state, and probably most of them wrong in principle.

. . . .

But I think the worst result of this centralized form of government which regulates cities from Columbus is that the people of the cities are left in a position where they have absolutely no control over their own destinies, and they are blamed for not taking an interest in the city government and for lacking in civic patriotism and righteousness. I tell you that the members of the legislature and of past constitutional conventions have been entirely responsible for that condition. Does it lie in our mouths to say that the people of Cincinnati or Cleveland or Columbus have been derelict in their duties when really they have had no control over their affairs at all? In order to stir up civic pride and political activity must there not be placed some feeling of responsibility upon the people of the municipalities? At present all they do practically is to vote for a mayor and councilmen occasionally, and then the mayor and councilmen are hemmed in by a lot of legal restrictions which say what they shall do or shall not do. Put the power in the hands of the municipalities so that they can govern themselves, and they will have no such excuse. They will know then that whatever ills they suffer are due to their own neglect, but at the present time they can conscientiously say that it is not their fault, that they have no control over their own destinies, and that is the reason I was so much opposed to the amendment offered by my friend, Mr. Anderson, this morning, which struck out really what seems to me to be the very thing we have been striving for.

. . . .

I have no patience with either side of that controversy. I have a contempt for those who can see nothing else in all the deliberations of this body but the wet and dry question. It seems to me the principle of self-government is ten times more important than this wet and dry question, which is eternally being flaunted here every time any kind of question is brought up. Let us be broader. Let us give citizens by the initiative and referendum real self-government, and let us also give the municipalities real self-government. We have already given the women the right of self-government. Now, let us go a little further. Let us strike the shackles of political serfdom from municipalities.

6 The War Years and After

THE YEARS between 1915 and 1929 were characterized by anxiety and turbulence for many Ohioans. The state's population swelled by almost a million, and the decade of the 1920s experienced greater economic expansion than any previous decade. Faced with the scourge of world war, the state responded to the national crisis with human resources, war materiel, and money. However, while willing to "make the world safe for democracy" abroad, many Ohioans had difficulty extending similar privileges of democracy to those among them who greeted the war with less than enthusiasm and who differed from the principles of the majority.

Women's suffrage and prohibition were two domestic issues that plagued the Ohio electorate for some time; voters remained confused and indecisive. After a flurry of plebiscites, each without a conclusive solution, the issues were resolved through federal constitutional amendments. On two occasions, for example—in 1912 and 1914—amendments to the state constitution granting suffrage to women had been defeated. A limited suffrage amendment was also turned down in a referendum in 1917. Two years later Congress passed the 19th amendment, and Ohio, through legislative action, was the fifth state to approve the women's suffrage amendment.

The issue of prohibition was no stranger to Ohioans. Beginning in 1874, with the organization of the Women's Temperance Crusade, the arguments for prohibition had been broadcast throughout the state. The cause was aided by the creation of the Anti-Saloon League in Oberlin in 1893 and further promoted when Westerville became the publishing headquarters for the league. However, though this mass movement existed in the state and gained strength through political action, Ohioans still rejected prohibition in some form five times between 1914 and 1919. The 18th amendment, accepted by the general assembly in 1918, was submitted to the voters the following year and defeated. It was only through a United States Supreme Court decision, which declared that legislative action was sufficient for amendment approval, that Ohio accepted the prohibition amendment.

Both of these issues placed many Ohio politicians in a dilemma. Atlee Pomerene, the mildly progressive Democratic United States Senator, was no exception: in 1914, when the Senate voted on the women's suffrage issue, and in 1917, when the upper house voted on the prohibition amendment, Pomerene defended his votes against both proposals. While personally favoring women's suffrage and prohibition, he could not forget the fact that he represented not himself but the people of Ohio. Therefore, based on the evidence that Ohioans had turned down the two issues through referendums, his vote reflected the opinion of the majority of voting Ohioans. Naturally, by 1922, when he was up for re-election, the prohibitionists and women who had supported prohibition joined to vote him out of office.

The country's entry into World War I touched the lives of almost every Ohioan. Nearly one quarter of a million men from the Buckeye State served, and 6,500 of them died in that service. The most famous group to serve was the 166th Infantry Regiment, comprised of the 4th Ohio, part of the 42nd Rainbow Division; it saw action in the Meuse-Argonne and Seden campaigns. Ohioans responded in nonmilitary ways as well. While generously supporting the several Liberty bond drives, Ohio counties organized war chests for emergency purposes and raised a total of $37 million. Through the organizational efforts of Governor James M. Cox, almost all aspects of domestic life were assembled to help the war effort. Food production was encouraged and food waste discouraged; labor was organized to prevent work shortages, and many students left colleges to work on the farms. The war years were trying, but those who aided the war effort did so willingly and unselfishly.

However, as was the case in the country's previous wars, there were those who viewed the international situation through different glasses and who were critical of the country's majority, even in the face of the war hysteria that gripped the state. Only one member of the state's twenty-four member delegation to the House of Representatives, Isaac Sherwood, voted against the war. German presses were suspected of being propaganda agencies for the German government. In Findlay a twenty-five-dollar fine was the penalty for speaking German publicly. Fifteen hundred members of the state's American Protective League took it upon themselves to guard the country's patriotic conscience and to search for slackers and German sympathizers. The state's Amish, Mennonites, and Seventh Day Adventists, mostly conscientious objectors, were harassed, were pressured to support the war effort with donations and labor, and were threatened with open violence. Probably the most objectionable episode of the war hysteria took place when Herbert S. Bigelow, the former president of the Ohio Constitutional Convention of 1912 and an outspoken critic of the war, was kidnapped by hooded men and taken across the Ohio River into Kentucky. There he was tied to a tree and horsewhipped for his opposition to the war. The unresolvable loyalty question of the Civil War again emerged: At what point does a democratic society cease to adhere to its basic principles in order to insure unanimity of support from its citizens?

Reactions to the disillusioning results of the war were quick to come to Ohio. Americanization committees, organized during the war, worked to forge a national uniformity. The Ake Law, which forbade the teaching of German below the eighth grade in Ohio's public schools and was encouraged by Governor Cox's message in April 1919, represented lingering antagonism toward all things German. During the "Red Scare," the general assembly passed the Criminal Syndicalism Act, aimed at Communists and labor agitators, which denied the use of crime, sabotage, or violence to promote political reform or industrial change. Nativism also received mild support in Ohio, and the Ku Klux Klan, robed and visible in the state, brought its wrath against the non-Anglo-Saxons within society.

During the 1920s, Ohio business, which had experienced setbacks during the Reconstruction period, expanded more than during any other decade. Labor, periodically striking against readjustments following the war, also enjoyed a period of prosperity. And the farmers, caught in postwar adjustments, shared in the prosperity of the 1920s, but to a lesser degree than other sectors of the economy. Optimism led to overspeculation, however, which dampened the boom of the 1920s, and by late 1929 Ohioans realized that the balloon of prosperity had burst.

Vote Against Women's Suffrage

ATLEE POMERENE

Mr. President, in the few remarks I shall make this afternoon I want it distinctly understood that I speak as a friend of woman suffrage, but I am unalterably opposed to this joint resolution. I do not believe that it is proper for the people of any State to deny to the people of another State the right to vote if they want it. I do not believe that it is the right of one State to force upon another State the obligation to vote if that State does not want it.

Probably 10 or 15 years ago in my own State of Ohio the women were given the right to vote on all school questions. Since that time not 2 per cent of the women of that State have exercised that privilege. When the law was passed I felt that it was simply the first step toward complete suffrage to the women of my own State. In my judgment, they have shown by the fact that they do not exercise it that they do not want the right to vote. If there can be any doubt about this proposition, it seems to me that there was a very clear expression of opinion in 1912, when the people of my State voted upon the question of amending the constitution. During that fall 42 amendments to the State constitution were submitted. Thirty-four of those amendments were adopted and eight were defeated. Those votes were discriminating in character. Some of the amendments were defeated by a very large vote; some by a very small vote; some were adopted by a very large vote and some were adopted by a very small vote.

There were less than 600,000 votes cast out of a total voting population of over 1,250,000. For these amendments which were carried the highest majority was 220,584 and the lowest majority 4,669. For those amendments which were defeated the highest vote against an amendment was 87,455 and the lowest was 1,079. On the woman-suffrage amendment, after a very strenuous campaign throughout the State, the vote was for the amendment 249,420, the vote against the amendment was 336,875. The majority against it was 87,455. In that campaign I had the privilege, because of engagements here in Washington, to speak only once, but I spoke in favor of woman suffrage and I voted in favor of woman suffrage; and if it is proposed again to amend the constitution of my own State I will vote for any amendment granting to the women of my State the right of suffrage; but because the people of my State have voted against it, do the people of some other State claim the right to say

From *Congressional Record*, Vol. 51, 63rd Congress, 2nd Session, March 5, 1914, pp. 4335-4337.

she shall have it? As one of those who voted for woman suffrage and on behalf of the 249,420 people who voted for it, I deny to Mississippi or any of the other Southern States the right to say that we shall not have it. On the other hand, on behalf of the 336,875 men who voted against it, I deny the right of Nevada, Wyoming, Colorado, or any other State to say that we shall have it, whether we want it or not.

I recognize the fact that the Congress has the right to pass this joint resolution if we consider it from the standpoint of power alone; but if we are to consider it from the standpoint of policy, I deny that it should be done. If because it is requested of Congress we shall say that no State shall discriminate against woman because of her sex, then, likewise, if someone sees fit to do it, a similar resolution could be presented denying to the States the right to grant women the suffrage. I would not do that; I do not believe that any Senator would present such a resolution; but if it were presented, what an outcry there would be from the States which have already granted the right of suffrage to women; and they would be justified. If they have the right—and they do have the right—to declare what shall be their own policy within their own boundaries, they ought not to claim the right to say what shall be done in other States where the environment and conditions may be entirely different.

Mr. President, there are, I believe, nine States that have granted to women the right of suffrage. In those nine States of Wyoming, Colorado, Utah, Idaho, Washington, Oregon, Arizona, Kansas, and California there is a population in round numbers of 7,800,000. If the proposition were to submit an amendment of this character to a popular vote in the United States, and it could be done under the Constitution, it would not be so objectionable; but let us analyze the figures for a moment and see what justice there is in it. None of us know it to be a fact, but I believe if it had been suggested at the time the Federal Constitution was adopted that the Government at large should control the right of suffrage and other local matters in the several States, the Constitution would never have been adopted.

In the 12 smallest States of the Union—North Dakota, Rhode Island, New Hampshire, Montana, Utah, Vermont, New Mexico, Idaho, Arizona, Delaware, Wyoming, and Nevada—there are 3,943,009 people, according to the census of 1910. In the 12 largest States—New York, Pennsylvania, Illinois, Ohio, Texas, Massachusetts, Missouri, Michigan, Indiana, Georgia, New Jersey, and California—there are 50,775,616 people, according to the census of 1910, out of a total population by that census in the 48 States of 91,972,266; so that the 12 States last referred to embrace more than one-half the population of the entire country. In the 12 smallest States to which I have referred there are less than 4,000,000 people. In those 12

States, with 3,943,009 people, they would have 12 votes in determining whether or not an amendment should be attached to the Constitution.

In the State of New York, according to the last Federal census, there were 9,113,614 people. In other words, the Empire State has about two and one-half times as many people as the 12 smallest States which I have named, and yet, when it comes to engrafting upon the Constitution of the United States an amendment of this momentous importance we are giving to less than 4,000,000 people twelve times the voice that we are giving to the more than 9,000,000 people of the State of New York.

Let us go further with this. Suppose, for the sake of the argument, that the people of the State of New York were unanimously against this amendment, with her 9,000,000 people, she would be powerless against the less than 4,000,000 people in the other 12 States. But, more than that—I am speaking now of the people as a whole—when it comes to this amendment, the people as a whole have no voice. There is no way by which we can count heads on this proposition. In the State of Nevada, the smallest State in point of population in the Union, where, according to the last Federal census, there were 81,875 people, there are, I am told, 75 members of both branches of the general assembly of that State. It is possible for a mere majority of a quorum in each house in the General Assembly of Nevada to adopt this amendment. In other words, a quorum of 75 people in both houses would have the right to say that the women of New York shall have the right to vote; and New York can not determine that question for herself, even though the voice of that State would be unanimously against the proposition.

Let me suggest, if we are to assume that this is a movement for moral uplift, that there is no movement in favor of morality at any time that dares or can afford to adopt unfair measures or unfair means to obtain it. I hope that my own State shall soon be added to the number of those that will give to women the full right of suffrage.

Vote Against Prohibition

ATLEE POMERENE

Mr. President, before the final vote is taken I desire to express briefly my reasons for the vote that I am going to cast upon this joint resolution.

I yield to no man in the desire to promote genuine temperance in my State and in the Union. I have tried to, and I think I always have lived a temperate life. I believe in living and letting live. I have an intense admiration for the genius of our institutions. I do not believe that the fundamental principles of our people have changed. I believe in democracy. I believe that the principles of democracy are best conserved when we deal with all subjects in a spirit of moderation rather than by following the extremist on either side of any question. I always try to have before me as my guide not the view of the extremist on any subject, but I am intensely interested in knowing what the average man in my State thinks, and I always try to keep before me a picture of the composite Ohioan as I see him. Now, the question is, What is my duty to my constituency as I am permitted to see it? That leads me to review for a moment the conditions as they prevail in Ohio, and I am going to beg the indulgence of the Senate for just a few minutes while I advert to them.

This is no new question in Ohio. We have had it before us for many years, and we will continue perhaps to have it for many years, whichever way it is decided. In the year 1912 most of us thought that the question was settled at least for a few years. That year we voted upon 42 amendments to the constitution. All but two or three were adopted. One of the amendments involved the question of licensing the saloon. At that time in our State we had residential local option, township local option, municipal local option, and county local option. When this vote came before the public most of those, and I think all of those who were leaders in the councils of the Prohibition Party, were opposed to the license amendment. There was only about 50 per cent of the total vote cast on the license amendment. There were for the license system 273,361 votes; against it, 188,823 votes. The majority for license was 84,538 [sic].

Again, in 1914, our people were called upon to vote upon the prohibition question. The election was held November 3, 1914. The vote against the prohibition amendment was 588,329; the vote for it, 504,177. The majority against prohibition was 85,152.

In 1915 we voted upon it again. The vote that year against

From *Congressional Record*, Vol. 55, 65th Congress, 1st Session, August 1, 1917, pp. 5640-5641.

prohibition was 540,377; in favor of it, 484,969; the majority against prohibition was 55,408.

Mr. President, at the present time in Ohio we have residential district local option, township local option, municipal local option, and there is now pending before the people of our State a prohibition amendment which will be voted upon this fall. Under the Ohio constitution our people have the right by petition to initiate an amendment to the constitution or new laws on this subject. They have full power, therefore, at any time to adopt prohibition or new legislation when they see fit so to do.

In my judgment, I must either ignore what seems to be the voice of Ohio, as evidenced by the result of the elections I have just referred to by voting for this amendment, or I must vote in favor of what I believe is the judgment of the people of Ohio by voting against it.

Have we arrived at that state of mind on this or any other question when the majority of the people in any State shall not have any voice in determining what changes in the fundamental law shall be proposed?

I know that the cry is made that it ought to be referred to the people, and many of the people in the country to-day are of the opinion that when we adopt this joint resolution and refer the matter to the States the people will have a right to vote upon it. Of course all men who are informed know that the people of the several sovereign States will have no opportunity to vote upon this amendment; but it is a question, under the plan proposed here, which will address itself solely to the legislatures of the several States, who may or may not be elected upon the prohibition issue, or who may be elected upon other issues quite as well as upon this one.

The State of Kansas claimed the right to vote as she saw fit, without let or hindrance by any State of the Union, when she decided this question for herself. The State of Texas claims that right. The State of Washington claims that right. The State of Michigan claims that right; and, sirs, if they had the right, it seems to me that the people of Ohio should have the right to determine the liquor question for themselves.

And now, if I may, in the few minutes allowed me, I want to call attention to another proposition.

In 1910 the 13 States of Nevada, Wyoming, Delaware, Arizona, Idaho, New Mexico, Vermont, Utah, Montana, New Hampshire, North Dakota, South Dakota, and Oregon had, all told, 4,657,052 people. The State of Ohio had 4,767,121. In other words, in the year 1910 Ohio had 110,069 more people than the 13 States I have named. Yet if this amendment is to be submitted to the States for their votes, these 13 States, with less population than the State of

Ohio, will have thirteen times as much voice as the State of Ohio in determining whether or not this amendment shall be added to the Constitution.

Again, 18 States—Nevada, Wyoming, Delaware, Arizona, Idaho, New Mexico, Vermont, Utah, Montana, New Hampshire, Rhode Island, North Dakota, South Dakota, Oregon, Maine, Florida, Colorado, and Connecticut—had, in 1910, 8,608,432 people; but the State of New York in that year had 9,113,614 people, or 505,182 more people than the 18 States I have named. Let me ask those who believe in democratic institutions since when has it come to pass that upon a question of this kind the principles of American government would permit these 18 States to have eighteen times the voice that New York shall have in amending the Constitution, if this amendment is to be submitted?

Inasmuch as Ohio in 1914 voted against prohibition by a majority of 85,152 [sic], and again in 1915, when a less vote was cast, by a majority of 55,408, thereby declaring her sentiments on the subject, how can I, as one of her Senators, vote for this resolution and put up to the people of the country the prohibition question in such form that we in Ohio will have only one-thirteenth as much influence in the adoption or rejection of prohibition as a fewer number of people in the 13 States of the Union to which I referred a moment ago, or thereby give to New York only one-eighteenth as much influence in determining this question as a fewer number of people in the 18 States which I have named? Surely the majority of voters in Ohio have some rights to be considered. Surely as their representative in the Senate I ought to bear this fact in mind in casting my vote.

Let me put the question in another form. If it were proposed to offer an amendment to the Constitution, the object of which was to permit the manufacture and sale of liquor in each of the States of the Union, would Senators representing dry States feel themselves justified in voting for that resolution because a substantial *minority* of the electors in their State wanted them to so do? Would not they feel bound by the *majority* sentiment in their States? If that be their position, am I less bound by the *majority* sentiment in my State? My belief is that in matters which are so intimately related to the habits of the people, each elector should have the same right to determine the question as any other elector, no matter what his views might be on the subject.

In my judgment the result will be much more satisfactory if this question is left to the people of each individual State to determine the kind of legislation they want upon the subject. For these reasons, in brief, I feel compelled to vote against the joint resolution.

Vote Against War

ISAAC SHERWOOD

Mr. Chairman, I can not keep faith with my people by voting for this war resolution in its present form. I will vote for it if the provision to authorize an army to be sent across the Atlantic to participate in this European conflict is stricken out. I will vote for a resolution to use the naval forces of the United States to protect American interests and safeguard our national honor on all the seas and oceans of the world. I agree with the distinguished and experienced gentleman from California [Mr. Kahn] that sending untrained and unseasoned soldiers into the terrible trench battles of the allies is wholesale murder.

We have said to Germany that we have an unrestricted right to send ships to English ports. The seas are free. We have said to England that we had an unrestricted right to send ships to German ports. The seas are free. We said to England that her blockade was "illegal, indefensible, and ineffective." Therefore we were not bound by it.

We attempted to send ships to German ports. They were halted by British cruisers, and because they were not armed and did not resist, they were not sunk but towed into Kirkwall and declared British prizes. All ships that attempted to go to Hamburg or Bremen were captured and millions of dollars worth of noncontraband goods were confiscated. A matter of $17,000,000 worth of meats was made the subject of peaceful settlement with the Chicago packers, so as to silence this influential element. But the ships of the American Trans-Atlantic Co., sailing in trade between our ports and South American ports, were seized and have recently been declared lawful prizes. All our differences with Great Britain were made a subject of peaceful arbitration. In upward of two years we have not sent any American ships to German ports. If we did so, and the vessel offered resistance, it would be sunk by the British Navy just as we have always held to be the right of a belligerent nation, and as we did in the war of 1812 and 1861-65, when every blockade runner was fired upon without notice and sunk in the Atlantic Ocean with all on board, no matter if citizens of neutral nations were on ships.

. . . .

While we are discussing the ruthless submarine warfare it is conceded that a mine is the most cowardly and destructive of all war's barbarities, much more so than the submarine, and yet England

From *Congressional Record*, Vol. 55, 65th Congress, Special Session, 1st Session, April 5, 1917, pp. 335-338.

mined the North Sea, one of the great oceans of the world, and also mined the harbors of several neutral countries and notified the world to keep out of that zone, and we kept out. Including Austria-Hungary and the coasts blockaded by Great Britain, we lost the markets for our products for over 175,000,000 people, and yet we submitted without breaking off diplomatic relations.

Germany has established a war zone not nearly so extensive as that of Great Britain, because it is only 20 miles from shore, and notified not only the United States but all the countries of the world that vessels entering that zone, consigned to ports of England, do so at their peril. This was not aimed at the United States alone or any other country, but strictly a measure of protection and notice to all the countries of the world, and yet these war-crazed enthusiasts, who talk about national honor, would make us believe that this submarine warfare is aimed at the United States.

Germany agreed to give up her submarine campaign provided England allowed ships to reach German ports from neutral countries, including the United States. This England refused to do. Germany thereupon intensified her U-boat campaign under the law of retaliation, because the neutral nations declined to protect the law of neutral shipping, and our Government refused to take part in a coalition of neutral powers to protect themselves against British aggression upon their rights. This is history, however. We then informed Germany that she must confine her submarine campaign to limits which we held to be dictated by laws of humanity and international usage, and Germany agreed on condition that we should compel Great Britain to return to the recognized principles for the safety of neutral shipping. This reasonable request Great Britain refused to grant.

Waiting in vain nearly a year for us to effect means to let neutral ships travel the seas unrestricted by British orders, Germany announced a certain date after which all ships would be sunk without notice if they attempted to invade the German war zone, but agreed voluntarily to provide for the safety of American ships through a defined passage in their journey to British ports. As a result of this, the President broke off diplomatic relations with Germany. And the President called upon all the neutral countries of the world to also sever diplomatic relations with Germany. But not one neutral nation responded.

We are now urged to war because Germany has established a war zone 20 miles from shore around the shore line of England. During the Crimean War England blockaded the port of Riga in Russia by war vessels 120 miles from the town. This exceeds the German blockade by 100 miles.

. . . .

The great Civil War ended with the United States holding the strongest and most valiant veteran Army in the world. But we did not go to war. Gen. Grant, then recognized as the foremost soldier in the world, was President; but he was not hysterical. He and his great Army and the whole American people had been saddened and sobered by war. And Gen. Grant in the White House was supported by able, sane, and experienced statesmen, and all our aggravating trouble with England was settled by arbitration. And who will say now that this was not best? At the distance of 3,500 miles the undesirable and dangerous German Kaiser looks the same to me as the great grandson of George III; in fact, all kings look alike to me. I am not willing to vote to send the gallant young manhood of America across the Atlantic Ocean to fight for either.

I remember well when Theodore Roosevelt was President of the United States the German Kaiser tendered an heroic statue of Frederick the Great to the United States, which tender was accepted with gracious thanks by Theodore Roosevelt, President, and the same statue, after due formality, was set up in the White House Park in the most conspicuous spot in the city of Washington—in front of the White House. It was dedicated with heroic ceremony. Frederick the Great was a friend and defender of George Washington, and the German nation ever since the organization of the Republic has been a constant and abiding friend of the United States; that during all our wars with Great Britain Germany has stood steadfast as our friend; that in the great Civil War, when Confederate ships were being built in English shipyards and driving our commerce from the seas and oceans of the world, Germany was our fast friend.

Germany furnished 300,000 soldiers to the Union Army, and such distinguished generals as Gen. Carl Schurz, Gen. Franz Sigel, and Gen. Osterhaus, and thousands of others who offered up their lives for the Union while England was trying to destroy the Republic. I am quoting from recent history.

. . . .

And now we are going to war as an ally of the one nation in Europe that has always been our enemy and against the nation that has always been our friend. This is the record we are making to-day. Posterity will judge our actions by this record.

I remember all this in that terrible conflict for four years, and it is burnt into my memory; and while my father was an Englishman, full bred, and my mother was a Scotch woman, full bred, I have been for strict neutrality in this great European conflict. I can not forget, because it is only a few months old, that the President of the United States was elected President because he kept us out of the European conflict. I can not forget, either, that in the speech made by the chairman of the Democratic national convention of 1916, his most forceful point in the declaration which called for the most enthusiastic applause was that we were not mixing and would not mix in this great European conflict, in this terrible holocaust of murder then in progress in Europe. I can not forget these things, because they are vital now.

Who are backing this powerful movement for war? Let me state. The report of the Du Pont Co., one of the manufacturers of explosives, shows gross receipts for 1916 of $318,845,685, and net earnings of $82,107,693. The company paid 100 per cent dividends on common stock and is constructing new plants to cost $60,000,000—getting ready for more war. The Bethlehem Steel Co. recently announced that it had placed $37,500,000 of foreign short-term notes as security for increased capital stock. New York and London financial interests are becoming identical. They are getting ready for more war, more human killings, for more bloody dollars.

Flour and potatoes are cheaper in London and Berlin, handicapped as they are by embargoes, than in the cities of the United States. This country has been drained of wheat, corn, and other food products for export to England and the allies, and we have had bread riots in New York and Philadelphia and Chicago, but we have not heeded the piteous cry of the hungry at home, while passing military appropriations liable to aggregate over three thousand five hundred millions to embroil this peaceful country in the most useless, destructive, and brutal war in all history, 3,000 miles away.

I have just been reading the Farewell Address of George Washington warning his countrymen to keep out of the struggles and conflicts of European empires. And while it is true that George Washington's sage advice and wise counsel is lightly regarded now by those who believe that war and not peace is the normal condition of our so-called Christian manhood, I still believe that George Washington was the greatest statesman and prophet of humane destiny since civilization was evolved in the womb of the dead centuries of barbarism.

Conscription

I have recently been reading a very valuable pamphlet by Prof. George Nasmyth, a noted writer on sociology, author of a book on social progress, and another valuable book, A Study of Force, as a factor in human relations. This pamphlet deals with the question of universal military training, or conscription, whichever you may call it. The argument for universal military service is that it treats the rich and the poor alike. This argument is not sound. Let me quote from Prof. Nasmyth, a paragraph that goes to the root of the whole question:

"Does universal military service involve equal sacrifice on the part of rich and poor alike? If both are killed, of course, both have made the last great sacrifice. But for the families of the two men the difference is very great. For the family of the poor man the loss of the bread winner means that the widow must go out to work; that the children must be deprived of an opportunity for education. For the rich man, on the contrary, no such sacrifice on the part of his family is involved. His wife is not compelled to go out and work; his children are not deprived of the opportunity of receiving a liberal education. A conscription of lives alone, such as is advocated by the believers in universal military service, is fundamentally unjust if the family, instead of the individual, is considered as the foundation of the Nation's life. But if conscription ever does become inevitable let us not add blasphemy to our other crimes by adopting militarism in the name of democracy. No; let us do it with the clear knowledge that we are dealing a death blow to the greatest experiment in democracy the human race has ever tried."

Besides, the rich man can purchase a substitute, but the poor man can not. He must go into the ranks of the killing and the killed.

. . . .

Those Members of Congress who vote for this war resolution to-day are taking an awful responsibility. If this resolution was to provide for the national defense against any threatened foreign aggression I would vote for it, but we all know it is not. The President, in the presence of both Houses of Congress and the Cabinet and the Supreme Court and the bespangled Diplomatic Corps, in a spectacular and elaborately staged event, read a message to Congress and the country, declaring his purpose to enter the European conflict in the interest of a world-wide democracy. Hence every Member on this floor knows that Germany has at this very moment declared officially that she desires peace and not war with the United States; that her war blockade of England and the allies' coasts is for self-protection. Her official warning was sent to the United States and all the neutral countries of the world to keep out of this established war zone. In violation of all the most sacred traditions of the past century and in violation of the most vital and sacred admonitions of George Washington, warning this Nation to avoid the conflicts of European empires; in violation of the Monroe doctrine, we are now about to plunge this great peaceful Nation into a kings' war in Europe. This, too, in violation of our most vital and sacred promises made to the American people less than six months ago to keep this Nation out of this criminal European conflict. We are going into a world-wide war, a war of kings and emperors and czars and sultans against kings and emperors and kaisers, in which the best manhood of Europe has already been ruthlessly slaughtered. In order to add to the horrid holocaust the stalwart young manhood of America are to be forced into the conflict, and we are going to rush them into this slaughterhouse against the best and highest ideals of this Republic—peace, progress, and prosperity, and a government of the people, by the people, and for the people.

. . . .

I am pledged to my constituents to use every honorable means to keep this country out of war. That was the main issue in my campaign, which culminated in November, 1916. The Republicans put up their most popular man with the largest campaign fund ever known. They started it with a great parade in which 20 brass bands were hired, and all the newspapers in my district were committed for preparedness. They claimed it was the universal sentiment and a patriotic sentiment. In every campaign speech I made I said, with all the emphasis I could command, that I regarded war as the greatest crime of the human race. I have been fourteen times elected to civil office, and have never accepted a dollar from an individual or a corporation as a campaign fund. I was elected last November from a Republican district with a majority approximating 13,000, the largest majority of any Democrat running in a Republican district on that issue. I would be violating my convictions and lacking in fidelity to the patriotic and stalwart men who sent me to Congress if I did not do my utmost to keep faith with my people.

As I love my country, I would use every honorable means to keep the young manhood of America out of this horrid holocaust of European slaughter. My experience in the Civil War has saddened all my life. I had my soul rent with indescribable agony, as I stood in the presence of comrades who were maimed, mangled, and dying on 42 battle fields of this Republic. As I love my country, I feel it my sacred duty to keep the stalwart young men of to-day out of a barbarous war 3,500 miles away, in which we have no vital interest. And I am earnestly inquiring what the harvest will be outside of a wholesale slaughter of the patriotic manhood of the Nation. As I love my country, if war is inevitable, then I will be found standing by the country as I did from '61 to '65, and I will go to the front if accepted as a soldier whenever or wherever duty calls.

Purely American

SIMEON D. FESS

Mr. Speaker, under leave to extend my remarks in the Record I insert the following:

ADDRESS DELIVERED BY S. D. FESS AT THE CHAMBER OF COMMERCE OF PITTSBURGH, PA., FEBRUARY 8, 1919.

Mr. Chairman and members of the Pittsburgh Chamber of Commerce, I am here to speak on at least one phase of the reconstruction problem.

However great was the problem of winning the war, the proper solution of the problems of peace is greater. The war came after two and one-half years of warning, which gave the Nation abundance of time to think of the task. When we entered it it was a problem of men and money, mobilized to give the maximum war ability. This was done in the usual American way. While all must admit it was wasteful, and wickedly so, the answer to all claims for economy and all charges of extravagance was "we must win the war."

With the close of the war the problems of peace are imminent and acute.

Under the stress of war we ignored the principles of sound business and finance to embark upon emergency legislation. While this was done as temporary measures to enable the Government to utilize the maximum ability for Government purposes, to a total disregard for individual rights, it offered an administration astonishingly friendly to socialistic tenets the open door to try out these socialistic doctrines at the behest of Socialist advocates and propagandists. So we are not surprised to find presented to us to-day on the part of the administration a request, if not a threat, and on the part of classes of agitators a demand, that these temporary and emergent measures for war purposes be made permanent law for peace purposes.

First Phase of Problem

This is the first phase of the reconstruction problems. Another phase more serious is the inevitable loosening of the ties of law and

From Simeon D. Fess, "Our Country is Not Large Enough to Shelter Any Citizen Not Truly American," *Congressional Record*, Vol. 57, 65th Congress, 3rd Session, February 11, 1919, pp. 131-134.

order, the giving way of the sheet anchor of peaceful government. This has permitted a phase of resistance to the organic laws of the land, which is reflected in numerous ways and divers places, not only in Europe and Asia but even here in America. The worst fruits of this disregard for order fully is found in Russia. The Bolshevist régime there can not be described to an American accustomed to respect for law. Here is a Government which but yesterday could stand out against the world. It was looked upon, and had been for many years past, as the greatest rival of the Anglo-Saxon. Many of our keenest students of world politics looked upon Russia as the one mighty rival of Great Britain. Students of political history predicted a conflict between the Slav and the Anglo-Saxon.

To-day, under the ban of a group of anarchists, whose fundamental theory of government is the abolition of private property, this mighty empire lies prostrate, with none so poor as to do her reverence. That doctrine with its poisonous virus breaking out all over Europe has shown its presence here in America, in more or less boldness since the war opened the door. Its fertile field is among the labor of our country, especially the ignorant foreign worker. It quite naturally feeds upon the misfortunes and pains of a people. It seeks the times of distress to fatten and increase its ranks.

. . . .

For the average American, for this is a foreign infusion, this doctrine is incredible. But I warn you men of business that it is taking a deeper hold upon our country than any of you perhaps conceive. It is rapidly spreading among the less well-to-do among us who are too prone to gather among themselves and turn a listening ear to the irresponsible agitator, who assures the aggrieved that their ills flow from their Government, which owes them a living upon terms of their own making. The toiler is told if he wants to work and must work he should work for himself or his Government, not any other employer. Recently a spokesman of the railway employees urged the roads should be run in the interest of the employees as against either the owners or the public. This is the Russian Soviet under which Russia is to-day prostrate. The toiler is told that the striking inequalities of our citizens as property holders is not due to individual differences but to a Government that wrongfully permits the inequalities. He is urged to demand in the name of equal possession that the Government be abolished and all denied any possessions. This doctrine refuses to admit of diversity of abilities and proposes to make all alike by leveling all to the plane of dispossession. It proposes to chop off the head of every citizen who, by his efforts and application, rises above the average standards.

Warning Is Issued

I warn the country against this frightful doctrine. No man can fail to see the food upon which it feeds, nor the growth it is bound to make unless met by a sound and well-organized campaign of education. All political parties ought to unite their agencies of information to dissipate by the light of education this nefarious and pernicious poison that is daily insinuating itself in our body politic.

. . . .

I believe that the American laborer is loyal to our spirit and institutions, and can not easily be turned against them, even in times of stress and storm induced by whatever cause so it is not such as may be avoided. But we can not overlook the importation of Old World principles and practices too often becoming insinuated into our labor circles from which are fomented outbreaks of lawlessness of various degrees. Within the past few weeks our Nation has witnessed outbreaks in many cities where were announced un-American doctrines and where the sight of the American uniform was hissed and our Government denounced.

Deportation Is Advocated

This country is great in its boundaries and offers vast areas for occupations and residences, but it is not great enough for two allegiances. We must make it known to every comer that unless he can subscribe to the doctrines of a real Americanism this is no place for him. I vote now to forcibly deport every man and woman who hissed the appearance of an American boy in khaki. I am ready also to forcibly expel every man and woman who refuses to subscribe to a full and unqualified allegiance to this country.

. . . .

While the world is set against autocracy we must avoid its extreme, bolshevism. Liberty under government, when the government is on behalf of liberty, is the solution.

This at once raises the question of our duty—now before us as a Nation just emerging from the world war, during which time in order to win the war we have made government everything and the individual nothing.

Liberty of industry is denied, and all business finds itself with the Government's strangle hold about its throat.

Our immediate duty, now that the war is over, is to get back from a war to a peace basis, which means to remove the Government's shackles on business.

When the real American doctrine is applied to present-day problems, people will demand the liberty of contract with the power of enforcement. Liberty without a corresponding responsibility is bolshevism. Enforcement of contract if no liberty was exercised in the making is autocracy. Both of these are un-American, and each is equally vicious.

Capital should be at liberty to invest, but in such a way as not to injure the public. Labor should be at liberty to discontinue a particular work, but not in violence to the injury of the public. The citizen should be at liberty to employ his talents, to apply his time to the best use of which he can make of his opportunities so long as not to interfere with or injure the public.

The function of the Government is to insure an equal opportunity to all its citizens in the rivalry of life.

. . . .

Government should not attempt to make all citizens of one mold, whether he be employer or employee. On the other hand, it should keep open wide the door of opportunity for every talent of every citizen. It should beckon to every citizen, whatever be his talent, his tendency, his tasks, so they be legitimate, to invite him to strive to excel, for this is the very essence of success of the individual and prosperity of a nation. The man who achieves should be commended. The man who fails should be stimulated to correct his mistakes in order to succeed, if possible. The Government should treat every man and woman as an independent, self-reliant, responsible citizen, not as a pensioner, not as a mere subject of paternalistic concern. Each citizen must be taught the fundamental doctrine of "sink or swim." That what he is is due to his efforts, not to paternalistic care; that he is the architect of his own fortune.

The door of opportunity must be left open. This is the real function of government. The success or failure of the citizen will therefore be his own, and the country must be made to recognize that fact in order to avoid producing on the one hand a nation of mollycoddles and on the other a nation of paternalistic dependents, both of which are equally bad.

If we fail to develop in the citizen this sense of self-reliance and responsibility, every misfortune growing out of indolence, idleness, or shiftlessness, to say nothing of waste and extravagance he will lay at the door of his government. This is the basis of anarchy and bolshevism.

. . . .

Dangers Always Imminent

These dangers, always imminent in times of distress, breed out of ignorance of economic principles and feed upon undisciplined passion so freely displayed in times of crises. To-day we see the same spirit of antagonism to law and all legal restraints rapidly spreading over the world. Congress was asked to vote $100,000,000 to feed Europe upon the specific representation that it will prevent the spread of bolshevism. This representation comes from the highest source. While all of us stand ready to assist the suffering in Europe we doubt the remedy proposed for the antidote of a cult of the type of bolshevism. Mere appeal through the stomach is at best but temporary, but the real remedy is the assurance that the time is here when respect for law must be compelled.

I have a few suggestions to make as remedies for this disease.

Open wide the door of opportunity for capital to invest in the enlargement of existent industrials and also in the development of new industries.

So soon as possible unshackle industry by the removal of hindering regulations, so that the war essentials no longer needed for war purposes can be converted into peace industries, and the nonessentials, discontinued during the war as of no value for war purposes, may be stimulated for peace purposes.

Let the Government, so soon as possible, cease to be a competitor in production in all such industries as can be carried on by private enterprise, thereby encouraging those who have capital to embark into production on such scale as the demands for the article will warrant. In other words, maintain the principle of private ownership and operation wherever possible under the law of supply and demand.

Legislation should be enacted to permit the development of hydroelectric power by private contract under such regulation as to amply protect the public. This increase of power in industrial development will enhance prosperity by increasing the output of labor, thereby multiplying the conveniences of life and reducing the cost of living.

. . . .

Our people can not be unaware of the modern cosmopolitan philanthropy which is styled the new internationalism by which we scorn at the idea of our legislation on behalf of our own people. The campaign now on to lose the American aspiration in a maze of European interests, to remove all economic barriers and legislate for the world rather than for America sounds well, but carries with it too much European customs and conditions of economy to suit a country whose laws and privileges have for a century seen an exodus from

Europe to America by a steady stream of immigration. The latest device for displacing a national policy based upon a real American spirit is the proposed constitution of the world, in which our national destiny is lost in international interests.

Nation Has Been Blessed

This Nation has been wonderfully blessed by the character of her laws and institutions, her principles, policies, and business freedom. Her industrial achievements are the wonder of all ages. Her captains of industry are the foremost of the world. Her labor is the best skilled, most independent, and prosperous. This has been made possible by the cooperative spirit between the employer and employee under a policy of protection of American labor against the cheaper European competitor. To this policy the country has committed the advocacy and leadership of a great political party. Its greatest proponent was the splendid leader of the American policy of protection whose memory we have so recently honored.

In this presence and upon this occasion when our thoughts are turned to the stupendous problems of reconstruction as affecting the labor situation of the Nation, and as would be reflected in the life and services of our martyred McKinley, we reaffirm our devotion to this American policy to protect American labor against the cheaper labor of the Old World, and will refuse to exchange a national policy for the new free-trade cult in which we are asked to cease legislation for our own people, to enter upon an international program of legislation for all the world. The country will take its stand firmly for an American policy of protection to insure steady employment of labor on an American scale to preserve the American standard of life. If Europe wishes to come to our standard we will rejoice in her decision. But until that is reached we will continue to maintain our policy of taking care of our own household first without any undue entangling alliances with foreign countries.

After the Germans

JAMES M. COX

April 1, 1919.

To the Members of the House of Representatives:

Under date of February twentieth, I directed a message to the General Assembly on the subject of the teaching of the German language in the elementary, or grade schools—public, private and parochial. In consequence of this message, the House adopted, February 24, H. R. No. 37, by Mr. Fouts, which, among other things, said:

> "*Be it resolved,* That this House does most respectfully petition the Governor to be, by him, placed in possession of facts showing in what manner and to what extent disloyalty and treason have emanated from or been fostered by the subjects taught in the schools of Ohio, and what class of schools, whether parochial, private, or public, have been most productive of existing evils, for the correction of which a remedy is demanded."

. . . .

I assert without reservation that the teaching of German to our children, no matter where they are being educated during their impressionable years, is not only a distinct menace to Americanism, but it is part of a conspiracy formed long ago by the German government in Berlin, and maintained openly in some instances, and insidiously in others, by individuals resident in America, but loyal in their allegiance to another land.

In order to make presentation of this subject as comprehensive as possible, I will make three definite accusations, and treat them in turn.

First: The German government maintained agencies in America for the exclusive purpose of holding en bloc, Americans of German birth or ancestry, in order as expressly stated to preserve Germanism in our country.

Second: The first and most important method adopted for the consummation of this plot was the teaching of German in every school possible.

Third: The text of these school books was not only treasonable, but it was deliberately made such.

From James M. Cox, "Special Message for the Teaching of German in the Elementary Schools," in James K. Mercer, *Ohio Legislative History*, III, (Columbus, 1920), pp. 71-89.

It would seem unnecessary to go into any elaboration on the subject of the Prussian conspiracy. Every man whose judgment is formed by an unprejudiced analysis of events, knows full well that the recent world-war was its direct result. For generations, the theory of the German superman has been implanted into youthful minds, germinated and developed finally into a conviction so concrete as to exclude any devotion whatsoever to the ideals of America. This doctrine has not only been preached to children in this state, but there was added here and there, as a logical corollary, the suggestion that the German destiny ultimately was the subjugation and domination of the earth.

. . . .

We have communities in this country which are not only distinctly German in their ancestry, but they live and feed on no tradition, historical or national, except that of their fatherland. It is a fact too notorious to be denied, that the German conspiracy was based in part upon the practice of deliberate falsehood and bad faith. At the instance of the kaiser himself, there was passed what is known as the Delbruck law. It provided that any man leaving Germany, and going into another country, could take the oath of a new citizenship, and still remain a legalized citizen of Germany, and a loyal subject of the kaiser, if he first made application either to the German government, or to any of its accredited representatives in the country in which he was then resident. In other words, he was to make false oath and render compliance by voice only, to domestic legal requirements, concealing within himself as no apparent disturbance to conscience, the certain knowledge that he was perpetrating a willful fraud in order to profit by the circumstances of his environment. That was the purpose of the individual.

. . . .

In other words, Germanism, to quote the language of Mr. [Theodore] Sutro, will die in America unless German can be taught to children. As Germanism dies, Americanism lives and grows, and the two terms in these days of increased official responsibilities, convey their own meaning so plainly that I need not remind you that we should preserve and nourish Americanism.

. . . .

So much for the purpose behind the teaching of German to the youths of the state. I ask you now to give your attention to what we find within the covers of the books from which the classes in German in the schools of Ohio were taught.

Andrew Fletcher once said: "If a man were permitted to make all the ballads, he need not care who made the laws of the nation." In other words, by a combination of rhyme and rhythm and tune and sentiment, the public mind could be so shaped as to render it impervious to a new doctrine. That the German propagandist considered the Fletcher maxim worthy of adoption is shown by the fact that through the pages of the text-books, we find songs of the fatherland, adulation of the kaiser, and the obtrusively insulting suggestion that the kaiser's heart was attuned to the design of the Almighty, and the ear of the Almighty always sympathetic to the appeals of the kaiser. With this machinery artfully adopted, the teacher of German in instances so numerous as to suspect the element of coincidence, was a German of the first generation. His purse he filled from American resource, but his heart was full of Prussian poison. In this connection, it could be stated that the teaching of German or of any other foreign language, is accomplished in considerable part through the colloquial process which made it an easy matter for Germans of the first generation, fluent as they were in that language, to procure positions in the schools. Hundreds of them in this state bought German bonds and so intense was their hatred of America that in the early days of the war, discretion was forgotten and remarks made in the school room were so overtly treasonable that public opinion demanded and procured their discharge.

In one Ohio city alone, forty-three teachers of German were called before the superintendent's staff. Sixteen of them were convicted of disloyalty and dismissed, two of them were suspected of being German spies. One of them declared publicly that those who were active in her trial, "would be glad to prostrate themselves before her and humbly beg for pardon when the war was over and the kaiser ruled America." In one city of the state, five hundred and forty minutes per week, or nine hours, were devoted to the study of German in the first four grades; from one hundred and twenty, to one hundred and forty minutes weekly, or two hours, were considered an ample time for the study of arithmetic in the first to the fifth grade, and the study of English grammar was given no time until the sixth grade was reached when it grudgingly received thirty minutes per week. In the eighth grade, German received more attention than any other study; in fact no other study received half as much time. The German students received only half the instruction in geography that the English scholars were given. They devoted twenty per cent less time to arithmetic, forty per cent less to history, and approximately fifty per cent less to the study of English.

A leaflet was printed on the work of the German propaganda in the schools of the city in question, and in it we find the statement that "many of the German teachers will not read a newspaper printed in the English language." In the text book, "Hier und Dort," used in Ohio Schools, we find that Washington is discredited. When that period of American history is reached, the text says that Washington lost the confidence of his countrymen, that the army knew no discipline, that it became disorganized, and that troops and officers were on the point of open mutiny, whereupon a German, Baron Steuben, appeared on the scene, saved the day and made America possible. It deals prejudicially with Lafayette, seeks to minimize the service he rendered to our cause, and makes invidious comparison between him and Steuben. You would expect that the brief selection on Washington's burial place would be free from anything German, but the last paragraph compares the simplicity of Washington's tomb, with that of Frederick the Great. A poem, entitled "From the Battlefield at Chancellorsville" is in the book, but we find that it was a German soldier who "lies dying at Chancellorsville." An article appears, called "Christmas," but it deals with nothing of the sacred tradition of that holy season; it tells only about the German celebration of Christmas, and says that when we sit down Christmas eve, we should remember that the celebration of Christmas was a custom kept by the German forefathers, and that we should have no Christmas trees now if the Germans had not brought the custom here with them.

. . . .

But I reserve the most disgraceful episode for the last, and I read to you now, a song that appears in practically all of the text-books, and which has been sung by thousands of our children. It runs:

"Hail to thee in victory,
Leader of the Fatherland!
Hail, Kaiser, to thee!
Feel in your brillant throne
The highest and greatest joy,
Darling of the people!
Hail, Kaiser, to thee.

"Not horse and trooper
Make secure the exalted height,
Where our prince stands!
The love of the Fatherland,
The love of the freeman,
Support the ruler's throne,
As a rock in the sea.
"Glow, holy flame!
Glow, and never die,
For Fatherland.
We all stand ready now,

"My country, 'tis of thee,
Sweet land of liberty.
Of thee I sing;
Land where my fathers died,
Land of the pilgrim's pride,
From every mountain-side,
Let freedom ring.

"My native country, thee,
Land of the noble free,
Thy name I love;
I love thy rocks and rills,
Thy woods and templed hills;
My heart with rapture thrills,
Like that above.
"Let music swell the breeze,
And ring from all the trees,
Sweet freedom's song.
Let mortal tongues awake,

Courageous for one man,
Gladly we'll fight and bleed,
For throne and empire.

"Be, Kaiser, long here with your
  people,
Pride of humanity.
Feel on your throne
The greatest and highest joy!
Darling of thy people,
Hail, Kaiser, to thee!"

Let all that breathe partake,
Let rocks their silence break,
  The sound prolong.

"Our fathers' God, to Thee,
Author of liberty,
  To Thee we sing;
Long may our land be bright,
With freedom's holy light;
Protect us by Thy might,
  Great God, our King."

I have included "America" for the purpose of contrast.

The thing that shocks our sensibilities is the fact that this sacrilegious Prussian production is sung to the tune of "America." Now let us compare it for a moment to the text of "America." You find in the German song, not a single reference to the Almighty. The words breathe almost a supplication to the kaiser, himself, whereas in "America", the whole sentiment is dedicated to God, to country, and to liberty, and no animate being is mentioned, save God himself. We are taught to render our thanksgiving to our fathers' God, the author of our liberty. The German song sung by our children in America not only pledges our youths to "Stand ready now, courageous for one man, Gladly we'll fight and bleed, for throne and empire," but the inference naturally would be that most things come from the kaiser, who is almost deified, and yet it is necessary, for reasons we do not know, that the time of the executive and legislative branches of this government should be taken up in considering the question of whether this ingenious disgraceful thing is to stop or go on. Some skeptic may ask whether the substance of these school books is just a mere hodge podge of bits of sentiment and fragments of history. Unfortunately, that is not the case. I bring you again to the recorded fact. Not only has German gold been used to maintain the teaching of German in our schools, but men have been given yearly salaries for the purpose of exclusively dedicating themselves to the task of supervising these text-books and seeing to it that the spirit of Germanism is kept alive.

I do not profess to speak from a perspective as wide as that formed by the experience of others, and by reason of this circumstance, I beg to quote from among the last words of Ex-President Theodore Roosevelt on the very subject which we are now discussing. He said:

"We have room in this country for but one flag, the Stars and Stripes, and we should tolerate no allegiance to any other flag, whether a foreign flag, or the red flag or the black flag. We have room for but one loyalty, loyalty to the United States. We have room for but one language, the language of Washington and Lincoln, the language of the Declaration of Independence and the Gettysburg speech; the English language. English should be the only language used or taught in the primary schools, public or private. In the higher schools of learning other modern languages should be taught on an equality with one another, but the language of use and instruction should be English. We should require by law that within a reasonable length of time, a time long enough to prevent needless hardship, every newspaper should be published in English. The language of the church and the Sunday School should be English.

"This war has shown us in vivid and startling fashion the danger of allowing our people to separate along lines of racial origin and linguistic cleavage. We shall be guilty of criminal folly if we fail to insist on the complete and thoroughgoing unification of our people.

"We are a nation and not a hodge podge of foreign nationalities. We must insist on a unified nationality with one flag, one language, one set of national ideas. We must shun as we would the plague all efforts to make us separate in groups of separate nationalities. We must all of us be Americans, and nothing but Americans; and all good Americans must stand on an equality of consideration and respect without regard to their creed or to the land from which their forebears came."

My proposition is that the Comings bill be so amended as to carry no limitations and that it be made unlawful for anyone anywhere in this state to teach German to the children in the grades, whether they attend public, private or parochial schools, it matters not. If there is no menace from the teaching of German to the impressionable youth in private or parochial schools, then by what process of reasoning do you gain the idea that it is a menace in the public schools? As the measure is now framed, it provides sequestered places where German propaganda will be sheltered by the arm of the law. It is the very thing in fact that has been resorted to in other places. For instance, as far back as 1904, when boards of education in some parts of the country, drove German out of the grades in the public schools, the German-American Alliance proposed, as is shown in "German-American Annals," that, "A new foundation could be built by establishing independent German schools, society and congregational schools, in which the language of instruction would be the German, and with English as the foreign language. Most church societies would welcome such an activity on the part of the central bund and would cooperate with it to all their power. These German schools could, under the leadership of German-American teachers, easily create as much or more than public schools."

I think you will see, therefore, that the very thing which you propose to do is precisely what the German propagandists would do, in their last extremity. Assured that you sense what is in the minds of those you represent, and that you intend your actions to be but legal expressions of their desires, I have no doubt that the Comings bill, passed through misconcept of the conditions about us, will be at once freed from the limitations which make it both odious and indefensible.

I make the further recommendation that teachers shall, by statutory direction, be compelled to take the oath of allegiance to this country. We have had our bitter experiences, and love for our children compels us in common prudence, to protect them from "the wolf in sheep's clothing".

JAMES M. COX,
Governor.

The Price for Criticism

HERBERT S. BIGELOW

THE FIGHT AGAINST PRIVILEGE
(From Mr. Bigelow's speech at the Liberty Theatre, New York, Jan. 13, 1918)

"Patriotism was not the motive for the assault. The assault was an act of revenge, perpetrated by the public utility interests of Cincinnati and the Kentucky cities across the river, and the purpose was to punish me, not for any sentiment or acts of disloyalty to the United States government, but my disloyalty to these monopoly interests, to which I plead guilty and of which I am proud.

"The trouble goes back to 1912, when, in the Constitutional Convention, we secured the Initiative & Referendum. No men were ever wise enough to make a constitution that would stay good long. We had just sense enough to know this so we made a constitution which the people could easily change. We invented workable provisions for the Initiative & Referendum, not only in the constitution of the state, but in the organic municipal law of the state.

"Big business campaigned especially against the Initiative & Referendum in the charter election which was held in September 1912. They loudly declaimed against these revolutionary doctrines,

From *The Outrage on Rev. Herbert S. Bigelow of Cincinnati, Ohio* (National Civil Liberties Bureau, 1918), 8-12.

as they were called, and charged we were assailing representative government, and turning the state over to anarchy and mob-rule.

"They might have forgiven us for this if we had failed, but the unpardonable sin was that we succeeded, that the people of Ohio laughed at what someone called their "well-organized despondency", and ratified these so-called revolutionary measures by over 80,000 majority.

"In the fall of this same year, 1912, I was sent to the Legislature from Cincinnati. I produced and got through the House, of which I was a member, a bill to revoke the Cincinnati Street Railway franchise, the notorious fifty year franchise that seventeen years before had been pushed through the Legislature by Mark Hanna and Joseph T. Foraker.

"But this, contumacious as it was, was not the limit of my disloyalty. I was personally responsible for filing a petition of ten thousand names to stop the passage of a twenty-five year franchise which the Council of Cincinnati had granted to the Kentucky street car lines. In the campaign on this franchise the corporation hung great streamers over all the crowded thoroughfares of the city bearing this legend: "Bigelowism versus Business. Which will you have?" The people answered that by defeating the franchise by 9,000 votes out of a total of about 60,000.

"The people of Cincinnati scored another victory against the public utility interests after that by defeating an ordinance to increase the charge for gas.

"So it happened that since we secured the two instruments of popular government we have made some use of them in Cincinnati on the average of once a year in combating the aggressions of the public utility interests. I have been looked upon as the ring-leader of the guerilla warfare, and I have been singled out for the bitter hatred and opposition of the interests and the newspapers which they control.

" 'That man Bigelow ought to be driven out of town.' 'He ought to be shot!' 'He ought to be tarred and feathered.' These expressions have been heard in the clubs and big business circles of Cincinnati for the last five years. These interests, emboldened by the war, figured that the public would jump to the conclusion that they were patriots.

"I will relate what happened, and let my hearers judge of the quality of their patriotism.

The Outrage

"On Sunday afternoon, October 28, I left the Grand Opera house and went to my office at the Odd Fellows' temple. After dictating copy on the peace prayer to the newspapers I went to the Metropole hotel to take supper with two friends. At 8 o'clock three of us boarded a York street car to go to York and Sixth streets, Newport, Ky., where I was to address a Socialist meeting.

"On my way I stopped at the office of the Enquirer and left the copy for Mr. Dean, the reporter who had asked me for it after the Grand Opera house meeting.

"The friends with me were Vernon J. Rose of Kansas City and Prof. E. J. Cantrel of Minneapolis, both of whom had spoken with me at the Grand Opera house.

"We arrived at the stop about 15 minutes past eight. A pleasant young man stepped up and addressed me, saying that they were afraid I was not coming and that they had just telephoned after me.

"I asked him his name, which I understood to be Mooney, and I introduced him to Mr. Rose and Prof. Cantrel.

"The entrance to the hall was on Sixth street, and I noticed some parties then gathered on the sidewalk, and around what appeared to be the door of the entrance. Seeing the men, I asked Mr. Mooney if there were prospects of a good meeting. He answered in the affirmative. But by that time I was up against some of the men in the crowd. A man standing near the building turned to me and said:

" 'Is this Mr. Bigelow?'

"I said 'yes,' and put out my hand to him. He took my hand and said: 'We want you to go over to headquarters before the meeting.'

"Instantly another man seized my left hand. They snapped handcuffs on both wrists.

"I said: 'Where are you going to take me?'

"A man on my right answered: 'To headquarters.'

"I made no response. I supposed they were Government secret service men. I preferred to rely upon my innocence of wrong and upon the justice of my Government. Resistance would have been likely to involve my friends with me in personal injury and serious charges, although I hardly formulated such a thought at the time.

"I was put in the back seat of a large machine, which was standing at the curb. My two captors seated themselves on each side of me and holding the handcuffs.

"Another man got in in the rear and stood in a stooped position, facing the crowd, with a revolver in his hand. The top of the machine was up and the curtains were quickly closed apparently by some one on the outside. There may have been a fourth man in the rear, for while the machine was started and began to pull away, some one tied a padded cloth over my mouth, and tied ropes around my feet. After that a bag was slipped over my head. In that position I rode with my silent companions over city pavements, across bridges, up and down hills, on country roads—some rough and some smooth—of course, I had no sense of direction, and little sense of time. But I could tell that we were riding at a high rate of speed, and while we were on city pavement, the horn was being sounded almost continuously.

"Finally the machine halted. There was a light from the rear which I could see through the bag, and I was deceived by that in supposing that we were near a city lamp. All sat motionless for a time. I heard an approaching train. This told me that we were near a railroad and I concluded that they were waiting to load me on the train. I speculated as to whether I should have to be exposed with the handcuffs on the train. Just before we came to a halt a man felt me over, apparently to discover weapons. He took from my overcoat pocket a box of candy which had been given me for my daughter.

"The sound of the train died away. There were whistles and movements. The curtains were pushed back. The man at my side seemed to be leaning out of the machine as though they were looking for confederates on the road.

"Presently my feet were untied, the bag taken off my head and I was helped to the ground. Though still gagged, I could see. It was a bright moonlight night. There were many men, from 25 to 40 perhaps, wearing white masks and aprons or skirts of the same material.

"These men appeared to be gathering from a line of automobiles in the rear. This explained the light I had seen through the bag. The machines that had followed had remained too far in the rear for me to hear them. One who acted as leader held aloft an electric light, though there was no need of lighting it.

"With a sweep of this object he indicated in silence that the company was to ascend the hill. It was a rather steep but short hill on which stood a little frame school house. I was led around the farther side of the building out to the rear. Before alighting from the machine my hands had been tightly fastened together.

"I was led to a tree and my hands were disjoined. Other line cords were tied to each handcuff and two men drew my arms by these ropes around the tree.

The Whipping

"Then the leader said: 'Off with his clothes,' and my arms were released sufficiently to enable them to take off my overcoat, coat and vest and suspenders. Then a man with what appeared to be a black snake whip, which I had seen while coming up the hill, stepped forward and took position to strike. He awaited the word of the leader, who said: " 'In the name of the women and children of Belgium and France lay on.'

"I was struck probably six or eight times, the man hauling off and swinging as if with all his might. When he stopped to rest, or for further command, he was ordered to continue. I can not be certain whether the same man or another continued the whipping. How many more times I was cut I am not sure, but not many, perhaps, ten or twelve in all.

"After this, while standing almost naked, a man began cutting locks of hair off the top and front of my head. Then something out of a large bottle was poured on my head and sopped over my hair. It smelled like crude oil, which it turned out to be.

"Permit the man to dress," the leader then commanded.

The Mob Departs

"This done, the leader began waving the men away. The most of them disappeared around the school house and I could hear the noise of starting machines.

"But before he left, the leader said: 'You are to remain there ten minutes after we are gone.' By this time I was stood up with my face to the side of the house.

"The leader further said to me: 'You are to be out of Cincinnati in 36 hours and remain away until the end of the war.'

"Two men were left to guard me. One pointed a revolver at me and ordered me to sit down on the cover of the cistern. Then he said to me, pointing the gun at me:

" 'You have been tried in the balance and found wanting.'

"I said: 'On what evidence?'

"He said: 'That is known by the company you keep. When we strike we strike at the top.'

"After more of this sort he announced to me that when they, too, were gone, I must stay here ten minutes.

"I asked him in what direction was home and how far away I was. He pointed in the direction in which we had come and said it was quite a distance.

"I asked him if I could walk home that night and he said 'No.'

"He told me that I should inquire my way at a certain farm house, the first house on the right.

"After he left I began to speculate on why they put oil on my hair. The only theory that seemed reasonable was that it was intended for identification later.

"I concluded that others might be waiting at that house to do a deed which the big crowd couldn't be trusted to witness, and that the oil was put on to make sure that the wrong man would not be assassinated.

"So I decided to go in the other direction.

The Journey Back

"I had walked about two hours when first one machine and then another came up in my rear. I eluded both of them; once I stepped into a field of standing corn. The second machine I escaped by climbing over a bridge and dropping down on a railroad track.

"I knew I was walking in the direction of Erlanger, as I inquired my way of a couple in a buggy, it occurring to me that if the pursuing machines were hostile they would probably learn from the couple that I had been directed to Erlanger. So when I reached the Lexington pike I turned on out, coming to Florence, better known as Stringtown on the Pike. I saw what was evidently the steeple of a Catholic church and determined to go to the house of the priest. While looking for this house I saw the sign of Dr. Grant, in Florence, and I knocked and the door of a Good Samaritan was opened unto me.

"I had never seen Dr. Grant before—he was a perfect stranger to me, but the doctor and his wife could not have done more for me had they been life-long friends. The most difficult part of Dr. Grant's ministration was a laborious shampoo to get the oil out of my hair. I reached Dr. Grant's house about 1:30 a. m., and thought it best not to betray my whereabouts by using the telephone that night. The doctor and I sat up the rest of the night and saw the sun-up.

"I had a much-relished breakfast with the doctor and his wife and little daughter. Then I telephoned to my family and found attorney Nicholas Klein at my house, searching for me. I told Mr. Klein where I was and he and a party came for me."

Ohio Klansmen

H. W. EVANS

Seventy-five thousand Ohio Klansmen with their wives and families gathered Thursday, July 12, at Buckeye Lake, near Columbus, Ohio, for the first state meeting of the Knights of the Ku Klux Klan in that state.

Imperial Wizard Dr. H. W. Evans, with his staff, was present as well as the leaders of the Klan in Ohio and adjoining states. The occasion was one of unbounded enthusiasm and plans were made for the advancement of Klankraft in this section of the country where the order is already of great strength.

The Imperial Wizard addressing the huge gathering spoke of the program confronting the Klan, outlining the objects to be achieved by the order. His address to the Klans of Ohio was as follows:

"In presenting a forward view for our great organization, it is eminently befitting that we should cast a retrospective eye over the past and mark the successive strides by which we have come to this great day in the history of our order. It is axiomatic and true that from the achievements of the past we may justly and accurately form a conclusion as to what is to come in the future.

"More than sixty years ago in the hour of our nation's greatest problem, there arose an organization which saved to a portion of our nation a white man's civilization and prevented another portion of our great nation from being used, through brutal passion, in a campaign of hatred against their blood kin. After a terrible fratricidal strife, the like of which the world had never seen, the American nation was preserved as a unit.

The Birth of the Klan

"The movement of the white citizens of a despoiled and broken Southland which preserved to many states in our nation the white man's heritage, passed into oblivion when the purposes for which it had been born were accomplished. The ideals and principles upon which it had been founded awaited another and a further need of the nation which knew how to use the principles, to erect an organization, and to function for God and country through it. When from the selfishness and ambitions of men and nations, the world war began in 1914, civilization was again menaced and there was grave danger that freedom would be crowded from her standing place and the world would retrace her steps down the cycles of time and all the things for which high-grade mankind has struggled would again be lost in darkness.

. . . .

The Klan is an organization founded upon the great fundamental ideas of helpful service from man to man, from man to country, and from man to God. Under this banner, if you will but keep your eyes ever on your leadership, if you will but keep your prayers ever ascending to Almighty God that strength be given to your leadership, if you will but be Klansmen as you yourself must interpret the true meaning of that sacred word, the ultimate success of our cause will be certain and the fruition of our utmost hopes will be absolutely assured.

. . . .

"The greatest necessity is that we save, enlarge and broaden our great free public school system under which the mass of our population is and must always be educated so that they can, with their own minds, properly understand and correctly gauge the ideas that are presented, the laws that are enacted, and the acts that are performed under their system of government.

Education Safeguards Liberty

"While the American Constitution holds it to be an inalienable right of every man to be free and holds one man the absolute equal of another, all men must recognize their responsibility under that right guaranteed them by the constitution for correct and positive action in all matters concerning their own and their country's welfare. So long as we have an educated people whose ideas have not been warped by the individual minds of their teachers and the organized efforts of agencies which seek their own purposes, an educated people whose minds have been led along the simple pathway of right and duty into a realization of what their minds and their consciences are for—that long will liberty be safe and sound government assured.

"The companion of education is necessarily the right of every free, rational, conscience-bound citizen of any country to give expression to his thoughts and ideas both in speech and in press, and thus by the continued exchange of ideas and dissemination of truth he will enlighten the whole people and bring common understanding to higher levels and greater possibilities.

White Supremacy is Age Old

"Now from the experience of centuries of mankind's history, the fact of white racial supremacy has been demonstrated in every age, under all conditions and everywhere upon the face of the earth.

"Sixty centuries ago when all the races of the world took an even start in their journey from barbarism towards civilization and from darkness to light, the races were free and equal, not only in the sight of Almighty God as human beings, but alike free for action and alike capable of performance, but while the inferior races, which are all the races except the white race, were dallying with the primrose paths of pleasure, wasting part of their existence in idleness, sensuality and laziness, the men of the white race were moving steadily onward with ever increasing strides towards enlightenment and truth.

"Thus from age to age, and from century to century, the distance between the races has ever been a widening distance.

"Today, it is futile to attempt by legislative enactment or national aid to develop inferior races beyond their natural endowments and capacities. It will still be impossible to hold the dominant race from further lengthening the distance between them and the inferior races of the earth.

"We must teach not alone the preservation of the purest and greatest racial blood strains the world has ever known, but we must teach the people of the dominant race to have a full and just appreciation of their duties under God and in the light of their past records and their consequent future responsibilities. For the people of a dominant race to be not only just and magnanimous, but kind and helpful to inferior peoples is a duty and responsibility of racial leadership. Thus, we must, through the enactment of just laws, just alike to all the people, be just to the people of less opportunity and consequently less ability. We must see that for every human being in this, our great country, the fullest opportunity for the enjoyment of liberty and the pursuit of happiness is afforded. This is a white man's burden, in a white man's country and I am bringing it to you as the greatest duty of the Knights of the Ku Klux Klan to correctly interpret and concretely perform it for God, for country, for family and for self.

"I bring to you no doctrine of hatred, either of alien people or religious sect, but I want to leave with you a message of genuine responsibility for your own development and genuine responsibility for your own action as you act along these lines.

"The doctrine of Klannishness is as old as man.

Israelites Had Klan

"When the children of Israel had been driven by famine into Egypt, they found themselves finally a despoiled and captive race. Under divine direction, and leadership of the uncrowned King of the Jews, Moses, they formed a Klan and all the glory of that great race was written from the spirit of Klannishness. When this Klan's strength, arrogance and might had led them away from the standards of right and the Klan became a menace to the world, God Almighty stayed its progress, but did not destroy it and so today we find that through the spirit of Klannishness, this race of people has been able to outlive the mistakes of twenty centuries and to retain a fraternalistic mind, a fraternalistic government, a monotheistic form of religion in spite of the progress of a redeeming Savior who through a doctrine of love has captured almost all the world.

"Nothing today bars the absorption of the Jew into the web and fibre of the Christian civilization except the Klan idea which has been innoculated into his blood and taught him for sixty centuries. Praise be to Almighty God the Klan today is a Christian organization and in its onward march it will take from the Klan of ancient days the things that have made it a menace to civilization, and step by step, it will force this alien Klan to either become incorporated in our body politic, through birth, training and religion, or they will have to depart from our fair land and return to whence they came and work out their destiny under less favorable circumstances and less favorable conditions in a place where they will not be a menace to freedom and the onward march of a conquering Christ.

"I cannot close without presenting for your careful consideration the most momentous problem of our age. The question before us today of immigration over-shades all other questions because of its relation to the fundamentals and the ideals of our nation.

"For one hundred and forty years, America has been a haven of refuge for the poor, the diseased, the maimed, the halt, and the blind; here they found a hospital for the cure of their minds, their bodies and their souls, in a land watered by the purest water of liberty, lit by the all-conquering rays of a clean God's sun; where prodigal nature had, with a lavish hand, prepared for man's happiness, prosperity and freedom in an immeasurable way and where opportunity lay as never before at any place or at any time in the world's history. Slowly we absorbed the alien populations of the world who came to us with a desire to find refuge, home and peace. We cured their ills and assimilated them into our body politic and went about our Master's business, but there came a time when men of ulterior motives and unclean minds,—men without character,— came to our shores and attempted to work out their purpose and their philosophies upon our fair land. Now when all the rest of the world is diseased, when there is no solidarity except ours, when all the balance of the world would like to find refuge beneath the Star Spangled Banner, we must protect the heritage given us by our forefathers against the infiltration of the distorted theories and machinations of the enemies of society.

"We must build up a superior race of men to carry the world's troubles upon their broad shoulders and in doing so, we must close the gates to the influx of the broken in body, the broken in fortune and the diseased in mind. We must set up a standard of visitation which requires that our guests shall be in mind, in spirit, and in life, somewhat our equal and which sets as the final standard of American citizenry the desired standard of native birth. Let us pass from this age to succeeding ages a standard so high that a native born American's proudest boast will be his birth right, just like, for many centuries, the proudest boast of the Roman people was, 'I am a Roman.'

"Let us demand a standard of high usefulness and let us grant citizenship only to those who are born to the heritage. Thus we will solve the problem of a dangerous assimilation and thus we will build up a national standard of character and of living to pass to succeeding ages and save our people from inoculation of false ideas, peoples, and Gods."

Cincinnati's Blacks

FRANK W. QUILLAN

Samuel J. Tilden, Democratic candidate for the Presidency in 1876, called Ohio a "d—d nigger State." The writer of this article, knowing that Ohio has the most interesting negro history of all the Northern States, spent the past summer touring Ohio and investigating the relations existing between the white and colored races today, to see whether the above statement is still true. I visited Cleveland, Akron, Columbus, Springfield, Dayton, Urbana, Xenia, Cincinnati, Hamilton, and many smaller cities, and talked with all classes of both colored and white people. My object was to learn the facts about what the two races think of one another, or more specifically, to find out how much race prejudice really exists. I believe that I started on the investigation unbiased, so far as it is possible for a man to be, and I desire to remain so, letting facts stand as they are. The negro question is a delicate one to treat, for the reason that there are two distinct classes of readers on the subject, one reading all on the subject that is favorable to the colored man and relegating to the waste basket all that is unfavorable, and the other doing just the opposite.

From Frank W. Quillan, "The Negro in Cincinnati," *The Independent*, LXVIII (February 24, 1910), 399-403.

The object of the writer of this article is to bring the two classes together on a common plane, to submit facts as to conditions, and let each reader draw his own conclusions.

While conditions vary in different cities, the following facts about the situation in Cincinnati are, in a broad way, typical of all the cities of Ohio, the nearest to an exception probably being Cleveland.

In the first place, no colored man is allowed to enroll in the Ohio Medical College, which is a branch of the University of Cincinnati, a public institution, nor can he enter the Eclectic Medical School. In fact, there is no school in the city where he is privileged to equip himself for the medical profession. If he leaves the city and secures his training elsewhere and then comes back again, he finds the door of opportunity closed. The colored doctor, no matter what his training has been or what his ability and standing may be, is not allowed to operate in the large City Hospital, a public institution maintained by taxation to which the colored people contribute their share. He is debarred from the Seton Hospital, on West Sixth street, and, in fact, from all hospitals save two small charity concerns. Colored people, received with reluctance into separate wards in the City Hospital, are refused the privilege of having a physician of their own race attend them.

Recently there came up the question of having colored men in the Health Department, and the Board of Public Service, which, of course, is made up of white men, handed down the decision that it would be unwise, as the colored sanitary officer would be compelled to call at the houses of white men during the latter's absence, and their wives would be made subject to insult in having to accept orders of a colored man.

There is not a negro to be found in the city fire department, which employs hundreds of men, all, of course, paid out of public taxation. The reason given for their absence is that white firemen will not work with them, as they would be compelled to eat and sleep alongside of them under the present manner of conducting the department.

The officers controlling the Municipal Bath House now forbid all colored people to bathe there. The privilege was granted for a short time recently under Democratic administration, but the house became practically a colored institution so quickly that the reform party had to withdraw the privilege.

All the popular parks, such as Chester, The Lagoon and Coney Island, exclude the negroes. Some of them have one "nigger day" each year, when the colored people are allowed to pass the sacred portals which are forbidden them the rest of the year. Some negroes are employed as waiters and porters at Coney Island, a leading park, six miles up the Ohio River. These are compelled to ride on the *deck* of the steamboat going and coming.

Hotels, restaurants, eating and drinking places, almost universally are closed to all people in whom the least tincture of colored blood can be detected. A colored man of education and culture, of unusual musical ability, and of great prominence among his people, told me that his wife was white enough to run the gauntlet, but that he was not, and that often when they happened to be down in the city at the noon hour he would send her into a white restaurant for her dinner, while he would stand on the curb and wait for her, or go to some cheap place for a "hand out," which he would generally have to take outside before eating. The same man told me that if he wanted a glass of beer he would have to go to some out-of-the-way place or low "dive" for it. The Bartenders' Union has passed a resolution forbidding its members to wait on a colored person, and they live up to it. On Fifth street, between Central avenue and Broadway, a distance of a dozen blocks, a colored man cannot enter a single saloon and buy a drink, or even a ham sandwich. W. P. Dabney, a colored man of education and of recognized ability in music and other arts, the Assistant Paymaster of the city of Cincinnati, handling tens of thousands of dollars annually, and paying it out to the Mayor, Chief of Police, and all other city employees, personally told the writer of the following experience: He and another prominent musician had, at much financial risk and trouble, secured a famous pupil of Rubinstein, an Italian, to give a concert in Cincinnati. After the concert was over the performer asked the committee to go to a saloon and have a drink with him. They all agreed and entered, the party consisting of the Italian musician, another foreigner, and the colored man, Mr. Dabney. The conversation at the moment happened to be about America, and the Italian was congratulating his companions upon their privilege of living in this land of the free. They sat down at a table and called for something to drink. The bartender could see but two at the table, and those the foreigners. The one real American, simply because his skin was dark (no, not that, or the Italian would have been unnoticed also), tho he was the trusted employee of a great city, was beneath the notice of a bartender.

At the Sinton Hotel, where Mr. Taft made his campaign headquarters, the colored man is not welcome even to standing room in the lobby. No matter how prominent he is, if he desires to see a white man on one of the upper floors he must take the freight elevator, or the lower compartment of the elevator, the "Jim Crow" compartment, we may call it.

The Pullman Car Company refuses to sell berths to colored people going South. Under stress, they will offer to put them in the drawing room, which costs more than they can afford to pay, and which if occupied would segregate them from the whites. Trains pulling out of Cincinnati for the South have their "Jim Crow" coaches, into which the colored people are asked to go. If they do not go willingly they are compelled to do so on reaching the Kentucky side of the Ohio river.

The Y. M. C. A. refuses them either active or associate membership. Recently some young colored men established a Y. M. C. A. on Walnut Hills, a prominent suburb of the city. The white Y. M. C. A. rose in holy wrath at this defilement of their name, and caused the colored organization to change its name to the Y. B(oys) C. A.

The Ohio Mechanics' Institute, probably the largest school of its kind in Ohio, has recently decided to deny them admission.

In the Children's Home, on Ninth street, another large public institution, colored children are permitted to stay but twenty-four hours, after which they are sent to the Colored Orphans' Asylum. The Automobile Club of America has decided to give orphans of cities in which there are branches of the association a free trip to the country annually. The Cincinnati branch two years ago forgot (?) the colored children. Last year, after a very heated public discussion of the matter, it was decided that there were not enough colored chauffeurs to draw them out, so they could not take them.

Theaters universally exclude the negro, or at the best give him a gallery seat, and that possibly at an advanced price. The large city workhouse, reformatories, city and county prisons, and hospitals, separate white and black as much as they possibly can.

The negro can neither rent nor buy a house in a decent section of the city without paying an exorbitant price. If he does succeed in buying a desirable piece of property, his white neighbors will endeavor by all possible means to get him out of it. Sometimes they even threaten his life, but more often they buy him out, generally paying him considerably more than the property cost him. This is expensive for the white man, but he maintains his price. Many negroes are taking advantage of this pride to better their financial condition, and many more would be doing the same if they had the capital. The following extract from a conversation with a colored preacher in one of the suburbs of Cincinnati will illustrate their attitude and their methods: "If I had a little money saved I would make the white folks pay for their prejudice. I would have some 'poor white trash' buy a lot in a fashionable neighborhood for me, and then I would declare my ownership and my intention to build. Immediately I would get many offers to buy, and when I could sell at a good profit I would let it go, and then I would buy another piece, and so continue. I could make a fine living in that way, far better than I can in the ministry, but I haven't the money to start with."

In St. James place, a fashionable residence district of Cincinnati, there lives a colored man of much prominence, being connected with the Southern Freedman's Aid Society and the Methodist Book Concern. The white neighbors have offered him big inducements to sell, but he, not being of the type represented above by the colored preacher, has refused all overtures and insists upon his rights.

But all of these prejudices, galling as they might be and would be to any white man, are small ones in comparison to one other. That other is the one that strikes at the law of self-preservation, strikes indeed at one of the basic principles of our life, namely, that every man should be permitted to earn his bread by the sweat of his brow, working in that pursuit best adapted to his ability. The colored man in earning his living is hampered on every side by race prejudice. The labor unions as a whole do not want him and will not have him, and their members will not work by the side of him. The result of this is that he is practically debarred from all mechanical pursuits requiring skill. He can join the hod carriers' union only, and this is due to the fact that not enough white men can be found to do the work. The bricklayers' union, the painters', the carpenters', the lathers', the plumbers', the barbers', the bartenders', the printers' unions, and many others deny him admission. The white man cannot employ them in any skilled work if he has so large a job that he has to employ white men along with them. The white men will not work with them, there are not enough colored people prepared to do the work to do it alone, and the result is that no matter how much the white employer himself is free from prejudice, his hands are tied, he must of necessity, generally speaking, refuse to employ the colored man in any skilled capacity. Many colored men who had come from the South told the writer that there was no such condition as this existing in the South; that if a colored man became capable of laying brick or doing carpentry work or any other skilled work, he was as freely employed in it by the whites as the white laborers themselves were.

Besides their being debarred from skilled labor, they are not employed as stenographers, bookkeepers or office men in any capacity except that of janitor. Not one is employed as teacher in the public schools, none are employed as clerks in stores or factories.

The post office work is open to them because of its being under civil service rules, and we find them generally measuring up to the possibilities in this line. In the Cincinnati Post Office there are twelve employed as clerks and twenty-eight as carriers, making a total of forty out of a grand total of seven hundred employees, or about 5 per cent., which is the per cent. of colored people in the city to the total population. In the police department there are twelve colored patrolmen out of a total of six hundred and ten, which is one-half their quota according to population. They get these places as policemen from the white people solely as a price for the colored vote.

The learned professions—the law, the ministry and medicine—are open to them, but the few who are brave enough to attempt these find that they can hardly make an honest living. The white people, of course, will not employ them, and, strange to say, their colored brothers are almost as much against them, but for different reasons, one of which is jealousy (a very strong race trait, as dozens of them themselves told the writer during the summer), and the other is lack of confidence. They will not respect the advice of one another, but will take the white man's every time, having learned during their days of slavery to look upon the word of the white man as law.

What are the causes of this strong prejudice in the city of Cincinnati? In general they are the same as are found in other cities of the State. The one big cause is that—"well, *just* because."

The other causes are:

(1) There is a large number of ignorant colored people coming in from the South, seeking the land of the free, where they can have "their rights," many of whom mistake liberty for license.

(2) When a negro commits a crime the newspapers always emphasize his race connection by such head lines as "A Big Black Burly Brute of a Negro" does such and such, and the whole race gets a share of the blame; while if the crime is committed by a white man, race is not mentioned, and the individual gets the blame.

(3) The mixing of the lower classes of the two races causes jealousy and ill feeling in these very classes, and much revulsion of feeling and fear in the higher classes.

(4) Cincinnati has always catered to the Southern trade and still does; therefore she adopts much of the South's attitude toward the negroes.

(5) An unusually large number of Cincinnati's population very probably has been in the South for a time and then returned to the North. It is almost the universal observation that such people, after their return, forever despise the negro.

(6) The white people constantly complain of not being able to depend upon the negro; they say he is shiftless, careless, and too prone to appropriate little things belonging to other people.

(7) The negro more and more is entering politics as a negro, and demanding rewards for the negroes, in the way of positions and public offices. Naturally they are meeting with strong opposition and much secret resentment. The following words from the New York *Tribune* of June, 1877, apply so remarkably well to conditions in Cincinnati and other cities thruout the State of Ohio that I quote it in full:

"If a delegation of red-haired gentlemen should invade the White House with a petition to be recognized they would at once arouse the hostility of bald-headed patriots as well as of those whose hair was black or gray, and there would be established a color line in hair, which would complicate the difficulties of civil service reform. It is equally clear that if a deputation of citizens who wear false teeth should demand some offices for their class, the citizens who gum it would combine with those who masticate their food with natural grinders, not only to the discomfiture of the fictitious ivory party, but to the peril of our institutions. Citizens of African descent should reflect before they commit like indiscretions. The political salvation of the negro depends upon his keeping out of politics *as* a negro. If he keeps everlastingly besieging the Executive Mansion in squads in order to have his color recognized he will succeed in establishing a very distinct color line. It will be a blessed day when negroes and white men both come to understand that appointment to office is not one of the inalienable rights of an American citizen, and when they can impress upon the gentlemen who are reforming the civil service that appointments are to be made solely for the purpose of transacting the business of the Government and solely upon the ground of fitness, and that race, color, previous condition of servitude, or present condition of politics are to be considered no more in the selection of place-men than they are in making out the tax list."

(8) The fact that so many negroes appear in the police court and prisons certainly hurts their cause greatly. According to the report of the Chief of Police of Cincinnati for the year 1905, there were 12,138 white people arrested and 3,107 colored. According to the census of 1900 there were 325,000 people in the city and 14,482 were colored. By a little study of these figures we see that in proportion to their respective populations there were five colored people arrested to one white, and we can also see that if the white people were as criminal as the colored, the police would have made the enormous number of 68,345 arrests that one year. In 1906 there were 11,284 arrests of white people and 2,658 of colored. There were remaining in the House of Refuge, the city prison for young people, on December 31, 1907, 238 white children and 95 colored. From the annual report of the Cincinnati workhouse for 1907 we learn that there were 2,414 white prisoners and 949 colored. About the same proportion has obtained for the last several years. From a study of these figures one must conclude that in recent years and in this one city, at least, the criminality of the negro has been fully five times as great as that of the white man.

Many "extenuating circumstances" might be offered to explain this difference, but the figures tell the more convincing story to the average man.

Many other causes possibly enter into the making of this condition of affairs in this one city. I have mentioned only such as came under my observation and such as throw extra light upon the facts presented. Here and there possibly I have appeared to favor one side and then another. I have tried very hard to present the facts and all the facts that I learned. May these help to better the relations between the two races.

Not So Dry

B. F. McDONALD

Hon. A. V. Donahey,
Governor of Ohio,
Columbus, Ohio.

Dear Governor:—
   I herewith submit to you in compliance with Section 6212-29 of the General Code the Fifth Annual Report of the Department of Prohibition of this State.
   For the period from September 1st, 1924, to September 1st, 1925, the administration of this department reports the following:

Inspections	4,289
Arrests made	3,862
Convictions had	2,093
Fines assessed	$645,155.00
Total fines collected under Crabbe Act	2,202,764.64
Total fines paid into State Treasury	1,101,382.32
Samples Analyzed	131

During the fiscal year ending June 30th, 1925, this department expended on the work accomplished the sum of $105,702.02.
   It will be noted that the number of inspections, arrests and convictions made through this department are but about half that of last year. This, due to the fact that during the past year we have had no card men working since the ruling of Attorney General Crabbe ruled out near one hundred such enforcement officers who were without expense to the State, being compensated through the local courts for the work they did. The results obtained, however, during

From B. F. McDonald, Prohibition Commissioner, *Fifth Annual Report of the Prohibition Commissioner,* (Columbus, 1925), pp. 3-5.

the past year by the regular inspectors has, in fact, exceeded that of any previous year.

During the past eight months under our direction more time and attention has been given to the apprehension of the chief violators such as transporters, operators of stills, and all those commercializing and dealing in illicit liquors in a large way. As a result of this action we have not apprehended so large a number of violators but we feel that our work has been, however, more effective in enforcing the prohibition law than formerly. I do not wish to convey the idea that we have not at any time molested the hip pocket bootlegger nor that such may feel that they will not be apprehended by men of this department in the future, but I do mean that the inspectors of this department have been directed to give their attention and have given their attention to the larger violators. We have since the first day of January, 1925, apprehended about 300 still operators, confiscated their stills and had the sentences thereon imposed, and since the first day of January, 1925, we have apprehended about 100 transporters, confiscated their cars, the same being sold and the proceeds thereof paid into the Treasury of the State and the treasuries of the various political subdivisions of the State and sentences imposed upon the violators.

W. J. Patrick, State Inspector in East Cleveland, Ohio, is possibly entitled to the credit of having gotten more stills in the same length of time than any other one inspector in the department. He reports to me that these stills are not found in barns, garages, store buildings, or other buildings outside homes, but almost without exception they have been found in private residences and many of these residences are among the finest in our state. One particular instance reported by Inspector Patrick was one taken from a fine residence on Lee Road, Cleveland Heights, Cleveland, Ohio. There were in this case two 50-gallon stills found, one on the second floor and one in the attic, 95 barrels of mash, and 395 gallons of finished liquor. This accounts, of course, to a great degree for the propaganda and resentment by bootleggers and their sympathizers against entrance into the private home.

. . . .

According to reports sent into this department out of the homes entered inspectors have found the law violated in four out of five entered, and in many cases where they found no specific violations they did find much evidence in the way of empty whiskey bottles, the odor of intoxicating liquors filling the house, and secret hiding places, trap doors, etc., evidently intended to conceal illicit liquors. The traffic in intoxicating liquors has been largely driven out of the public place of business and is to a great extent today carried on from residences, which, under the law, ceases to be a bona fide private dwelling when used for trafficking in intoxicating liquors. Unless curbed by the forces of the law the liquor traffic will continue to be carried on from the homes to an ever growing extent and we may fully expect propaganda against invasion of the home to be continued by the bootleggers and their sympathetic friends. You will note, too, that all those interested in this propaganda are opposed to the law and the constitution and are going their limit to break it down. I believe in protecting the sanctity of the home, but when a residence is used primarily as a distillery or a bootlegging joint under the guise of a private home, it must suffer the consequences.

Steubenville and Jefferson County still continues one of the worst places for violation of the prohibition laws, and in fact all laws as reported to me by the inspectors in that section.

Since the 1st day of February of this year, I have kept two of my twenty regular men working almost constantly and continuously in that county and they have reported to me that they have made many arrests in Steubenville, taken them before the Mayor of Bloomfield and fines have been assessed aggregating $30,000.00 and from the county aggregating $50,000.00. They have reported to me that gambling is boldly carried on and drunks upon the street are unmolested by the police or other enforcement officers. In several places in the City of Steubenville iron doors and walls were installed in an effort to resist the invasion of the state enforcement officer. It has been necessary, too, for me to keep two men spending most of their time in Scioto County, owing to the inefficiency of the County Sheriff's office of that county.

In the City of Martins Ferry, in Belmont County, much complaint was made about the laxity of law enforcement, and as you will recall, charges involving certain city officials were made and placed before you, which were by you remanded back for hearing before the Civil Service Commission of that city with request from you that I aid the City Solicitor in the prosecution of these charges. This was done, consuming in all near a week's time and resulting in the removal of the Chief of Police, two patrolmen and the suspension of another. Reports coming to me from that city are now encouraging.

7 The Depression Years

FOLLOWING THE YEARS of prosperity, the depression years of the 1930s were frustrating and uncertain for most Ohioans. With wages cut, or jobless, or in need of some assistance to provide for person and family, Americans had to come to grips with the failure of an economic system that offered few guarantees of financial security. At first private philanthrophy or local governments tried to offer aid to the needy; however, it quickly became apparent that assistance on a massive scale was necessary to bring relief to the unemployed and the helpless. Without seeking any permanent solutions to the relief question, the Ohio General Assembly created a crazy quilt of relief legislation. As the situation worsened, the federal government poured money into the state. Despite the apparent need for outside assistance, Ohio's top politicians, both Democrat and Republican, placed principles above opportunity and mounted the ramparts to defend the state against the encroachment of federal power.

To be sure, local, state, and federal agencies spent money to aid the victims of the Depression in Ohio. Between 1932 and 1939, for example, the federal government spent $175,000,000, the state spent $97,000,000, and local government provided $40,000,000 in direct relief. These amounts did not include contributions from private sources. The government moneys, however, were expended without benefit of coordinated programs, were sought by competing rural and urban demands, were criticized by balanced-budget-minded state administrations, and were hampered by a social mentality that was enthralled by seventeenth-century English poor laws. Nearly sixteen months after the bottom fell out of the American economy, the state began to deal with the Depression as a state-wide problem. Governor George White, in an attempt to determine the extent of the Depression, established the Governor's Voluntary Relief Committee, which had the responsibility of surveying the relief situation. Earlier, the emphasis for relief had been placed on local government agencies, including the local school districts, which were required to provide shoes, clothing, medical supplies, and other necessary items for school children. While the governor did attempt to finance a relief program through sales taxes and taxes on luxuries, his efforts were resisted by the business interests in the state.

There was also experimentation conducted in Ohio to relieve the plight of the unemployed. For instance, twelve factories that had been closed early in the Depression were opened under the Ohio Relief Production Units, Incorporated, a program begun in 1934 and financed by federal grants. Plants in Delaware, New Bremen, New Philadelphia, Dayton, and other cities were operated by workers who had been on relief. They produced items such as chairs, clothing, blankets, and china—products to be distributed to the needy. However, the scheme was short-lived; by May 1935 the factories in the program were ordered closed.

In January 1933, for the first time since 1917, a Democrat-dominated general assembly convened in Columbus. No doubt encouraged by the Roosevelt administration, the legislators passed the O'Neil-Pringle Minimum Wage Bill, which, while not all-encompassing, established minimum wages in limited areas. Through the use of the initiative petition, Ohio also accepted an old age pension plan in November of that first year. Farmers were also assisted, and the painful problem of foreclosure was eased. It was not until late in 1934 that a graduated sales tax was passed, which placed part of the burden on those who had enough money to be consumers.

Perhaps the most dramatic political difficulties that arose during the Depression were the colorful but embarrassing skirmishes that took place between two state administrations—one Democrat and one Republican—and the Roosevelt administration. In 1935, Democratic Governor Martin Davey, and again in 1939, Republican Governor John W. Bricker, criticized the national administration for heavy-handed bureaucratic measures in its relief work in Ohio. Because of promises to the public of greater economy in state government, both governors wanted the federal government to increase its relief payments to the state's needy while allowing the state to administer the programs. Davey was charged with political corruption by Washington, and the state's relief program was federalized. In fact, for a period of time all federal moneys coming into the state were stopped. Bricker, on the other hand, while not charged with personal corruption, was embarrassed by the national press and the national administration by charges that Ohioans were starving in Cleveland. Indeed, while the charges were long in both controversies, the proof was short; at base the difference was in economic philosophies and disagreement over the role of the federal government in local affairs.

Not only was there a change in the role of government during the

1930s, but organized labor battled during the depression years to change its stature and to organize itself in the major industries in the country. Between 1929 and 1936, there were 802 strikes in Ohio, dealing with everything from petty grievances to the major issue of union recognition. By 1937, the Congress of Industrial Organizations, having split earlier from the American Federation of Labor, attempted to organize the steel industry. After having no difficulty with big steel, labor encountered the smaller companies—such as Republic Steel and the Youngstown Sheet and Tube Company—and their refusal to recognize labor in their plants. During the summer of 1937, workers in Youngstown, Niles, Massillon, and other mill towns walked out; during the weeks of the strike violence occurred. While labor employed the use of the strike and mass picketing, management, under the direction of Tom Girdler, president of Republic Steel, fought back with anti-union measures. Not only willing to fight labor but also eager to punish labor's ally, the Roosevelt administration, Girdler employed the Mohawk Valley formula, which organized public opinion against union members and made labor appear unpatriotic. The strike itself was ugly, but labor's objectives were won and the unions' voice in political affairs could no longer be ignored.

Thus, during the 1930s, Ohio's society was changed by the impact of the expanded federal power and the influence of labor in both politics and the economy. The government in Washington took on larger dimensions, and state and local government could no longer cope with issues that were national in scope. Because of its important status in an industrial state, organized labor in Ohio became an important ingredient in state politics, and it became difficult indeed for a candidate to secure an office without labor's support.

The Need for Money

UNEMPLOYMENT COMMISSION
Down to Destitution

The mere dollar deficiency does not arouse such strong protest from receivers of relief, however, as do the methods of relief giving. Be it said that we are not herein attacking the relief agencies—public or private. What can they do with such limited funds? They, indeed, are the first to deplore the methods they are forced to use to keep our unemployed alive.

Soup kitchens, bread lines, commissaries, made-work, share-the-work movements, all of these have become by-words describing the results of the present depression. But the implications in human suffering behind those words are not realities to those who have not experienced them. Destitution, as the state which a family is almost required to reach by the regulations governing our relief-giving, becomes significant only in terms of individual cases.

A charity worker tells a typical story of a man with 3 children living just outside of an Ohio city. He owns his home; a skilled mechanic—he has had no work for 18 months; his only means of getting around to find a job is an old car for which he paid $50 in the days when he was working and which formerly carried him to and from work. He and his wife and children are hungry. They need clothing, fuel, gasoline for the car so that the father can look for work. An appeal to the charities brings investigation. This family is not destitute. A car, even two alarm clocks in the house testify to that. No relief can be given until the man sells his rickety old means-of-looking-for-a-job, which at the present is worth less than $5 to anyone but him. He must even give or throw away one alarm clock. The grocery order which he receives after he has done this gives his family a poor two meals a day, perhaps only one.

. . . .

Distribution by Commissary

In Dayton, orders on retail grocery dealers were formerly used, but a commissary was opened because the first method was too expensive, and the funds available were too small to fill the need in that way. In a large 6-story warehouse food bought in carload quantities is dispensed to the jobless who have proved that they are in need. To this "charity warehouse" come the unemployed to carry

From The Ohio Commission on Unemployment Insurance, *Studies and Reports*, Part II of *Report of the Ohio Commission on Unemployment Insurance*, (Columbus, 1933), pp. 137-150.

home on sleds, wagons or in their arms, potatoes, beans and canned corn, tomatoes and spinach, apples and prunes, coffee and a butter substitute. Eggs for illness, milk or cocoa, beef or pork are also included. For 2 adults and 2 children, the relief amounts to from $22 to $25 a month, that is from $0.16 to $0.21 a day per person.

The Dayton Parent-Teacher's Association asked that children be fed at school, and it is an interesting comment on amounts of relief that practically every child who needed to be fed at school came from a family which was on the charity list.

The township trustees of Venice in Seneca County announced in July, 1932, that those asking for relief must "sell or kill or give away" all dogs and pets. Owners of automobiles leave their license plates with the trustees of the county funds while receiving help. These are merely further indication of the pauperization requisite for receiving help.

From a system of giving grocery orders to the needy, Canton changed to the commissary after a careful study of it. The public contributed subscriptions and voted public bonds. Producers gave their surplus, which was collected by community help. Goods were bought by a committee of wholesalers through Canton concerns. Milk, bread, clothing and fuel were supplied through local vendors, and a shoe merchant assisted the Community Store by purchasing wholesale shoes, fitting and issuing them through his store. Mr. Luntz, President of the Canton Welfare Federation, holds that community cooperation is responsible for the success of their Community Store. The standard order of groceries issued for families including 2 adults and 3 children for a week is as follows:

I lb. bacon square	2 lbs. macaroni
I lb. fresh beef	4 lbs. rolled oats
2 lbs. hamburg	I jar peanut butter
½ lb. cheese	I box sal soda
I lb. lard	2 quarts of milk delivered daily
I lb. oleomargarine	3 tall cans milk
I lb. soda crackers	½ lb. dried corn
I dozen eggs	5 lbs. parsnips
½ lb. cocoa	2 lbs. lettuce
½ lb. coffee	2 lbs. carrots
10 bread tickets	3 lbs. white sugar
I box matches	I peck potatoes
I No. 2½ can tomatoes	5 lbs. pastry flour
I can corn syrup	2 cakes toilet soap
I can tomato paste	2 cakes laundry soap
I pt. vinegar	
I lb. seedless raisins	

The order is varied from week to week, and costs on the average $.08 a day per person. This is a much lower rate than the expense of feeding through retail grocery stores. The 3,600 families being fed at the Community Store are assigned times to come so that they do not have to stand outside in line waiting for their "dole" of food. This food is in return for work.

. . . .

Dayton's Production Units

A Dayton group had the foresight to plan work for the unemployed on a practical local basis. As a result of this preparation by the Character Building Division of the Community Fund, Dayton has the Dayton Association of Coöperative Production Units in operation.

Because of this scheme some of the unemployed in Dayton are working, but not for wages. About 450 families are organized into 7 Production Units, varying in size from 50 to 110 families. The emphasis in these groups of unemployed is on production, although barter exists among the units and between individual units and outside individuals or groups. For instance, the East Dayton unit barters bread for groceries from the city Community store.

Besides producing bread, East Dayton mends shoes, builds furniture, makes dresses and shirts and cans goods. The Home View Unit (negro), the first unit formed, also produces clothing. Its active members number 45, and the men among them make soap, cut wood and in the summer cultivate the unit's common garden. An old colored woman spins yarn on an old-fashioned wheel, and the women upstairs in the Home View Unit house use the yarn to tie comforts. The Belmont Unit is building its own quarters out of brick from the city dump, and in the basement of this new building complete shoe machinery will be set up. The unit expects to swap shoes for soup with the Columbia Conserve Company.

Each of the 7 units has elected its general manager, executive committee and needs committee. The latter decides, after discussing it with each member family, what the relative needs of the families are and supplies them from the storeroom of the unit. A minimum number of hours at work is required of each active member, but the return to that member is measured in terms, not of hours spent or of goods produced, but of family needs.

Ohio's Relief

DAYTON FROST

Development of State Responsibility, 1931

No official recognition of the ravages of unemployment or drought was made by the State of Ohio until the latter part of 1930. This period saw the first attempts at some organized expression on the part of the state in behalf of the hunger, cold, destitution, and despair which were daily becoming more acute and more widespread.

The Governor of the state at that time, caused the formation of a voluntary Governor's Relief Committee, for the purpose of studying the situation through existing state departments. This committee, which was continued by the next administration, was composed of the directors of all state departments and a representative each from the American Red Cross and the American Legion. Later, similar relief committees were formed in many counties, each committee in turn being composed of representatives of local governmental groups and interested public and private agencies. All members served without pay and were responsible for keeping in close contact with the local situation.

The directors of state departments caused extensive reports to be made by the traveling supervisors of their respective departments. The need, as evidenced in these reports, later became the basis for the acceptance of legislation then being sponsored by several state departments. Two of the bills suggested were passed during the regular session of the 89th General Assembly. They were: (1) Senate Bill 81 passed February 11, 1931 and (2) House Bill 102 passed March 11, 1931. These two acts, together with the experience gained in their administration, were used as guides in drafting the later, more comprehensive emergency relief laws passed in 1932.

Senate Bill 81 supplemented Section 7777 of the General Code and provided that "When any board of education is satisfied that a child, compelled to attend school, is unable to do so because absolutely in want of shoes, clothing, medical attention, or other necessities, and those upon whom he is dependent are unable to support or care for themselves and the child, the given board of education shall provide such necessities as may enable the child to attend school. Upon satisfactory proof that any board of education has no funds available to meet such needs, the state director of education shall authorize the board of education to purchase such items and pay for such other necessities to the extent of the amount of money that he has approved in each individual case, and the state director of

From Dayton Frost, *Emergency Relief Administration in Ohio: 1931-1935*, (Columbus, 1936), pp. 21-28; 149-152; 205-210.

education shall authorize payment of such items from any monies appropriated for distribution by him for such purpose."

For the purposes of this section $50,000 was appropriated from the general revenue fund. The provisions of the act, however, were not effective after July 15, 1931. A later appropriation by the State Emergency Board made available an additional $15,000 for this purpose. The total amount spent from the entire $65,000 came to $56,251.39 and was encumbered by local boards of education.

. . . .

It should be noted here that state supervision of expenditures was very meager and state participation in local administration practically nil. There was, nevertheless, a faint expression of a recognized responsibility. This, together with the acknowledgment of obligation expressed in House Bill No. 102 passed the following month, laid the foundation for more extensive participation by the state.

The issuance of bonds for poor relief purposes was in itself somewhat of a departure from the usual proceedings in Ohio. Through the provisions of the Pringle-Roberts Act, nevertheless, any county, city, or township could, upon completion of the legal requirements, sell bonds or notes for such purposes. A maximum of one-twentieth of 1% of the issuing subdivisions' tax duplicate was allowed.

Poor relief purposes as outlined in Section 1 of the act included: mothers' pension payments, temporary support and medical care of transients, maintenance of the county home or the children's home, the expense of placing children in foster homes, direct relief to the indigent, burial of the indigent, and hospitalization.

. . . .

In the fall of 1931 Ohio received as its share of the proceeds of charity football games held in Chicago some $30,000 for poor relief purposes. While this money represented in effect, funds from private sources, the entire amount was made available to the Governor's Relief Committee for distribution. The bulk of these funds was spent for food, shoes and cloth which was made into garments locally by volunteer groups. All supplies were, of course, for the exclusive use of needy school children and were delivered for the most part to southeastern Ohio counties during the winter of 1931-32. The amount received from the games was later increased by an additional $25,000 appropriation from the State Emergency Board.

Emergency Legislation, 1932

From these small, unrelated beginnings the new State Relief Commission was evolved. The events leading up to actual legislation, however, were more decisive.

At a meeting in Columbus, the Mayors of Ohio' large cities drafted and presented to the Governor, their plea for assistance with a burden which was becoming increasingly impossible to support through local efforts alone and with local budgets either public or private. Community fund executives, directors, executive secretaries, and boards of responsible private relief agencies, added their reports of the impossible task facing them if state or federal aid were not made available immediately. Both national and state indexes of employment were headed downward. Factories were either closing or producing on part time schedules, and payrolls were shrinking. Extreme pessimism and despair were reported from every quarter, while newspapers carried daily reports of riots, plundering, evictions, stranded families, even suicides which were a result of the severe industrial depression enveloping the state and nation.

. . . .

Housing

Although the State Relief Commission was specifically set up to cope with the emergency relief situation, and although the Commission itself, and the general public took cognizance of the seriousness of the shelter problem, there were neither sufficient available funds nor adequate policies to meet the situation.

In the winter of 1932-1933 landlords were protesting because they felt they were being doubly penalized. They were housing relief clients for which they were being compensated inadequately, and, in addition, were expected to pay taxes promptly and maintain the property. Many landlords filed suit for eviction and many more threatened to do so. Because of this unsatisfactory situation between landlords, clients, and relief agencies, it was felt that a law which would remit the taxes on property occupied by relief clients would do much to solve the difficulty from the viewpoint of all concerned. Such a law, (Senate Bill 200) was passed by the Ohio Legislature on March 22, 1933, approved April 6th, 1933, and filed in the office of the Secretary of State on April 10th, 1933. It became effective on June 10th, 1933.

Although some of the metropolitan counties readily adopted resolutions putting into effect the provisions of this act, the landlords were still somewhat dissatisfied. Effective September 1, 1933, the State Relief Commission of Ohio formally placed into effect supplement No. 4 to Federal Emergency Relief Administration rules and regulations No. 1, governing payment of rents. This supplement provided that a small cash allowance could be granted by the county relief administrations in addition to the issuance of tax warrants for the payment of rent to owners whose property was occupied by indigent persons.

. . . .

The law and these provisions eased the situation but much confusion and dissatisfaction on the part of landlords still existed because of a lack of understanding on the part of public officials.

The Family Service Division in March, 1934, therefore, established a Housing Department which had the responsibility of effecting a better understanding of the law and its functions with boards of county commissioners and county relief administrations. Problems resulting from the administration of the law were brought to the attention of this department, which in turn secured uniform interpretations from the office of the Attorney General and from the State Relief Commission. Since the Annat Law and its supplementary cash payments allowed by the State Relief Commission were important features of the relief system in Ohio, it was used generally and for the most part effectively in every county which had a shelter problem.

The Housing Department at this time developed a Relief Housing Repair Program. This program was based upon the contemplated use of relief labor together with necessary materials to restore suitable housing properties to a sound and tenantable condition. The cash allowance granted by the State Relief Commission and the provisions of Amended Senate Bill No. 200 were a fundamental part of the scheme. Any property owner could make application to the county relief director for the benefits of the plan if his property was vacant or if occupied by a family entitled to rent relief. It provided for the rehabilitation of such properties in exchange for the use of such properties in housing unemployed families. The control of each of such properties was assigned to the county relief administration for the period of time necessary to allow the equivalent of the cost of the labor and materials needed for the repairs, plus the cash allowance, to be returned in rental value.

The repairs were made under the direction of the Works Division of the State Relief Commission and later of the Federal Emergency Relief Administration in Ohio. This repair program, as conceived and set up by the State Relief Commission, later became the model for a national program and was approved as such by the engineering division of the Federal Emergency Relief Administration.

Selection of Men for the Civilian Conservation Corps

Launching the Program. When, on March 31, 1933, the President signed the Act of Congress authorizing the establishment of the Civilian Conservation Corps, he was faced with an emergency of serious proportions. Action had to be taken to mobilize existing organizations in a cooperative effort to place one-quarter of a million young men at work within the following three months. It was natural, therefore, that the President should call on every available public relief and private welfare agency in an attempt to locate with the least possible delay, those boys who met both the qualifications of need and of fitness for vigorous outdoor work. Consequently, CCC selection work became an immediate concern of the State Relief Commission of Ohio.

The Federal Emergency Relief Administration had not yet come into existence in April, 1933, and the task of supervising the selection process was assigned on a national scale to the Department of Labor. In view of the fact that the Department of Labor had no adequate local organizations in the several states, it seemed most logical to appoint the state relief administrators (in all states where there were such) as agents in this work. For Ohio, the Secretary of Labor appointed the Executive Director of the State Relief Commission to fill this position.

Inasmuch as the Relief Commission was at that time a small organization which was distributing state relief funds to counties without intensive supervision, it did not possess any adequate state-wide organization through which it could operate quickly and surely in response to a sudden request for 12,536 juniors (18 to 25 years of age) and 1,084 "local experienced men". It was necessary, therefore, to designate Red Cross agencies, private welfare agencies, and municipal officials in addition to the chairman of county relief committees as agents of the Department of Labor and the State Relief Commission. The field representatives of the Relief Commission were instructed to cover the counties in their districts quickly and locate the most appropriate agent or agency to do the work of selection. Within three weeks the Commission had an organization established with a selecting agent in each county of the state.

The actual acceptance and enrollment operations for these 13,620 young men were held between May 26 and July 1, 1933. They were given preliminary physical examinations at "acceptance stations"—usually National Guard Armories—and were examined more thoroughly when they reached camp. Large numbers of them were sent to Fort Knox, Kentucky, to undergo a "reconditioning" period preparatory to strenuous work, for many of the boys were seriously undernourished and needed a "breaking in" period.

During this early selection work it was thought inadvisable to make strict eligibility regulations permitting selection of boys from relief rolls only, partly because of the fact that there were huge numbers of very needy people for whom no relief was being provided and partly because the enrollment work had to be done so quickly that thorough investigation of the financial circumstances of each family could not be accomplished in the brief time available. Preference was given, of course, to those who were definitely known to be on the public relief rolls. In spite of the hasty selection work, however, the class of boys was good and their need was unquestionably great.

By July, 1933, Ohio had filled its quota of 13,620 young men. The main rush was over.

. . . .

It is obvious that the program in Ohio has assumed important proportions. Over 68,000 Ohio boys, 17-28 years of age, have been enrolled in the Civilian Conservation Corps during the three years of its operation. Most of these boys fall in the younger age groups. Until the fall of 1935, when the minimum age requirement was reduced from 18 to 17 years, approximately 37% of all the boys going into CCC camps were 18 years of age and two-thirds of all the boys were either 18, 19, or 20. Only 1.5% of them were 28 years old. After the reduction of the age minimum to 17 years, the concentration of younger boys in camp became more pronounced, as would be expected. Three-quarters of the boys were 20 years of age or younger, and only one-quarter were 21 to 28, inclusive.

Inasmuch as each CCC enrollee is required to send $25 per month to a needy dependent, called his allottee, the allotments of fifteen or twenty thousand boys represent a sizeable amount of money and are a very appreciable factor in reducing the relief loads of the respective county relief administrations. It is estimated that nearly $5,000,000 in the form of CCC allotments was returned to parents and other dependents of Ohio enrollees during the year 1935 as a result of the work done by the boys. This is in addition to the $5.00 per month received by the boys in camp and the large expenditures for the food, clothing and shelter of the boys in camp. The various county relief directors in the state have seemed especially appreciative of the CCC program in recent months when their relief loads were more than they could handle adequately with the funds at their disposal.

In addition to the monetary benefits it is important to mention briefly the other benefits derived by CCC boys from camp life and the part played by the Federal Emergency Relief Administration in attempting to help the boys continue the progress begun in camp, after their return. From a social work standpoint, it is hard to conceive of a more wholesome combination of factors for young boys than is brought together in this CCC program. Besides reducing markedly the crime and delinquency rates, camp life builds the boys up physically, teaches them to work, and frequently gives them valuable vocational and avocational training. With the thought that these CCC boys are due for a difficult and frequently discouraging time after their return from camp, the Federal Emergency Relief

Administration has encouraged the local selecting agents to do all they can to help the boys readjust themselves to their local communities.

Controversy Over Relief

MARTIN DAVEY

Gov. Martin L. Davey tonight carried his relief administration controversy with the federal government direct to the people of Ohio. In a speech broadcast over the state he charged that "autocratic federal control" of relief administration in the state "extends even to the expenditure of money furnished by the state of Ohio."

Says It Was Campaign Issue

The text of the governor's address follows:

"There has been so much misrepresentation through unfriendly channels and partisan opponents regarding the relief situation in Ohio that it has become necessary for me to go directly to you, the people of this state, with a clear statement of the facts. These clever and none too scrupulous opponents have attempted to divert the minds of the people from the real issues, and have tried to charge me with the very things of which they themselves are guilty.

"Many of you will recall that I made an issue of this relief situation in the campaign last year and discussed it with perfect candor in almost every county in Ohio. I made a solemn promise to the people of Ohio to correct the abuses and to eliminate the waste and inefficiency.

"Soon after the inauguration I discovered that the state government of Ohio has no power whatever in connection with the relief program. All the rules are made by theorists in Washington and other theorists in Columbus who are the agents of the federal government. All policies are determined in Washington and executed through their Columbus agents.

From *Cleveland Plain Dealer*, March 10, 1935.

Can't Correct Evils, He Holds

"The so-called state relief director has been required to get approval of every little act from the federal agents. The so-called state relief commission had no power to operate, except under the direction and with the approval of the federal agents in Columbus, acting on instructions from Washington. This autocratic federal control extends even to the expenditure of money furnished by the state of Ohio.

"Therefore, neither myself as governor nor any agent of the state of Ohio has the slightest possibility of correcting any of the evils and waste and inefficiency that give rise to such widespread complaints. I am wholly unable to keep an earnest campaign promise to clean up this situation.

"For these reasons, I have requested Mr. Hopkins, federal emergency relief administrator, Washington, D.C., to assume the full public responsibility for the things that he does behind the scenes. He and his agents exercise complete control, and I insist that they must assume public responsibility. I will not continue to take the blame, which is state-wide in its scope, with no power to correct the causes of these complaints.

"All that I am now asking is that Mr. Hopkins be frank enough and courageous enough to put his own name on the front door as general manager. This act will not change the situation one particle, because he is the autocratic general manager, anyway, behind the scenes. I am asking that he admit it publicly.

Calls Walls of Highest Grade

"It is not my purpose to evade responsibility, because I have never been guilty of such a thing in my life. I was perfectly willing to take all the blame that goes with executive power, but when there is not the slightest power lodged in the governor to correct the abuses and the waste I am not willing to assume public responsibility for what is going on.

"In order to do the kind of job that seems so necessary and urgent I selected as state relief director one of the highest grade men in Ohio—a man of fine intelligence, unimpeachable integrity and great executive capacity. He is a man whom I have known for many years, and who has the universal respect of the many thousands who know him. He happens to be an independent Republican, and I thought that this fact would guarantee us against any charge of partisanship.

"Mr. Hopkins finally accepted him reluctantly, but Mr. Walls, fine gentleman and great executive that he is, found his hands completely tied, because the federal agents in Columbus continue to decide every little move. I am insisting that the federal authorities pull the curtains aside and let the public know that they, and they alone, are running this show.

"This brings us to another important point. There are too many theorists in this relief setup. These theorists have developed a set of requirements for case workers that eliminate almost everyone who is not a graduate from a college or university and who has not had special training in welfare work. The result is that most of the persons employed on a salaried basis in the last year or more have been young college girls, most of whom have been reared in protected circumstances and who have little or no practical experience with life.

"Nearly all of you citizens of Ohio who are now listening to this discussion would be barred from these salaried positions, no matter how desperately you might need the employment, or how well qualified you are from a practical standpoint. Just consider your own situation. You have intelligence and good character. You have had to battle with the problems of life. This experience has given you a large measure of common sense. It may be that you desperately need employment. You don't want charity. You are willing and anxious to work to earn your livelihood.

"And yet the job that you so seriously need, and for which you many times pray, must be given, under the rule of the theorists, to some young, inexperienced person, who comes from a family of wealthy or well-to-do people and who has taken up social welfare work as a temporary adventure.

"There are literally tens of thousands of the finest citizens in Ohio of mature years who need this work and who could do a much better job from a practical standpoint. This includes heads of families, former business and professional men and women, widows with children to support. But no matter how fine and useful a life you have lived, no matter how capable and industrious you may be, all of you are barred from these relief jobs, and some young theorist who probably does not need the work is put in your place.

"The serious situation in the Ohio relief program may not be well known in the larger cities, because most of the people there are not in a position to see what is going on. But the people in at least 75 of the 88 counties know what I am talking about.

"One of the most serious complaints in most of the counties in Ohio is the fact that strangers have been sent in there to administer their relief problems—strange administrators, strange case workers, who do not know the local people and their history. The result is that some of the most needy and worthy citizens are neglected and subjected to humiliation.

"Many people who have lived lives of industry and thrift are forced to sell their little remaining property and give up their little life insurance policies before they can have bread. At the same time the chiselers who are always persistent, get on the relief rolls. Of course most of the people on relief are worthy and ought to be there.

"The whole philosophy under which this relief program is administered puts a premium on pauperism and penalizes thrift. It humiliates the industrious citizen who has a little something left but who has no bread in the house.

Quotes Township Officials

"One of the things most urgently needed in this relief program is to put the administration of it back where it belongs—in the hands of the respected civic leaders and township trustees who know their people. Only in this way can the program be administered on a proper basis of humaneness and economy.

"At this point I wish to read a significant telegram sent to Mr. Hopkins by the president and secretary of the Township Trustees and Clerks of Ohio, an organization representing over 5,000 elected local officials.

" 'The Ohio State Association of Township Trustees and Clerks, composed of publicly elected officials throughout the 1,339 townships in the state, is opposed to the present centralized relief setup as it is being administered in Ohio. Township officials have had years of experience in performing their duties under the laws of Ohio in caring for distressed people. From such experience and from close contact with existing conditions, we agree with our governor, Martin L. Davey, that the present system is cluttered with waste, inefficiency and unnecessary red tape.

" 'As representatives of the taxpayers in our respective townships and as public officials interested in the welfare of distressed people, we urge federal action to remedy this deplorable condition. It is unfair to demand further taxation of our people, knowing such conditions exist. We desire to co-operate and work with the federal government in bringing about a proficient and economic administration of relief funds, but we vigorously protest conditions now existing in Ohio.'

"This policy of sending strangers into most of the counties of Ohio as administrators and case workers is responsible for many of the conditions that give rise to complaint. Let me give you a few illustrations.

"Some reliable friends of mine came in the office last week from one Ohio county and told me that the relief administrator there had frequent drinking parties in the office at night and kept the lights burning with his parties until late hours.

"Reliable friends from another county told me that the stranger in charge required the girls in the office to go out on parties with him in order to keep their jobs.

"Some equally reliable friends give me the interesting information that in one of the larger cities the stranger in charge there is intoxicated much of the time and follows the same tactics with the women employes.

"And yet we are powerless to correct any of these conditions until the state relief director is able to sell the federal agents the idea that something simply must be done.

"From another county, the report comes to me from reliable sources that some two or three dozen people have just recently been taken off the relief rolls who have been regularly employed and not entitled to relief.

"Township trustees tell of the excessive relief load in language like this: 'When we were handling relief in our township we had 23 people on relief. And now they have 83.'

Deposit Checks, He Says

"From other sources I learn that certain people are depositing relief checks in their postal savings accounts. I learn, also, that in some cases some unworthy people secure grocery orders and sell them for cash at a big discount, to use the money for other purposes.

"Let me make myself entirely clear. The great majority of the people receiving relief need it and deserve it. And I applaud with enthusiasm the humane purposes of this program. It is right for the government to help its good citizens who are in distress through no fault of their own. And I am for that part of the program 100 per cent.

"One of the worst causes that give rise to complaints is the excessive number of silly reports that the case workers are required to make. Of course, every safeguard should be thrown about the expenditure of public funds, and no worthy public official would want it any other way. But after this has been done, most of the other reports are so superfluous, impractical and theoretical that they are absurd. It takes at least half the time of the case workers to make out this multitude of reports. Some of the workers spend nearly all of their time making out reports, and of course, they report what the higher officials want to see.

"The result is that they have very little time to go out and visit the people whom they are supposed to serve. Tens of thousands of the people on relief are not visited oftener than once in two, three or four months. The case workers cannot hope to know conditions because the whole picture can change in that length of time. No wonder these conditions continue to exist that give rise to complaints.

Only 2 Things Needed, He Holds

"In many instances there are as many as a half dozen case workers calling on people in one city block. There is probably some theoretical reason for this like the difference in temperament of the people called upon, but that is a perfectly silly idea.

"This problem of relief is a very practical one. It involves two major questions. First, do the people really need relief, and, second are they actually entitled to it? This program needs to be simplified so that the case workers can have time to call on the people and find out these simple facts eliminating all the foolish and irrelevant questions that they are required to ask.

"The program of the relief workers needs to be systematized so that they can see more people per day and see all of their people much more frequently. It needs to eliminate the impractical theorists. The relief program ought to avail itself of the fine citizenship of this state, men and women of intelligence and character and experience with life, and some maturity of judgment, people who are industrious and will go out and do the work with a genuine interest in the problem.

"However, the chiselers ought to be eliminated, and the carelessness and waste should be brought to an abrupt stop. One friend of mine told me of a case where a man and his wife own four houses, living in one and receiving rent from the other three. The wife works at housework and the husband is a janitor. And yet they are receiving relief, to which they are not entitled.

"At the same time there are many cases of the finest citizens in Ohio who are temporarily in distress and who cannot receive attention to their problems because of the everlasting delays in the work of investigation. Then when these worthy cases finally are reached, after exasperating and distressing delay, they are subjected to humiliation and required to sell everything they have left and be reduced to pauperism before the unpractical and inhuman relief program will give them a little bread and butter.

"What are the causes of these conditions. One cause has already been discussed, this policy of sending strangers into the counties who do not know the people. Another has already been discussed, the policy of employing as case workers only young, inexperienced theorists.

"From Cincinnati comes the complaint that some of the relief officials are citizens and residents of Kentucky, that one of the relief officials is not an American citizen but a British subject and that many of the people on relief are not citizens of Ohio but have come from other states because it is easier to get on relief here than where they came from.

"Relief conditions in Toledo and Youngstown are known to be bad. The strangers that were formerly put in charge in those cities have been guilty of lax methods. Perhaps a public investigation in those cities would be a wholesome thing, and I am inclined to believe that such public investigations might prove more than interesting.

. . . .

Wants "Disillusioning Evidence"

"The relief program in Ohio costs $10,000,000 a month. Cleveland has about one-sixth of the population and is using one-fourth of the money in spite of the fact that employment is said to be substantially on the increase. I realize that Cleveland has been hard hit in the depression, industrially and also through large bank failures. But there are many other cities and towns that have been hit just about as hard and in the same way in proportion to population.

. . . .

"Now comes the question of civil service as applied to relief workers. May I call your attention to the name under which the national relief program is conducted, the Federal Emergency Relief Administration? This was supposed to be a temporary emergency undertaking. It was not intended to be a permanent structure. God forbid that it should have to be.

"No Need for Civil Service"

"For this very reason the relief workers were not put under civil service in any state in this Union. Why should they be? There is not the slightest justification for attempting to set up a permanent relief organization. If the recovery program works, as we have reason to hope and expect, the relief problem should rapidly disappear for the most part.

"Do you, the taxpayers of Ohio, want a good many thousand additional employes saddled on your backs permanently by putting them under civil service? Do you not have struggle enough out of your impoverished resources and income to pay present taxes and interest and upkeep expense and have some thing left for food and clothes and other necessities?

" . . . My own judgment is that as rapidly as possible this whole relief program ought to be put in charge of the local communities to be administered by respected citizens in co-operation with elected officials. This hypocritical talk about the sacredness of civil service as applied to the relief program is a clever piece of trickery to divert the attention of the people from a bad situation.

Denies Playing Politics

"Another example of hypocrisy and malicious misrepresentation is the untruthful charge that I have been trying to play politics with the relief program for the exclusive purpose of finding jobs for Democrats. Well, suppose we see what the situation is.

"In Miami County, down in southwestern Ohio, there are eighteen salaried employes in the county relief office. All eighteen of them are Republicans. Not one Democrat among them. I ask you, in all fairness, is this non-partisan? Up in Logan County, in west-central Ohio, there are 27 salaried employes in the relief office and just one lone Democrat receiving $60 per month. I ask you again, is this non-partisan?

"Down in southeastern Ohio we find a similar situation in Noble County. With 22 salaried employes there are only four Democrats. Is that non-partisan? In Carroll County, over in eastern Ohio, there are 22 salaried employes and only four Democrats among them. Would you call that non-partisan? Up in Youngstown there are 262 salaried employes and only sixteen Democrats.

. . . .

"Worse than this, I could show you an imposing list of active Republican politicians holding these salaried jobs, and never permitting the Democrats of Ohio to have a fair break. I can produce plenty of evidence that these Republican politicians are regularly playing politics with the relief program.

"What makes it a virtue for Republican politicians to play politics and to practically exclude the Democrats from participation? What makes it such a crime for the fine Democratic people of Ohio to ask for a 50-50 break on this program?

. . . .

"If Mr. Hopkins wants to tolerate the abuses, the waste, the inefficiency and the favoritism, he has that right; but he must take his place before the people of Ohio as the one solely responsible. I am absolutely unwilling to take the blame for the intolerable conditions which he alone controls and permits to exist.

"We have a grave financial problem that I want you, the hard-pressed taxpayers of Ohio, to be familiar with and to ponder very seriously. By close planning the state government can just barely balance its budget. Under our Constitution we cannot borrow money in excess of $750,000 without a vote of the people and all of that borrowing power was exhausted in the last administration. Therefore, we have no borrowing power unless the people wish to provide it by a popular vote. We cannot coin money. We cannot pick it off the bushes. The only way we can get money for the state is through taxation.

"The federal government requires the state of Ohio to furnish $2,000,000 per month for relief. That makes $24,000,000 a year. Only $9,000,000 of this has been provided. Therefore, we have a deficit of $15,000,000 if we are to continue to contribute our portion of the relief funds for the balance of the year.

"In addition to this, we must somehow provide another $6,000,000 for old age pensions because only half enough has already been provided; in addition to this, there is an urgent need for $5,000,000 or $10,000,000 to eliminate the fire traps in the state institutions and provide additional facilities where they are so seriously overcrowded.

Calls Schools Liberties' Citadels

"But more than anything else, we must somehow produce an undetermined number of millions more for the schools of Ohio. Our schools are probably the most important public institutions we have. They are the citadel of our liberties. They cannot be permitted to close or be seriously curtailed. The Constitution of Ohio guarantees and requires education for our children. However, in order to make sure that our schools will continue to function it will take more millions of dollars than are now in sight.

"I do not propose to shirk the responsibility that lies in the governor's office to help provide a program and the necessary revenues to carry on these essential things. But I believe that we have no moral right to ask the hard-pressed taxpayers of Ohio to take on an additional tax burden unless we practice economy and eliminate waste and unnecessary cost everywhere.

. . . .

"But here we have this wasteful and inefficient relief program, into which we are required to pour another $15,000,000 that must be wrung from the hard-pressed taxpayers of this state on orders from Mr. Hopkins. He says, in so many words, that unless we furnish $2,000,000 a month he will not furnish the $8,000,000 that he has been sending to Ohio.

"My answer to him is this. If you will be courageous enough and fair enough to eliminate the inexcusable waste and inefficiency in the Ohio relief program the people of this state will be willing to dig down into their thinly-lined pockets and contribute their share through new taxes, if necessary, to maintain a businesslike, economical and humane relief program in this state.

"My friends, I have tried to make this situation and the vital issues involved just as clear as my command of the English language will permit. There are vital issues involved. There are important principles at stake. It is my purpose to be the champion of equal justice, of economical and humane government and of common sense and the enduring virtues in public affairs.

"I propose to stand firmly as the protector of the taxpayer of Ohio against waste and inefficiency and loose management. I propose to remain steadfast in that position, and will welcome the support of all straight-thinking people in Ohio."

More Controversy Over Relief

JOHN W. BRICKER

I doubly appreciate this opportunity to meet with you tonight, because it affords me the high privilege of assuring you all that *Ohio is still there!*

We have not been taken over by the White House or the Department of the Interior.

It will be my official duty, in the course of these brief remarks tonight, to correct these critics of Ohio with facts from the official records of Ohio.

. . . .

When I took office last January there was a deficit of over forty million dollars. I know that is petty cash as deficits go in Washington, but it is the biggest one Ohio ever had.

From Address of John W. Bricker, Governor of Ohio, The Ohio Society of New York at the Pennsylvania Hotel, New York City, New York, December 16, 1939. John W. Bricker Papers, Box 74, Ohio Historical Society, Columbus, Ohio. Reprinted by permission of John W. Bricker.

Faced with that financial picture and bound by platform pledges to provide adequate relief, balance the budget, and impose no new taxes, the legislature met and the new administration was inaugurated. I consider platform pledges and campaign promises binding obligations and those promises and pledges are being kept.

During this year, Ohio will meet the increased needs of an expanded educational, health and welfare program to the extent of over eight million dollars more than was spent last year, and at the same time will reduce the deficit by more than eight million dollars. Every obligation of the state incurred this year has been paid promptly when due. We have changed Ohio from a deficit state to a pay-as-you-go state.

. . . .

This year the state pay roll and office maintenance costs of all state departments will be nearly ten million dollars less than last year. Through these savings Ohio has met all the requirements of government, has been able to make increased contributions for education, relief, and old age pensions,—and that without one cent of new taxes or any increase of existing taxes.

I come now to the subject of relief. Because of propaganda, false statements and political interference from the outside a great deal of attention has been directed to Ohio relief in the past few weeks. At the beginning of this year we improved the system of administering relief in Ohio and provided for the distribution of funds granted by the state upon a basis of need rather than geography. Many counties in Ohio have practically no relief problem. Under the preceding administration they had been receiving relief grants from the state to the detriment of those communities that did need the funds. A complete investigation was made by the Legislature, extensive hearings were held, and based upon past experiences and anticipated needs, the Legislature appropriated ten million dollars for each year of the biennium to be distributed directly to local governments for relief.

As a part of Ohio's relief program the Legislature reduced the vote required this year on relief levies in cities from sixty-five per cent to fifty per cent. It also authorized the use of twenty-five per cent of the local government's auto license tax fund for the purpose of relief. It also eliminated restrictions on the use of certain local revenues and thus made them available for relief purposes. Thus the Legislature greatly enlarged the potential resources of local communities available for relief.

Let it be understood by all that the responsibility for work relief has been assumed and is now controlled by the federal government, operating largely through WPA. Even in that program controlled and

administered by the federal government, local communities are required to contribute. During the past year WPA employment in Ohio
has been cut by Washington fifty-three and six-tenths percent while
the average reduction for the whole United States for the same
period was only forty-three and nine-tenths percent. That discrepancy is not justified by any consideration of relief needs. That
picture would indicate that Ohio is being punished. Why? Is it
because Ohio voted Republican last year?

That, however, is not the most sordid aspect of the political
manipulation of WPA by Washington. In Cleveland in October of
1938, a congressional election year, during the month immediately
preceding election day, there were seventy-four thousand two hundred and twenty-five on WPA. A year later there were less than thirty
thousand on WPA in Cleveland; a cut of over sixty per cent. The
biggest cut in Ohio WPA employment was in Cleveland, the very
place that relief needs are greatest. The state has recognized this fact
and has distributed this year, thirty per cent of the state's total relief
appropriation to Cleveland's county although that county contains
only about thirteen per cent of Ohio's population.

Throughout all these months, by resolution and by visits of the
mayor of Cleveland to the national administration, requests were
made, demands were sent that this discrimination by WPA against
Cleveland must cease. As this process of punishing Cleveland continued after the election last year, the state relief rolls in Cleveland
steadily increased. They increased from fifteen thousand seven hundred and forty-four cases in October, 1938, to twenty-eight thousand
and sixty cases in October, 1939. Keep ever in mind that WPA is the
federal program and direct relief is carried at the cost of the state and
local communities.

In addition to this discrimination against Ohio and particularly
Cleveland there was another unfair, and I think premeditated, action
on the part of the Federal Works Progress Administration. In Cleveland and elsewhere in Ohio others than employable relief clients were
placed on the WPA rolls, although the federal law requires that
preference shall be determined on a basis of relative need.

You have probably all read the President's statement at his press
conference last week in which he said that substantially all of
Cleveland's employables who were willing to work were being taken
care of under WPA programs.

Here are the facts: Out of a total of twenty-five thousand persons
employed by WPA the first ten months of this year in Cleveland only
nine thousand four hundred and fifty-four persons were employed
from the active relief rolls—only a little over one-third.

In October alone this year, out of twenty-eight thousand on the
direct relief rolls in Cleveland, there were six thousand eight hundred

employable persons certified for WPA, but not employed by WPA. These are the figures, and these are the bald facts of the employment on WPA of those not in need of relief, while thousands of employables are on relief and must remain on relief.

When the state welfare director initiated a program to remedy this situation in WPA at Cleveland, and insisted that employable relief cases should be given preference in WPA employment—and that political patronage must cease—the promise was made that these things would be done.

I hope those promises will be kept.

Upon the insistent demands of the state administration, upon the revelation of discriminatory treatment which Cleveland and Ohio have received, the federal government seemed suddenly to realize the vulnerability of its position. So after the state had made available in cash approximately four-hundred and fifty thousand dollars additional for Cleveland, and after the city had its proceedings under way for the issuance of over a million dollars of relief bonds, as suggested by the state administration—then, with a flourish of sensationalism, in rushed the federal government with carloads of food and allotments of WPA funds which should have been available months ago.

Ohio this year has increased her appropriation for general welfare and public assistance out of state and local funds. Ohio and Cleveland have taken care of their people, but the federal government has failed miserably in Ohio. There are only two answers to be given for this discrimination. It was either a deliberate attempt to unfairly cut the WPA employment in Ohio as a punishment for not voting right last year, or as an embarrassment to a Republican administration. Possibly it was for the purpose of creating such a situation that the federal administration, with a demagogic gesture of rushing to the rescue, could take credit where blame was due.

The people of America must awaken to a realization of how far this federal administration will go in playing politics with human misery and relief—how far it will go in its attempt to smear the good name of a state or an administration which dares to do a good job financially as well as in social service.

The issue is clear-cut! Shall relief, including work-relief, WPA, or whatever it may be called, be administered honestly, fairly, with due regard to the needs of the people, or shall it be administered as a political racket—padding the WPA rolls in election years, and forgetting the needs in non-election years, carrying the burden so the federal government can take credit when a national election is on, and passing the buck back to the states and local communities in the other years? This is a question which the American people must answer; and in it is involved a fundamental question of public morals. . . .

There have been attacks made on Ohio, and on me personally. Most New Dealers have contempt for any government authority or public official who does balance a budget, who does administer relief honestly, who does save public money, or who shows any interest whatever in the taxpayer. No, it is the political discrimination of the national administration against Ohio—obviously for the purpose of discrediting a state administration—that caused the trouble.

This is the story of federal relief for seven years. First it was C.W.A., next it was F.E.R.A., then it was P.W.A., and finally it was W.P.A. At every change the states were supposed to alter their programs to conform to the most recent experiment out of Washington. In these transitions the needy suffered unnecessarily.

The Nation is confronted, therefore, with a demand for a constructive and stable national program of public assistance. The system of Federal control and domination in each relief area of the United States should be reformed. Work relief programs in the various states should be administered locally, and financed by local, state and federal participation, with the assistance of federal grants in the same manner as prevails in all other public assistance programs.

. . . .

As Governor of Ohio, I do not propose to condone with official silence a scheme of political manipulation which threatens the very integrity of the ballot, simply because that scheme has been bundled up in the glittering trappings of official demagoguery and offered to the nation in the name of relief.

It is not in my heart to flinch before a public crack-down from the White House simply because I have refused steadfastly to permit the administration of public assistance in the state of Ohio to become the football of disgraceful partisan politics in Washington, New York, and the Department of the Interior.

Farming in Ohio, 1932-1937

JOHN McSWEENEY

Mr. Speaker, I have asked leave to extend my remarks to include a report of the Department of Agriculture under the Agricultural

Adjustment Administration relative to the farming situation in Ohio.

Since my earliest service in the Congress from 1922 to 1928, when I was a member of the Committee on Agriculture, I have been deeply interested in some type of agricultural program which I thought would benefit the farmer without being harmful to the other diversified interests of Ohio. In fact, I was among the few Representatives from Ohio who supported the McNary-Haugen bill, which I felt at that time was a very fine agricultural program. During my present service in the Congress as Representative at Large I have supported many of the agricultural bills. I have been somewhat worried as to the results of this legislation, which, like any other legislation, will have its faults. But I am inserting this report from the Department, which gives me a great deal of encouragement and makes me feel that the plan has been of some benefit.

I am sure the milk producers, the poultrymen, and others will feel that these statistics are at least encouraging. I am anxious for suggestions from my fellow citizens of Ohio as to how the present program could be improved or changed for their benefit.

The report is as follows:

I. Comparison of Data

Farm cash income in Ohio rose from $157,138,000 in 1932 to $355,553,000 in 1937, an increase of 126 percent. Indications are for an income in 1938 considerably lower than in 1937. Of the 1937 income, $8,813,000 was in Government payments to farmers.

Ohio's Part in the National Gain. The extent of change in the economic situation of Ohio farmers during the 1932-37 period is indicated by the greatly increased income from the leading farm commodities produced in the State.

Ohio dairymen's income from milk rose from $42,569,000 in 1932 to $77,890,000 in 1937. This was a gain to producers of $35,321,000.

Cash income of corn-hog producers also showed encouraging upturns from 1932 to 1937, increasing $55,648,000, or from $34,442,000 to $91,090,000.

Poultry producers likewise profited from increased income during this period. Cash income from chickens and eggs in 1932 was $24,173,000. In 1937 it went up $14,640,000 to $38,813,000.

Ohio beef producers' cash income in 1932 was $12,169,000. In 1937 it advanced 182 percent to $34,362,000. This was a $22,193,000 gain.

Income of Ohio farmers from other commodities showed similar

From John McSweeney, "The Farming Situation in Ohio, 1932-37," *Congressional Record,* Vol. 83, 57th Congress, 3rd Session, pp. 2846-2849.

increases from 1932 to 1937. Wheat income rose from $8,471,000 to $35,500,000, a $27,029,000 gain. That from oats increased $840,000; that from hay, $2,830,000; that from potatoes, $2,175,000; that from apples, $3,041,000; and that from sheep and lambs, $3,118,000.

Price changes from 1932 to 1936 on the leading farm commodities in the State, which brought about a considerable part of the increased income indicated above, are shown below:

Table 1.—*Average prices received by Ohio farmers for commodities listed, in 1932 and in 1936*

Commodity	Unit	1932	1936
Wheat	Bushel	$0.47	$1.05
Corn	do	.32	.99
Oats	do	.18	.44
Barley	do	.25	.71
Rye	do	.32	.79
Buckwheat	do	.44	.88
Potatoes	do	.53	1.16
Hay (all)	Ton	[1] 4.70	[1] 11.40
Apples	Bushel	.64	1.25
Hogs	Hundredweight	3.70	9.90
Beef cattle	do	4.65	7.10
Veal calves	do	5.60	9.00
Chickens	Pound	.111	.159
Butter	do	.21	.32
Eggs	Dozen	.141	.217
Wool	Pound	.10	.29
Tobacco	do	.067	.146

[1] Dec. 1 price.

Farm Real-Estate Values Up. Along with rising farm income, Ohio farm real-estate values have mounted and taxes have declined. In this State the decline in value of farm real estate per acre, which began in 1921, halted for the first time in the year ending March 1933, when it stood at a low of 59 percent of pre-war. From this low the estimated value per acre rose to 75 percent of pre-war for the year ending March 1937. Ohio farmers as a whole, therefore, found their real estate worth about 27 percent more early in 1937 than in the first quarter of 1933.

Fewer Ohio farmers were forced into sales or transfers of their lands and more were able to make voluntary transactions. The number of forced farm sales per thousand declined from 34.1 for the year ending March 1933 to 14.4 for that ending in March 1937. Voluntary trades and sales during the same period increased from 16 to 36.3 per thousand farms.

Bankruptcies among farmers in the United States numbered 2,479 in the year ending June 30, 1937, according to an analysis by the Bureau of Agricultural Economics based on reports to the Attorney General. This number represented a 58-percent decrease from the 5,917 bankruptcies in the fiscal year ending June 30, 1933. In Ohio during this period they dropped from a total of 644 to 146.

In 1932 taxes on Ohio farm real estate reached what was probably their all-time peak in relation to value, when they stood at $2 per $100 of value. By 1936 they had fallen to $1 per $100. Figures for 1937 are not yet available.

Farm Wage Rates Higher.   Wage earners on Ohio farms, as well as landlords and tenants, found their income increasing. On April 1, 1933, the average monthly farm rate per person with board was $15.75. Four years later it was $26.75, having advanced 70 percent above the 1933 level.

II. Agricultural Adjustment Programs the Basis

The production-adjustment programs of the A. A. A., with other recovery measures, were the basis for the marked agricultural change from 1933 to 1937.

Under these programs 236,988 crop-adjustment contracts from Ohio farmers were accepted by the A. A. A. Of these contracts 27,648 were tobacco, 110,200 corn-hog, 13,065 sugar beet, and 86,075 wheat.

Under the terms of these contracts Ohio farmers shifted many acres from the production of soil-depleting cash crops, in which price-depressing surpluses existed, to production of other crops which were soil conserving or soil improving in nature.

The agricultural adjustment programs, from their beginning in 1933, were concerned with good use of the land as well as with adjusting production to effective demand. It was recognized from the start that relieving a portion of the farm land from the soil-exhausting burden of surplus-crop production offered a chance to put this land to soil-conserving uses which farm specialists for many years had been advocating.

Adjustment contracts included provisions encouraging beneficial uses for acreage taken out of surplus crops. The first corn-hog contract—that for the 1934 crop year—authorized use of the rented acres "for planting additional permanent pasturage; for soil-improving and erosion-preventing crops not to be harvested; for resting or fallowing the land; for weed eradication; or for planting farm woodlots." The first wheat contract contained similar provisions regarding the rented acreage.

In the 1934 crop year, the first in which adjustment programs were in full operation, the Nation's farmers agreed to shift their production on nearly 36,000,000 acres, or one-ninth of all the cultivated land in the country. Farmers in Ohio shifted more than 590,000 acres from corn, wheat, and tobacco. Of the 36,000,000 shifted acres in the United States, about one-third was put in pasture or meadow crops, and one-third into emergency forage crops and crops that supplied food and feed for home use. The remaining one-third was fallowed to conserve moisture and control weeds, planted to farm wood lots, or left idle. The acreage left idle was very small.

Adjustment measures were undertaken only after cotton, tobacco, wheat, and corn-hog producers had indicated their approval by means of democratic referenda.

Ohio farmers further evidenced their cooperation in the early adjustment programs by their votes in four referenda on these and related measures. During the first 2 weeks of October 1934 corn-hog producers were asked whether they favored an adjustment program for 1935. In this referendum Ohio producers numbering 16,753 voted for a program, while 12,704 voted against. A Nation-wide wheat referendum was conducted on May 25, 1935, in which producers were asked, "Are you in favor of a wheat-production control program to follow the present one which expires with the 1935 crop year?" In Ohio 20,407 votes were cast, with 14,688 favoring the program.

In the summer of 1935 producers of flue-cured, burley, fire-cured, dark air-cured, and cigar-leaf tobacco were asked whether they favored a production-adjustment program to follow the one which expired with the crop year 1935. Burley producers in Ohio favored a program for 1936, by a vote of 3,332 to 510. Cigar-leaf growers favored a 1936 program by 2,360 to 218. The last early adjustment referendum held in Ohio was that conducted on October 26, 1935, in which corn-hog producers were asked whether they favored a corn-hog program for 1936. Returns showed 35,116 in favor of such a program, and 6,237 opposed.

The result of these A. A. A. programs and of the droughts of 1934 and 1936 was to reduce price-depressing surpluses of most major farm commodities to approximately normal carry-over levels.

. . . .

Under the adjustment programs through December 31, 1937,

rental-benefit payments to producers of farm commodities were: Tobacco, $2,331,183.60; rye, $42.92; corn-hogs, $24,683,664.56; wheat, $6,262,922.72; and sugar beets, $1,409,174.02.

III. The Soil-Conservation Programs

Because the national economic emergency of 1932-33 was due largely to burdensome surpluses of farm commodities, the Agricultural Adjustment Act of 1933 had emphasized production-control as a means of restoring farm purchasing power and thereby relieving the emergency. By 1936 farm purchasing power, based on cash income from marketings, was about 40 percent greater than for 1932. Because of the adjustment programs and two severe droughts, surpluses had been considerably reduced. This lessening of the emergency, and the Supreme Court's decision in the Hoosac Mills case on January 6, 1936, which invalidated the A. A. A. production-control programs, paved the way for a long-time soil-conservation program. This program was based on the Soil Conservation and Domestic Allotment Act, approved February 29, 1936, which emphasized soil conservation rather than production adjustment.

. . . .

The 1936 Agricultural Conservation Program. About 4,000,000 farmers in all parts of the Nation, members of about 2,700 county conservation associations, participated in the 1936 agricultural conservation program. Under this program two types of payments were offered to farmers for positive performance in conserving and improving their farm land. Soil-conserving payments were made for shifting acreage from soil-depleting to soil-conserving crops in 1936. Soil-building payments were made for 1936 seedings of soil-building crops, and for approved soil-building practices.

. . . .

In Ohio about 126,700 farmers, organized into 88 county associations, participated in the 1936 program. Of the total Ohio cropland, about 63 percent, or 8,091,400 acres, was covered by applications for payments. The acreage diverted from soil-depleting crops (10,854 from tobacco and 448,737 from other crops) totaled 459,591 acres. Soil-building practices were put into effect on about 2,006,530 acres, as follows: New seedings of legumes and legume mixtures, perennial grasses for pasture, and green-manure crops, 1,859,114 acres; fertilizer and lime applications, 147,264 acres; and forest tree plantings, 152 acres.

For their positive soil-conserving and soil-building performances in this connection Ohio farmers participating in the 1936 program received $9,708,084 in conservation payments, including county association expenses.

REA in Ohio

HAROLD K. CLAYPOOL

Mr. Speaker, I desire to speak upon the improvement in conditions with the farmers of the Eleventh Ohio Congressional District brought about by the present Congress, with special reference to the rural electrification program. Private capital has in the past been able to bring to the city dweller the innumerable benefits of electricity. It became necessary, however, because of divers conditions, for the Government to extend these benefits to the farmer.

As a representative of a district with large agricultural interests, it has been a pleasure to participate in the efforts of this Congress to assist the farmer when we extended for 2 additional years the 3½-percent loans through Federal land banks and when we passed the new agricultural bill. This latter bill may need some revision after the light of some experience in its operation leads us in the direction of improvement in its terms. Something had to be done for the farmer, and if the agricultural bill does not provide the remedy in its existing form, we must then make the necessary changes.

The flood-control bill will contain an allotment of over $8,000,000 in the Eleventh Ohio District for control of floods and incidental benefits to the farmers of the district.

No utilization of the forces of Nature has brought so much comfort and happiness to the people of the world as has the adaptation of electricity to the necessary work of mankind. All credit must be given originally to the great inventive minds which made possible present uses of electricity and those who assembled the private capital to originate and promote its various uses. This Congress can claim credit for furthering this progress by the extension of electrification to the farmer to the extent that in Ohio alone $7,566,525 is

From Harold K. Claypool, "Rural Electrification in the Eleventh Congressional District of Ohio," *Congressional Record*, Vol. 83, 75th Congress, 3rd Session, p. 3173.

authorized to be expended therein. I am pleased to say that more than one-seventh of this amount has gone to the Eleventh Ohio District, which I have the honor to represent. When this program was inaugurated, electricity was available to only a little more than 10 percent of the farms in my district. When we have completed the projects for which loans have already been approved, 50 percent of the farms in my district will be able to secure electric service; and, with pride in that achievement, I will not be content until the benefits of this boon to the human race has been extended to every farmhouse desiring it.

My district has been especially fortunate in securing loans of over $1,000,000 for rural electrification, despite large over-subscription of money available from the Government. I was pleased to actively support an additional appropriation in the independent offices appropriation bill for this purpose of $40,000,000, which will be available after July 1. Later, in the recovery bill, I assisted in inserting an item in that bill making $100,000,000 more available for rural electrification, so that a total of $140,000,000 will be available for this purpose for the year beginning July 1, 1938.

The two cooperatives in my district are the South Central Rural Electric Cooperative, Inc., with headquarters at Lancaster, and the Inter-County Rural Electric Cooperative, Inc., which serves Ross County. The first was organized by outstanding and progressive farmers in Fairfield, Perry, and Pickaway Counties, and a movement is now under way to bring the farmers of Hocking County into this organization, which I hope may be completed soon. It has been a pleasure as the representative in Congress of the Eleventh Ohio District, to present their applications for loans for the construction of rural electrification projects, which efforts have been very successful indeed. The South Central Cooperative has obtained a total of loans of $438,000, making available electricity to about 1,000 farms in Fairfield County, 300 in Pickaway County, and 350 in Perry County, a total of 1,650 in these 3 counties.

The Inter-County Rural Electric Cooperative, Inc., has obtained loans which added to its pending application for $267,000 will make $645,200 available for this cooperative, making possible electricity for much over 1,000 farms in Ross County. Thus a total of 2,650 farms in the Eleventh Ohio District are extended the benefits of electricity.

American cities today and for many years past have enjoyed the light and power provided by this great industry of electricity with which the great names of Benjamin Franklin and Thomas Edison have been so closely connected and which industry has been promoted by the great industrial, financial, and political leaders of our country—and if this Congress can by pushing these benefits of light and power into the American farmhouses and thus lighten the burden of the producers of food for America it will, in my opinion, be entitled to a pardonable pride in this accomplishment.

Little Steel Strike, 1937

ARTHUR P. LAMNECK

Mr. Chairman, in his immortal Gettysburg Address, Abraham Lincoln said:

> Now we are engaged in a great civil war, testing whether that nation or any nation so conceived and so dedicated can long endure.

Little did I think that the day would come in my time when I should feel under a solemn duty to arise in my place in this House and give utterance, in my humble way, to a similar statement. Yet that is exactly why I stand here today, seriously disturbed because I know only too well that few of you will realize without my explanation the parallel which I am about to draw.

I refer to the present controversy between capital and labor which is sweeping this country like wildfire. I solemnly assure you that in my opinion the issue involved is just as vital to the future of my country and your country as any issue of the War between the States, just as "testing" whether our Democratic capitalistic form of society can long endure. And you have only to pick up your daily paper to learn that the issue is being fought out in a civil war, with all the violence and bloodshed, all the usual implements of any civil war.

My interest in the situation centers in the steel strikes now going on. It has been aroused for two reasons: First, because the most aggravated, the most unhappy, and the most menacing conditions exist in the State of Ohio which I represent in this House; and second, and much more important, because I feel that the very foundations of our National Government are threatened by the sinister implications which these strikes carry.

Let me first make myself clear as to my attitude toward labor.

From Arthur P. Lamneck, "Debate over the Little Steel Strike, 1937," *Congressional Record*, Vol. 81, 75th Congress, 1st Session, pp. 5749-5753.

I have said on the floor of this House on previous occasions that a laboring man has the right to strike when he wants to, work when he wants to, and quit when he wants to. He has the right to select leaders of his own choosing, free from any coercion or direction on the part of his employer, to negotiate in his interest. I do not believe that there is a person in this country who has given this any thought who would not agree generally with this proposition. I go further, as does the law, and claim that the employee has the right to use peaceable means of persuasion to influence his fellow workers to his way of thinking.

However, my personal belief is that there should be a justifiable reason for striking. If the laborers' wages are not sufficient, if their hours are too long, if their working conditions are improper, they have the right to complain, to protest, and to strike if they want to, in the hope of rectifying these conditions.

But the strikes to which I now refer do not involve these issues or any other issues which can really be said to require the invocation of that specious and much-abused phrase "human rights." I claim that no workingman who is interested in the future of this country and is a patriotic American citizen should strike unless there is a justifiable reason and a reason basically connected with his work.

. . . .

I say that no workingman who will strike without a just and sufficient cause is a patriotic American citizen.

Let me next give you a little background on these particular strikes which I am discussing.

These strikes involve the Republic Steel Corporation and the Youngstown Sheet & Tube Co., whose principal activities are in the Mahoning Valley in the Youngstown district of Ohio. Inland Steel is also involved and now Bethlehem has been drawn in. They have no strikes in my congressional district, therefore my comments on the situation are based entirely upon a firm conviction that if these strikes are permitted to go on and if the communistic forces, with their growing strength in this country, are permitted to destroy property and hinder people who want to work, it will lead to disastrous results.

. . . .

I should like to tell you in detail how the present controversy arose, but time will not permit. The issue has been repeatedly set forth in the public press. There is only one issue, and that is whether the companies involved shall sign a contract binding them for the period thereof to stated terms of employment in general accord with the provisions of the Wagner Act. The union has not asked the

National Labor Relations Board to hold an election to determine whether it controls a majority of the workmen in any plant or company. The corporations have no such right.

So the issue has been drawn, not over wages, not over hours of work, not over vacations, not over working conditions, but purely and solely on the question of whether or not the companies involved shall sign a written contract binding them to bargain collectively.

. . . .

But the question may be asked, Why do the steel companies object to signing a contract? Because obviously, in the first place, they are not obligated by law to do so and cannot legally be so obligated. But, second, and this is the essence, because they are absolutely convinced from their long experience in dealing with labor that the signing of the first contract marks the first step in future demands for more burdensome contracts, finally ending in a demand for a contract embodying the closed shop and the check-off. If this comes, they say, God help the steel industry; I say God help this country.

. . . .

What does labor say to this question? Does John L. Lewis deny his ultimate objective is the closed shop and the check-off? No. On the contrary, he has made it abundantly clear in recent months that this is a goal toward which he is relentlessly driving. I say "a goal", not "the goal", deliberately, because neither I nor anyone else can say today what his real, full future objectives may be. As a matter of fact, they may well be shaped by the amount of power which he can gather to himself.

How far they may well go is even today fairly apparent.

. . . .

But in the State of Ohio the Mahoning Valley presents throughout its extent the spectacle of plants besieged by lawless mobs in the guise of picket lines—the peaceful picketing which the law permits. But in those localities where workers of their own free will have elected to stand by their posts there are daily, nay, hourly, occurrences which we in the peaceful atmosphere of Washington cannot even begin to appreciate. Let me tell you about Niles and Warren. Several thousand men are at work in these plants. Others would like to return to work but dare not. These plants are surrounded day and night by a cordon of strikers and their sympathizers, armed with lethal weapons. These men have used every means at their command to prevent loyal workers from entering or leaving the plants. They have shot to kill at workers attempting to slip in under cover of night. They have threatened and coerced the wives and children of men in the plant. They have by threats of violence prevented the railroads serving the plants from taking cars in or bringing them out, thus restraining interstate commerce and breaching the Federal laws. In the early days of the strike they held up United States mail trucks and prevented them from delivering food, clothing, and newspapers mailed to persons in the plants. Such an act is a clear violation of the Postal Code of the United States. Latterly the local postmasters have declined to accept packages containing such articles into the United States mail, on the pretext of a technical rule of the Postmaster General or in the theory that danger would be involved in attempting to deliver them against the will of the strikers.

In other words, the Federal mail service at these points is virtually controlled by the wishes and commands of a group of men engaged daily in breaches of law in every direction.

. . . .

Is there any more important human right than the right to work, the right to furnish support for a family? What differentiates the Government's boasted obligation to see that the unemployed are provided for from the Government's apparently forgotten obligation to see that those who are willing and able to work—who are even willing to fight for the right to work—are protected in this right?

Yet if the newspaper quotations of statements of Post Office officials are to be believed, and there seems no reason to doubt them, the Post Office Department first defends its position on a legalistic ground which rivals in sophistry the worst arguments of those social classes which are daily being held up to public shame and censure by proponents of the "more abundant life."

Its second line of defense is the fact that conditions surrounding the strike-bound plants present dangers of physical violence to men and equipment which the Post Office Department cannot afford to risk. Its Budget might be unbalanced if some of the mail trucks were damaged or destroyed.

Have the processes of law and order sunk to such a low degree in this country that the United States Government is to be deterred from the discharge of its duties by the menace of a group of self-willed men?

. . . .

It is my purpose now to make clear to you, as I see it, the full significance and the necessary implications of these strikes and of the present labor movement in the United States.

First let me say to you that it is my firm belief that the time has arrived when those of us who form the legislative and executive branches of the Federal Government as well as those to whom has been entrusted the government of the States affected, must take cognizance of this situation and act with all our power to keep it within bounds. As surely as I stand here if, recreant to our trust and blind to our plain duty, we fail to act and to act promptly, our children and our children's children will rue this day.

One opportunity, one crying demand for firm and positive governmental action, has come and gone unheeded. I refer to the recent sit-down strikes when governmental authority actuated by an alleged high regard for human rights and fear of bloodshed gave apparent sanction to the taking over of private property without due process.

In the sit-down strikes there was violated the sacred right of private property. Decrees of established courts to that effect were derided by the ravishers and unenforced by executive authority charged with that duty.

There was a sign of relief throughout the country when these outrages were apparently ended, ended with the open and brazen violation of fundamental rights which had occurred unpunished and unredressed. What was the result of the policy, this policy of high regard for human rights? Today, within a few months of the so-called truce, we have before us the spectacle of even greater excesses. We have labor, in the form of the C. I. O. led by the ambition-ridden John L. Lewis, going to far greater lengths than the sit-down strikers, not in pursuit of higher wages, not in pursuit of shorter hours, not in pursuit of better working conditions, but seeking only to impose by force upon employers the performance of an act which even the one-sided Wagner Act does not require. And as a necessary part, the course of such autocratic and unwarranted demands subjecting their fellow workmen, who will not join hands with them, either to the penalty of not working at all or to staying at work, which they have freely chosen to do under conditions of indescribable hardship.

The opportunity presented by the sit-down strikes to make clear once and for all the fact that law and order must prevail in this country regardless of who is affected thereby, has come and gone. Now, we are confronted with an even more urgent call. Not only is the right to the peaceful possession of one's property threatened but the right to work without molestation at the job of one's choice is being denied.

If we fail to heed this call, what next?

I urge upon the municipal and State authorities that they do everything in their power within their several jurisdictions to see that their laws are obeyed and that the property rights of their citizens, including particularly the right to work, are protected, let the results be what they may. I invoke their most anxious, their most prayerful consideration of the fact that if they fail in this crisis they are furnishing the most effective possible ammunition to that school of thought whose constant effort today is to take from the powers of the State governments and add to those of the central government. No more persuasive argument exists than the shining example of failure by you to meet such an emergency as now exists.

I call upon the executive branch of our Federal Government to put an immediate stop to the flagrant and open violation of Federal statutes which, through the medium of the daily press, have become a matter of common knowledge throughout the country. The sovereignty of our Government is being openly flaunted and held up to ridicule by a group of self-willed men bent upon their own purposes without any regard whatever for our country's laws, who will go just as far in their disregard for law and order as the authorities will permit.

This is the first step to anarchy.

Failing action by the executive department under present laws, I call upon this House, this Congress, to enact legislation making it mandatory upon those charged with the enforcement of our laws to take those steps which are so evidently necessary now to preserve our form of government and to stop the further progress of these elements in our society which are so obviously bent upon a program of destruction. [Applause.]

Little Steel Strike, 1937

MICHAEL J. KIRWAN

Mr. Chairman, as a new Member, this is my first attempt to address the House.

When my colleague, Mr. Lamneck, told about the labor conditions which prevail in Ohio he was speaking of my district. I represent the Nineteenth District of Ohio, where the strike is going on.

Let us not confine our discussion to this strike, but let us go back to the first major strike in this country, which occurred in 1893. Let

From Michael J. Kirwan, "Debate over the Little Steel Strike, 1937," *Congressional Record*, Vol. 81, 75th Congress, 1st Session, p. 5753.

us consider the strike in Chicago, the Pullman and railroad strike, and recall how the troops shot the strikers down that day. Let us move on to the steel strike, a couple of years afterward, and remember when Carnegie paid Frick $1,000,000 to break that strike. It will never be forgotten how the Pinkerton detectives on a boat shot down those strikers on the river banks.

Frick went to the hospital after Carnegie paid him a million dollars to break that strike. He become melancholy from thinking over what he had done and the lives that had been lost there. When he came out of the hospital he and Carnegie became bitter enemies. Carnegie sent a messenger to him and undertook to bring about a reconciliation. You remember his reply, "I will see you in hell; we are both going there." This was Frick's reply to Carnegie in 1896 or 1897.

Remember the next strike of the coal miners in Pennsylvania in 1902, when 149,000 workers with 500,000 dependents were on strike. The 6 months of victorious strike freed labor from slavery.

Let us move on now to Colorado and consider the coal and fuel company strike there. We had a fellow named Roosevelt as President. Teddy, I think, was his first name, or they called him that. Remember when they burned the houses that these miners lived in and then loaded them in box cars, transported them to the plains of Kansas and left the women and children out in Colorado to starve.

I am asking my colleague from Ohio [Mr. Lamneck], if he is in the House—in fact, I throw this challenge at him—show me anywhere in the world during the last 160 years, as long as this Government has been functioning, where they have committed a crime like that. Consider the other nations of the world. There was only one thing to equal it, and that was when Turkey gathered up her stray dogs in Constantinople and loaded them on a boat and put them out on an island, and the whole world complained about that, but you did not hear any complaint in 1903 or 1904, when they moved out these miners and left their women and children to starve.

At the turn of the century, if you asked for your rights, you were called an anarchist, and later, in 1910, a Socialist. Everything moved along until 1919, when, if you stood up for your rights, you were called a Bolshevik. Today, if you protest for your rights, they will call you a Communist or a Nazi-ist, or one of those terms; but go to the La Follette hearings, if you want information, and find out who was branded a rat or stool pigeon for giving information against labor. Look at the names appearing in that hearing and you will find that they were all good American names and not one of them from Russia.

I belong in the steel district, and last Sunday the only paper in that town, which is serving 300,000 people, in a front-page editorial was telling the owners to sign up with the men; that they had carried the thing too far; that the men are right. [Applause.]

The men are right; and every strike that we ever had in this country, whether the men lost or won, within 2 years at the latest, the companies put into practice what the men went out on strike for.

In 1919 Mr. Gary, chairman of the board of directors of United States Steel, said you could not put 8 hours a day into the steel plants, that it would never work, but it did work.

Look back on that Colorado strike, when John D. Rockefeller sent his son out there because he wanted a report on what was happening, and when young John D. reported to his own father, from that time on it made a good man out of Rockefeller and a credit to the Nation, as was his son also. He sold the holdings he had out there, and the Standard Oil is one of the best companies to work for in the country today. You are pensioned at 60 years of age, from the president on down.

Where was your Government in those days that it did not take a hand in keeping law and order, when they let those men and women starve? They starved in the anthracite region for 6 months. That was Teddy Roosevelt. He never took a hand. Where was he in 1903 and 1904, during the Colorado strike? He never took a hand.

We are complaining a lot about the steel situation. This reminds me of an old story that Walter Kelly, the Virginia judge, used to tell. Coming up through the Southland he stopped to watch a crowd of youngsters playing ball. He asked one of the boys who was chasing the ball, "What's the score, sonny?" The boy replied, "Fifty to nothing." Kelly said, "They are lamming the life out of you." The boy quickly replied, "Nope; we haven't had our turn at bat yet."

For 50 years labor has been chasing the ball. It begins to look like labor is beginning to have its turn at bat.

8 The Incredible Forties

WITH THE TRAGEDY of Pearl Harbor in December 1941, Ohioans were called upon to sacrifice for a world war and to face the consequences of reconstruction for the second time in the twentieth century. Society in the Buckeye State felt the impact of the technological advances that were made in industry, education, and government in order to fight the war. As prosperity returned through war contracts, women left their homes to work in war plants, and new in-migrants, specifically blacks and Appalachian whites, moved to Ohio's industrial centers seeking jobs and security. Many of the problems that arose during the reconstruction period were similar to the ones following World War I, and in some instances easier solutions were found by local government agencies. However, the seeds of many problems of the 1950s and 1960s were planted during the war years.

Over 800,000 men and women from Ohio served in the military forces in some capacity. Ohioans participated in all theaters of operations, but of particular note was the 192nd Tank Battalion, composed largely of men from northwestern Ohio. Shipped early in the war to the Pacific, this unit fought bravely against the Japanese invasion of Luzon in the Philippines and was among the American units that ultimately surrendered to the Japanese at Bataan. Twenty-three thousand Ohioans who served during World War II were killed.

Two years after the war began, large numbers of both Italian and German prisoners of war were held in POW camps within the state. The largest camp was located at Camp Perry along Lake Erie. By October 31, 1943, over 1,000 Italians were kept under guard; eight months later, the first German prisoners began to arrive in Ohio, and by August 1945 over 5,500 German POWs had arrived. Camp Perry was not the only location for POW camps. Between October 1943 and the end of the war, Italian and German POWs were kept at Defiance, Celina, Bowling Green, Marion, Fletcher General Hospital in Cambridge, Fort Hayes, Crile General Hospital in Cleveland, Wilmington, Dayton, and the Erie Proving Grounds, LaCarne. Prisoners were used as agricultural laborers and as workers in food processing plants in northwestern Ohio. By the middle of 1946, all POWs had been removed from the state.

The war years were prosperous ones for many Ohioans. Employment opportunities opened for men and women in the defense industries, and lucrative federal defense contracts poured into the state. There were 933 key war industries in Ohio, employing nearly 1,000,000 workers. In addition, one half of the state's 10,000 manufacturing companies produced some war materiel. The major cities, including Canton, Cincinnati, Dayton, Hamilton, and Toledo, enjoyed the benefits of war production; and Akron, which prospered through its aviation and rubber industries, expanded rapidly. It was reported that twenty-seven cents of every dollar spent on army military aircraft came to Ohio.

As men entered military service, a manpower shortage developed in industry. Training programs at the federal and state level worked to provide trained personnel for the war industries, and the public schools also contributed to help solve the problem through vocational education programs. For the first time, women entered industry as laborers. By 1943 it was estimated that one out of every five workers in defense plants was a woman, and as the war progressed, five out of every six new employees were women. Ohio's farmers also contributed to the war effort, and as prices rose they too shared the prosperity of the war years. By late summer 1945, farm incomes had risen 191% over what they had been in 1939. The state's agricultural activities were coordinated by the Ohio War Agricultural Committee, which was comprised of representatives from state government, the Farm Bureau Federation, the Grange, and members of the farm press. Quotas on food production were lifted, needed farm labor recruited, and planting schedules planned. To meet the growing need for food on the domestic scene, a Victory Garden program was encouraged at the local level. By the war's end, nearly 2.5 million gardens were being planted, which represented $150,000,000 in farm produce.

Following the war, many problems that had faced the state and the nation revisited the Buckeye State. As prices began to soar and wages dragged behind, labor unrest was predictable, and a rash of strikes plagued large and small businesses. Toledo, hoping for as little difficulty as possible, sought solutions to labor unrest before it started. Problems of housing shortages, high prices, and race relations also faced state and municipal government. In Cleveland, under the leadership of Mayor Frank Lausche, programs were inaugurated during the war which eased the American black and the newly arrived Appalachian laborer into the local labor market. These programs were successful, and during the war and into the reconstruction period racial tensions were at least lessened in Ohio's largest city.

Similar to the "Red Scare," which began shortly after World War I, a fear of Communism emerged full-blown on the national scene in the mid-forties. Apprehensive of adverse political effects on the national administration, President Harry S. Truman began an investigation of government employees in 1947, seeking American loyalists. The investigations, however, uncovered no hardened Communists in the government, although there were several resignations. The states, including Ohio, joined the redbaiting bandwagon, and fears of entrenched Communists in government and local school districts excited numbers of people over the state.

The 1940s were years of sacrifice, hard work, and frustration for many Ohioans, but the return of prosperity helped to ease the pain of the crisis period. The impact of big government was felt throughout the state, and because they had been conditioned to the expansion of the federal government during the Depression years, Ohioans accepted the planning of the war years. However, because of the effects at home of the war, which produced new migration patterns, housing shortages, high prices, inflation, women laborers, and many other problems, Ohioans spent the next two decades seeking solutions to issues that were rooted in the 1940s.

Ohio and World War II

JAMES H. RODABAUGH

The story of Ohio in World War II is a record of the faith of a people in its country and confidence in its ability to win; of magnificent popular support of the mobilization program for total war; and of the effective cooperation of varying and conflicting interests for the general welfare. Ohio's record is not unique in respect to faith, support, and cooperation. Her people contributed generally only in proportion to their numbers and to the State's productive resources in the nation's totals. In order further to place ourselves in proper perspective, we must remember that the people of other nations, great and small, gave the lives of their men and women and turned the full force of their productive power to the defeat of the Axis nations. With these relationships in mind, we may say that Ohio played a great part in 1) winning the war; 2) proving the essential unity and strength of the national democracy; 3) and discovering the productive potential of this country.

Ohio contributed her full share on all fronts, at home and abroad. We were most conscious, of course, of the battle fronts, where more than 600,000 sons and daughters served in the armed forces. More than 200,000 Ohioans were members of the naval services; some 400,000, therefore, were members of the forces of the army. A number of army units were originally composed largely of Ohio men. For example, there was Co. C, 192nd Tank Battalion, composed of men from Port Clinton and northwestern Ohio, which resisted the Japanese invasion of Luzon and was captured on Bataan. The 174th Field Artillery Battalion won a niche among the heroic Ohio outfits in the Siege of Brest and the Battle of the Bulge. The 112th Engineer Combat Battalion was the first engineer unit to arrive in Great Britain after the entry of the United States into the war. This outfit, originally part of "Cleveland's Own" 112th Engineer Combat Regiment, fought on Omaha Beach, Normandy, on D-Day, assisted in the liberation of Paris, and participated in the historic dash across France and Belgium which caused the disintegration of a major portion of the German armies. There were other Ohio units which won fame on the field of battle, including the 254th Engineer Combat Battalion, the 987th Field Artillery Battalion, the 107th Cavalry Group, the 151st Medical Battalion, the 2nd Battalion of the 372nd Infantry Regiment, Companies B, C, and D of the 131st Quartermaster Regiment, the 191st Engineers Company, Companies

From James H. Rodabaugh, "Ohio's War Record," *Communikay*, IV (April, 1946), 2-6.

Pioneer, A, and B of the 637th Tank Destroyer Battalion, and the 166th Infantry Regiment.

. . . .

All elements of Ohio's population contributed to the Allies' success on the battle fields. Approximately 9% of Ohio's people went into the armed services. The Negro population which comprised about 5% of the total Ohio population furnished 6% of Ohio's soldiers in World War II. More than 10% of the Ohio Negroes went into the armed services through the draft. The Jewish people, too, gave their full share to the forces of the United States Army and Navy. It is estimated that close to 20,000 Jewish men and women, about 12% of the total Jewish population in Ohio, were in the service. This accounted for nearly 3½% of the Ohioans in World War II.

. . . .

Total mobilization demanded a program for increased food production. The federal and state departments of agriculture organized to encourage the farmers toward greater efforts. The guarantee of a certain market and good prices also contributed to the increases. When Selective Service and industry drew men from the farms, labor assistants were set up in the offices of the County Agents to help provide farm workers. An emergency farm labor program brought Jamaicans, Mexicans, Barbadians, and other workers from the South into Ohio. By 1943, also, prisoners of war were being used. In 1944, 8140 farm laborers were imported, and during the past year 6936. These workers were used mainly for work in connection with seasonal crops which called for hand labor, such as tomatoes, vegetables, fruits, and sugar beets. Thousands of townspeople and young people from the public schools of Ohio also took their turns in the fields.

As a result of the increased efforts on the farms, and in spite of declines in acreage under cultivation, agricultural production in Ohio between 1940 and 1945 experienced an overall increase of 30%. The production of wheat and corn each went up approximately 45%; soybeans, 127%; oats, 20%; eggs, 25%; and chickens, 15%. Hog numbers in 1944 had increased 35% above the 1939-41 average; milk cows increased 11% and other cattle, 16%. All grain-consuming animals increased by 1944 22% above the 1939-41 level. At the same time the production of truck crops increased by 9% in the five years of wartime. Vegetable production was increased by the Victory Garden campaign inaugurated in 1943. In the past three years there have been a total of 2,570,562 Victory Gardens in Ohio, which produced vegetable crops worth over $150,000,000.

It is interesting to consider the socio-economic result of this increase in farm production. By the end of the third year of war, August 1942, agricultural income in Ohio had risen 88% from the income at the beginning of hostilities. By August 1945, as compared with August 1939, agricultural income was up 191%, or had almost tripled. Increased incomes were experienced especially on meat animals, dairy products, grains, poultry, and eggs. Ohio farm prices, as a whole, increased nearly 90% above the 1935-39 averages, while prices paid by farmers increased by about 50%. The social effect of this increased income to Ohio's rural population becomes even more significant when it is considered with the probable reduction of farm population through the draft and the migration of farm labor to industrial centers.

Ohio's great record of contribution to the war effort was made in industry. The manufacture of iron and steel and their products, vehicles, metal and metal products other than iron and steel, and rubber products experienced the largest increases during the war. It was in the manufacture of iron and steel and their products that the Middle West was really the world heartland of this war. Iron ore came by boat from the great Mesabi Range through the Lakes to various ports. It was this carrying trade that lifted the Great Lakes tonnage to 184,155,384 net tons in 1944. This figure was 2½ times greater than all the war cargoes carried that year by America's Atlantic-Pacific ocean-going merchant vessels. The number of Ohio's employees in the iron and steel industries jumped from 273,166 in June 1940 to 445,000 in June 1943, an increase of 63%; the number employed in the manufacture of vehicles increased from 45,536 to 244,210—an increase of 436%; the number in the manufacture of metal products increased from 37,497 to 86,806—or 131.5%; the number in rubber manufacturing increased 56%—from 46,626 to 72,643. In the three years 1940 to 1943, total employment in Ohio's major manufacturing industries increased 68%—from 754,886 to 1,268,685. All employment in Ohio increased 55% above the 1935-39 level by August 1943. From that time there was a steady decline of 31% by November 1945.

The increase in electric power production in Ohio is apparent from the following figures: During the first six months of 1940, the production was 4,408 million kilowatt hours; during the first half of 1945 it totalled 7,898 million kilowatt hours. The production of bituminous coal in Ohio rose 82% between 1939 and 1945.

Up to May 1945 Ohio industries had received war contracts to the value of nearly 18 billion dollars. Aircraft and ordnance were the major classifications of Ohio war contracts—contracts valued at 5 3/4 billions being let for aircraft, and 4 2/3 billions for ordnance. These combined contracts amounted to 58.2% of the total. Shipbuilding ranked third in value of war contracts with $1,450,000,000 worth being let to Ohio companies. Ohio ranked fourth among the states in the amount of war contracts, with 7.8% of the total. Michigan, New York, and California surpassed her.

Among Ohio's cities Cleveland industries received the largest war contracts with a total value of $5,000,000,000. Aircraft accounted for $1,200,000,000 of this, with ordnance and shipbuilding contracts each reaching a sum of a billion dollars. Aircraft contracts accounted for $2,000,000,000 out of Cincinnati's total of $3,400,000,000 in war contracts. Akron ranked third in the value of such contracts, with $2,100,000,000—most of the contracts going for rubber and aircraft. Dayton's contracts reached $1,700,000,000; while Youngstown, Toledo, and Columbus each received contracts totalling over a billion dollars. The figures cited are intended only to give some indication of the tremendous increase in industrial activity in Ohio during World War II.

The expanding labor market was accompanied by increasing wages. Between 1940 and 1943 Ohio manufacturing wage earners' average annual earnings increased 65%—from $1529 to $2524. By the beginning of 1945, these wage earners were averaging $53.00 for a 46 to 47-hour week. In general, however, wages declined 11% during 1945 from the 1944 level. By the end of the year the average was down to $44.76 for a 42-hour week. Between 1940 and 1943 clerical workers in manufacturing increased their annual earnings an average of 36%—from $1732 to $2354. At the same time salespeople (not traveling) increased but 32%—from $1859 to $2455. At the end of World War I there was still nearly a 24% differential between the wage earners and salespeople. The point is that wage earners are receiving greater incomes as a result of the present war, and that clerical workers and salespeople, whose incomes have not risen proportionately, have fallen—so far as their economic position is concerned—into the proletariat. Whether or not this will reflect upon their political and economic attitudes is an interesting question for the future.

The demand for labor opened the gates for white women and Negroes. In 1940 the Negro accounted for 2½% of the total employment in war industries; in 1945 he accounted for 8.2% of the total. In the year previous to our entry into World War II, the United States Employment Service in Ohio placed only 3% of its Negro registrants in manufacturing industries; in 1944, when six times as many Negroes were placed in jobs by the U.S.E.S., 55% of them went into manufacturing. In 1940 the Negro supplied 2% of the skilled workers in Ohio industries; by 1945 he was furnishing 8%. Although Negroes received larger incomes than before the war, they were still, in general, in the lower income brackets. The result was that in the recent strikes the Negroes were the chief group to apply for relief. The Negro also made gains in participation in a number of labor unions, especially in the C.I.O. Thousands of women also went to work during the war period, being employed especially in aircraft industries, precision work, and sales and service industries. In Columbus the number of women workers reached a peak of 38% of total employment in July 1945. After V-J Day 70 to 80% of those applying for unemployment compensation were women. In July 1945 in Columbus women were drawing an average wage of 80 cents an hour in industry, 50 cents in service trades, and 5 to 6 dollars a day for household labor; by January 1946 these wages had reduced by approximately one third, except in service trades. Office workers, too, who were demanding $125 to $150 a month had dropped to $100 to $150 a month average.

In Ohio by August 1943 total payrolls had increased 198% above the 1935-1939 level. This includes, of course, increased wages, 55% greater employment, and more manhours worked. Since that peak was reached there has been a reduction to 123% above the 1935-39 level by November 1945. During the war another economic revolution was in the making. In 1939 salaries and wages absorbed 66% of industrial income; by 1944 they absorbed 72%. At the same time proprietors' and property incomes reduced from 27% to 23%. Other income, i.e., from pensions, relief, and social security programs, reduced from 7% to 5%. The question is, of course, how far the middle incomes, i.e., the property and proprietors', may or can be reduced before the owners surrender their controls. The exigencies of war narrowed the owners' and investors' margin by more than 11% and extended the differential between incomes of salary and wages and property and proprietors' by nearly 26%. Thus, as far as income is concerned, the wage and salary earner is absorbing an increasingly larger share.

Ohio's POW Camps

REPORT

A preliminary survey of the possibilities of establishing a Prisoner of War Camp in Defiance County was made in July 1944 at the request of the Ohio War Manpower Commission. The proposed camp was to be a branch of the Prisoner of War Camp located at Camp Perry. From this survey it was determined that a definite need for prisoner of war labor existed in the Defiance area and that the former Civilian Conservation Corps camp located on East Second Street would be suitable for about six hundred prisoners.

Under the command of Captain Frank Bodenhorn one hundred and thirty German prisoners of war were sent from Camp Perry to Defiance on August 4, 1944. A tight guard was established around the area until the prisoners completed building a barbed wire fence eight feet high around the stockade site. Flood lights and guard towers were also placed around the entire compound. This work required three sixteen-hour work days.

The residents of Defiance made an immediate and lasting impression on the American personnel. The Defiance Chapter of the Red Cross, represented by Edward F. Wanley and Mrs. Helen Lawler, called on the Commanding Officer before the convoy had completed unloading and offered their services. Several local groups, the Red Cross, Rotary Club, Public Library, and many individuals jointly fitted up a day room for the guards before the camp had become fairly settled. The citizens of the community cooperated with the personnel of the camp throughout the period that the camp was activated.

After the camp was established it was necessary to erect three additional buildings, a barracks and a mess hall for the guards and a mess hall for the prisoners.

The camp was established to provide labor for the tomato fields and canning plants in the immediate vicinity. At first there was little demand for the labor, but after a few farmers had used some of the prisoners and found that they did good work and were not to be feared, the demand increased by leaps and bounds. The original plan was that not more than six hundred prisoners of war would be kept at Defiance for a period of three months. When, however, it was learned that their services could be used the year around, the camp was winterized. At the peak of activity in the fall of 1945, there were some eight hundred prisoners in the camp. Since the barracks were not adequate for this number, tents were erected between the hut-

From "Prisoner of War Camp—Defiance," *Communikay*, V (September, 1946), 4-5.

ments for about three hundred prisoners of war. The farmers in the Defiance area used the prisoners to pick tomatoes, to harvest wheat and corn, to fill silos, and to build fences. This labor was also used to increase industrial production in the community. One select group completely manned a large plant using only a few civilians as supervisors. Others worked in canning plants, tile mills, fertilizer factories, feed mills, furniture factories, trailer factories, and packing plants. During the period the prisoners worked in Defiance and the surrounding territory, they earned for the United States Treasury some five hundred thousand dollars.

No difficulties were experienced in handling the prisoners during the period of activation. One prisoner did become despondent and committed suicide by drowning in the Maumee River on August 20, 1944.

After the camp was closed on December 15, 1945, the Army turned over to the State of Ohio all buildings which had been erected, including a wash room complete with plumbing and water heaters, two mess halls complete with tables and ranges, some thirty space heaters, two large refrigerators, and considerable other equipment. It was felt that the cost of moving this property would exceed its value and the state officials were anxious to secure the material for use by state troops.

Ohio's Sacrifice

REPORT

New Activities Resulting From the War

Highway Ordnance Company. In 1942 the Ohio Department of Highways was requested by Charles Upham, Engineer-Director of the American Road Builders' Association, to secure personnel for new ordnance companies for the United States Army. Mr. Upham's request came at the direct behest of the Army, which was seeking to

From "Report of the Ohio Department of Highways," *Communikay,* V (July, 1946), 2-8.

tap the road building industry's vast reservoir of skills essential for ordnance type of work.

. . . .

In August 1942 Paul E. Boyer of Anna, Chief Mechanic for the Department in Division Seven at Sidney, was selected by Army officers as Captain. During September while the other officers reported to Camp Perry for training Captain Boyer interviewed over 700 applicants for the company at various points in Ohio until 180 officers and men had been chosen.

Now known as the 528th Ordnance Company, these Ohioans spent the summer of 1943 on maneuvers under simulated combat conditions. Upon completion of the maneuvers, the company moved to Pine Camp, New York, and in November an official card was received by the Department giving the new address of the unit as A.P.O. 4915, New York.

Help the Farmer. In the last week in May 1943 the farmers of Ohio were confronted with an unusual condition. Incessant rains during the month of May had prevented the plowing and preparation of land for the planting of corn and soy beans and the time was fast approaching when these crops should be planted in order to mature before early frosts. This condition was particularly aggravated in the northwestern and central western portions of the State.

Coming at a time when every effort was being expended to help out in the war effort by increasing food production, this condition became a matter of serious concern. Officials of the Department of Agriculture, the Ohio State University Agriculture Extension Service, and the Department of Highways formulated a plan to use Highway Department tractors in critical areas. This plan was supported by the Governor and put in operation.

. . . .

Access Roads. Since 1940 the Department has given considerable aid in the analysis of the highway transportation requisites of dozens of war plants which had been newly constructed or substantially enlarged to produce materials of war. In addition to this, the Department developed detailed plans, placed the work under contract, and supervised the construction of those roads deemed essential to the war. One hundred and ninety-six miles of access roads have been constructed at a cost of $20,000,000. These roads, while providing rapid and safe access to war plants, were selected and designed to fit into continuing post-war use.

Strategic Network of Highways. The Strategic Network of Highways is composed of main roads connecting termini selected by the General Staff of the United States Army and considered to be of chief importance in the mobilization of armies and supplies in time of war. There are 1381 miles of the Federal Aid Highway System on the Strategic Network in Ohio. Periodic examination of the Strategic Network is made to determine its adequacy in regard to pavement, berm, and bridge widths, and also bridge and pavement loadings in accordance with army standards. As the result of recent and proposed construction, there are only five inadequate structures left on the Network and all of these are within municipalities.

. . . .

The use of asphalt and tar products for roads and highways was restricted and controlled from July 1, 1942 until September 1943. This restriction was placed in effect by Recommendation No. 45, issued by the Petroleum Co-ordinator for War. During this period the State Highway Department handled and transmitted to the Public Roads Administration requests for 2740 individual projects for the counties, cities, and state. The restrictions imposed by this order reduced the amount of bituminous material used on highways and driveways sufficiently to permit the pavement of military airports and roads used primarily for the transportation of war material.

Bridge Capacities. The War Department in 1942 requested the Director of Highways to furnish a statement of the capacity of all bridges over 20-foot span in Ohio for the purpose of routing military vehicles. Data on the 5,543 State Highway bridges was furnished quickly from the bridge records. Many of the 14,337 bridges on county and township roads, and city streets, required special surveys. Departmental engineers, in co-operation with county engineers, completed the work to the satisfaction of the War Department in less than four months.

. . . .

Salvage and Scrap Activities. When war was declared in December 1941 the Highway Department, realizing that various materials would become critical, emphasized the salvaging of all scrap materials and the disposal of material unsuitable for its own use. In line with this situation, a man experienced in the salvage and scrap business was placed in charge to make as much of this material available as soon as possible.

Iron scrap is classified as heavy melting, bridge, iron, No. 1 and No. 2 grades, cast iron, cutting iron, miscellaneous sheet iron, borings, and turnings. Non-ferrous metals, such as brass, copper, aluminum, and lead, carry a separate classification. During the years 1942 and 1943 the Department disposed of the following scrap: scrap iron—6,700,000 lbs.; non-ferrous metals—65,000 lbs.; scrap rubber—

115,000 lbs.; scrap paper—22,000 lbs.; scrap storage batteries—2,100 units.

In addition to the collection, classification, and disposal of scrap materials, some materials which in ordinary times, due to their low cost and availability would be considered scrap, were reclaimed for re-use. This is particularly true of used grader blades, structural shapes, steel drums, cans, paint buckets, and other miscellaneous items. This reclaimed material approximated a total value of $15,000.00.

Conservation of Tires and Gasoline. After December 1941 when the tire situation became critical the State took decisive action to insure that its tires were giving the utmost in mileage. Unless rigid conservation measures were put into effect, essential service to the public would suffer through lack of tires on which equipment is kept rolling. Speed of vehicles was reduced to a maximum of 40 miles per hour by the use of governors. This was before the 35 mile per hour limit was set by the Federal Government. The State speed limit was later reduced to 35 miles per hour in compliance with the National policy.

Early in 1943 in order to conserve tires and gasoline the State Highway Department instituted a program in mileage reduction for all State owned automobiles. A goal was set and departmental mileage budgets were established. Railroad and bus travel was encouraged and a "share-the-ride" plan, with a clearing house for all State travel, was established. During 1943 a reduction of 14,342,854 miles was made, a decrease of 32.5% from 1941. This represented a saving of 950,000 gallons of gasoline at 15 miles per gallon and a saving of 2,300 tires at 25,000 miles per tire. This accomplishment is the result of a desire by the personnel of all state departments to co-operate to the full extent in the conduct of the war.

. . . .

License Tags. Until 1943 Ohio issued two plates for each vehicle, except trailers; one to be attached to the front of the car and the other to the back. These plates required nearly 1400 tons of steel annually. In order to save this steel the 1943 licenses were issued in the form of gummed paper stickers for the windshield. The steel plates issued in 1942 remained on the cars during 1943. These stickers served their purpose in the conservation of vital steel but after two years service many of the 1942 plates were in poor condition. Thus, in planning for the 1944 licenses, it was decided again to use steel plates, with one plate only for each vehicle and that to be attached to the rear of the car.

Highway Patrol. In addition to the normal activities of the Patrol, the war brought on many added responsibilities. Early in

1941 it became apparent that the services of the Highway Patrol would be needed in the national defense. Military transport surveys were made and bivouac facilities for troops were arranged in each county of the state. The Federal Bureau of Investigation sought the assistance of the Highway Patrol in rendering protection against espionage, sabotage, and subversive activities. A group of experienced officers were selected and assigned to conduct investigations requested by the F.B.I.

In 1941, 15,037 man hours were devoted exclusively to the national emergency by the Highway Patrol. Between the time that war was declared and the end of 1944, an additional 107,850 man hours were devoted to the same purpose. The declaration of war by the United States made necessary the establishment of twenty-four hour patrols in the vicinity of all large airports, vital bridge facilities, and Army and Navy establishments.

Equality in War Industry

CLEVELAND

Equality Campaign

Political pressure exerted in Cleveland for local drive to foster employment of Negroes in city's war industries

"Equality," guaranteed to American Negroes by the 14th and 15th amendments to the Constitution, is reaffirmed in the Selective Service Act. It was also reaffirmed by President Roosevelt a year ago in Executive Order 8802, better known among Negroes than among whites, which stated:

> " . . . there shall be no discrimination in the employment of workers in defense industries of government because of race, creed, color, or national origin, and I do hereby declare that it is the duty of employers and of labor organizations in furtherance of said policy and of this order to provide for the full and equitable participation of all workers in defense industries without discrimination because of race, creed, color, or national origin."

From "Equality Campaign," *Business Week* (May 9, 1942), 70-72. Reprinted by permission.

Pressure Exerted—This week the economic equality front opened up in Cleveland, in a vital sector of war industry. Mayor Frank J. Lausche, who has his own city War Production Committee, was importuned by Negro leaders to be the spearhead of a local drive to promote the employment of thousands of colored men as trainees for skilled machine jobs, and of thousands of colored women on war assembly lines.

The metropolitan Cleveland area, which contains about 1% of the national population, also contains about 1% of the U. S. Negro population. Three members of the 33-man city council are Negroes. In other public offices racial recognition is personified in a member of the city civil service commission, and in one assistant city law director, Charles White, a Harvard graduate. The white Republican leader of the city council, Herman Finkle, owes political strength to his ability to influence Negro voters. Such varied factors, in the opinion of many observers, make Cleveland a favorable proving ground for the nondiscrimination decree.

Between the Wars—Negroes came to Cleveland in large numbers to meet industrial demands of the last war. They remained to swell the city relief and WPA rolls when hard times came knocking.

During WPA's most swollen months of 1938, 80,000 Greater Cleveland families were supported by government-made work and another 20,000 lived on city relief. About 20% of these 100,000 family units were Negroes. Today, Negroes make up 40% of the 14,000 Cleveland families who are left on WPA and city relief. Negroes, their leaders complain, are the last to be hired and the first to be fired.

In War Industries—Thousands of Negroes are now employed in Cleveland war industries. The U. S. Aluminum Co.—Alcoa subsidiary—has the largest quota, about 2,000. National Bronze & Aluminum Foundry Co., which bounced right back into production after a disastrous fire last fall, has another 1,000. National Malleable & Steel Castings Co., Ferro Machine & Foundry Co., Westinghouse Electric & Manufacturing Co., and the steel mills in Cleveland all number their Negro employment in the hundreds. All of these, however, hire them for "hot work," that is, for work in foundries or for other heavy labor in metal production and fabrication.

Thompson Products, which next to Republic Steel has become Cleveland's biggest employer of labor, also has become the city's largest employer of Negroes in semiskilled jobs.

Internal Difficulties—The most logical objection to hiring Negroes in war industry, according to George Merritt Washington, Cleveland secretary of the Urban League, is that such a change in policy may cause internal plant difficulties. When this objection was raised first, he said, he discounted it immediately, but experience has shown otherwise.

In one Cleveland plant which he named, there is an urgent need for additional workmen to meet war schedules. The management was ready to begin hiring Negroes but the local A.F.L. Machinists' Union entered a strenuous protest. None have been hired there, to date.

At White Motors, protests by some union members (C.I.O.'s United Auto Workers) were overruled and the company a few months ago began hiring Negro plant workers for the first time in its history. As an organization, the C.I.O. Auto Workers Union stands for nondiscrimination.

Official Attitude—The War Production Board has a Negro employment and training branch, headed by Negro Robert C. Weaver, a government career man with a Harvard Ph.D. In Cleveland the other day Weaver said:

> "The primary responsibility for ending racial discrimination in war industry rests with employers. Employers are the ones who must take the initiative. If there are union objections to hiring Negroes, industry can handle the situation. Appeals can be taken to the President's Committee on Fair Employment Practices if necessary."

Whenever Negroes are inducted in war industry under WPB's aegis, they are inducted with the cooperation of labor. Otherwise, the new employees would be deviled out of their jobs by their fellow workers.

At this stage, WPB has had almost no complaints that Negroes were being hired at sub-standard wages.

War and Migration

JACK YEAMAN BRYAN

What sort of people are in-migrant war workers? What health and social problems do they create? After the war is over, will they put a special burden on social services? These questions have been bothering residents of Cleveland, Ohio, where emotion and prejudice have seriously influenced community attitudes toward newcomers to the city.

Therefore, the Cleveland Welfare Federation decided last September to make a systematic inquiry for use in future planning as well as in directing public opinion towards an informed understanding of the situation.

. . . .

Guesses Proved Wrong

One striking discovery was the disparity between popular ideas about newcomers and the considered opinion of informed observers. For instance, it is commonly supposed in Cleveland that hiring for war industries has swelled the city's population enormously. Actually, in-migrancy has failed to offset the loss of those who have left for service in the armed forces. While more than 135,000 Clevelanders have already left for the wars, the sugar ration count indicates that only about 100,000 newcomers have arrived since 1940. Housing officials believe the in-migrant total may now be as high as 120,000, but even this figure indicates a temporary shrinkage in population.

The study also revealed a notable disagreement between the average person and the informed observer about the characteristics of these newcomers—what sort of people they are, their assets and liabilities as residents of our city. The man in the street is apt to regard them—particularly those he has never met—with the distrust and suspicion he reserves for all foreigners and other strangers. He has a mind-set which tends to regard the least desirable elements as typical. Though he agrees that newcomers are needed for the war plants, he considers them as "riff raff" that the city would do well to get rid of as soon as the emergency ends.

This low estimate, of course, has its base in an economic fear. When jobs become scarce, the outsiders may remain as competitors. If relief again becomes a critical need for the employable, they may become competitors for that also.

It is common to link in-migrancy solely with precarious and inferior economic status—to think of in-migrants only as unskilled workmen. But many executives and professionals now holding war-connected positions have migrated to Cleveland since Pearl Harbor. They, also, must be classed as in-migrants along with the manual laborer.

It is true, however, that the proportion of in-migrant laborers to the more skilled and professional workers has increased as the emergency has lengthened. In many war industries major and minor executives, together with skilled workers, arrived early to help set up war production in specialized lines. They were followed soon by un-

From Jack Yeaman Bryan, "The In-Migrant 'Menace'," *Survey*, LXXXI (January, 1945), 6-9. Reprinted by permission.

trained workers. Even so, it is a mistake to suppose that recent newcomers are nearly all manual laborers. An upward trend has been noted during the past year of new arrivals among social workers, teachers, nurses, physicians, and other professionals.

Another common misconception is that in-migrants include an alarming percentage of girls and women "on the loose." Actually, the woman's bureau of the Cleveland Police Department has found surprisingly few unattached girls among the in-migrants. The great majority of girls among the newcomers have come to Cleveland as part of established family groups.

Although single persons have dominated large American migrations in the past, the present war-connected shift of population appears to be principally a movement of families. At least this is true of the picture in Cleveland. Furthermore, the new families closely resemble the average local family in size, numbering about four members. If the man seeking employment in war industry does not bring his family with him, he usually sends for them as soon as he is established.

Statements are frequently heard to the effect that a very large share of in-migrant war workers are Negroes. One of the reasons that people have this impression is that more Negroes are employed in the downtown area than formerly, and that colored residents have more money with which to shop in the big stores. Actually, the proportion of Negroes among Cleveland in-migrants is slightly less than 18 percent.

Another prevalent error is the supposition that the majority of white immigrants are "hill-billies" from rural sections of the South. Investigation showed that comparatively few of them have come from south of the Ohio River. At two of the largest housing projects for war workers, white families new to Cleveland were found to come preponderantly from nearby areas—in Ohio, Pennsylvania, and Michigan, with much smaller numbers from such states as West Virginia and Tennessee.

Records of 499 families at one of these projects were studied with particular care. Although thirty-two states are represented among the residents in that project, 135 of the sample were Clevelanders. An additional 155 were from Ohio outside Cleveland, 59 from Pennsylvania, 56 from Michigan, and the rest from more distant states.

With the Negroes the situation is different, the majority being from Alabama, Georgia, and Tennessee. However, most of them come from urban, not rural, areas of these states. Therefore many, already accustomed to city living and to working in industry, have a background which favors easy adjustment to city life.

The degree to which in-migrants may be expected to affect

postwar social and health problems evidently hinges on three points: the number who will remain, the amount of employment open to them after reconversion, their capacity to follow standards of behavior acceptable in an urban community.

Will Migrants Remain?

Most close observers queried were of the opinion that a majority of the Negroes will tend to remain, whereas white people from rural areas will tend to go back to their place of origin. The reason the rural white is expected to return is that he is apt to have difficulties in adjusting to a big city. His roots in his home community are deep, his relatives perhaps numerous, and he had always been able to "worry through" hard times there. Besides, he has an established liking for the country. He is, therefore, inclined to stay in the city only so long as the wages are high.

Among the Negroes, those who were brought in by labor caravans have generally not liked what they found and many have failed to stay for any appreciable time. With those who came in on their own accord, however, the situation is different.

A rather large number are from urban areas in the South, but few have any particular attachment to the towns they have left. They have come north because they already had relatives or friends here.

Furthermore, once settled, they regard Cleveland as a better place than the southern city they left in which to educate their children and improve their condition generally. Even in a depression, many believe, their lot would be much better than in the South. According to resident Negro leaders, if the present practice of keeping jobs open to Negroes is continued after the war, 70 percent will stay; if prewar discriminations in hiring are resumed, at least 50 percent will stay.

The study uncovered completely opposite views on the part of employers regarding the efficiency of Negro workers and the desirability of keeping them on the payrolls when the emergency ends. The experience of downtown drug stores and restaurants which have hired Negro help on a catch-as-catch-can basis has not been happy. Several industrial plants, too, especially those which have used caravan-hiring, have had unfortunate experiences.

On the other hand, some of the largest plants have found Negroes so satisfactory in many kinds of work that they plan to avoid any discrimination whatever in the future. Two large manufacturers of airplane parts, for example, have found Negroes as good workmen as whites, and more careful to avoid absenteeism. Moreover, they have not been troubled by friction between whites and Negroes in working hours.

These antithetical views stem from dissimilar hiring policies. The two plants which have had successful experiences have both hired on a selective basis with the cooperation of established Negro organizations. Thus, men and women known to be most reliable were brought in first to set the pace and provide leadership and training for later employes. Equally important, these plants have kept the possibility of promotion open, and this has encouraged more efficient effort. In short, their reasons for avoiding discrimination in the future come from evidence in their own experience that non-discrimination is a good policy.

By contrast, the plants which put the lowest estimate on Negro workmen have generally attempted to use them only in the least desirable jobs, such as foundry work. Their chance of promotion is negligible. The turnover is accordingly high, the efficiency low. Consequently, officials in such plants consider their negative feeling toward Negroes confirmed and will continue to hire them only so long as the labor shortage requires it.

. . . .

Troubles

In some of the large housing projects there has been considerable friction between established citizens and in-migrants. For instance, some residents complain that in-migrant children are permitted to run wild. Many of them are not really "bad" as yet, but are neglected by parents from rural or semi-rural areas, who are not used to keeping a sharp eye on their youngsters. Other conflicts grow out of neglect of yards, careless housekeeping, leaving garbage about in cardboard boxes, and the like. But most trouble of this kind is due simply to an ignorance of city customs and of the requirements for public health in crowded areas.

School officials, too, have their troubles with in-migrant children. Many of them who have come from rural areas have had to be set back a year or so in school. They resent this. If they are from outside the state, they may have stopped attending school in their home communities and do not like being forced to enroll again under Ohio's more exacting attendance laws. The result is that some of them are not easy to manage.

. . . .

On the other hand, there has been no increase in the tuberculosis rate in the city. The current absence of a rise, of course, may be the temporary result of improved economic conditions. Despite shortages, high wages do allow people to buy wholesome food, warm clothing, and sufficient fuel. If these gains should disappear, a postwar rise in the tuberculosis rate might be expected.

On other counts, too, signs point towards trouble ahead. Despite all that may be said to demonstrate that in-migrants are less of a "menace" than commonly pictured, it would be a grave mistake to underestimate the special problems which they bring to the community's welfare services.

Of the 2,440 new patients getting free clinic treatment at Charity Hospital in 1943, 18.4 percent had been in the Cleveland area less than one year. The net number of newcomers for that year was 57,000 or less than 5 percent of the county's population. Thus from 5 percent of the residents came about 18 percent of the clinic treatment cases. Consequently, the in-migrant group was responsible for more than three times as much free clinic care as long term residents.

What Cleveland Thinks

All of these facts have helped bring about a new point of view toward the future of the newcomers who have come to Cleveland during the war. Time only will tell, of course, how many of them will remain. The most conservative guess is 20 percent—with the probability of a larger proportion. But undeniably, those who do remain will constitute a net addition to our population. Many of them will have problems requiring service from health and social agencies. These agencies are already carrying excessive loads, and the financial problem is becoming increasingly difficult.

Nevertheless, Cleveland agencies now consider it a gross error to think of the problems brought by in-migrants as not belonging to Cleveland. Any person who stays as long as a year has probably lost residence elsewhere, and is legally a Clevelander. His problems are to be accepted as Cleveland's.

. . . .

Instead of disowning the in-migrants as a menace from the outside, instead of sitting back and hoping that at least the worst of them will leave, Cleveland is beginning now to make plans for helping them fulfill the opportunities of good citizenship.

Industrial Peace in Toledo

GILBERT BAILEY

Toledo, Ohio.

In a period of growing concern over the problem of labor disputes, more and more attention is being focused on the so-called "Toledo Plan" of labor conciliation. This northern Ohio city has developed its own home-remedy for strikes and it has worked so well that St. Louis and Louisville have adopted the same system. And other cities, which have been struggling ineffectually against strikes and shut-downs, are beginning to take notice of Toledo's record. So I came here to find out what the Toledo plan is and how it is working out.

It is a simple idea. Toledo, instead of taking its labor troubles to higher authority, set up its own labor conciliation group of eighteen prominent citizens, with management, labor and "the public interest" all equally represented. These men try to settle local disputes as you would settle a family quarrel. When a controversy occurs, the eighteen citizens bring the disputing parties together immediately and try to keep them together until all possibilities of a peaceful settlement are exhausted, meanwhile bringing the force of public opinion to bear on the argument. The idea is to set up community interest as a moderator between labor and management and to establish a closer relationship between their leaders.

The reasons why such a simple plan should work in Toledo are not at first evident to the outside observer. This is not the kind of city where you would expect to find industrial peace right now. It is a factory town of 300,000 people, with 40 per cent of its wage-earners working in manufacturing plants. Known for the manufacture of glass, jeeps, food products, stamping, tools and dies, Toledo has a variety of other industries producing about $400,000,000 worth of manufactured goods each year.

It is a tight labor town, with about 90 per cent of its industrial wage-earners militantly organized. UAW-CIO's "Local 12" alone has 50,000 members, ranging from jeep builders to biscuit makers, and a six-story headquarters almost as elaborately appointed as any industrial office in town.

Toledo also has a well-established name, dating from the Auto-Lite strike in 1934, as a testing ground for labor strife. As one city

From Gilbert Bailey, "Toledo Offers a Plan for Industrial Peace," *New York Times Magazine*, (November 24, 1946). Copyright © 1946 by The New York Times Company. Reprinted by permission.

official put it, "We used to air-condition our factories by throwing bricks through the windows."

. . . .

By treating labor disputes as a community problem, the Labor-Management-Citizens Committee, as it is called, has succeeded in giving labor-management relations a personal quality which is rare in other communities. As evidence of common faith in the plan, forty-three unions and 267 employers have asked for "Certificates of Participation."

. . . .

It took several months to lay the groundwork for the Toledo Plan. The idea began to take shape last year when the Mayor appointed the Labor-Management-Citizens Committee, six men each from management, labor and the citizenry, including the presidents of four corporations, three ministers, a judge, a college professor, the Vice Mayor and most of Toledo's top labor leaders. They met every two weeks at a hotel, put their feet under a table and talked about labor-management troubles and the possibility of dealing with them as a joint civic problem.

For seven months they talked and argued about the rights of wage-earners and the rights of factory owners and on the old issues— the closed shop, slow-down, hiring and firing policies—they came out about where they started. But they did reach agreement on one important point: in all disputes the interest of the community comes first. Perhaps of far more importance, leaders of industry and labor got acquainted for the first time.

. . . .

When a strike impends, the committee goes right out and takes a hand in trying to prevent a work stoppage. One labor member and one industrial member usually see the parties involved and try to sell them the idea of a peaceful settlement. Most of the top labor leaders and heads of industries know one another by their first names and they try to settle their disputes as quickly and informally as possible.

When a strike is actually called, one of the committee members gets in touch with the disputing parties and offers the city's conciliation services. If they accept—acceptance is voluntary—the chairman appoints three men to hear the case and make a recommendation for settlement.

Last summer when traction employes struck for higher wages and the city faced an indefinite tie-up, committee members met with the union and the company nine days out of eleven; the controversy was settled on the eleventh day. With one exception, it was the longest strike Toledo has had since the community took over its labor-management problems.

This strike was in progress on the day I arrived in Toledo, and it afforded a good opportunity to see the Toledo Plan in operation on what was described as "a tough case." Two hundred men had walked out of the Libby-Owens-Ford (Plaskon) plant after an impasse in collective bargaining. A picket line had been thrown around the factory and, inside, quantities of raw plastic were in various stages of spoiling.

The main issue was whether the factory had to have a swing shift to produce plastic economically. At heart it was a conflict between a worker's right to eat breakfast at a reasonable hour and industry's determination to keep the plastic flowing. Company experts were prepared to show that plastic must be a continuous "three-shift" operation, while the union leaders were holding out for two shifts so their men could have fixed working hours. After seven days of strike, the dispute was brought to the Labor-Management-Citizens Committee, or the "LMC," as it is known.

In this particular case, Judge Amos Cohn, the LMC chairman, was sitting as the public member of the three-man conciliation panel.

. . . .

The panel session, held in Judge Cohn's courtroom, was already in somewhat heated session when I arrived, and the CIO leader and a plastics operations expert were winding up their opening arguments. The company had accused the union, among other things, of setting "up a roadblock to scientific and industrial progress in Toledo," and the CIO spokesman became so vehement about swing shifts that the judge had to call him down. He was still simmering when the meeting adjourned for a cooling-off period.

During the recess the community panel proposed informally that they should all join in and visit the plant on a fact-finding tour. Immediately the whole party of about twenty-five people—panel, shop committee, company experts and officials—piled into automobiles and started for the Plaskon plant to find out if it really took a swing shift to make plastic. The picket line was removed to make way for the party.

We spent an hour going through the plant, while an operations expert explained, step by step, why it took three shifts of men on duty around the clock to keep production up. At the end of the tour, the union and the company were able to agree on a possible compromise settlement: a few key men on a swing shift, enough to keep essential processes going.

. . . .

How could such a disarmingly simple notion have any effect on labor-management disputes? Merely by getting together around a table and talking, the leaders of labor and industry discovered that they do have interests in common on the community level. Obviously, misunderstandings could be avoided, time wasted in bluffing and pointless demurring could be saved, and some strikes averted if factory owners and labor leaders understood one another.

. . . .

Some of the more conservative supporters of the Labor-Management-Citizens Committee prefer to regard the Community Group as an experiment rather than a discovery. And there are some skeptics. I talked to one labor organizer who refused to believe that community interest, no matter how well it was exploited, could compete with economic self-interest. "In my opinion, the whole thing would break down if a certain labor leader decided to walk out," he said.

I went around to see Vice Mayor Mike DiSalle, the man who fathered the original idea, pushed the plan through the City Council and served as the chairman of the Toledo Labor Management Citizens Committee until he took a leave of absence to run for Congress. He has predicted that "strikes will be a rarity in Toledo in six months" and he firmly believes that the Toledo plan could be applied in other cities. Two things are necessary, in his opinion, to make it work: first, a willingness on the part of labor and management leaders to sit down and talk about their differences; secondly, the active support of civic groups, newspapers and public opinion.

Not Under the Bed

CHADS O. SKINNER

State's 3,500 Communists Analyze News Just Like Joe

Here is the lowdown on the Communist Party in Ohio as it was obtained not by looking for Reds under the bed, but by talking to the Party's head men:

The Party (and a Joe Stalin special curse on one who would spell the word with a lower case) has only 3,500 members in the state.

The Party's state headquarters is at 2083 E. 4th Street, fourth floor, in one room where quite a few of the comrades could gather for instruction, are pictures of Nicolas Lenin and Abraham Lincoln on opposite walls.

Sectional offices of the Party are in Youngstown, Akron, Toledo, Bellaire (the coal mining capital of Ohio), and Cincinnati.

Defends Negroes

The Party has organizers in Columbus, Dayton, Mansfield, Lorrain, Sandusky, and Canton.

The Party "pitches in"—and does so with a vengeance—wherever it considers the rights of minority groups, notably Negroes, are being infringed. The Party stands for "full rights" for Negroes.

The Party conducts schools at which members are instructed in the problems of the day, and sometimes in the fundamental tenets of Karl Heinrich Marx, the German Socialist and philosopher, whose writings are the basis of the "class struggle" the Communists are carrying on.

The Party does not exactly set up "front" organizations or order members to get into units of the Congress of Industrial Organizations or the American Federation of Labor; but its espousal of the cause of men who work for wages produces Communist adherents in trade unionism.

The high command of the Communist Party in Ohio "reads everything," including such non-Communist publications as the *Plain Dealer,* and is a darn sight better informed on current events and trends than most leaders of the Democrat and Republican parties.

While disavowing official connection with Commissar Stalin's Soviet Russia, the Party, "in making an analysis of the events of the day comes to the same conclusions as the Party in Russia."

These data were gathered from Arnold Johnson, state head of

From *Cleveland Plain Dealer,* **August 10, 1946.**

the Party, who was patently nonplussed when a representative of the capitalist press, as the comrades call all papers other than the *Daily Worker,* sought an appointment with him; from Gus Hall, cochairman of the Ohio branch of the party and a navy veteran of World War II, and Mike Davidow, Cuyahoga County secretary of the Communist organization, who is an army veteran and was in on the invasion of Okinawa.

The Staff

These men have a staff consisting of Abe Lewis, Communist organizer in the Cedar-Central area of Cleveland that is heavily populated by Negroes; Martin Chancey, state secretary of the Party; Andrew Onda, chairman of the Mahoning Valley district; Joe Friedman, Akron chairman; Anton Ckrchmarek, Ohio Valley chairman; Robert Dunkel, Cincinnati chairman. The fiery Onda, incidentally, spearheaded the Communist "hunger marches" on City Hall early in the depression of the 1930s.

"We don't send men into the ranks of labor unions," Johnson asserted, "but men in trade unionism join the Party because of what we stand for."

Hall remarked that an analysis of the Communist roster in Ohio showed that "our trade union membership is almost equally divided between A. F. of L. and C. I. O. unions."

Johnson said his party had members who were "active in virtually all kinds of organizations throughout the state."

"We pitch in wherever minorities are fighting for their rights," Johnson said. "You can bet on that. We urge everywhere that all organizations support antilynching measures."

Some of the Ohio comrades attended last month's meeting of the National Committee of the Communist Party at which the organization set these tasks for itself:

1—To launch a circulation drive for the *Daily Worker* and the *Worker,* the latter being the Sunday edition of the former.

2—To organize mass actions against inflationary price rises and high rents; to initiate and co-operate in movements for the reopening of wage negotiations.

Out for Votes

3—To mobilize the party and labor for support of the candidates, platforms and aims of the labor-progressive candidates in the coming November election.

4—To launch a new drive for the breaking of diplomatic and economic relations with Franco Spain.

5—To rouse the nation for withdrawal of all United States troops from China and the halt of American aid to the Chiang regime which is "waging civil war."

In the Communist state headquarters, when this reporter visited it, Comrade Johnson's stenographer was wearing a red, white and blue dress and typing away at a desk over which hung a calendar issued by one of Cleveland's most conservative capitalist institutions.

More About Ohio's Communists

CHADS O. SKINNER

Few Hands, But Deft, Hold Hammer of Reds

The Communists pack weight in labor unions and in organizations fighting the battles of minority groups that is far out of proportion to their numerical strength in Cleveland, in Ohio and the nation.

That is because the Communist Party instills the techniques of leadership in the comrades.

It is because the party carries on continuing research into economic and trade union problems of the day. It equips the comrades with arguments, if not facts, for parliamentary maneuvering in the pinkish organizations to which Communists belong.

Furthermore, whenever a "cause" develops that is down the Communist alley, the Commies get in there and fight harder than the people whose cause is at stake.

They Do Effective Work

One of the ablest leaders in the Negro community here, no Communist himself, put it this way.

"The Communists are the only ones who come to our people's aid in situations like those in Georgia where the lynchings of Negroes

From *Cleveland Plain Dealer,* August 11, 1946.

recently took place. It's not the churches or other non-Communist organizations that give us assistance; it's the Communists who come in with propaganda and who work harder than most of us. And they don't try to disguise the fact that they are Communists. When you're in a desperate fight you can't take too hard a look at your allies."

A mortal enemy of Communism, a person who has made intensive inquiry into the party structure and tactics, said it would be folly to deny that the Communists, despite their minority status, do effective work in the unions and associations they are in "because they have the benefit of the party's research department which concocts their resolutions and prepares their arguments."

This authority on the Communist party locally and nationally said the widely held belief that the followers "infiltrate" labor unions is fallacious.

"The Communist organization," he remarked, "is a political party that appeals to the working class, and with that appeal it obtains a certain number of members who are already in labor unions, A. F. of L. and C. I. O."

There are Communists, too, in such "liberal" organizations as the Cleveland chapter of American Youth for Democracy, which is currently charging that the proprietors of the Euclid Beach amusement park are abridging civil rights by refusing to permit Negroes to go swimming or to dance there.

Frank Hashmall, 28-year-old graduate of the College of the City of New York, who heads the chapter, said so himself.

Hashmall reported that the A. Y. D., in collaboration with the United Negro and Allied Veterans of America and the National Negro Congress, had been instrumental in supplying the basis of four suits filed recently in Municipal Court, alleging that the Euclid Beach management had violated a little known Ohio civil rights law by refusing two Negro couples the right to dance at the amusement park.

The suits were filed by Jerry Land, who told this writer that he is a member of the Communist party. He is in a law partnership with his mother, Mrs. Yetta Land, who was long one of the most militant women Communists here or anywhere else.

Asks $500 Damages

Land said that his litigation asked $500 damages for each of the four young Negroes he represents. The case probably will not be heard for several months. The American Youth for Democracy chapter, which has been picketing Euclid Beach, may not technically be a Communist "front" outfit, but you can wager quite a few bob that Commies are in its picket line.

When I asked Hashmall what his political philosophy was he answered:

"My political philosophy is basically that we have to extend democracy quickly and thoroughly."

Johnson's Candidacy

"Are you a Communist?" I inquired.

"I am in favor of the extension of our democracy," he replied. "There are Communists in our organization."

One of the most spectacular "incidents" involving a Communist was the endorsement last fall of the central body of C. I. O. unions of the candidacy of Arthur Johnson, state head of the party, for the Cleveland Board of Education. At that time a spokesman for the anti-Communist bloc of the C. I. O. body told his colleagues the endorsement of Johnson was "dynamite" and that the C. I. O. and its Political Action Committee simply could not endorse "a top Communist for a top educational office and get away with it."

Good at Debate

The endorsement was finally rescinded. Johnson was soundly defeated, but the more sanguine Communists asserted that the 58,000-odd votes Johnson got represented the party's strength in Cleveland. Johnson himself said the party had only 3,500 members in all Ohio.

One person who has studied Communist technique said that comrades who are in the same trade union "carry on a continuous secret cause," and can knock the spots off non-Communist colleagues in free style debate and in getting their views incorporated into parliamentary resolutions.

"I don't like the Commies," this critic remarked, "but don't forget that they stand for the betterment of labor and most of their proposals inside union councils are sound. But, of course, they drag in a lot of dead cats that represent just plain Communist propaganda."

Larry Doby

GORDON COBBLEDICK

There's No Need to Guess About Larry Doby; He Will Be Accepted if He Proves Big Leaguer

CHICAGO, July 5—People are doing a lot of unnecessary guessing as to how Larry Doby, the Indians' newest rookie, will be accepted by his teammates and by the customers.

He will be accepted by both groups if he proves to be a good ball player and a good human being, and will be rejected by both if the opposite is true.

How do I know? Well, the Cleveland Browns of the All-America Football Conference signed two Negro players last year, to the deep consternation of their rival teams. There had been no colored boys in the white professional league and it was evident that all except the Browns intended to keep it that way if possible.

Today, something less than a year later, every team in the All-America Conference is beating the bushes in a desperate effort to find a good Negro football player or two—another Bill Willis or another Marion Motley. Several have succeeded and the others are still trying.

The white members of the Browns themselves, several of them from the deep South, were not exactly elated when they learned that Willis and Motley were to be their teammates. But that changed, too, just as the feeling of the other clubs in the league changed.

Southerner Takes Seat Between Willis and Motley

At the Bowling Green training camp late last summer I saw the hungry behemoths storm into the Falcon's Nest, a sort of student union, for lunch one day. Willis and Motley filled their trays and took places at a table, leaving an empty chair between them. There were a dozen other empty chairs, but the man who took the place between the two colored boys was Gaylon Smith.

Smith hails from Mississippi, where Messrs. Bilbo and Rankin wave the banners of white supremacy, but it was apparent that the fact that Willis and Motley were on his team was good enough for him.

In one of the early games of the season, in Chicago, the Rockets undertook to "get" the Negro stars. The Browns' reaction cost them a substantial amount of yardage in unnecessary roughness penalties,

From *Cleveland Plain Dealer*, Sports Section, July 6, 1947.

but they taught the Rockets a lesson. Willis and Motley were their teammates, and a punch on either's nose was a punch on the nose of a Cleveland player and was so considered by the Browns.

The All-America Conference plays a round robin home-and-home schedule, with each team meeting every other team twice. The first time around, resentment against Willis and Motley was evident in every opponent. The second time around this feeling was notably absent. The boys had been accepted as first-rate football players, and as first-rate football players were respected by friend and foe alike.

Robinson Is Accepted by All N. L. Clubs

Jackie Robinson is another reason why the guessing at the reaction to Doby's presence with the Indians is unnecessary. The Brooklyn Dodgers didn't particularly want Robinson as a teammate and it is no secret that they would have borne up under the blow if he had failed to make the grade.

But he has made the grade, has earned his spurs as a bona fide big leaguer, and as such has been accepted gladly by his own team and by all others in the National League. The occasion happily has not risen, but it is a safe bet that in the event of physical trouble between Robinson and an opponent, the Dodgers would be fighting on Robinson's side.

The reports on Doby suggest strongly that he is a ball player of considerable talent. Whether he is ready for the major leagues remains to be seen. The wildest-eyed rooter for the Negro leagues does not advance the claim that they are as fast company as the white majors, but colored people believe that there are several players in their leagues who are capable of playing with the white boys.

Unlike many of the greatest Negro stars, Doby has youth on his side. If he shows the need of further experience he will be farmed out. He can't be sent to Baltimore or Oklahoma City, the Indians' principal farms, but several cities would be glad to get him.

But whether or not he makes good, the barriers are down and the big leagues of baseball are open to the colored players. Some who come after him will make the grade. And the game will be better for it.

9 At Mid-Century

THE 1950s have been described by recent young Americans as the feel-nothing-do-nothing decade. It could be speculated that, because of the Depression, World War II and its reconstruction, the cold war, atomic weaponry, and the Korean War, society could stand few more crises. Popular notions and conjecture aside, however, society and government were faced with problems that reflected growth and prosperity despite economic recession in the decade. Ohio was a microcosm of America during the 1950s. Continued population growth, urbanization, suburbanization, and industrialization diminished the importance of agriculture in the state's economy. At the same time, government had to assume greater responsibility for service facilities and expanded social services. The decade was neither quiet, unproductive, nor unresponsive; rather, it was one in which people identified the problems associated with growth and expected a greater amount of positive action on the part of government.

Ohio's population reached 9,706,397 during the 1950s, an increase of 22% over the previous decade. Businesses also expanded and consolidated into larger corporations. Accompanying this growth were the sprawling effects of suburbanization, which placed greater demands on the services offered by older cities and generated greater responsibilities for newly incorporated municipalities. Consequently, in order to meet the added costs of governing, state and local governments were preoccupied with a constant search for new sources of revenue during the decade. Industrialization, urbanization, and suburbanization also had their effects on agriculture in Ohio. Besides taking labor from the farms, the construction of highways, factories, homes, and shopping centers removed valuable land from cultivation. During the 1950s, Ohio lost 22,285 farms, reducing farm acreage by over 1,000,000 acres. For example, the completion in 1955 of the Ohio Turnpike, which stretched for 241 miles across northern Ohio, removed 25,000 acres of rich land from production, representing a loss of 2,500,000 bushels of corn.

The shift in population from the farms to the urban areas promoted a crisis in a state legislature that was already suffering from rural-urban jealousies. The Hanna amendment of 1903 had given to each county—regardless of population—one representative in the general assembly. The rural bloc of legislators could outvote their urban colleagues, even though by 1950, because of the population shifts, the majority of Ohioans lived in metropolitan areas. In the state legislature, a rotten borough system had developed: as a result, legislation needed for the cities had difficulty passing the legislature. The issue of fair representation was raised during the 1950s, but because of both personal and partisan politics the system was not reformed until the 1960s.

During the 1950s, state government assumed responsibility for large capital improvement programs and expanded social services. Recognizing the importance of a new and efficient highway system to connect its industrial centers, the state spent $500,000,000 on highway construction alone. In order to keep pace with the benefits of modern medicine and to provide for the more unfortunate in Ohio's society, it financed expanded social services. At the same time, educational and research facilities at the university level had to be expanded to aid industrial expansion and the technological explosion. Therefore, in 1955, Ohioans approved a bond issue of $150,000,000 to aid capital improvements in these areas. While the state was running pell-mell toward complete industrialization, conservationists recognized that the environment as well as society was paying the price of economic expansion through ecological destruction. In the 1950s, state agencies such as the Department of Health began to study the effects of industrial pollution on man and his environment. In 1951, the Deddens Act, passed by the general assembly, created the Water Pollution Control Board, which studied and offered controls over municipalities and industries that used the state's water system as a dumping ground for waste materials. The state agencies responsible for such controls wanted the 1950s to become the decade for pollution abatement.

Ohio's government was certainly willing to cope with problems resulting from rapid economic expansion and prosperity. The larger role of government, both as a regulator and as a provider, meant greater economic support as well as a conscientious commitment for social improvements. The people of the 1950s, weary from nearly a decade of continued crises, were perhaps convinced to work toward improved conditions in more subtle ways than those of preceding or succeeding decades.

Population Change

REPORT
Rural-Urban Migration Patterns, 1940-1950

When the definition of rural areas of Ohio was held constant as they were for 1940 we find a heavy migration of population into rural areas. Rural areas had a net population gain due to migration of 225,946 between 1940 and 1950, while urban population had a net gain of only 17,524. The migration gain rate for the state was 108 per cent of the rural population in 1940. There was an excess of rural births over rural deaths, or natural increase amounting to 248,558 for the decade.

The pattern of increase in rural areas, however, indicates a strong suburbanization movement of population in counties which have large cities or those adjacent to such counties, rather than a general increase in rural farm population. Most of this increase comes from urban people who are so designated in the new definition of urban in the 1950 census, but to understand what has taken place in rural areas, it can be seen more clearly when the 1940 definition is held constant.

The net migration increase received by the urban population of the state was only 17,524, while the rural increase due to net migration was 225,946.

The natural increase in urban areas was 546,967; that for rural was 248,578. When the increase due to migration and the natural increase are totaled urban areas increased 564,491 and rural 474,524.

Migration: Agricultural Factors

The strong trend of movement of population toward the rural areas located near-by highly urban areas in Ohio indicates that the factors in intra-state migration are a result of the agricultural and industrial developments over a longer period of time than the decade. In contrast to the kinds of "pushes" and "pulls" operating on a population in a state with a larger proportion of rural people the factors in the kind of migration which took place in Ohio seem to take on different aspects.

For one thing, Ohio has had an urban population more than equal to its rural population for almost half a century. The large number of metropolitan areas comprising 100,000 or more persons have existed since well before World War II, and these areas have

From Wade H. Andrews and Emily M. Westerkamm, *Rural-Urban Population Change and Migration in Ohio 1940-1950*, **Research Bulletin 737, November, 1953, (Wooster, 1953),** 33-40.

been attracting the rural farm population by means of job opportunities and higher levels of living since the urban development of the state began. While the number of farms in Ohio has continued to decline in the past decade, the trend of the past ten years represents only a late stage in a development which was already well under way by 1940. There has been the usual rural to urban migration as is shown in the non-metropolitan areas but also there has occurred the event which seems to be peculiar to the decade under discussion. This event may be called the reaching of a "saturation point" of urban areas, and the overflow of resident non-farm population into the adjacent rural metropolitan and non-metropolitan areas.

An analysis of several agricultural variables serves to explain the agricultural forces in the movement of rural farm population. The trend in agricultural factors in Ohio corresponds in most respects to that of the same factors in other states, however, the preponderance of suburbanization in metropolitan areas tends to affect, in some instances, the way they are related to population movements.

Reduction in Number of Farms

From the available data it is known that the decade reflects a movement away from farms in the number of farm-operator families. The reduction in the number of farms varied in non-metropolitan areas from 9 to 23 percent with an average drop of 13.7 percent. In metropolitan areas the range was from four to 33 percent with an average drop of 18.9 percent. The reduction averaged about 15 percent for the state as a whole.

In addition, increased mechanization of farms resulted in a reduction in the need for hired farm labor. This decrease in hired farm workers can be inferred from the reduction in farm wage expenditure by nearly 30 percent between 1939 and 1949, after allowances are made for the increase in farm wage rates.

. . . .

The state as a whole experienced more than 66 percent of its reduction in number of farms during the last half of the decade. The same kind of difference holds for the reduction in farms during the two halves of the decade for both metropolitan and non-metropolitan areas, even though the actual rate of decrease for metropolitan areas is higher for both five year periods than the rate for non-metropolitan areas.

It is likely that there are several important forces affecting the reduction in the number of farms. It may be postulated that some of these forces are different between metropolitan and non-metropolitan areas. In metropolitan areas the exodus of urban people to the suburban areas has changed the use of much of the land from farms into residential areas either subdivisions or individual residences and industrial areas. In non-metropolitan areas the reduction seems to be more related to the enlargement of the size of farm units. This parallels the increased level of living and the decrease in rural population.

The greater reduction in number of farms in all areas of Ohio after World War II can also be interpreted in terms of the impetus which the movement already under way was given by the general economic prosperity in this country and the resulting employment opportunities offered by large metropolitan areas during the post war period.

Improved opportunities for urban work has attracted many rural people. Improved farm prosperity has enabled better farmers to enlarge their farms by buying out those wishing to leave. Such reasoning is only hypothetical but appears to have plausible basis in the data.

Rise in Farm Levels of Living

For Ohio the average farm operator level of living index in 1950 was 148, which means that the farm level of living in the state was about 50 percent better than the United States average in 1945 (index of 100). The average in 1950 for the United States from the same index was 122. Between 1940 and 1950 the index for Ohio increased 31 percent.

These changes for the state did not occur evenly. Largest gains during the decade were made by those areas which had low levels in 1940. In 1940 the indexes of western Ohio counties averaged about 130 or 17 index points above the state average of 113, whereas the southeastern counties indexes averaged about 88 or 25 points below the average level of living for the state. By 1950 we find that although the western part of the state still enjoyed the highest levels this difference had been considerably reduced. Gains for the decade in western counties were about 25 index points; for southeastern counties the gains ranged from 43 to 65 points.

During the period 1940 to 1945 the western and northeastern parts of the state gained quite rapidly but from 1945 to 1950 improved only very little. Southeastern Ohio, however, had, for the most part, greater gains in the five year period following the war.

Tyranny in Ohio

HUBERT H. HUMPHREY

Saturday, July 1, 1950

Mr. President, Members of the Senate will recall that in the course of the debate on S. 1728 I made reference to the fact that State legislatures were in the main not as democratic nor as representative of the people as other legislative bodies in America. In that connection I was interested in an article appearing in the July 1, 1950, issue of the United States Municipal News published by the United States Conference of Mayors. It reprints an editorial from the Akron Beacon Journal and goes on to refer to another editorial appearing in the Milwaukee Journal on the same subject.

I ask unanimous consent to have these excerpts from page 51 of the publication printed in the Appendix of the Record.

There being no objection, the article was ordered to be printed in the Record, as follows:

[From the United States Municipal News]

Tyranny in Ohio

The United States Conference of Mayors met in New York City last month and adopted a number of resolutions, one of which read as follows:

"*Resolved,* That since equality of representation is the most vital and fundamental principle of democracy and inequality of representation is a tyranny to which no people worthy of freedom will lightly submit; and in order that cities be accorded the fair and equal representation in the various State legislatures to which they are entitled as a matter of justice and right, the 1950 Annual Conference of the United States Conference of Mayors urge upon the States where fair and equal representation does not exist to correct this condition which is utterly repugnant to the basic concept of democratic processes of government by initiating action leading to reapportionment at the conclusion of the 1950 population census, or, in those States not having constitutional or statutory provision for reapportionment on the basis of population, to sponsor the constitutional or statutory amendments necessary to make such reapportionment possible."

From a speech by Hubert H. Humphrey, "State Legislatures," *Congressional Record*, Vol. 96, 81st Congress, 2nd Session, p. 4951.

Are Ohioans unworthy of freedom? The "tyranny" of unequal representation has existed here ever since 1903 when the Ohio Constitution was amended to give every county, no matter how small, one State Representative. For 100 years prior to 1903 Ohio had enjoyed representative government.

Representation became unequal as soon as the 1903 amendment went into effect and the inequality has been growing more pronounced ever since. In the 1951-52 legislature, Vinton County's lone representative will speak for some 11,000 citizens, while each of Summit County's four will represent 100,000.

It is conservative to say that two-thirds of the Ohio House represent only one-third of the people.

We doubt that any other State in the Union is guiltier than Ohio of tolerating the tyranny which the Conference of Mayors deplores.

Here, a constitutional amendment is necessary to restore representative government. This could be done, though with some difficulty, by circulating petitions and initiating an amendment for the voters' consideration—perhaps as early as 1951.

There is another and perhaps a better way. The people are scheduled to get a chance to vote in 1952 on whether they favor the calling of a constitutional convention—the first, by the way, since 1912 and the third since the present Constitution was adopted in 1851. If the people's answer is yes, legislative reapportionment doubtless will be one of the main subjects taken up by the convention. Reapportionment arrived at in this way might be sounder than reform accomplished by means of an initiated amendment.

Of course, there is no certainty that a vote for holding a constitutional convention will be followed by approval of the convention's proposals. The work of the 1873-74 convention was rejected by the people. And there is no certainty, even, that a majority will favor the holding of a convention. The last time the question came up, in 1932, the decision was against a convention.

Still, it seems to us that the cities, having endured inequality of representation for almost 50 years, can afford to wait until 1952 to find out whether they must push for amendment of the Constitution by petition and referendum. In the meantime, city officials should begin to consult with political-science experts with a view to having a satisfactory plan ready to present either to a convention or to the people.

In our view there is no question that the Ohio system, wherein a population minority controls the legislature, is undemocratic. The penalty which this system has imposed is the necessity of compromising principle. Too many times bills which would benefit the majority have been blocked until rewards were forthcoming for the overrepresented minority. Ohio's fantastically complicated and illogical tax system can be blamed in large part on the logrolling which goes on, necessarily, in a lopsided legislature.

The tyranny of unequal representation is too solidly entrenched to be overthrown at a single stroke. But if we consider ourselves worthy of freedom, we should begin to organize our rebellion now.— Akron Beacon Journal.

Communists Again

UN-AMERICAN COMMISSION

This is the first report of the Ohio Un-American Activities Commission submitted to the members of the 100th General Assembly and the Governor of the State of Ohio pursuant to sections of the Ohio General Code, passed on June 1, 1951, and approved by Governor Frank J. Lausche on June 18, 1951, creating an un-American activities commission in the legislative branch of the government.

. . . .

What Is Communism?

Any investigation of Communism must be predicated upon an understanding of what Communism as it exists today really is. To arrive at such a definition, it is essential that we view the activities of the Communist Party in the light of present day facts, not obscured by the double-talk of Party sympathizers or idealized by starry-eyed reformers. The Communist Party is an international conspiracy, directed from Moscow, and having as its goal the violent overthrow of our democratic form of government. The Commission's sole concern with individuals and organizations has been with the part they play in this conspiracy.

. . . .

Clear and Present Danger

Slowly but surely, the American people are beginning to recognize Communism and the Communist Party for what they really are.

From *Report of the Un-American Activities Commission, State of Ohio, 1951-1952*, I, (Columbus, 1952), pp. 14-34.

Too long Communists and their apologists have been successful in creating the illusion that Communism is a vague dream of economic utopianism and Communists are a handful of crackpots pursuing a vain illusory will-o'-the-wisp, all to be tolerated as a necessary evil in a land devoted to freedom and liberty. This view persists, even in the face of the stark and unpalatable fact that the Communists to date have taken over one-fifth of the land surface of the earth and manifest control over one-third of its peoples.

The clear and present danger of the Communist Party lies in the role it will play in the event of an actual shooting war with the Soviet Union.

. . . .

If such a war should come to pass, there would be certain advantages definitely on our side and certain advantages which would as definitely lie on the side of the Soviet Union. We would have no superiority of manpower; that advantage would lie with the enemy. We would certainly have no greater zeal or ardor for a war; that is not a trait of a peace-loving people. It is doubtful if we would have any advantage in new weapons of war. Our one solid advantage is the superiority of American industry, the ability of our plants to out-produce the factories of Russia and her satellites, the ability to step up production to provide the tools of war without completely disrupting our economy. It was this circumstance which turned the tide of World War II in our favor and will inevitably be the deciding factor in any future struggle.

It will be the task of the American Communist Party to minimize or neutralize this advantage. To that end, the Party will have to fight its battle in our factories, shops and mills, to foment crippling strikes, to delay production schedules, to bring our machinery to a halt and to destroy the instruments of production by sabotage.

. . . .

The strong concentration of basic industry within the State of Ohio ranks this State probably in second place among the areas that must be destroyed or seriously crippled to further the Soviet war effort. Our industries of machine tool, rubber, steel, automotive parts, and coal are the backbone of the nation's strength, and coupled with our expanding atomic energy program make crystal-clear the reason for the Communists' concern with Ohio.

There are three groups whose presence in Ohio constitutes a threat to the security of our industries and our war potential. The first group is numerically the smallest but the best trained for their purposes. These are the Communists who are graduates of the International Lenin Institute in Moscow to which promising Communists from all over the world were sent for training in Communist theory and practice. The courses of study, according to a witness who was himself a graduate of the International Lenin Institute, included, besides such courses as the philosophy of Marx and Lenin, dialectical materialism, history of the Russian Communist Party, study of the Comintern, and trade unionism; also the teaching of practical methods of sabotage and psychological warfare. Sabotage included guerilla warfare, suitable for civil insurrection in a struggle for power, use of dynamite and various other forms of explosives, wrecking machinery, crippling power plants, disrupting communication and transportation systems; all against the day when such knowledge and training was to be used to advance the Soviet cause throughout the world. The classes actually constructed black powder bombs, experimented with stick dynamite, made TNT, studied detonators and fuses, certainly not for mere divertissement and it was never so intended.

. . . .

The second group, numerically stronger and only slightly less-trained, are those Communists or sympathizers who fought in the International Brigades in the Spanish Civil War and retain allegiance to the Veterans of the Abraham Lincoln Brigade. Not every member of the Brigade was a Communist, but the Communist Party did most of the recruiting and today anyone still a member of the organization, Veterans of the Abraham Lincoln Brigade, is under Party discipline and subject to Party loyalties. The Ohio Communist Party Year Book for 1937 hailed 150 Ohioans fighting in Spain. The Spanish Civil War was the proving-ground for tactics of guerilla warfare and sabotage on a large scale, and American Communists got additional schooling in sabotage methods.

The third group whose presence in Ohio contributes to the present danger are the rank and file members of the Communist Party who have no special training in sabotage methods, no special techniques, but who need only their slavish devotion to the Soviet Union to be of material assistance to the cause.

. . . .

Labor

From its earliest inception in the United States, the Communist Party preached the necessity of rooting itself in the trade union movement to reach the great bulk of workers throughout key industries. At the Eighth Convention of the Communist Party of the USA, held in Cleveland, Ohio, April 2-8, 1934, it was resolved:

"The Communists in the trade unions must undertake to bring the program and policies of the Party before the masses. A struggle must be conducted against all opportunist deviations which wish to limit the struggles of the trade unions to purely 'trade' questions. The trade unions as the basic mass organization of the workers must fight for all the needs of the workers. This, of course, cannot be achieved through a sectarian commandeering of the masses. The Communists must win the workers for such a struggle on the basis of utilizing every economic struggle for broadening the outlook and perspective of the workers to revolutionize them, and win the best elements to the Party."

. . . .

The studied insidious campaign of infiltration into the trade union movement reached its climax in 1949 and 1950 when the CIO, at its national conventions, expelled eleven international unions as being Communist-controlled and Communist-dominated. Such drastic action was not lightly taken by the CIO.

. . . .

Most important of these unions in Ohio were the International Union of Mine, Mill and Smelter Workers; International Fur and Leather Workers; United Office and Professional Workers of America; and the United Electrical, Radio and Machine Workers of America.

. . . .

The importance of the electrical, radio and machine industry cannot be overstressed. Its military products include: motors and essential equipment for jet planes; guided missiles; radar; complex control for planes, tanks and submarines, multiple types of communication and signal equipment; and atomic energy machinery. It has been properly characterized as the most sensitive industry in the entire field of defense production.

. . . .

Of particular concern to Commission members was testimony indicating plant operators were willing, even eager, to deal with Communist unions, because such unions would "make cut rate bargains with employers to maintain their base." Testimony indicates that such unions adopt a conciliatory attitude toward management in order to be sure they are not pushed out of the plants. Plant management, so shortsighted, is literally playing with dynamite, with dynamite which one day may destroy their plants and do serious damage to the security of our country.

James B. Carey, Secretary and Treasurer of the CIO, and President of the International Union of Electrical, Radio & Machine Workers (IUE-CIO), commenting upon this hearing of the Ohio Un-American Activities Commission in his testimony before the

Senate Subcommittee on Labor and Labor-Management Relations, said, "We charge that in encouraging and assisting the survival of UE, the multi-million dollar corporations of our industry have committed something very close to treason. And it may well be that the nation will never know the full extent of that treason until we find ourselves locked in military combat with a totalitarian enemy whose fanatical adherents and stooges had the run of the industry."

Youth

Another of the more alarming aspects of the Communist Party Program is its concentration on youth. This is not a recently developed program, but is basic in the Communist scheme.

· ·

The effort to subvert American youth and to win it to a foreign ideology is continuing. Communist youth organizations have succeeded one another; as each has fulfilled its function, or become clearly identified for what it really is, and therefore lost its effectiveness for the cause of Communism, another has taken its place. In the recent past, the Young Communist League (YCL) was succeeded by the American Youth for Democracy (AYD) which in turn has been replaced by the current Communist youth organization, the Labor Youth League (LYL). The LYL is not a Communist-front organization; it is actually "the youth-arm of the Communist International in the United States, set up on the orders of the national board, who receives their orders from the Kremlin."

· ·

Communist Party Goes Underground

Much has been said and written concerning the danger of passing legislation against the Communist Party which might drive the Party underground. Evidence before the Commission has made it clear that the Communist Party has already gone underground. It was the decision of the United States Supreme Court, upholding the constitutionality of the Smith Act and sending the top Communist traitors to federal penitentiaries, that sent the Party scurrying underground.

· ·

The effect of this pronouncement in Ohio was immediate. According to John Janowitz, a meeting of the branch of the Communist Party in Cleveland to which he belonged was hurriedly called on June 22, 1951, by Sam Reed, a Communist Party functionary. At that meeting, Reed explained the Party was going underground and all literature should be either destroyed or stored; no meetings with more than one or two members should be held; no phone calls would be made concerning Party activities, and no phone calls made to any Party functionary. The witness particularly said there was no indication that the Party was disbanding or abandoning its end and aims.

. . . .

Numerical Strength in Ohio

In view of the strict secrecy in which the Communist Party has cloaked its membership during the present period, figures showing numerical strength in any locality are of little real significance. There is no such thing as a "card carrying Communist" today. Party membership books were destroyed in 1947, membership cards were destroyed in 1948 and none have been issued since then.

For security reasons the Party has dropped from membership for various reasons persons who might not stand up in time of crisis. Others have severed their connections because of fear of exposure, loss of jobs, public scorn and possible prosecution. While these cannot be counted on the rolls of the Communist Party, they may well be ready to return to activity if increasing Party strength bolsters their waning courage. They have not necessarily been disillusioned or cast out the Communist ideology. Others have been deliberately dropped from membership to form a reserve corps to function only in the event of a general round-up of all Communist Party members. This is to insure that a new Communist Party can rise even though all on the Party rolls are interned. It is obvious that not every Communist is then included in registration figures, but it would be mere conjecture to guess how many more should be added to include all the various categories.

As FBI Director J. Edgar Hoover has said, "The numerical strength of the Party's enrolled membership is insignificant. But it is well-known that there are many members who because of their position are not carried on Party rolls. . . What is important is the claim of the Communists themselves that for every Party member there are ten others ready, willing and able to do the Party's work."

The best figures available indicate there are 1300 Communist Party members on the Party rolls for 1952 in Ohio. About half of these are in the Cleveland area. There are 200 Party members in central and southern Ohio, and about 400 in the industrial centers of Toledo, Akron, Youngstown, Lorain, Ashtabula, and Norwalk.

. . . .

Front Organizations

. . . .

Certain organizations in Ohio cannot escape the label of Communist front organization. These include the Ohio Bill of Rights Conference; American Committee for Protection of Foreign Born; Ohio Freedom of the Press Association; Ohio Labor Conference for Peace; Defense Committee for Victims of the Ohio Un-American Activities Commission; Labor Youth League; and the International Workers Order, to name but a few. The Commission has not compiled a list of Ohio front organizations for general dissemination.

The question immediately is posed, is there any way that a Communist front can be recognized? There can be no single test, no hard and fast rule, no infallible yardstick to measure any group, but there are certain signs which might give indications to an interested observer as to the true character of any such organization. Does the group consistently espouse the cause of Soviet Russia and criticize the policies of the American government? With every shift in the Communist Party line, does the organization make a corresponding shift in sentiment? Does the Communist press regularly praise the organization and feature its activities? Does the organization consider matters far afield from its stated objectives and purposes? Are its programs studded with known Communists, sympathizers or apologists? Does the group, avowedly non-partisan, engage in political activities and consistently advocate causes pushed by Communists? Does it sponsor causes, campaigns, petitions, or other activities promoted by the Communist Party? Does the organization permit itself to be used as a sounding board for Communist doctrines? Does its literature follow the Party line? Does it use the peculiar terminology of the Communist double-talk in its literature, resolutions or news releases? Have outstanding leaders in public life openly renounced affiliation with the organization?

Mental Hospitals

JAY W. COLLINS

Social Service

The mental health program in Ohio is faltering because of a shortage of Psychiatric Social Workers. The system is badly out of balance because the essential functions which are their lot are being completed in only minor degree.

This breakdown in organization causes a staggering cost in human misery, a deceleration in the spirit of the program, and a financial loss to the tax payers that is beyond estimate.

It is understatement to say that this situation is serious. It is critical.

The shortage of Social Workers is more serious than the shortage of any other category of mental hospital team member.

The main reason for this cry of alarm is the fact that there are untold thousands of patients in our state mental hospital who would not be there if there were enough social work specialists to arrange for their release to families, homes, or jobs. There are hundreds of patients re-admitted each year who might have remained in normal society if Psychiatric Social Workers had been available to help them maintain adjustment and attain a stabilized medication program. There are hundreds of patients who would have approached mental recovery more quickly if Social Workers had been available to help relieve personal tension-producing problems during their most critical days of hospitalization, and there would have been innumerable less relapses had the patient's families been properly oriented to the role they must play in aiding the adjustment of their relative who returned to the family either on trial visit or as a discharged patient.

There are 3000 patients in our hospitals who need not be there!

This is not an alarmist figure. It represents the composite opinion of Clinical Directors, Superintendents, and Social Workers—the people who are closest to the problem. The actual figures for estimates of the Clinical Directors and Superintendents was 2991. The estimate of the Social Workers was 3367. If we were to consider the maximum estimates of each, there are over 4000 patients in the hospitals who could be enjoying a normal life if enough Social Workers were on roll to work out home-going arrangements for them.

Further Social loss and extended hardship comes from the fact that a shortage of social workers often causes a delay in the obtaining of information which the doctors need to evaluate the conditions of a patient, thus causing delay in treatment of the patient.

Numerous other obstacles to proper patient care were observed and will be examined in some detail as we assess the social work section of the hospital program.

Staffing. These figures indicate the extent of shortage: there are 30 Social Workers for about 700 patients at the Psychiatric Institutes, a ratio of one to 23 patients; there are 80 at prolonged-care hospitals to serve 32,682 patients, a ratio of one to 408 patients; there are 58 at the other Receiving hospitals and State Schools to serve 10,228 patients, a ratio of one to 176 patients.

The overall ratio is one Social Worker to each 259 patients!

From Jay W. Collins, *A Report to the Governor; The Mental Hospitals of Ohio, 1959,* (Columbus, 1959), pp. 15-160.

By American Psychiatric Association standards, we need 477 Psychiatric Social Workers today. We now have 168.

· ·

The Food Service Situation

The food service story is an amazing one. It has elements of luster and pathos. It can be described as progressive and waning in the same paragraph. It can be cited as one of the bright spots in the mental hospital system or it can be viewed as somber and murky. Basically, it is a tale of doing much, but not enough, with little.

First let us put the problem in perspective. State prolonged-stay mental hospitals have 56¢ per day to feed each patient three meals. Receiving hospitals are allowed 79¢. The tuberculosis hospital can spend 65¢ per day on food. The adequacy of these figures will be discussed after the dietary operation and problems are described.

· ·

Dining Rooms. There are three types of dining rooms: patient cafeterias, employee cafeterias and cottage dining areas. The atmosphere in each is greatly different. Employee cafeterias are the best—and show what can be done by interested management. Good lighting draperies, plants, good furniture, good dishes and silverware are usually provided for employees.

Not so for older patient cafeterias, though the newly-built ones are delightful. A few hospitals, Lima and Longview for example, have re-done some patient cafeterias with excellent results. The rest are just fair, and the one at Cleveland State can only be classified as a disgrace. *There is no acceptable reason for failing to make patient dining areas pleasant;* lack of funds and painting personnel are the usual reasons given, but this raises questions as to the priority of use of such funds and painters as were available and used for other purposes. The installation of window ventilation fans would aid conditions in many cafeterias.

Cottages and ward dining areas often compare with the patient cafeteria at Cleveland State. Many smell of old food, have bad lighting, peeling paint, rickety furniture, wobbly chairs, unsanitary floors, and inadequate sinks. Attendants admit that cockroaches are not unusual visitors. Several pleasant cottage dining areas were noted; some of which had been supplied with draperies by the attendants.

· ·

Overcrowding

Replace senile patients. At least 10% of our patient population consists of senile patients who do not require psychiatric care and who cannot benefit from treatment with any known remedy because of the organic nature of their disease. Their presence in the prolonged-care hospitals reduces the effectiveness of the staffs in treating cases that can be improved. In Cleveland State alone there are at least 600 such persons, causing a deplorable crowded condition that is unparallelled in the state, but existing to a lesser degree elsewhere.

These people need housing. They need clothing and food and safeguarding and entertainment and medical attention for physical problems.

It is submitted that their best interests would be served, as would the best interests of other patients in our crowded hospitals, if senile patients were transferred to a new type of unit to be built by the state, a colony or village type, with one-story buildings partitioned so as to provide a small private room for each patient. There could be grouping of patients by condition so that those who require but little attention or help could have semi-self-care units with only minimal staff available. There would be no need for the variety of specialists who are needed to improve mental patients—psychologists, occupational therapists, psychiatrists, etc. A few general practitioners would be an adequate medical staff.

Some units would require food service in them, but many patients could go to central dining room. It would not be necessary to construct an expensive hospital building for the physically ill, for sick patients could be transferred back to the state hospital of which they serve as a branch. Having the same administration staff for both the sponsoring hospital and its branch would reduce unit costs. Specialized staff could be sent to the branch hospital as needed.

Further effort need not be undertaken here to describe the operating potentials. The point is that less expensive care could be given, the units would be less costly to build, and removal of a number of senile patients would relieve over-crowded conditions in the other hospitals.

Psychiatrists agreed that this is practical. They feel that such units should be built close to cities so that aged patients might benefit from stimulation of such relationship. The probability of community volunteer assistance and family interest would be enhanced by being near metropolitan areas. Further study should be given to this proposal. . . .

Pollution 1955

RALPH E. DWORK

Progress against pollution is a story of pipes and people.

It is a story of construction of efficient modern facilities to treat the wastes of municipalities and industries for the protection of our waterways.

It also is the story of large groups of people tackling one of the big problems of our time—a problem which has many social and economic as well as technical ramifications.

We are making rapid progress against water pollution in Ohio. We are making that progress because people have become aware of the seriousness and danger of water pollution, and the people have determined to do something about it.

It is impossible to sit on the Water Pollution Control Board of Ohio and not realize that we are in the midst of an era of tremendous change in thinking about the disposal of wastes from our communities and factories.

People representing industries and municipalities come before the Board in a spirit of cooperation and joint effort. It is true that there are difficulties to be worked out—questions of time, of economics, of financing. But there are no disagreements on the goal.

The people of Ohio want clean streams. They are willing to make sacrifices, if necessary, to have clean streams.

. . . .

The Water Pollution Control Board is dealing in its permit control program with a total of 496 municipalities, 34 county sewer districts, and 634 industries.

In each of these groups significant progress is being made toward the proper treatment of sewage and other wastes to prevent pollution.

Of the 496 municipalities, 210 now have sewage treatment plants. Of the 34 sewer districts, 27 have disposal plants. Of the 634 industries, 433 have some form of waste treatment. Some of these treatment facilities are not adequate as yet, but steps are being taken to improve those that are not satisfactory. At the same time, rapid strides are being made toward the installation of treatment where none has yet been provided.

In the case of industries, it should be noted that the word "treatment" as used in this report also includes other corrective

From Ralph E. Dwork, "Pollution 1955: a report of progress," *Clean Waters in Ohio*, III (Spring 1955), 2-12.

measures or internal process changes which help to control or eliminate polluting wastes.

Let me give you some facts to indicate the progress that has been made this last year.

During 1954, facilities for satisfactory treatment of sewage and industrial wastes were completed and put into use by 11 cities, 8 villages and 67 industries. Some of these were new, some were improvements.

At the present moment, 30 cities, 12 villages and 106 industries have such facilities under construction.

Another 22 cities and 54 villages have completed detailed plans for approved sewage plant construction. These communities are working now on financing arrangements.

The remaining 17 cities, another 30 villages and 197 industries are at present working on design plans for approved treatment.

. . . .

Recognizing that conservation of other resources than water can be a big part of this program, the Water Pollution Control Board has cooperated with industries seeking methods to extract valuable by-products from wastes.

Throughout its work, the Board has been guided by a philosophy which can be summarized in two words, "minimum" and "reasonable." It has sought to set "minimum reasonable" time periods—minimum, from the viewpoint of those suffering as a result of water pollution; reasonable, from the viewpoint of those who must expend effort and money to abate pollution.

That the people of Ohio are willing to spend money in the fight against water pollution has been well demonstrated. In the last three general elections, voters of 62 communities approved the issuance of more than $67,000,000 in tax bonds for sewage treatment. And that is only part of the municipal financing picture. Twice again that amount of money has been made available through the issuance of unvoted bonds in communities where sewer service revenues will be used to finance sewerage projects.

Visualize for a moment the human element, the people involved in the passage of these bond issues. Educational programs were necessary in every one of the towns—the cooperation of newspapers, radio and television stations, distribution of pamphlets and posters, community meetings and speeches. The Water Pollution Control Board was able to give some assistance in these educational programs but the major burden fell on local civic groups and individuals.

Consider the numbers of people living in the municipalities where sewage treatment construction projects are under way right now. There are 355,000 in the towns building new disposal plants. There are 2,722,000 in the communities which are enlarging and replacing outgrown sewage plants. Over three million people altogether.

. . . .

Here is a good place to mention again the special cooperation which has been shown by industry in this program.

At the start, the Water Pollution Control Board began bringing groups of industries into the program by a series of compulsory hearings. After several of these hearings, representatives of industry suggested that a voluntary approach be tried. They felt that the compulsory hearings, with attendant publicity, indicated to the public that industry was reluctant to join in the anti-pollution program. They felt that industry as a whole was desirous of cooperating.

The Water Pollution Control Board agreed to try the voluntary approach with industry. The hearings were discontinued. Instead, a series of dates or deadlines was established for the various groups of industries to come into the program by voluntarily applying for permits and accepting the conditions of permits issued by the Board. This new approach was a complete success. Every industry, asked to come into the program by this method, complied. Of the 634 industries in the program now, more than half have come in under this voluntary, cooperative basis. Included in this voluntary group are some of the largest industries in the state—steel, oil, coal, textiles, rubber, paper, chemicals.

There is no question of goals between the Water Pollution Control Board and industry. All are agreed that water pollution must be ended. The questions remaining are largely those of timing.

. . . .

Ohio is involved in an eight-state compact for cleaning up the Ohio River. Only a few years ago every city and village on the Ohio from Pittsburgh to Cairo was dumping raw sewage into the river. Now a large number of them have built or are building sewage treatment plants. In Ohio, Cincinnati has completed one, and is building the second of four projected plants. Ironton and Powhatan Point have completed new disposal plants. Steubenville and Marietta have plants under construction. Portsmouth and New Boston should have their plants under construction this spring, and East Liverpool perhaps later in the year. Other cities and villages on the Ohio River in Ohio are working on plans or financing arrangements for sewage treatment.

Lest the people at the other end of the state think that the pollution problems of Lake Erie are being neglected, we can report that Cleveland and Toledo are constructing improvements to their sewage treatment plants, and that Ashtabula, Lorain and Port Clinton are building new plants. Nearly ready to start construction of new sewage treatment plants are Painesville, Willoughby and Sandusky. Other communities are working on designs and financing.

Fighting water pollution is a complex and long-range job.

It has been said before but it bears repeating that "we have been 150 years in creating this problem and we are not going to solve it overnight."

The Water Pollution Control Board has not tried to set a definite deadline for the ending of water pollution in Ohio. That would be impossible. But it was said here last year that 1960 was beginning to look like a good target date, that by 1960 most of the aims of the Water Pollution Control Law might be accomplished. This year, 1960, still looks like a good target date.

Mine Pollution

CLEAN WATERS

The discovery of coal in Southeastern Ohio decades ago was a blessing to residents of the area. It gave them a major industry, jobs and wealth.

Today it also gives them a headache.

The thousands of mines—abandoned mines as well as the active ones—have caused the formation of an acid discharge which has literally destroyed hundreds of miles of recreational streams.

This is of serious concern to residents of the area. Recreation could be a big business for them today. To many, this is the most beautiful part of Ohio, hill land still fifty percent in forests and woodland, ideal for the impounding of lakes and the creation of parks. But the water in the streams that would fill the lakes has been so acid in many locations that fish have disappeared and even aquatic vegetation has been destroyed.

Coal mining is still a big business in the area, and nobody wants to lose it. But other industry would be welcome, too. However, most industrial plants need water; they cannot use acid water.

From "From Fool's Gold to Stream Pollution," *Clean Waters in Ohio*, V (Summer 1956), 2-6.

And while this hilly area is not the best part of the state for farming, there are many good farms in it. Some of the farmers would like to irrigate their lands for better crops, but they can't use acid water either.

So, the mine acid problem is a serious one from many viewpoints.

The sad part of the story is that nobody yet has come up with a practical method for the prevention of either the formation or the seepage of acid from coal mines.

. . . .

Source of the acid in mines is the oxidation of sulfuritic materials which are natural constituents of coal and the rocky strata around the veins of coal. There are several of these materials, but the most common is iron disulphide, usually termed pyrite. It also is known as "fool's gold" because of its pale, brass-yellow color and brilliant metallic luster.

Disturbance of the cover of the coal during mining operations exposes these sulfuritic materials to the air. While so exposed they are oxidized by the atmospheric oxygen into iron sulfate and sulfuric acid. The result of this reaction is apparent to the eye as white or yellow deposits on the exposed areas. These deposits would stay there except for the water.

Water following normal underground channels invariably gets into mines. This is the same water which ordinarily feeds wells and springs. The excavation made for removal of the coal severs the natural channels. The water takes the path of least resistance by flowing through the mine. On its way it picks up the iron sulfate and sulfuric acid.

Adding to the problem is the fact that much of the acid mine drainage today comes from mines which were worked out or abandoned years ago. The companies which worked the mines have gone out of existence in most cases. Ownership of the surface lands above the mines usually has changed too. There is therefore no clear-cut responsibility in these cases, even if a satisfactory method for preventing the acid formation was available.

During the 1930's an attempt was made at sealing these abandoned mines with the use of WPA labor. The aim was to prevent oxygen from getting into the mines to combine with the sulfuritic materials in the formation of acid. Thousands of mines were sealed in Ohio, West Virginia and Pennsylvania. Some beneficial results were reported at the time. But it was found in most cases that oxygen still got into the mines.

. . . .

The 101st Ohio General Assembly in 1955 appropriated $30,000 to the Water Pollution Control Board for cooperation with the Ohio Coal Industry Water Pollution Committee in a study of the acid mine waste problem.

Raccoon Creek, which rises in Vinton County near Lake Hope and Lake Alma and flows into the Ohio River near Gallipolis, was selected for the study because it is an example of severe damage from acid mine water. Through much of its length, Raccoon Creek—once a popular fishing stream flowing through forest area—now is almost completely sterile, containing neither plant life nor fish.

The Coal Industry Water Pollution Committee has employed Dr. S. A. Braley, of the Mellon Institute, Pittsburgh, to make preliminary studies. The Water Pollution Control Board has provided Dr. Braley with credentials which authorize him to make his surveys on private lands where necessary.

Recently Dr. Braley made a partial report based on limited studies conducted during the fall and winter. He indicated the extent of the problem when he said that the acid getting into Raccoon Creek comes from literally thousands of sources, including many mines, tipples and gob piles abandoned years ago, as well as from some active mines, and even from acid-forming sandstone in some areas.

"The problem will have to be attacked at the source of the acid," he said. "It seems almost hopeless, and I doubt if anybody would say that the acid can be eliminated completely. But it can be minimized if we attack some of the major sources."

Ohio's Future in Higher Education

EDUCATION COMMISSION

Warnings are constantly being made that our nation must prepare for the doubling of today's enrollments in the next 12 years. This means that our college population will be six million or more in 1970, in contrast to three million at the present time.

In Ohio certain forecasters predict a situation equally acute.

From the number of college students now enrolled and the probable number of college-age youth in 1970, it can be anticipated that in 12 years Ohio may also expect approximately double the number of full-time students enrolled in 1955. In the opinion of some this is too conservative. Commission members and their advisors, however, decided on this conservative estimate because of the solid base it furnished for all of their recommendations.

. . . .

The most potent fact overshadowing the future of higher education in Ohio is the tremendous and continuous increase in population. From 1950 to 1956 the population increased by 13 per cent; that is, from 7,947,000 to 9,006,000. During this six-year period we had not only a native increase of 773,439 but also an in-migration of 285,934. The U. S. Bureau of the Census predicts that by 1970 Ohio will have 12,258,000 people, thus becoming the third most populous state in the nation, after New York and California.

. . . .

The cost of any adequate program of expansion, of course, will be large. All of this emphasizes the need for imagination and care so that the cost of the new facilities as well as the expenses of students can be kept to a minimum. The pattern of the future will doubtless deviate somewhat from that of the past. More dormitories will be built to house students; but because of higher living expenses, plus an increased desire by many to attend college while living at home, a larger percentage of students is looking forward to attending what can be considered "commuter colleges." Because of this, more attention must be devoted to new undergraduate facilities on a local basis.

. . . .

Quality, the Top Priority

Democracy must remain on good terms with both average ability and talent. After the individual has demonstrated his abilities in the earlier competitive stages of his education, he must be encouraged to broaden himself in the great and accepted areas of knowledge. Emphasis should be placed on such intellectual skills as mathematics and English. In addition, students should have available strong courses in the natural sciences, history, languages, social studies, literature and the arts. After all have had an initial experience of a year or two in each basic area, those who demonstrate sufficient talent should be

From The Ohio Commission on Education Beyond the High School, *Ohio's Future in Education Beyond the High School,* (Columbus, 1958), pp. 17-66.

urged to continue in the direction most suited to their major interests and abilities.

When democracy has done its best to provide appropriate educational opportunities for all, the individual will still, of course, risk failure. Indeed the problems of increased enrollments call for increased responsibility of the individual for his own education.

. . . .

Many questions are immediately presented. Who shall go to college? What should be the nature of the college preparatory work? How should students be selected for college? How can there be better articulation between high school and college? How can the transition from high school to college be most successfully made? How far and how fast should we attempt to raise the academic standards at both levels?

In attempting to spell out possible solutions to these and other questions in the recommendations accompanying this report, the Commission suggests that the General Assembly give consideration to modifying the Ohio Revised Code, which now provides that any graduate of a first class high school be admitted to a state university without examination. Many persons and groups with whom the Commission met believed a modification of this statute would go far in helping upgrade the work being done by students both at the high school and college levels.

. . . .

Education has been one of the greatest forces which have made our country what it is today. The need for it is now greater than ever before. It must neither be neglected, approved "as is," nor destructively changed. It means more than research and scientific knowledge; it means respect for man, and freedom of the individual. Its goal is wisdom, the product of experience, and it flourishes most when carried on close to the people. Education must be a brilliant beacon leading to higher standards of living, to peace in the world, to individual happiness and well-being for mankind. The quality of education, therefore, deserves top priority in planning for the future.

Mathematics, Science and Engineering

To be pertinent and timely any report on education in 1958 must from necessity emphasize instruction in mathematics, science and engineering. Our nation and the world needs gifted and well-educated graduates in these fields. International competition makes them essential to national leadership and possibly even to survival. A scientist or engineer must be, among other things, a well-educated man. Basic general education, therefore, is needed by all engineers or we will start developing future leaders without proper understanding of the world we live in. Today, the demand for excellence in mathematics and science transcends all other issues in this field.

. . . .

Financial Implications

The instructions which members of the Ohio Commission received included no special reference to the financial implications of possible recommendations. This was appreciated greatly because it gave members freedom to study and analyze all suggestions and recommendations without constantly asking, "Will the cost be excessive?" No meeting ever occurred, however, without some discussion of the financial implications of the various proposals. We were conscious that the costs of all recommendations from necessity had to be reasonable and within the ability of our citizens to meet them. Nevertheless, we could not be unmindful of certain economic facts pertaining to the future of our state. Ohio has now become the second state in the Union in respect to the dollar values added to raw materials in the manufacturing process. In addition, because of enterprising leaders and skilled workmen, its geographical location, research, power resources and developments, raw materials, the St. Lawrence Seaway and the Ohio River Valley development, Ohio will inevitably grow in wealth and population. This expansion will increase both enrollments and demand for large numbers of well educated men and women in all fields of activity. Any worth-while plan for education beyond the high school must necessarily consider these significant factors.

Point 14 of the premises adopted by the Commission was carefully written as follows to explain our attitude toward increased costs:

"We recognize that comprehensive plans for meeting Ohio's present and future needs in higher education can only be achieved through the provision of vastly increased financial resources, but we likewise accept the obligation to think and plan in terms of the highest efficiency of arrangements and of the most rigorous possible economy in cost to the citizens of Ohio."

. . . .

The following quotations from Dr. Russell's carefully prepared report "Meeting Ohio's Needs in Higher Education" merit repetition in this study.

"Ohio's Part in the Nation-Wide Program of Higher Education"

"It is helpful first to look at the program of higher education maintained in the State of Ohio as a part of the total national picture, before proceeding to the details relating to the facilities and services of the various Ohio institutions. In order to evaluate the contribution made by the Ohio institutions to the total national program of higher education, it is necessary to have some measure of the general position that Ohio occupies in the life and economy of the nation. This position may readily be expressed in terms of the percentage that Ohio is of the national total on certain significant factors. For example, the United States Bureau of Census reports data that indicate Ohio had 5.5 per cent of the total civilian population of the country in 1955.

"On most economic factors, Ohio is in a relatively fortunate position. In 1953 the state produced 9.1 per cent of the value added by manufacture in the entire country, though only 3.2 per cent of the value of agricultural products came from Ohio in that year. This would indicate that Ohio has an economy more mature and more highly industrialized than the average state. Ohio residents in 1954 had 6.0 per cent of the total personal income of the nation, and 6.7 per cent of the total income tax paid to the Federal Government originated in Ohio in that year. Ohio had 5.6 per cent of the total retail sales of the nation in 1955, and 5.7 per cent of the assets of the national bank and savings and loan associations of the country were in Ohio in 1953. Motor car registrations in Ohio in 1954 were 5.6 per cent of the total in the United States. In the case of each of the items of data cited above, the figure for the latest year available has been used.

. . . .

"From these data, the conclusion is drawn that Ohio might be expected to carry at least 5.6 per cent of the total national load in higher education. This figure is only slightly above the level of the civilian population and it is at or below the level of the various economic factors listed. It is exactly at the level of retail sales and motor car registrations in Ohio.

"The performance of the State of Ohio in higher education may be measured also by the technique of noting the percentage relationship which its services bear to the national totals.

"The first measure of Ohio's service in higher education is the number of educational institutions maintained in the state. For this purpose the listing of the U. S. Office of Education Directory for

1955-56 was taken. This is a definitive list, recognized nationally and internationally, of all institutions that may be properly classified as 'higher education.' Ohio has 61 such institutions listed, out of a total of 1,855 in the Directory, making Ohio's percentage 3.3 of the national total. This is substantially below the 5.6 level needs.

"Another approach to an estimate of the adequacy of the number of institutions of higher education maintained in Ohio is through a computation of the number of young people of college age per institution. Thompson's data from 'College Age Population Trends 1940-1970' have been used in these computations. Ohio has one recognized institution of college level for each 6,313 persons of college age in the state. The average for the entire country is 4,356 persons of college age for each institution of higher education. The only states that have a larger college-age population per institution than Ohio has are Alabama, Wyoming, Louisiana, West Virginia, and Arkansas.

"Many people in Ohio have long believed that the state is blessed with an abundance of college-level institutions. In fact, the notion is widespread that the state is 'over-colleged.' But, measured by the standards of its total civilian population, its college-age population, and its economic resources, Ohio does not maintain nearly as many centers where higher education is available as is generally the custom throughout the country.

"The financial support of higher education is another factor on which Ohio's attainment may be compared to that of the country as a whole. For this purpose the latest available statistics published by the U. S. Office of Education have been used, showing the expenditures for current educational and general purposes in the institutions for higher education for 1951-52 (these are the latest published data available at present). The Ohio institutions, publicly controlled and privately controlled combined, have 4.0 per cent of the total expenditures for current educational and general purposes in the institutions of higher education in that year. By this measure, it is clear that the Ohio institutions do not enjoy as strong financial support as would be expected from either the size of the state's population or its economic status. To achieve the 5.6 percentage level in financial support suggested as the norm for Ohio, the institutions of this study would have had to make expenditures of some $31,000,000 more than they spent for educational and general purposes in 1951-52.

"The shortage in financial support for the current programs of higher education is characteristic of both the publicly controlled and the privately controlled institutions in Ohio, though it is more pronounced in the latter than in the former group. The publicly controlled universities in Ohio have expenditures equal to 4.3 per cent of the national total for publicly controlled institutions. The privately controlled colleges and universities in Ohio have expenditures for current educational and general purposes equal to only 3.6 per cent of the national total for privately controlled institutions. To reach the 5.6 per cent level the publicly controlled institutions would have had to expend in 1951-52 for current educational and general purposes approximately $13,500,000 more than they did spend, and the expenditure in the privately controlled institutions in that year would have had to be increased by about $17,500,000 to reach the 5.6 level suggested as the standard for Ohio.

"The conclusion that Ohio does not support higher education as well as the average for the country as a whole is supported by another set of data. For the entire United States in 1951-52 the current expenditures for higher education were 0.99 per cent of the total income received by individuals, but for Ohio this percentage was only 0.70."

. . . .

Various articles and monographs support Dr. Russell's findings and stress these points: 1) Great inequality exists among the states in the support of higher education. 2) Public support from tax sources frequently bears little relation to states' ability to pay for higher education. 3) States should increase their aid to publicly financed institutions of higher education according to their abilities to pay for such education and the outlook for growth. 4) Support of privately financed institutions must be increased even more.

Ohio's support of higher education is low particularly in relation to the population and wealth of the state. In 1955 the personal income per capita in Ohio was $2,054—well above the national average of $1,846. Only 10 other states had personal incomes per capita higher. In the same year per capita state expenditures on higher education were $7.50—considerably below the national average of $9.93—and Ohio ranked 36th among the states in such expenditures.

10 The Inconclusive Sixties

THE 1960s witnessed more of the economic growth and expansion of governmental responsibilities begun in the 1950s—with its accompanying increased expenditures. Despite campaign promises by James A. Rhodes for austerity in government, he introduced the largest budget in the state's history after he was elected governor in 1963. Conditioned over the years by the more active role played by government, and overwhelmed by the magnitude of the problems measured in costs and management, the people turned more to both state and federal agencies for assistance. A growing governmental framework of departments, divisions, and agencies was established to attack the problems in Ohio. As the decade ended, however, and the people were frustrated by international events, the effects of government action in many cases were inconclusive.

One area of the state that was discovered during the 1960s was Appalachia. In order to deal with the economic problems found in those eastern and southern Ohio counties included in national Appalachia, the Ohio Office of Appalachia was created and housed within the Department of Urban Affairs. Plagued by the lack of a taxable economic base, the Appalachian region in Ohio was behind the rest of the state in many services, including education, medical care, shopping facilities, and highways. While it recognized that outside financial support was necessary, the state's objective was "to foster the evolution of a diversified, self-sustaining economy" for the Appalachian counties.

Probably no other operation better illustrates governmental participation at the local level than the state's work with the urban areas. The Ohio Department of Urban Affairs became the major clearing house for dealing with the dilemma of simultaneous growth and decay in Ohio's cities. Created in 1967, this department was to be the coordinating agent to help solve community problems. Within that new department were seven divisions: Intergovernmental Services, Urban Development, Legal Services, Public Finances, Opportunity, Appalachia, and Law Enforcement Planning. These agencies began to deal with urban problems on a full-time basis in an attempt to rescue the state's metropolitan areas from total human and physical deterioration. Although the state worked with the cities, help may have been too late for some. During the 1950s, the larger metropolitan areas had been abandoned by middle-class whites, who fled to the suburbs. With a reduced tax base, the cities found it difficult to finance service facilities. At the same time, black migration had stepped up, and the increasing number of blacks—many of them unskilled—crowded into already deteriorated ghetto areas. The state organized to deal with the urban problems, but the frustration of Ohio's blacks had already reached a boiling point. During the latter half of the decade disturbances took place in Dayton, Akron, and Cleveland. The 1960s ended with an urban truce but no conclusive solution.

One social innovation of the 1960s was the strengthening of government's role in the protection of individual civil rights, especially among minority groups. Following the famous 1954 desegregation case, and encouraged by the blacks' own active search for identity, Ohio passed an updated civil rights law and created a civil rights commission in 1959. Through its annual reports to the governor, the commission pointed out discriminatory practices in both the public and private sectors of society, and labored to offer equal opportunity to all Ohioans. Urban blacks were not the only ones to attract state attention in the quest for human dignity. From 1954, enough migrant laborers had been transported from the American Southwest and Florida to the rich farmlands in northwestern Ohio to prompt state action. By 1964, eighteen thousand immigrant farm laborers, 90% of whom were Spanish-speaking, were housed in 527 camps in ten counties to harvest tomatoes, sugar beets, and pickles—products valued at $15,000,000. In its concern with living and working conditions, sanitary facilities, pay, education, health, and spiritual growth, the state, along with churches and public service organizations, helped to provide a better way of life for a segment of America's society that had failed to gain its full share of the nation's prosperity.

In an effort to meet the need for highly trained personnel in the industry of the state, and at the same time to provide for equal opportunity to its citizens, Ohio expanded its higher education facilities during the 1960s. The Rhodes administration began a mortar and bricks program that expanded existing universities, absorbed new institutions, and created a branch campus system that located higher education within thirty miles of nearly everybody's door.

The 1960s concluded with increased government participation in all sectors of human life. The expenditure of moneys and the creation of bureaucratic agencies were anticipated to be the panacea for all ills. Yet, these twin antidotes did not cure the patient, and it has been speculated that big government, large expenditures, and an expanded bureaucracy were merely inevitable results of modern, industrialized society. Nevertheless, the problems that plagued the state during the 1960s were no longer localized and isolated as unique to Ohio, but were part of the larger national scene. Despite increasingly comprehensive governmental action at both the state and federal levels during the decade, solutions to the problems of late twentieth-century society remained all too elusive and inconclusive.

Appalachia Ohio

REPORT

Natural Features

Land features are the greatest common denominators to Ohio
Appalachia. The unglaciated Kanawha Plateau, which rises to over
1400 feet, straddles twenty-four of the twenty-eight counties. The
relief is undulating to rugged with narrow valleys and some steep
ridgetops. Only in the far western counties of the region is the relief
fairly level. The underlying sedimentary bedrock is limestone covered
with sandstone and shale. This covering is much more shallow in the
west, so erosion of the less resistant limestone produced broad plains.
Slower erosion in the middle and eastern sections created high hills
with deep valleys.

Most soils are characterized by residual sandstone and shale, are
often quite shallow, and in areas of steep slopes are considerably
eroded. Many areas are thus not well suited to cultivation although
soils are generally fertile. With Ohio Appalachia occupying 33% of
the State's total land, in 1965 it only received approximately 15% of
cash receipts from farming in the State. Agricultural use is primarily
related to smaller pasture and dairy production. High yields of grain
and hay may be produced on the more gentle slopes if conservation
practices such as contour strip cropping or terraces are used.

The generally fertile soils and ample rainfall in all seasons have
provided good conditions for the growth of woodlands. In 1960 an
estimated 37% of Appalachia Ohio was covered by woodland, much
of this concentrated in the middle south. Major forest types are
beech and maple in the east and southwest, and mixed oak with
hickory and pine elsewhere. From an industrial standpoint, the more
valuable hardwoods include white and red oak, hard maple, black
walnut, tulip poplar, basswood, hickory, and beech. However, with
the increase in wood pulp conversion industries, many other species
have assumed definite commercial values. While potentially the
Appalachia region has quite a valuable resource in its woodlands,
actual productivity has been hurt by poor cutting practices and
management in the past. However, excellent stands of timber are
being restored, especially in the extensive State and National forests
in the area.

Ohio Appalachia is also quite rich in mineral resources. Much of
this wealth has already been tapped, yet large amounts remain. Five

From Ohio Department of Urban Affairs, Ohio Office of Appalachia, *Appalachia Ohio: A Plan for Development*, (Columbus, 1969), pp. 7-14.

Appalachia counties rank as major producers of bituminous coal: Harrison, Belmont, Jefferson, Coshocton, and Tuscarawas. Production in 1965 of coal in Appalachia Ohio was 36,681,000 net tons. Other minerals which are mined or quarried in the area include stone (4,727,000 net tons, 1964), sand and gravel (4,584,000 net tons), and clay (1,955,000 net tons). Other valuable minerals in the area include oil, lime, salt, peat, flint, fuller's earth, phosphorus and pyrite. Wealth in mineral resources, however, has produced many problems because of poor mining practices. Unreclaimed strip mines and acid leakage are two of the more serious results.

Ohio Appalachia is bordered on the south and east by the magnificent Ohio River and has three major Ohio streams passing through: the Muskingum, Hocking, and Scioto Rivers. Many other smaller streams feed into these or directly in the Ohio River, thus providing considerable potential for water supply, industrial and power use, recreational use, and scenic enjoyment throughout the region. However, these streams also present significant problems: pollution and flooding. Besides municipal and industrial sources of water pollution, there are silt and mine acid pollutants which contribute to the problem, destroying water life, its scenic and recreational enjoyment, and its use as a water supply. Flooding problems are even more serious with many large urban concentrations in the narrow valleys. Aided by plentiful rainfall and large drainage areas, these valleys are often subject to floods of various intensity. The construction of many multi-purpose water impoundments is helping solve these problems by slowing down flood waters and is aiding flow in drought periods.

The natural features of the area present an impressive potential for recreational and scenic enjoyment. The hilly to rugged topography, the large areas of natural woodlands, the narrow, deep valleys with scenic rivers and man-made lakes provide an attractive and potentially exciting outdoors for nearby metropolitan concentrations. Even the mineral riches of the region could be used as an asset for recreation attraction.

. . . .

Urban Development

Because of the rugged terrain and problems in transportation no major metropolitan centers have formed in Appalachia Ohio. Historically, many small farming and some mining villages were formed throughout the area, primarily as small service centers within convenient travel distance of the rural residents. As industrial development and more specialized services occurred, certain small centers grew much more rapidly than others because of competitive advantages. These advantages included such attributes as highway, rail, or river transportation, and the availability of coal, water power, quality timber or agricultural products, and other natural resources. However, no one center has had enough of these attributes to develop into a large concentration such as Cincinnati, Columbus, or Pittsburgh.

The level and pattern of urbanization are very important to understanding the existing potentials and problems of a region. Urbanization in the U. S. as a whole is directly related to increasing national economic growth and prosperity and, perhaps, to some extent is a cause of it. In the U. S. as a whole, 70% of the population was classified as urban in 1960, increasing from 40% in 1900. Compared to this, Appalachia was 47% urban in 1960 and Ohio Appalachia was 38% urban. Urbanization allows and fosters specialization and efficiency in economic production and social and economic services.

. . . .

The lack of large urban centers in a region thus greatly contributes to loss of local spending, to outmigration, and to a limited quantity and quality of local services.

. . . .

Population

Population growth occurred early in Appalachia Ohio and has slowed down considerably since 1900. Comparisons with growth for Ohio and the United States as a whole show that it has not been keeping pace with the rates of growth for these larger areas and has in one 10-year period (1940-50) declined in population. Projections of Appalachia Ohio's 1965 estimated population, 1,154,000, do not show any significant change in these trends.

Although some growth is occurring in the region, its very slow rate reflects a trend of outmigration. In other words, natural increases are occurring (i.e., the difference between births and deaths) but more persons are moving out than are moving in.

. . . .

Outmigration is a reflection of the region's inability to provide sufficient job opportunities and other attractions for the region's natural increases. It is also closely related to the lack of large urban centers in the region which, according to national trends, are attracting by far the largest increases in population. While outmigration in itself may not be an undesirable condition, i.e., it is a necessary adjustment to changing regional economic conditions, it is the selectiveness of migration which presents the most significant problem for Appalachia Ohio. By far the largest proportions of migrants are

Past and Projected Population
(in thousands)

	Appalachia Ohio	Ohio	Appalachia Ohio As % of Ohio	U.S.A.	Appalachia Ohio As % of U.S.A.
1900[a]	903	4,158	21.7	75,995	1.19
1910	940	4,767	19.7	91,972	1.02
1920	974	5,759	16.9	105,711	.92
1930	989	6,647	14.9	122,775	.81
1940	1041	6,908	15.1	131,669	.79
1950	1035	7,947	13.0	150,697	.69
1960	1120	9,706	11.5	179,323	.62
1965[b]	1154	10,564	10.9	193,795	.60
1975[c]	1228[c]	11,453[c]	10.7	219,366[d]	.56

(a) 1900-1960, from U. S. Bureau of Census.
(b) Estimates from *"The Appalachia Region—A Statistical Appendix,"* Appalachian Regional Commission.
(c) From *"Ohio Population,"* Economic Research Division, Ohio Development Department, 1968.
(d) U. S. Bureau of the Census, Current Population Report, (Series P-25, No. 359), 1967 (series C).

persons between ages 0 to 10 and ages 20 to 30. *In other words, it is typically young marrieds with young children who are moving out.* This represents a serious drain on the very attractive young labor force and potential leaders of a community.

. . . .

Economy

The Appalachia portion of Ohio reached its peak about 60-75 years ago in terms of the productivity of its resource-based industries, such as agriculture, forestry, and mining. Much of this area was the first settled part of Ohio. It was easier to reach by river 150 years ago than were other parts of the State.

. . . .

In many cases, the foundations for industrial activity that continue to the present day were established during this early period. The forests were first utilized by the agricultural settlers and, along with limited iron ore deposits, later formed the basis for a charcoal iron industry that flourished in the late 1800's. Today the forests are a source of raw materials for the essentially small-scale wood products industries in these counties. Natural gas, in conjunction with the clays and sands of the area, sparked the manufacturing of clay and glass products. These earth raw materials remain important, along with salt deposits which have attracted chemical manufacturing plants to the Ohio River Valley. Perhaps the greatest raw material has been coal. It has brought manufacturers directly, and indirectly through cheap electric power, to several parts of the region, even though coal mining as an economic activity has diminished in importance.

The recent economic structure of the Ohio Appalachia region is reflected in the region's employment by industry group. The region is heavily oriented toward manufacturing activity and secondarily toward trade and services.

. . . .

Agriculture and forestry, mining, and manufacturing, form a set of basic industries that produce and sell products to markets outside the immediate area and thus potentially bring in "outside dollars". Growth in this sector of the economy can have a large multiplying effect on the total economy, including corresponding or even much greater growth in the other employment groups listed above. During the period 1950-1960, losses in agriculture-forestry and mining employment were so large they were not even offset by a healthy increase in manufacturing employment. Mining and agriculture have been declining nationally primarily due to changes in technology. Appalachia Ohio as well as all of Appalachia, with a large concentration of these types of employment, suffered even much more than the remainder of the Nation.

. . . .

Manufacturing, by far the largest industry group for the region, is definitely one of the most important as it contributed over 20,000 new jobs to the region in the 1950's. By 1960 the region's proportion in manufacturing employment was still less than the Ohio average but considerably higher than the average for the U. S. as a whole.

. . . .

However, statistics on value added per manufacturing employee show that Ohio Appalachia is much stronger in its productiveness than Appalachia as a whole, and is even stronger than the U. S. as a whole. Furthermore, Appalachia Ohio's productiveness is on a more rapid upswing than either Appalachia or the U. S. This high increase relates to substantial increases in employment for 1950-1960 in such high-value added industries as food products, printing and publishing, chemical products, electrical and other machinery, and transportation equipment.

. . . .

That certain weaknesses do exist in the overall economic health of the region is apparent in recent per capita personal income estimates for the area. Per capita personal income is not only quite low compared to the U. S., but it is even lower than the Appalachia average and is increasing at a slower rate.

. . . .

Likewise, another result of the region's economic problems is the high unemployment rate. For 1960, the unemployment rate for Appalachia Ohio was 7.3% compared to 6.8% and 5.1% for Appalachia and the U. S. respectively. Again, this is a reflection of large decreases in mining and agriculture employment (and to a lesser extent in railroad employment) upon which the region has been historically dependent. The workers cannot easily be assimilated into the regional economy. Most must either migrate to large metropolitan areas where there are (or they think there are) appropriate employment opportunities, retrain for employment skills in demand, remain unemployed, or leave the labor force. More recently unemployment rates have decreased nationally, to an estimated 3.8% in 1967 and are less in Ohio Appalachia and Appalachia than before, 5.2% and 4.6% respectively.

. . . .

The total manufacturing sector in Ohio Appalachia would have gained 6,121 employees between 1960 and 1966 if it had grown at the same rate as the Nation. The manufacturing sector would have increased by an *additional* 7,245 employees (i.e., its industrial mix growth) had each of its specific activities experienced a level of growth comparable to their respective national industry rate. Thus, if national and specific industry growth forces had operated in Ohio Appalachia as they did nationally, manufacturing employment would have grown by 13,366. Yet, total net change in manufacturing employment (1960-1966, for activities present in both years) was only 874. Consequently, local conditions were unfavorable to the extent that 12,491 potential manufacturing jobs (i.e., regional share growth) were not realized.

As indicated earlier, the apparent adverse change in local conditions may in fact be attractive to other types of manufacturing activities. During this six-year period, while employment in existing activities (shown in the above table) realized a gain of 874 (for an opportunity loss of 12,491), new activities locating in Ohio Appalachia added 8,063 employees (not shown in the above table). Thus, a total employment gain between 1960-1966 in new and existing (1960) plants was 8,937.

In order to better understand this large opportunity loss and the types of industries responsible, detailed shift analysis by industry type will be presented for each of the sub-regions in Ohio Appalachia. One general conclusion which can be drawn from the above statistics is that most of the region's industrial growth problems stem not from a slow growing industrial mix but from local deficiencies. In other words, many of the local industries nationally are rapidly growing; but because of local problems, local growth is not keeping up.

New Emphasis for Education

JOHN C. ULLERY

WE FACE A CRISIS . . .

The Problem . . . Attitudes . . .

The appointment of this Task Force indicates the Governor's recognition of a gap between the need for and the availability of vocational and technical education in Ohio.

The Task Force also noted a significant divergence in attitudes. The Task Force was encouraged by the attitude of classroom teachers to the problem. They see almost daily the frustration of students dealing with an educational system that leaves the student only two choices: a college education or a generalized education that seems to have no direct value to the student.

The student attitude is reflected in a 25 percent dropout rate between kindergarten and 12th grade. The present system of education is not relevant to the needs of 75 percent of students who will not earn a vocational diploma or an associate or higher degree.

The Task Force feels this frustration stems from an attitude of education that neither recognizes individual abilities nor provides programs based on individual needs.

. . . .

From John C. Ullery, *A Report by the Governor's Task Force on Vocational and Technical Education,* (Columbus, 1969), pp. 1-9.

Many education leaders do not see the necessity of change from their present programs, tending to downgrade employment-oriented education. The Task Force feels this has come about because vocational education unfortunately was for years the dumping ground for the slow learner, the disciplinary problem student and other "unwanteds" on the educational assembly line.

Industrial leaders know the school system is not producing graduates who are immediately employable and productive. Therefore they are particularly unwilling to hire a teenage male until he has some experience and can show a good work record. Few education programs in Ohio are now able to fill his need.

Many parents have not been concerned about the system of education because their leaders were not concerned. Most have accepted that going to college is the prime measure of success. Parents seldom look upon success in employment as proof of accomplishment.

. . . .

Ohio's present educational system, after 160 years of development, leaves much to be desired with respect to preparation of young people for full and productive lives. The Task Force noted these items:

1. 30,000 drop-outs and force-outs a year. Every five years this adds at least 150,000 untrained, unskilled and largely unemployable persons to the labor market.
2. 83 percent of the unemployed in Ohio are under 35 years of age.
3. 50 percent of these unemployed did not finish high school.
4. Nearly 50 percent completed high school but still cannot find work.
5. 28 percent of Ohio's unemployed young people have never held a job.

The Task Force found these figures particularly distressing because 1968 is a period of full employment. Many employers are working employees overtime in order to meet demands for their products.

. . . .

Last year, for example, Cleveland Public Schools graduated 6,211 pupils, but 4,722 dropped out of Junior and Senior High Schools.

Ohio has led the nation in industrial development. However, future development is threatened unless we have a trained and skilled labor force in adequate numbers available for industry. Ohio industry can upgrade some present employees and can import some skilled craftsmen and technicians from outside the state. However, it would be far better if a ready pool of skilled workers could be supplied from the ranks of Ohioans who now lack necessary skills but who are trainable.

One of the biggest potential sources of skilled labor in Ohio is our youth. Yet last year only five percent of the 150,000 graduates were employment-trained or skilled to a degree acceptable to employers.

WE FACE A CRISIS . . .

The Problem . . . Programs . . .

The programs of education today are often not relevant to the student's needs. Most programs within elementary and secondary education in Ohio have changed very little in this century, even though Ohio has moved from an agrarian society through an industrial phase to the rapidly advancing technological society that we live in today.

By 1980 Ohio job needs will be as follows:

45 percent of employees will need specific employment training—a Vocational Diploma.

25 percent of employees will need a Technical or Academic Associate Degree.

20 percent of employees will need a College Degree (Bachelor's Degree or higher).

10 percent of employees will need a High School Diploma or equivalent.

The educational system today produces the following:

Untrained

45 percent who will have a high school diploma without job training.

25 percent who will drop out of the system with no training.

Trained

15 percent who will have a College degree—job related.

10 percent who will have a Technical or Academic Associate Degree—job related.

5 percent who will have a Vocational Diploma—job related.

These figures show the present educational programs are not reflecting the employment needs of the student, or the needs of those adults beyond school age who are untrained or under-trained to fill available jobs.

The Task Force concluded there is little correlation at the primary and secondary levels between future employment opportunities and current education programs. There is no effective effort by colleges and universities to supply the kinds of teachers needed to staff an employment-oriented education system.

The Task Force found little, if any, liaison between the planners in public education and private vocational and occupational schools.

The Task Force was able to find no significant liaison between the planners in public education and industry. The present programs give a boy or girl, who cannot achieve at the rate of the college bound or who does not want to go to college, only two alternatives. The first is to drop out of school at the earliest opportunity and be unemployed; the second is to hang on and finish a general course, then become unemployed or underemployed. As long as the problem is ignored the school systems will continue to dump hundreds of thousands of untrained young people into a society constantly becoming more complex and technically demanding.

Senior Citizens

AGING COMMISSION

Summary

What are the problems of *Ohio's Senior Citizens?* Essentially, they relate to income, to physical and mental health, and to housing.

They are no different, except in degree, from problems of Ohio's junior citizens. Yet these differences are extremely important. They are important because the proportion of older people is rising. They are important because the aged are less able physically and financially to solve their own problems. They are important because the

From Governor's Commission on Aging, *Ohio's Senior Citizens*, (Columbus, 1960), pp. 1, 25.

needs of senior citizens increase as their health and resources decline. They are important because changing patterns of life have shifted more of the responsibility for finding solutions to the community at large.

. . . .

Background

Financial and emotional insecurity, ill health, loneliness, unsatisfactory living arrangements—some or all of which plague many older people—present serious challenges to society. Needs, of course, are not confined to any age or economic bracket. Financial problems are nevertheless basic and extensive among older persons.

Years of useful service, as well as contributions of skill, talent, leadership, wisdom, and experience are lost through short-sighted views which arbitrarily classify people as aged at a given figure—usually 65. The 65 and over group has grown from three million throughout the nation in 1900, to 16 million currently. Nearly one out of ten of Ohio's population is in this age group. Over one-half the estimated 856,000 live in Ohio's eight most populous counties. In some areas, notably counties in Southeastern Ohio, the proportion of the total population who are 65 years of age or older runs as high as 16 to 18 per cent.

Efforts have been made to lighten the senior years through Social Security, private retirement and insurance benefits, public assistance, golden age clubs, housing for the indigent, and various health and home-service projects. Such activities, however, do not adequately meet or solve the many problems which have arisen.

Recognizing the national scope of these problems, the first White House Conference on Aging will be held in Washington, D.C. in January 1961, to develop recommendations. To implement national goals, Ohio's Governor Michael V. DiSalle appointed a seven-member Governor's Commission on Aging with a Staff of three, six consultants, an Interdepartmental Committee, and various Advisory Committees—to conduct conferences, collect information, and prepare reports. They were asked to identify major unmet needs, and to develop recommendations.

. . . .

Income Maintenance

Needs of older people differ only in degree from those of other groups. They require sufficient income to provide at least minimum basic diets, suitable living arrangements, proper clothing, adequate health care, social and recreational opportunities.

One measure of minimum needs of the aging is the standard

allowed by the Ohio Department of Public Welfare in its Aid for the Aged program. This amounts to $1,242 per year for individuals living alone—exclusive of medical care. The average for medical care in 1959 was approximately $117. Without including other special allowances, the minimum amount for wholly dependent persons could total over $1,351 per year. The average income of three out of every five persons aged 65 and over in 1958, however, was less than $1,000 per year.

For every 83 men aged 65 and over, there were 100 women in the same age group. The women, however, received less in income than the men. Three out of every four of the aged women had less than $1,000 in money income. Only one out of three of the aged men had a similarly low income.

The low income position of families whose heads were 65 or over ($2,666 median) was disclosed by comparison with families with heads 55 to 64 years of age. The median for the latter was almost twice as high.

Most persons 65 and over received income from one or more of the following sources: employment, Old Age and Survivors' Insurance (Social Security), public assistance (Aid for the Aged), government, railroad, or veterans' pensions. Payments from industrial and private plans, private annuities, savings and investments represented other sources of income.

Nearly one-half the 65 and over group in Ohio received Social Security as of December 1959, averaging $77 per month. Approximately 10 per cent were recipients of Aid for the Aged, averaging around $60 per month. More than 26,000 among those receiving Aid for the Aged were also on Social Security. Some 1,500 persons 65 and over who got Aid to the Blind were among the recipients of Social Security payments.

Employment

The most satisfying source of income for able-bodied workers of any age is that derived from productive employment. Work is the cornerstone for the institution called life.

Values of employment to the aged cannot be overestimated. It means activity, dignity, status. It means accomplishment, companionship, independence.

Older workers have encountered increasing barriers in finding and keeping employment.

. . . .

As of June 1, 1960 there were 29,000 out of 111,000 men and 12,000 out of 49,000 women seeking employment through the Ohio

State Employment Service who were 45 years of age or over. Many older workers do not register for jobs, according to county reports, because "they know they will not be hired." Once separated from their jobs, older workers tend to remain unemployed.

An analysis of job orders filed with the Service revealed that more than one-half called for applicants not over 55 years of age. Forty per cent requested candidates up to 45 years of age.

A number of steps have been taken to help alleviate the problem. These include:

1. The Ohio State Employment Service in the Bureau of Unemployment Compensation offers a "Service to Older Workers Program" through which specialized help is given. In addition, promotional campaigns endeavor to overcome prejudice.

. . . .

Financial Programs

Ohio's major contribution to the study of problems of the aging, perhaps, was a special survey of financial programs for the retired.

. . . .

The survey was conducted by questionnaire to a sample of 3,200 Ohio employers. Some 1,900 returns were received. Based upon these returns, an estimated one million Ohioans were found to be covered by industry pension plans. Over 1.3 million were covered by health insurance plans, and a similar number by life insurance plans. Around 590 thousand, however, were not covered by any financial program. Adequacy of the various plans, of course, varied widely.

The rapid growth of private pension plans is a comparatively recent development. Only 6 per cent of the 1,274 plans reported by Ohio employers existed prior to 1938. One-third were set up since 1954.

. . . .

Relatively few firms offered pre-retirement counseling or assistance. About one-sixth of the firms which had one or more financial plans for older or retired employees, conducted individual counseling sessions. One out of ten distributed retirement literature. A scattered few gave legal advice, or medical examinations, or enrolled retirees in service clubs. One-seventh invited them to company functions. Less than 5 per cent, however, maintained retired-employee clubs, held social or educational meetings with them, or permitted their use of medical or recreational facilities.

Health

Most older people who are not in institutions are physically able to carry on normal activities. Their health problems vary more in incidence than in kind. The rate of disabling chronic illness rises, however, when economic resources may be relatively low.

Health services, in general, endeavor to provide the highest level of physical, mental and social well-being for the entire community. Emphasis for older people is on maintenance of successful, independent living, in accustomed surroundings. Concentration on preventive health measures, early detection and prompt care seem to warrant greater attention. Home-care programs, in the long run, cost less and bring far greater benefits than institutional care.

. . . .

State departments most concerned with health problems of the aged are the Department of Health; Department of Mental Hygiene and Correction; and the Department of Public Welfare. In the Department of Health, the Division of Chronic Diseases is a center for planning and developing projects, apart from direct concern for health needs, facilities and services.

. . . .

With the goal of improving nursing home care, responsibility for licensing and regulating such homes has been recently assigned to the Department of Health.

. . . .

Mental health needs of older persons, according to the Department of Mental Hygiene and Correction, are identical with those of the younger. In December 1959, there were nearly 8,500 patients 65 or over in Ohio mental institutions. Approximately one-half could be cared for elsewhere. Cooperative efforts with the Division of Aid for the Aged (Department of Public Welfare) has moved some of the eligible older patients from mental hospitals to foster homes.

. . . .

The Division of Aid for the Aged paid out over $10 million for medical care in 1959. The medical care program is limited, however, to treatment of known illnesses. Only recipients of general financial assistance are covered. Medically indigent persons are not eligible.

. . . .

Housing

People of all ages strive for independence. Increasing numbers of older men and women seek comfort and shelter outside the homes of their children. The aged as a group, however, are less able than others to compete for adequate housing. Great difficulties are reported by older persons with marginal incomes. Housing which is available at prices they can afford is often unsuitable physically, psychologically, and socially.

Living quarters for the aged should embrace many safety features. Such features, however, are rare except in low-rent public housing designed for the aged and available only to those with low incomes.

The Cleveland Metropolitan Housing Authority pioneered in designing housing for the elderly. Its Cedar Apartments includes elevator service, first-floor space for a Golden Age Center, program and cafeteria facilities. Another pioneering project, soon to be built, will embrace a diagnostic unit operated by the nearby Mt. Sinai Hospital.

A survey of Housing Authorities in Ohio disclosed 2,770 units, with specially designed features for the elderly, being planned or built. They include both elevator apartments, and one-story rows.

. . . .

Because of chronic illness or other disability, some of the older population require institutional care. Rest homes with adequate facilities, staff and rehabilitative programs are in short supply. On the other hand, some have to remain in such homes merely because of shortages of alternative housing and service.

Living arrangements in most County Homes are unsatisfactory. Most such Homes are old, dilapidated, overcrowded, and understaffed.

Non-profit fraternal, church and labor groups have led the way in providing homes for the aged. The Federal Housing Act of 1956 has encouraged building by these groups. Few private contractors, realtors, or others have undertaken such projects.

. . . .

Recreation

Older people often have an abundance of free time. Healthful recreation not only satisfies genuine needs but also offers an escape from loneliness and boredom. Productive use of leisure helps men and women to grow old gracefully. It can be a lifesaver for humanity, and a taxsaver for the community.

A survey of Ohio's recreational resources disclosed no uniform pattern of services. Public recreation and voluntary agencies sponsored most activities for the aging. Others, however, were religious organizations, labor unions, civic and social clubs, private organizations, housing authorities, and commercial enterprises. Program content varied from discussion clubs to lecture series, from card games to "socials", from sightseeing to fine-arts exhibits.

. . . .

Education

Life expectancy beyond 65 has increased markedly. The added years may offer deterioration and vegetation, or enrichment and fulfillment. Meaningful mental, physical, and social activity yields by far the better alternative.

Education can enrich the lives, both of the young and the old. Formal and informal education are needed to prolong employment, to develop new skills, and to promote physical and emotional stability.

There are many unused educational resources in every community which can contribute to the health and happiness of senior citizens. The public schools, beginning to inaugurate adult education programs, have not yet contributed their full potentials. State laws and the State Department of Education, however, encourage efforts in this direction.

A survey of Ohio colleges and universities focused attention on institutions of higher education. Most consider responsibilities almost solely to the growing youth population. Others believe they have moral obligations to serve adults as well.

Less than one thousand persons 65 and over were enrolled in formal classes in Ohio's colleges and universities. Of these, over 700 were enrolled in one school, the University of Cincinnati. More than 100 were registered at Miami University, at Oxford. The rest were scattered among eleven other institutions of higher learning. Only a handful reduced fees or simplified admission procedures for older persons, to encourage their enrollment.

Family Life and Religion

The young are dependent upon the old, and the old upon the young. A firm basis for security requires mutual respect. Changed patterns of family life, however, have altered children's attitudes and obligations for the physical, spiritual and emotional well-being of their parents. Older persons have unwittingly been cast into less useful, less meaningful, and less satisfying roles. Attitudes are reflected in the trend toward confining the aged to rest homes, nursing homes and mental institutions.

Religion, concerned with ethical as well as spiritual values, has some responsibility for influencing attitudes. Yet churches themselves may not fully recognize the special needs of the aged. By teaching respect for older persons in emphasizing "Honor Thy Father and Thy Mother", by helping to reward older people with social status and emotional satisfaction, and by helping them to understand youth, religion can draw the generations closer together.

Organized religion also plays a significant role in the welfare and social service areas by organizing programs such as friendly visitors and golden age clubs. A comprehensive picture of the extent of church programs for the older population is lacking, however.

Discrimination in Ohio, 1960

CIVIL RIGHTS COMMISSION

PREFACE

Background

The Legislature of Ohio has twice within a span of 75 years adopted major civil rights laws. In 1884, following the U.S. Supreme Court Decision which invalidated the Federal Civil Rights Laws (109 U.S. 3 (1883)), a statute was enacted commonly referred to as the Ohio Public Accommodations Law which with only minor changes remains currently in effect (Sections 2901.35 and 2901.36, Revised Code of Ohio).

In 1959, the 103rd General Assembly enacted a civil rights law "to prevent and eliminate the practice of discrimination in employment against persons because of their race, color, religion, national origin or ancestry" and created the Ohio Civil Rights Commission to enforce this newly defined civil right and define other powers and duties of the Commission. Among the powers and duties defined are the sections of the Revised Code cited on the preceding page.

For clarity of understanding, the general purpose of civil rights laws is to insure that all persons, irrespective of their race, color, religion, national origin or ancestry have legal rights protecting them

From Ohio Civil Rights Commission, *Discrimination in Public Accommodations in Ohio,* (Columbus 1960) pp. 5-18 from abuse, or denial of privileges or opportunities commonly enjoyed or exercised by all other persons. The long history of such laws began with the adoption of the Thirteenth, Fourteenth and Fifteenth Amendments to the U.S. Constitution. There have since been enacted hundreds of civil rights statutes by Federal, state and municipal governments; historic decisions rendered by the U.S. Supreme Court; and executive orders issued by U.S. Presidents and Governors of many states.

. . . .

Reasons for the Survey

Because the public accommodations law has a 76-year history and its effectiveness has frequently been questioned, the Civil Rights Commission decided upon a study to determine:

1. Whether the present law is adequate to the needs of current problems in the area of public accommodations.

2. Whether the application of the law needs broadening, redefinition, or changes in its administration.

While these two broad concerns constituted sufficient reason for the Commission to review the civil rights law which had been in effect for 76 years, additional reasons for survey and evaluation of the public accommodations law developed from:

1. An increasing number of cases filed under the statute being brought to the Commission's attention accompanied by observations and complaints that the intent of the law was not being achieved.

2. Interracial tension caused by picketing of restaurants claimed to be discriminatory in Xenia, Lorain, and Cincinnati.

3. Availability of data in this area of discrimination which could be obtained with a limited staff in a reasonable period of time.

. . . .

DISCRIMINATION IN PUBLIC ACCOMMODATIONS IN OHIO

. . . .

Summary of Findings and Conclusions

Discrimination in public accommodations and places of public service based on race, color, religion, national origin or ancestry exists in Ohio despite a law declaring such discrimination to be illegal. It exists in big cities and smaller communities and to a greater degree in communities of southern Ohio than in northern Ohio.

The principal recipients of discriminatory treatment are Negroes, dark-skin Puerto Ricans and Mexican-Americans. In few instances were persons of the Jewish faith, and even more rarely of the

Catholic faith, discriminated against in public accommodations or services.

Experienced observers believe that discrimination in this field is more widespread than available data indicates because of unreported cases caused by either lack of knowledge of statutory prohibition or lack of confidence in the law.

The treatment accorded principally non-whites ranges from restrained or unfriendly acceptance to complete denial of service which may be accompanied by antagonistic rebuffs and upon occasion, physical assaults.

. . . .

Places of Lodging Services. Convention hotels in big cities, in the main, were in compliance with the law. Moderate-priced hotels on the fringes of downtown areas or hotels in areas of racial transition were frequent violators of the law. Several suits were cited as having been brought against hotels connected with resorts. Motels are often listed as refusing service.

A complaint was received directly by the Commission relative to a family seeking accommodations at a prominent summer resort hotel in Ohio. A letter of reservation for rooms at the hotel was sent in advance containing half the cost of the facilities. The hotel in question had assured the wife that adequate facilities were available for the weekend sought for the accommodations. The family consisting of father, mother and three children arrived at the hotel, but were prevented from going to the hotel building by a private police officer who told the family that they would not be accommodated in the hotel because of their race. Upon the insistence of the mother that she had a reservation paid for as required by the hotel, the guard permitted the mother to walk to the registration desk requiring in the meantime that the car with the remainder of the family pull off to the side of the roadway leading to the hotel. After a stormy scene in the manager's office, the hotel finally insisted that they had received no reservation. Later, it was claimed that the reservation and the pre-payment had been returned. The complaint received by the Commission stated that other patrons of the hotel who were white and claiming no prior registration were accepted during part of the period that the colored family was being denied admittance. The family filing the complaint reported a letter was later received returning the money and indicating that no reservations could be furnished for the hotel during the time in question.

The National Medical Association, a Negro association of doctors, attempted to schedule their annual convention in a large city but were refused convention facilities in a hotel especially suitable for arrangements of displays commonly found at such events. The hotel in question refused accommodations on the days desired by the organization even though it was admitted that there was no conflict in date with any other convention group. But the time desired by the National Medical Association was on the days in the week when there were somewhat more white patrons who might be occupying the hotel. The NMA believed that it was offered second-class treatment and explored the legal protection offered by Ohio statute. It found that because it was an association, it could not invoke the statute. Ironically, when the convention was held, many delegates were able to stay at the hotel as individuals.

. . . .

Places of Food and Beverage Services. As in the case of lodging, convention hotels in big cities were seldom cited as refusing service to minority groups. Again, the moderate-priced, second-class restaurants and those located in areas of racial transition were frequently cited as violators. Occasionally, supper clubs were listed, along with party homes and restaurants specializing in banquets and special affairs.

A restaurant was cited as having accommodated a company party which included one Negro, following which the proprietor advised the company their patronage was no longer desired if Negroes were to be included in the groups.

A prominent civic club composed of Negro women made reservation at a restaurant to celebrate its anniversary. When the group arrived and it was discovered that they were colored, they were told that no reservation was recorded and that the restaurant was too busy to accommodate them.

. . . .

In a newspaper account, a Negro woman protesting the proprietor's refusal of service in a restaurant resulted in the police arresting her on a charge of disorderly conduct. No Commission investigation was made in this case, but general reports indicate that arrests on disorderly conduct charges are often resorted to by those intent on maintaining discriminatory practices.

In a pending suit, a prominent Negro civic leader, investigating complaints of discrimination against a neighborhood bar, was personally denied service. Two bystanders who overheard the heated discussion between the Negro and the proprietor followed the Negro outside and assaulted him. A $500 damage suit has been filed against the proprietor.

. . . .

Places of Recreation. Of the seven major categories, this one evoked the largest number and the most vehement complaints on refusal of equal services, notwithstanding the fact that public recreation facilities are generally open to all without regard to race, creed, or color. Common complaints were against roller skating rinks, bowling alleys, dance halls, swimming pools, bathing facilities, golf courses and boating facilities.

The most unusual report came from one city where the roller skating rink was made available to Negro patrons two nights each week after 12:00 midnight. The proprietor was quoted as saying that he made this concession "to assist in keeping the Negro youths off the streets."

A mother with two small children was denied admission to a roller skating rink on a Saturday morning because it was not the day set aside for Negroes.

. . . .

Several large commercial recreation areas in the state admit Negroes on special days or refuse their admission on certain days or restrict their patronage to certain activities within the park.

One large park having a fairly good record concerning racial practices denies Negroes admission on "Kentucky Day" and "Tennessee Day." All white people are admitted without question.

. . . .

Participation in bowling has various ramifications. At one public school a Negro pupil signed up for the bowling team. He was told by the teacher in charge that Negroes were not accepted at the bowling alleys and that he should withdraw so that other students could bowl. The Negro obliged and the school team was organized. One white student withdrew in protest to the arrangement.

In another community, local unions refused to admit Negro members to their bowling teams because of the racial exclusion policy of the alleys.

. . . .

A Negro couple went to a nearby commercial fishing pond one Saturday morning. They were denied admission and told that Negroes fished only on Mondays, Tuesdays and Wednesdays.

Mr. —— took his children to swim in the public pool located in an all-white neighborhood. The management let the water out and a "near-riot" resulted.

. . . .

Transportation Facilities. Fewer complaints were lodged against public transportation than any other category. However, in two cities it was reported that taxi cabs are reluctant to pick up Negroes during the rush hours in downtown sections.

This was explained on an economic basis. Since Negroes in these cities live away from the downtown section, a Negro passenger would be looked upon as a potential long ride which would mitigate against greater income from several short runs. In another instance, taxi cabs are used to haul passengers from the airport. Negro passengers are avoided based on the fear that they would limit the number of passengers a driver could put in the taxi on one trip.

. . . .

The experience of an out-of-town funeral director was recounted in the daily press. According to this article, the funeral director had made arrangements by telephone for burial in the cemetery. He arrived prior to the funeral and checked all final details. While awaiting the cortege, the funeral director was re-contacted by the manager of the cemetery and was informed that the open grave for which he had contracted could not be occupied because it was learned that the corpse was a Negro and the grave was located in the white section of the cemetery.

Numerous hospitals were cited as discriminating in one form or another against Negroes. One incident was cited of a mother having a baby in the corridor of the hospital because the rooms designated for use by Negroes were occupied while at the same time several other rooms were vacant.

In another community, a woman in a maternity ward was moved on the complaint of a white patient to the hospital officials. It is the practice in this hospital to move Negro patients whenever a white person complains.

A report from another community indicated that the doctors have little difficulty in getting Negro patients admitted to hospitals. However, the hospitals have segregated wards and Negroes are frequently put in these wards regardless of ability to pay and severity of illness.

. . . .

Discriminatory Advertisement. The matter of discriminatory advertisement has its effect. It is reported that trade-discount coupon books were being sold to Negro and white residents, although the books carried a number of coupons for beauty salons, restaurants, dancing studios, and the like which were closed to Negroes.

Conclusions on Effectiveness of Current Statute. The experience of citizens in securing relief against discrimination under Section 2901.35, commonly known as the Ohio Public Accommodations Statute, under the criminal or civil provisions of the Statute, varies by geography. The outcome of the cases often reflects a bias by juries and/or public prosecutors, as well as police officers in their role as witnesses, toward the concept of equal public accommodations for all Ohio citizens, regardless of the evidence of the discriminatory treatment.

The range of data collected indicates that there is a grave number of incidents of violations of the Civil Rights Statute. It is also reported that legal action is seldom taken. The current law is an unwieldy, uncertain provision for helping to assure citizens of their rights.

In small communities, it is reported that local police officers are especially reluctant to enforce the public accommodations law. Furthermore, "outside" attorneys are reluctant to accept cases due to the disproportionate time and effort involved. The law, therefore, is rendered meaningless for minority group persons so situated.

The law as presently constituted is virtually useless to travelers discriminated against while in Ohio enroute to distant parts, due to the requirement of local court appearance. Further, the reluctance on the part of local authorities to prosecute cases under the law frequently renders a hardship on citizens when discriminated against because of their inability to pay attorney fees and court costs. The statute is clearly outmoded and ineffective in accommodating the rights to equality of access to public accommodations and services for all well-mannered and orderly persons regardless of race, religion and national origin.

The present statute has no provision against discriminatory practices where based on religion, national origin or ancestry. The freedom of movement enjoyed by persons of darker skin, though not Negro, who with increasing frequency are travelers in the United States, may not be deemed covered by the language of the law since it refers only to "color and race."

. . . .

Recommendation

The Ohio Civil Rights Commission finds that the denial of full and equal use of public accommodations and services, because of a person's race, color, religion, national origin or ancestry is detrimental to and in conflict with the interests and welfare of the people and government of Ohio.

The Commission believes that problems involving the rights of citizens requires a search for solutions within law and is in keeping with the traditions of American democracy. The Commission recommends to the 104th General Assembly that it enact legislation with effective enforcement provisions and procedures to the end that full enjoyment of public accommodations and services shall be the right of all regardless of race, color, religion, national origin or ancestry.

Farm Laborers with Accents

MIGRANT COMMITTEE

Origin and Purpose of Committee

The migrant worker has been playing an increasingly important role in Ohio's agricultural economy as many growers are almost totally dependent on this mobile labor force to help plant and harvest the crops. Their services are needed during the critical periods when the success or failure of handling a crop is contingent upon having an adequate labor supply. Ohio is a highly industrialized state and no longer are there sufficient qualified local agricultural workers to meet the heavy demand for harvest hands in certain areas of the state.

It is not only imperative that the workers be at the place of need when they are needed, but it is also important to the workers, as their earnings are governed by the number of days they are employed during the season. It is estimated that this domestic migrant labor force in Ohio each year numbers approximately 10,000 workers.

Migrant agricultural workers in our state are those whose principal income is earned from seasonal farm employment and who, during the course of a year's work, may move numerous times, often through many states. These workers and their families have the same basic desires and needs as the residents of Ohio. They would like steady employment to support their families, a good home in which to live, schools for their children, church and recreational facilities, health and welfare services, and an accepted place in the community.

In many instances, the migrants have not realized their desires. Many states and communities have found that united efforts are necessary to develop programs to help solve the problems of these workers and their families. The interrelationship of the problems is such that it requires coordinated action and effort on the part of state agencies and all interested groups or individuals.

It is recognized there may be a number of approaches to help solve the problems; however, the best approach is a Governor's Committee on Migratory Labor where all activities can be coordinated.

A committee composed of representatives of various interests was organized by the Governor to utilize the existing resources and to plan new programs on a state-wide basis. This group is working on the many problems in an effort to improve the social and economic

---

From Governor's Committee on Migrant Labor, *Report on Domestic Migratory Labor in Ohio*, (Columbus, 1958), pp. 2-10.

welfare of our migratory farm workers. It is due to the deep concern of individuals, church groups, civic organizations, and state agencies that the members of the Governor's Committee on Migratory Labor are combining their efforts in developing more effective programs to help resolve the problems confronting the agricultural migratory worker and the users of this mobile labor force.

This resume illustrates some of the ways the Governor and the Committee members are attempting to mobilize and coordinate the efforts of the people in Ohio in developing constructive programs for migrant workers and their families.

Migrant Report—United Church Women of Ohio—1957

The United Church Women of Ohio, working in cooperation with the Division of Home Missions of the National Council of Churches, have been actively supporting the Migrant work for many years. We designate the month of March for the promotion of the work and for the raising of funds for the coming season.

The Migrant Ministry is carried on in the following areas: Norwalk, Hartville, Lucas Co., Sandusky Co., Wood Co., Ottawa Co., and Putnam Co., with one or more staff, including volunteers from the community, working in 141 different places. In 1957 there were 14 members on the seasonal State staff with one part-time member of the National staff and 170 local volunteers.

Each area reports some outstanding development for 1957.

Lucas Co. The outstanding development in this area was the "CHILD CARE CENTER" which was started because of the interest and concern of various interested groups and individuals. Some time ago the people in Toledo talked of a Child Care Center but only after a number of years did it become a reality. The State Child Welfare Department of Ohio in cooperation with the Welfare Department in Toledo made the school a possibility. The Migrant Committee of Lucas County has a real interest in this venture. Our migrant staff helped in securing the children for the school and worked in the nursery. The parents were happy to send their children and the response was good.

Another new feature of the program was the teen-age club. The club met once a week with 20 to 30 young people attending. Several of the churches gave leadership to this club, as well as providing games, refreshments and worship services.

There was the unusual fine response to the Sewing Club by the women. Family nights with recreation and films were continued on the farms and in the camps. Whenever possible these evenings were closed by a worship service.

Sandusky Co., Fremont. This is a varied program for the fact that work is done on 52 different camps and farms, of which 29 received extensive program. The variety of crops makes for a number of locations during the summer.

The staff leadership in this county was good. A program was provided in the morning, the afternoon and each evening. This meant driving many miles each day to reach the various locations.

. . . .

Wood Co. Generally the attitude of the farmers is good in Wood county. The farmers realize the workers are necessary and they treat them as people. Part of this is due to the fact that there are small camps on many of the farms. The farmers enthusiastically welcome the Migrant Ministry program for their workers.

This fall some of the children from the Wood County Canning Company as well as children from a family in the Walbridge area enrolled in school.

In former years some of the children and adults have attended the churches. Several families, now permanent residents, have joined the local churches. There is generally a better attitude toward the people in Wood county than in some areas.

This is one county where the Health Department is starting to work with the agencies within the county to improve the situation of the migrants. Members of the Wood County Migrant Committee are on this interagency committee.

The program consisted of a Bible School, Harvester program, distribution of clothing and family nights. In this area one of the important parts of the work is the visitation that must be done to reach the people on many of the farms.

. . . .

Hartville. This is one of the most fertile migrant fields because the people stay 6 months and in this period real progress can be made with a group of people.

The negro people that work in the Hartville area during the summer months work for the same farmers in Florida during the winter. This gives the people some feeling of security because they do know that they have work the year round in two states.

In two years this program has grown rapidly. Last year the program lasted 4 weeks. This year we planned a 6 week program and at the end of the period the people wanted to extend the time.

The people in the community are willing to give of their time and talents to make a program meaningful to the migrant people. Because of the local people helping in many ways some of the children attended the Bible School of one of the Mennonite churches. A male quartette sang at the services in the Church of God. Surely, the work of the volunteers had made these people feel that they wanted to be a part of the local church.

The Stark County Milk Producers provided free milk for the Bible School. Stark County Dairy Council provided literature and posters on nutrition. Ladies Guilds and Women's Societies furnished cookies and refreshments.

A nurse visited the camps occasionally to talk to the children and take care of minor ailments.

The largest single project of the period was the Vacation Church School which was held in the evenings to enable the older children to attend. Ten volunteers from the local churches taught in the school as well as set up the program.

Sunday services were held in two of the camps. Mr. Robert Stewart from Canton assisted in the services when possible.

A weekly Newsletter was sent to the growers, the church people and other interested people.

. . . .

Report of the Work of the Catholic Church Among Ohio Migrants

Like other groups and agencies in Ohio, the Catholic Church was at first unaware of the implications to herself of the truckloads of workers who pulled into Northern Ohio during harvesttime and bent to the work of hoeing and picking Ohio field crops. The Church had to be deeply concerned with the migratory problem because, of the total migrant population in the United States, one million Spanish-speaking workers are of the Catholic Faith.

Even a casual visit to a camp was enough to convince a priest or lay worker that this rootless people had picked up a nestful of problems in its wandering. Some of these problems could be attacked and solved on the local level, others had to be met nationally, but all were specialized evils endemic to migrancy. With this in mind, a national organization called the Bishops' Committee for the Spanish Speaking was set up as early as 1943. It has continuously attracted to its membership an array of experts on every phase of migratory labor. The major effort of this group has been the spiritual welfare of migrant workers. However, convinced that it is difficult to pray on an empty stomach, the Committee has spent a great deal of labor in behalf of the economic and social betterment of those in the migrant stream. The following are examples of Committee efforts.

1. It has created an atmosphere of understanding between the supply states of the Southwest and the work areas of the

North by sponsoring joint conferences, publishing information on the cultural background of the Spanish speaking, etc.

2. It has arranged a program whereby Mexican priests come North to serve as chaplains caring for the needs of their own people.
3. It cooperates with agencies of the State and Federal Governments to ameliorate inhuman conditions wherever they are found among these people. For example, the Committee for the Spanish Speaking spoke out forcibly before a congressional committee and in the press against the present Bracero Program. It felt that U. S. agricultural workers were being discriminated against when their wages were depressed by flooding the market with foreign labor.

Of the 10,000 migrants who work in Ohio field crops each summer, the majority are Texas Mexicans. Of these, 95% are Catholic. The greatest concentration of Ohio migrants is in the Diocese of Toledo, but some population spills over its boundaries into the Archdioceses of Cleveland and Cincinnati, and the Diocese of Columbus. Thus, the Catholic parishes in Ohio and more especially in the North and West have a great responsibility to care for the spiritual and material needs of their neighbors from the South.

The Ohio Councils of Catholic Men and Women in cooperation with their pastors have developed an apostolate to migrants. The program is centered in the various parishes, each parish being responsible in the main for the care of migrants living within its boundaries.

Men and women of the parish are organized to teach in the camps. They supervise the distribution of clothing and food to those who are in need. They work with the parish priest to perform many services; for example, furnishing transportation to the Health Clinics, recruiting nurses, providing playground facilities for children, "selling" the community on the importance of accepting the migrant as a fellow citizen.

Training courses are held periodically on a regional basis to acquaint the teachers with the rudiments of Spanish, to help them understand the customs and background of the Spanish migrant, and the personality problems that can develop when people are constantly shifted from place to place.

From June to October, five Spanish speaking priests work full time in the service of Ohio migrant workers and their families. The presence of the "padres" is perhaps the greatest single factor in making Ohio seem like home to the Texas migrant.

The Catholic Church enthusiastically supported the formation in Ohio of the Governor's Committee on Migrant Labor. The migrant problem is so complex that its solution demands more than desultory "do-goodery." The Governor's Committee has pulled together the efforts of many groups. Surveying the problem from several angles, the Committee was able to set reasonable goals and make steady, concerted progress that would have been impossible to any agency or organization working alone. The Governor's Committee created a spirit of understanding and cooperation that has caught on among all groups involved in work with migrants. The Catholic Church is happy to be a partner in this cooperative effort. Catholic hospitals and parish churches have offered their facilities and personnel in cooperation with the various County Health Departments to bring professional care and health education to migrants in Ohio. Priests in various parishes have worked with Farm Placement Personnel to iron out problems in camps and to help find employment for migrants during slack work seasons. In conjunction with the State Departments of Education and Welfare, summer schools were conducted during June and August to afford migrant children an opportunity to catch up on school work they had missed because of moving from place to place during the regular school year. Remedial work in arithmetic, spelling, and reading given by qualified teachers was well-received and proved most beneficial.

Ohio holds an enviable position in the migrant picture because of its diversified agriculture, but perhaps even more so because the field crops industry of this state is sincerely interested in the welfare of the people who work for them. The Catholic Church in Ohio realizes its responsibility to assist whenever possible in making Ohio an inviting spot for farm labor. It is grateful to the packers and growers who have cooperated so wholeheartedly with the programs it has initiated. In return, it pledges to support legitimate efforts of the field crops people to maintain an industry that is so beneficial to the communities and farms of our state.

The Catholic Church has an important part to play in fostering the spiritual and material welfare of migrant workers, but it must play this part in chorus with many people and many agencies, each contributing in its own way to a better life for our migrants. Perhaps, the words of a grateful mother writing from Texas sums up the meaning of all this:

San Antonio, Texas

Dear Father,

Hello! How are you? How are the kind nurses and sisters at the Hospital? They are real nice people ... I kind of miss them and wish I was over in Ohio. Honest to goodness that was a state I really liked. You may not believe me, but it was the only place they have treated us nice and that was the only place I was at ease.

I hope to go there to live when my girls grow a little more . . .
Georgie and Popeye Garcia send you their regards.

Yours truly,
Carmen M.

"Honest to Goodness" a lot of dedication and lot of service from many quarters made that cry of gratitude possible. The Catholic Church in Ohio is proud to be a part of this dedication and service.

Shoot-Out in Cleveland

LOUIS H. MASOTTI, JEROME R. CORSI

Introduction

On the evening of July 23, 1968, shots rang out on a narrow street in Cleveland's racially troubled East Side. Within minutes, a full-scale gun battle was raging between Cleveland police and black snipers. An hour and a half later, seven people lay dead; 15 others were wounded. Fifteen of the casualties were policemen.

For the next 5 days, violence flared in Glenville and other East Side neighborhoods. Arsonists heaved fire bombs into buildings; teenagers smashed store windows and led mobs in looting. The police lashed back, sometimes in blind fury. In the smoldering aftermath, 63 business establishments were counted damaged or destroyed. Property losses exceeded $2 million.

In human and dollar costs, the Glenville incident was not the most serious event in the recent tide of racial violence in America. But it differed sharply from the current pattern of violence in significant, instructive ways. Indeed, it established a new theme and an apparent escalation in the level of racial conflict in America.

Racial clashes have produced bloodshed and property damage before. Most recent outbreaks, like the Detroit riot of 1967, were

From Louis H. Masotti and Jerome R. Corsi, *Shoot-Out in Cleveland: Black Militants and the Police*, (Washington, 1969).

initiated by blacks—itself a deviation from earlier patterns—but the hostility was directed toward property, not persons. (Sporadic sniper fire—less of it than originally believed—occurred during major disorders in 1967, but long after the violence had expressed itself in property damage.) The Glenville incident was different; it began as person-oriented violence, blacks and whites shooting at each other, snipers against cops. And apparently alone among major outbreaks of racial violence in American history, it ended in more white casualties than black.

Moreover, the Glenville incident occurred in the first major American city to have elected a Negro mayor and in a city that had been spared serious disorders during the volatile summer of 1967. Because of Carl B. Stokes' success in preventing violence after the assassination of Martin Luther King in April 1968, Clevelanders looked upon him as a positive guarantee against future racial disturbances in their city. Yet the violence occurred, and the Glenville incident raised disturbing questions for other American cities with increasing Negro populations that can expect to have Negro-led governments in the future.

Lastly, Mayor Stokes introduced a new technique for quenching the violence. At the urgings of black leaders, he placed control of the troubled neighborhoods in their hands, barring white policemen, National Guardsmen, and white nonresidents from the area. After one night's trial, the policy was altered; police and National Guardsmen were brought into the area, chiefly to protect property. Born in controversy, carried out under complicating circumstances and with only partial success, the technique of "community control" during riots is still a matter of dispute as to its effectiveness.

Why did it happen, especially in Cleveland? Was the Glenville incident the result of a vast conspiracy to "get Whitey" or the sudden, unpremeditated act of a few individuals? Who is to blame? Will it happen again—in Cleveland or elsewhere?

Prelude to the Shooting

In the early years of the Republic, Cleveland was a small inland port settled by New Englanders who had moved westward, with a smattering of German merchants and Irish workers along the docks on the south shore of Lake Erie. Far into the 19th century, Cleveland kept the complexion of a New England town. In the years following the Civil War, however, surging commercial growth and industrialization brought to Cleveland an influx of immigrants from eastern and southern Europe. By 1910 these immigrants and their children made up 75 percent of the central city's population. Separated from the old inhabitants by language, customs, and religion, finding the doors to power and social acceptance closed to them, the immigrants retreated to ethnic enclaves of their own. Gradually they gained power in the city's politics, but the enclaves and ethnic loyalties remained. Later in the 20th century, especially after World War II, growing Cleveland experienced an influx of Negroes out of the South and Appalachia. In time, blacks constituted a sizeable but powerless and excluded minority in Cleveland.

The recent history of the Negro struggle for equality in Cleveland parallels that of other American cities. In the early 1960's, when the civil-rights movement was gaining force in America, several small groups were formed in Cleveland. As elsewhere, white participation was welcomed, and a white minister and his wife were among the prime organizers of the Cleveland chapter of the Congress of Racial Equality (CORE) in 1962. By 1963 there were some 50 separate civil-rights groups in Cleveland, ranging from the moderate National Association for the Advancement of Colored People (NAACP) to CORE (then considered radical) to the Black Muslims (then, and now, even more radical).

In the spring of 1963, the Cleveland NAACP made a move toward establishing unity among the various groups. Its efforts to unite with the more militant groups may have been less an expression of a new militant spirit than of the political instinct to keep alive and enhance its own standing in the community. The effort succeeded; out of a series of meetings during the hot nights of June emerged a new coalition, calling itself the United Freedom Movement (UFM). Its integrated membership included inner-city ministers, leaders of the Jewish community, traditional Negro leaders, and some of Cleveland's new breed of angry young black men.

At best, the new alliance was tenuous. Much of its success would depend on how well it could assure cooperation and unity from so many diverse factions. A balance would have to be struck between moderate and militant approaches. And to survive, the UFM would have to demonstrate that it could produce results.

The UFM's first confrontation, over the hiring practices of contractors building the city's Convention Center, ended in no victory. In the fall of 1963, the alliance turned its attention to the city's school system. Although many Negro children were bussed to alter the segregated system, there was evidence that receiving schools contrived to separate these children from the white students. Relatively few of Cleveland's schoolchildren were in integrated classrooms. The UFM set a list of demands before the Board of Education, with a deadline of September 23 for compliance. The Board and UFM representatives met in a series of closed meetings, and on deadline day basic agreement seemed to have been reached. UFM spokesmen, however, argued that informal agreements in closed session were not official and binding. The following evening, after hearing a report from the steering committee, UFM members voted to picket the Board of Education.

The Board of Education responded to the picketing by scheduling a public meeting September 30, at which it promised to take steps toward "fullest possible integration consistent with sound educational practice" in the receiving schools. The board also promised to create a Citizens' Council on Human Relations to encourage true integration. For the moment, the UFM was triumphant.

By January 1964, UFM leaders concluded the board was not living up to its promises. Meetings with the board only deepened the frustration. To escalate the pressure, the UFM decided to take its picket lines to schools where black children were being bussed. The first two demonstrations, on January 29, brought forth angry mobs of whites. At one of the target schools, demonstrators were forced off the sidewalk as a mob tried to push them in the path of passing automobiles. The next day, a demonstration planned at Murray Hill School, in the heart of Cleveland's "Little Italy," produced a more serious confrontation. At 9:30 a.m., when the demonstration was scheduled to begin, a crowd of angry whites had already surrounded the school. Many were young, and many had been seen at the demonstrations the day before. Reports that the mob had formed deterred the demonstrators from attempting to march on the school. Sensing that the demonstrators would not march, the crowd moved to a busy intersection in Little Italy and began to attack Negroes driving by in their automobiles.

Throughout the day, the mob remained and continued to attack those perceived as "enemies"—enemies that included a number of newsmen. At about midday, the mob attempted to charge the area where the demonstrators had assembled. While police lines checked the advance of the crowd, the demonstrators left to assemble at another location several miles away. By late afternoon, any thought of a march on Murray Hill School was out of the question.

The Murray Hill incident was the UFM's fiery baptism and a clear signal of the deepening rift between Cleveland's blacks and whites. It was also a demonstration of the powerlessness of the Negro community, as evidenced by the official response from City Hall. Mayor Ralph Locher took the position that the school question was outside his jurisdiction. And while the violence lasted, he considered requesting an injunction against the picketing. The police were also a bitter disappointment to the civil-rights leaders. There had been no arrests despite the fact that for an entire day the Murray Hill mob roamed the streets beating Negroes, newsmen, anyone who enraged them, and throwing rocks and bottles at passing automobiles.

The rift grew even deeper when, on February 3, 1964, demonstrators staged a sit-in at the Board of Education building. Police forcibly removed them the next day. The UFM had already lost the sympathy of City Hall and the Board of Education; now the news media became disenchanted. The protest had gone "too far," it had become too "radical," the limit of tolerance had been reached. The community reaction also opened wounds within the UFM itself; while the more militant members were demanding further and more extreme measures, the NAACP faction openly worried about the consequences of the heightened level of protest.

On February 4, the UFM won a temporary victory. The Board of Education agreed to immediate diffusion of the bussed students on a level designed to induce integration. In March, however, it was evident that the board was pushing forward the construction of three schools in the Glenville area, the black neighborhood that was to be the scene of racial violence in 1968. These schools would, by their location, introduce segregation into the school system once more.

UFM demonstrators, on April 6, joined the Hazeldell Parents Association, a group of Glenville residents, in picketing one of the school construction sites. A new tactic was introduced: demonstrators threw themselves into construction pits and in the way of construction equipment. The next day the demonstration was carried to another construction site. The tactics remained the same. The only difference was the result: the Reverend Bruce Klunder, the white minister who had helped to organize the local chapter of CORE, placed himself behind a bulldozer and in the confusion was run over and killed.

Police sought to end the confrontation by dragging demonstrators away. As word of Klunder's death spread, however, further violence became inevitable. Bands of angry Negroes roamed the streets, looted stores, and battled police late into the night. Klunder's death would be long remembered in Cleveland's black community.

Blocked by a court injunction against further interference with school construction, the UFM—over the objections of its conservative members—turned to a new tactic: a boycott of the schools. On Monday, April 20, about 85 percent of the Negro students in Cleveland's public schools stayed home. The boycott was a Pyrrhic victory. Nonattendance of blacks at predominantly white schools was precisely what many white parents wanted. The boycott had not been important in terms of money, power, or lasting prestige—the important "values" of the power structure.

In succeeding months, a new superintendent of schools, Dr. Paul Briggs, significantly reduced the crisis. Briggs shifted emphasis from integration to quality education in each neighborhood. The shift undercut the efforts of the UFM. The emphasis on quality education in their own neighborhoods gained increasing acceptance in the

Negro community, especially as the concept of "Black Power," with its emphasis on racial separatism, found more and more adherents.

* * *

"Black Power" gained in popularity in the black community during 1965, but it sent shivers of anxiety into the white enclaves of Cleveland. That summer, Clevelanders witnessed on their television sets racial disturbances in other cities, including the riot in Watts. In the fall of 1965, several organizations of black militants emerged in Cleveland, led by black nationalists. Traditional organizations such as the NAACP, and now even CORE, had increasing difficulty generating support from the white community. The only organization that continued to provide moral and financial support to the black groups was the Council of Churches, and its resources were limited.

In view of the mounting tensions between the white and black communities, outbreaks of violence were not wholly surprising. Beginning early in 1966, gang fights and physical assaults plagued the Superior-Sowinski area. The Sowinski area, like the Murray Hill area, has been a white ethnic enclave in Cleveland's troubled East Side. As with the Murray Hill area, antagonism toward Negroes runs high in Sowinski. The Superior area bordering Sowinski is predominantly Negro.

The attacks and gang fights continued throughout the Spring. Negro youths were responsible for some of the assaults, white youths for others, but to the Negro community it was apparent that police responded much more quickly and effectively when the victims were white. "If you're going to beat up those niggers," a policeman is said to have told a white gang, "take them down in the park [Sowinski Park] where we can't see it." On Wednesday evening, June 22, two Negro youths were attacked by a gang of whites. A crowd that gathered at Superior Avenue and 90th Street confronted police with their complaints, describing the attackers and pointing to the car they had ridden in, but the police made no move to investigate. Some of the angry crowd threw rocks and bottles. Negro leaders met with the police the next day; the police responded to their grievances by saying they had problems all over the city, that they were understaffed and overworked, that not every incident could be investigated, that incidents like Wednesday evening's attack occur all the time in racially mixed neighborhoods.

Violence broke out again Thursday evening. A Negro youth was shot, according to eyewitnesses, by two white men in a blue Corvair. The description seemed to implicate the owner of a supermarket on Superior Avenue. Since the police would not take any action, Negro youths took the initiative: the supermarket was burned to the ground. Other white-owned businesses were harassed during the evening's disturbance.

After still another night of violence, Mayor Locher met with Negro residents of the troubled area on Saturday, June 25. He promised to investigate their grievances. The tension subsided, at least for the moment.

* * *

Superior Avenue, scene of the June 1966 disturbances, is a broad thoroughfare that carries Cleveland officeworkers home to the comfortable suburbs of East Cleveland and Cleveland Heights. South of Superior Avenue, roughly embracing the numbered streets between the seventies and the nineties, is the neighborhood of Hough (pronounced "huff"). It is a residential area of deteriorating framehouses, old apartment buildings, dwellings vacant and vandalized, occasional small shops, and neighborhood bars. Since the mid-1950's, Hough has been a predominantly Negro slum.

On the evening of July 18, 1966, a sign appeared on the door of a bar at 79th and Hough Ave.: "No Water for Niggers." Residents of the area were enraged. A crowd gathered. The manager of the bar and another white man paraded in front of the bar armed with a pistol and a shotgun. Police arrived and, in their attempt to "disperse the crowd," began to push and shove individuals from the vicinity of the bar. Nearby stores became the targets of rocks. The crowd began to spread; the Hough riot had begun.

For one full week Cleveland was immersed in mass civil disorder. In many ways the violence resembled the earlier violence of Watts: looting, vandalism, burning, sniping. Initially, it was contained in a small area: between 71st Street on the west and 93d Street on the east, and including half-a-dozen blocks north and south of Hough Avenue. On July 20, the third night of violence, sporadic damage was reported in a much wider area, including parts of Kinsman on the south and Glenville on the east. It included thrown fire bombs, some looting, and attempts to divert the police with false fire alarms.

The damage in Hough was extensive. Before rainfall hit Cleveland on Sunday night, July 24, and the violence subsided, four persons (all Negro) had been killed, countless others injured, and whole blocks of buildings had been nearly totally leveled. More than 2,200 National Guardsmen had been called in to patrol the streets. And if Cleveland's racial relations were becoming polarized before the Hough riot, there was no doubt that the split was profound after it was over.

The grand jury of Cuyahoga County, in special session, began its investigation of the disturbances on July 26. In its report, issued August 9, the jury blamed the disorders on—

a relatively small group of trained and disciplined professionals at this business . . . aided and abetted, wittingly or otherwise, by misguided people of all ages and colors, many of whom are avowed believers in violence and extremism, and some of whom also are either members of or officers in the Communist Party.

The conspiracy theory and the suggestion of Communist domination readily found adherents, and Mayor Locher congratulated the grand jury for having "the guts to fix the approximate cause which had been hinted at for a long time, that subversive and Communist elements in our community were behind the rioting."

Few in the black community were persuaded by the grand jury report. They could not fail to note that no Hough residents sat on the panel, and that the foreman of the grand jury, Louis B. Seltzer, editor of the *Cleveland Press,* was being sued at the time of the investigation by a black nationalist leader for calling his organization a "gun club." Suspicions of bias were fed by the report's references to the black leader, Lewis Robinson, as one dedicated to "inciting these youths to focus their hatreds" and to "indoctrinating them with his own vigorous philosophy of violence."

On August 22, a biracial review panel, composed wholly of citizens associated with the Hough area, began its own investigation. Their report concluded that "the underlying causes of the rioting are to be found in the social conditions that exist in the ghetto areas of Cleveland."

"To many," they noted, "it seemed almost inevitable that such neglect and disregard would lead to frustration and desperation that would finally burst forth in a destructive way." As to the influence of Communist agitators: "We would believe that an individual living in such poverty as exists in Hough needs no one to tell him just how deplorable his living conditions are."

A week later, controversy over the causes of the rioting reached into the hearing rooms of Washington. Testifying before Senator Ribicoff's committee investigating urban problems, Mayor Locher was confronted with the U.S. Attorney General's conclusion that "it would be a tragic mistake to try to say that the riots are the result of some masterminded plot." Mayor Locher, however, persisted. Locher argued: "I would disagree with the statements of the Attorney General, and I would wholeheartedly agree with the conclusions made by the grand jury report."

*   *   *

There matters stood at the end of the long hot summer, a war of conflicting viewpoints hardened to a standstill as autumn arrived and quietly passed into winter. Then it was 1967, and perceptive observers looked ahead to another summer of racial violence in Cleveland. As early as April 6, a *Cleveland Plain Dealer* reporter noted: "Even very rational, very hopeful men and women believe that Cleveland will be on fire this summer."

Like a seismograph picking up faint tremors that warn of a major earthquake, the April newspapers recorded a number of fires on Cleveland's East Side that may have been set by arsonists, and a series of lootings around 105th Street, eastward of the scene of the Hough riot. The Cleveland Subcommittee of the Ohio State Advisory Committee to the U.S. Commission on Civil Rights visited the Hough area and saw there ample evidence of the poverty and frustration that would breed another riot.

> Store fronts are boarded up. Unoccupied houses have been vandalized. Stench rises from the debris-filled basements of burned-out buildings. Litter fills street curbings. Garbage and trash are scattered in yards and vacant lots. Recent surveys indicate that in some census tracts as much as 80 percent of the 16-21 age group is unemployed or school dropouts and that 25 percent of the midyear high school graduates seeking work are unable to find jobs.

The subcommittee's report noted that women in Hough were paying high prices for low-quality food in neighborhood grocery stores, using welfare checks that were inadequate for a decent standard of living. The State government, the report charged, has been indifferent to the plight of Hough residents, so have the local authorities.

> The policeman, if you can find one, still shows little interest in vacant houses being stripped of equipment during daylight hours, or the prostitutes on parade, or the accosting of resident mothers and daughters walking home.

The national media shared the prediction that Cleveland was ripe for burning. In late June, Roldo Bartimole, a *Wall Street Journal* reporter, and Murray Gruber, a faculty member of Western Reserve University, published an article in the *Nation* entitled "Cleveland: Recipe for Violence." Their conclusion: "All the elements for tragedy are now present in this city, self-proclaimed 'Best Location in the Nation.' It may be too late for Cleveland, but there are lessons here for other cities that want to avoid disaster." A month later, in the *Saturday Evening Post*, staff writer John Skow noted: "It is hard to find a city resident who believes Cleveland will go unburned through the summer."

And yet, it didn't happen. While Tampa, Cincinnati, Atlanta, Newark, and Detroit experienced major disorders during the summer of 1967, the lid stayed on in Cleveland. Even Martin Luther King's peaceful efforts to press for better jobs for Negroes met with indifference in the Negro neighborhoods of Cleveland that summer. Scorned by the mayor as "an extremist" when he arrived in April, King announced in May that Cleveland would be a "target city" for the Southern Christian Leadership Conference. His most severe tactic against employers discriminating against Negroes would be a boycott of their goods. King's campaign accomplished few of his aims, yet no one turned to violent means to abet his cause.

*   *   *

Explanations for Cleveland's quiet summer of 1967 abound. One contributing cause, perhaps of minor importance, was the channeling of hopes and grievances through the electoral process. Carl B. Stokes, a Negro candidate who in 1965 had come within 2,100 votes of becoming the mayor of Cleveland, was again challenging the incumbent, Ralph Locher. Having come so close, Stokes in 1967 had the avid backing and earnest hopes of Cleveland's black community.

In 1965 Stokes had run as an independent and gained an advantage from the multiplicity of candidates. This time he was forced into the Democratic primary race. Seth Taft, grandson of President Taft and a prominent Cleveland Republican, had threatened to withdraw as his party's candidate if Stokes ran as an independent, for Taft calculated that he would be a certain loser in a three-way race. Stokes, on the other hand, calculated that since he would have to run against Locher in either case, it would be easier to defeat him in the primary, when a lower turnout of voters could be expected.

Stokes was correct. In the primary election of October 4, he defeated Locher by a plurality of 18,000 votes. The decisive factor was the size of the Negro turnout. Although Negroes constituted only about 40 percent of the registered voters, 73.4 percent of them voted in the primary. Only 58.4 percent of the white voters cast ballots in the primary.

The campaign between Stokes and Taft was well fought. Both hired professional help for campaign promotion and poll taking; both made personal appearances and speeches frequently and throughout the city. They met in a series of televised debates in traditional Lincoln-Douglas style.

In the end, Stokes won, becoming the first Negro mayor of a major American city. His victory was initially interpreted as Cleveland's triumph over racial bigotry, an indication of a new openmindedness in American race relations. Examination of the voting data reveals this interpretation as optimistic. Support for Stokes was concentrated in the Negro wards, where he received 95 percent of the vote. In the predominantly white wards he received only 19.3 percent of the vote, and his support was lowest in the three wards with the highest concentration of white ethnic groups in the city.

As a Negro mayor, Stokes was the subject of critical scrutiny by the public and of high expectations from those who had felt ignored by previous, "machine" administrations. His first few months in office were wrecked with difficulties; there were minor political scandals involving some of his early appointees, and public squabblings among others of his administration. The turning point for Stokes came in the wake of Martin Luther King's assassination on April 4, 1968. While other cities erupted in violence, Stokes took to the streets to keep his brothers "cool," effectively invoking the help of black nationalists in keeping the peace. Cleveland stayed quiet, and white citizens of Cleveland were satisfied that in Mayor Stokes they had an effective guarantee against further racial disorders.

Many Clevelanders realized that there would have to be substantive changes in the Negro ghettoes, and they stepped forward in May to support the mayor's new program, "Cleveland: Now!," a campaign to raise $11,250,000 to finance programs ranging from youth employment to rehabilitation of housing to downtown economic development. Some of the projects were eligible for Federal matching funds, and on July 2 Vice President Humphrey came to Cleveland to announce a $1.6 million grant to the Negro-run Hough Area Development Corporation for a program to help small businesses in the riot-torn neighborhood. By then, pledges to the "Cleveland: Now!" campaign from businesses and citizens had reached the $4 million mark.

With optimism, and with a sense of satisfaction over progress being made, Cleveland entered the summer of 1968. But some who could see beneath the calm surface were not optimistic.

. . . .

A Midsummer's Nightmare

Glenville, lying near the northeast corner of Cleveland, is a neighborhood of two- and three-story houses with broad front porches and small front lawns. In the 1940's Glenville was a largely Jewish area; today it is very predominantly Negro. Except for pockets of deterioration, it stands in tidy contrast to the Hough area, lying to the west.

For Patrolman William Kehoe, performing traffic duty on the East Side, July 23, 1968, was a slow day. Shortly after noon he called headquarters for a possible assignment. Lt. Edward Anderson, traffic coordinator for the Cleveland Police Department, assigned him to check an abandoned automobile in the Glenville area. . . .

The car, a 1958 Cadillac, was on Beulah Avenue, between East 123d Street and Lakeview. The left front tire was flat; to Patrolman Kehoe, it appeared the car was a "junk car" that had not been driven for some time. Neighbors confirmed that the car had been there many days; none had any idea who owned it. At 1:25 p.m., Kehoe placed a parking ticket on the abandoned car, then filled out a routine report for the tow truck division of the police department.

Kehoe expected that the car would be towed away before the evening rush hour. But William McMillan and Roy Benslay, operating tow truck No. 58, had other assignments that kept them from the pickup in Glenville until dusk. They arrived on Beulah Avenue in their uniforms, which resemble standard police uniforms except that the jackets are of the Eisenhower type. Clevelanders commonly assume that the tow-truck operators are policemen, but in fact they are civilian employees and carry no weapons.

What happened next has been recounted by McMillan. After Benslay backed the truck up to the Cadillac, McMillan emerged from the cab to check the license plate number against the assignment card. "The next thing I knew I was shot in the back. I turned around and saw a man with a shotgun firing from the side of a house on the corner of Lakeview."

McMillan ran to the front of the tow truck to take cover. A second shot hit him in the right side. "Another sniper was firing from the bushes just in front of the truck." Benslay, crouching in the cab of the truck, radioed for help. Then the shooting stopped.

"A Negro with a carbine in his hand walked up the sidewalk and stopped just across from me," McMillan told a reporter several days later.

"Are you one of the sons of bitches stealing cars?" the Negro asked him. McMillan pleaded that he was unarmed and rose from the street to show that he had no weapon. The Negro raised the carbine to his shoulder and took aim. McMillan ran toward 123d Street. As he turned the corner, another bullet hit him in the right side. McMillan kept running.

Halfway along the block a Negro woman shouted to McMillan and offered him refuge. Inside the house he telephoned the police department, but the lines were busy. When he heard sirens, McMillan left the house and walked northward on 123d Street. After turning right on Oakland Avenue he spotted a squad car, which rushed him to a hospital.

McMillan identified the Negro with the carbine as Fred (Ahmed) Evans [a black nationalist leader].

He also offered an explanation of the event. "The snipers set up the ambush and used the tow truck as a decoy to bring the police in," he said. "They had their crossfire all planned. We all were sitting ducks."

McMillan's ambush theory found ready acceptance. Many Clevelanders, and at least two national news magazines, accepted it unquestioningly. But other events of that grim Tuesday, and the accounts of other eyewitnesses, cast doubts upon the ambush theory.

*   *   *

Ahmed [Evans] lived in an apartment in a two-story, red brick house at 12312 Auburndale, a block and a half from the scene of the tow-truck shooting. On the evening of July 23, shortly before the tow-truck incident, he had visitors: George Forbes, the city councilman from Ahmed's area, and Walter Beach, a former halfback for the Cleveland Browns, who was the director of the Mayor's Council on Youth Opportunities. According to a summary of events, issued later by the mayor's office, the meeting lasted from 7:50 p.m. to 8:05 p.m.

Forbes and Beach had come from a meeting at City Hall where Ahmed had been the subject of anxious discussion. The meeting, which began at 2:30 that afternoon, had been called by Inspector Lewis Coffey of the Cleveland Police Department. Coffey had intelligence reports, which the police department had obtained chiefly through the Federal Bureau of Investigation, that warned of an outbreak of violence planned for Cleveland the next morning, July 24, at 8 a.m. The central figures in the outbreak would be Ahmed and his group, the Black Nationalists of New Libya.

Ahmed's group, according to the reports, had been assembling an arsenal of handguns and carbines and stashing them in Ahmed's apartment. Some of the group had gone to Pittsburgh, Detroit, and Akron on Sunday night to collect semiautomatic weapons; a further trip to Detroit was planned for Tuesday evening, July 23. In addition to the Wednesday morning outbreak, the reports added, there was the possibility of simultaneous outbreaks in other Northern cities. In Cleveland, five Negroes would be the targets of assassination: Mayor Carl B. Stokes, Councilman Leo Jackson, William O. Walker (publisher of the Negro newspaper, *The Cleveland Call & Post*), Baxter Hill, and James Payne. Four of the targets were prominent Negroes; the fifth, James Payne, was the patrolman Ahmed had been found guilty of assaulting.

The truth of these reports was questionable. Police doubted that a trip to both Pittsburgh and Detroit had been made in one night. The reports came from a single individual, a member of Ahmed's group who apparently was not an infiltrator but a man accustomed to selling information to the FBI and the Cleveland police. Other intelligence sources did not corroborate his story. Those who had talked to the informer on the telephone suspected he was under the influence of drugs.

The reports were serious enough, however, to warrant considerable attention. On Tuesday morning, Cleveland police checked various aspects of the intelligence reports. They learned that on Monday, black nationalists had been in Higbee's, a downtown department store, examining high-powered deer rifles with telescopic scopes. Nationalists had been seen buying bandoliers (links of ammunition for automatic weapons), canteens, and first-aid kits from a downtown army surplus store. There was some uncertainty whether the nationalists included Ahmed or any of his group.

Mayor Stokes was in Washington, D.C., that day, participating in a discussion entitled "Is the Big City Dying?" In his absence, Clarence James, the law director (a position similar to city attorney or solicitor) participated in the City Hall meeting as "acting mayor." While the meeting was in progress, Mayor Stokes placed a routine call from Washington to his office. Informed of the potential trouble, he told James to telephone Baxter Hill, the director of Pride, Inc., a community self-help organization, and a member of the Community Relations Board. Unable to reach Hill, James summoned to the meeting Councilman George Forbes, who was also familiar with Ahmed and his group.

Discussion turned from the intelligence reports to tactics for coping with the developing situation. There were no grounds for arresting Ahmed and too little to establish "probable cause" for obtaining a search warrant. By the laws of Cleveland and Ohio, mere possession of handguns or rifles is not illegal. While possession of automatic and semiautomatic weapons *is* illegal, there was only the informer's report to indicate that Ahmed and his group possessed such weapons. Even if there had been something in the informer's story to establish probable cause, he could not be used to testify without "blowing" his cover.

According to the informer's story, Ahmed and his group were planning a trip to Detroit Tuesday evening to obtain illegal automatic weapons. That being the case, Inspector Coffey advised, the police should establish a surveillance near Ahmed's house. Furthermore, it ought to be a moving surveillance, not a stationary one—roving police cars rather than parked ones. Ahmed's neighborhood was residential, his and nearby streets were narrow, and a parked car full of men—especially if they were white police officers—would attract notice. Moreover, Ahmed often stationed guards at his home to watch for police, sometimes sending them on "patrols" to hunt for police on nearby streets. Enough cars were available for an effective moving surveillance, and the police department would assign to the task as many Negro officers as it could.

One other aspect of the informer's story demanded attention. Although police investigation had failed to find confirming evidence of an assassination plot, a decision was made to provide a security guard for the five Negroes mentioned as potential victims.

Councilman Forbes and Walter Beach agreed to talk to Ahmed, to try to cool him down and work out a solution to his known grievances. Forbes and Beach knew, as many others knew, that Ahmed was angered over apparent discriminations against him in recent weeks. With the grant he had received from "Cleveland: Now!" funds, Ahmed was in the process of refurbishing a dilapidated and long-vacant store on Hough Avenue, converting it into an Afro-American culture shop. After investing considerable effort on the cleanup, he was notified by the white landlord that he could not use the store. And now he was being evicted from his apartment on Auburndale. After legal proceedings, a 24-hour notice was served by bailiffs earlier on Tuesday. (The apartment actually was not his; it was rented by a 16-year-old who had taken the African name of Osu Bey.)

After the City Hall meeting broke up about 6 p.m., Forbes and Beach drove toward the East Side. On the way to Ahmed's home they stopped on Superior Avenue at the Afro Set, a shop and gathering place for young militants. Harllel Jones, leader of the Afro Set, was not there, but Forbes and Beach talked to one of the young members of the group who agreed to accompany them to Ahmed's home. The three drove eastward on Superior Avenue, then turned south on Lakeview. At the corner of Moulton Avenue, which is close to the intersection of Lakeview and Auburndale, they saw an unmarked car "full of white people." It was glaringly evident that the police had established a stationary surveillance rather than a moving one. In fact, another surveillance car was facing Ahmed's apartment building from the opposite direction, parked where Auburndale joins East 124th Street. Both cars contained only white officers; both were in plain view of Ahmed's home.

Beach steered his car left onto Auburndale and parked in front of Ahmed's apartment building. As the three men emerged from the car, Ahmed called to them from a narrow passageway next to the building. In a backyard conference, he poured out his apprehension about the police surveillance. There were, he said, even police on the roof. The police had harassed him before; he was afraid the surveillance was leading up to another incident of harassment. He urged Forbes and Beach to try to get the surveillance removed. The men also discussed Ahmed's eviction problems, and Forbes and Beach promised to do what they could.

When the conference ended, the visitors felt they had satisfied Ahmed. As they were leaving, he told them to give a message to Mayor Stokes: "Tell the Big Brother downtown that everything is going to be all right."

Forbes decided that there was nothing he could do at the scene to have the surveillance removed. As a councilman, he knew the police who usually work in his district, but the surveillance teams were from a special unit. He judged they would not recognize him or listen to him.

. . . .

Forbes and Beach returned to the home of Harllel Jones, this time finding him there. While they were talking, a member of the Afro Set came in to report that shooting had begun in Glenville. Forbes called the mayor. Stokes already had the news. The emergency call had come from Safety Director McManamon. The Glenville disturbance had been ignited.

*   *   *

Who shot first? And at whom? Various accounts of where, how, and why the shooting started have appeared. Even after extensive investigation, questions remain unanswered.

. . . .

By the testimony of the surveillance teams . . . they were the first to be fired upon, not the tow truck. Rightly or wrongly, Ahmed regarded the obvious presence of the surveillance cars over several hours' time as threatening. The tow truck, it now appears, was not the deliberate target of a planned ambush but arrived at the wrong place at the wrong time. Inspector Lewis Coffey took this view in an interview published in the *Plain Dealer* 3 days after the event. According to Coffey, the tow truck arrived on Beulah Avenue "almost simultaneously" with the initial shootings at the surveillance cars. "Then he gets it."

. . . .

Of the sequence of events on Beulah Avenue during the evening of July 23, there were several eyewitness reports. Not all of them accord with the claim of William McMillan, the tow-truck operator, that he was shot very soon after arriving at the abandoned car. Residents of the area have reported seeing the tow-truck officers examining the automobile for a period of time before the outbreak of shooting. A man and his wife drove by the tow truck as McMillan was getting out to examine the Cadillac. They drove to the intersection of Lakeview, turned left and proceeded two blocks to Superior, turned left again, and in that time heard no shots. Other witnesses claim that the tow-truck operators were confronted by an individual who seemed to argue with them. This individual walked away, only to reappear with the snipers some time later. One resident interviewed claimed that the individual who confronted the tow-truck operators then walked away and made a telephone call. Such a call could have been directed to Ahmed and also could have prompted the movement from Ahmed's home or given it direction after the movement had started.

The official police log lends weight to the evidence, supplied by the accounts of surveillance-car activity, that the movement away from Ahmed's house, and some of the actual shooting, occurred before McMillan was shot. The tow truck placed its call for help at 8:28 p.m. The first radio report of shooting came 4 minutes earlier in a conversation between the dispatchery and Car 604 (which was not one of the surveillance cars). Car 604 gave its position as 123d and Beulah. Since this is close to the location of the tow truck, it tends to support the conclusion that the tow truck was inadvertently trapped in the crossfire between police and snipers.

A puzzling claim was made in a chronology of events released by the mayor's office at the press conference on August 9. According to this chronology, at 8:15 p.m. the tow truck "gets [a] call" to pick up the abandoned Cadillac. This invites the inference that some citizen had telephoned the police department Tuesday evening with the intention of luring the tow truck into a trap. Except in response to dangerous accidents, it is not usual operating procedure for a tow truck to be instructed by headquarters to go immediately to tow a car. And it has been established that the automobile had been examined earlier on Tuesday and the tow-sheet report prepared then.

Against theories of an ambush or well-planned conspiracy stands the evidence that on Tuesday evening Ahmed was annoyed and apprehensive about the police surveillance. He expressed such sentiments to Walter Beach and George Forbes. He had memories of police violence in Akron. "So we armed ourselves. And what followed was chaos."

In an interview published in the *Cleveland Press,* August 2, Ahmed offered his version of his movements after leaving the house:

> I was heading for the Lakeview Tavern [at the corner of Auburndale and Lakeview] when I heard some shots coming from the end of the street. Then one of the brothers passed me running. Some policemen in a blue detective's car opened up with a machinegun and he was dead. So I ran into a yard and I began trading shots with a policeman behind a parked car. I couldn't hit him. I wasn't coming anywhere close to him. And then my carbine jammed.

According to Ahmed, he then hid in bushes and tried to fix the carbine, but without success.

In an interview for this study, Ahmed said that he had rounded the corner and was walking on Lakeview when he heard the first shot. When he went to investigate, he saw the tow-truck operator running along Beulah. Then, he said, he heard what sounded like a submachinegun blast; he later concluded that this was the fire that killed Amir Iber Katir, one of his followers. (The account by Lt. Miller and the observations of a radio reporter who arrived at the scene support the conclusion that the first person killed was a black nationalist. The coroner's autopsy revealed four bullet wounds: the right chest, right thigh, left leg, and left thigh.) Ahmed has con-cluded: "We were ambushed, not the police."

An eyewitness recalled that Ahmed came down the street very coolly. By the time he got to Beulah, the shooting had begun. Ahmed, said the witness, was carrying an automatic weapon, and when he reached the corner he started firing.

> Ahmed himself, he came down later. On his side, and when he came down with the automatic rifle or machinegun, whichever it be, his rifle drowned all the other guns. . . . He came down peacefully. He came down the left side of the street and when he turned the corner, that's when all hell broke loose.

Ahmed has admitted that he did not have total control of the situation. There were many nationalists involved and he was only one. "I had come to be the leader. But the night of the 23d, there was no leader. After we got our guns, it was every man for himself."

*   *   *

In the 1-hour period between 8:30 p.m. and 9:30 p.m. on Tuesday evening, at least 22 people were killed or injured in the raging gun battle between police and snipers. The major shooting occurred along Lakeview Avenue between Beulah Avenue and Auburndale, a distance of less than 300 yards, and ranged no more than a block each way on side streets.

The area is no place to hold a shoot-out. Lakeview itself is narrow. The side streets are even narrower, and some of them jut at odd angles. Houses are close together, sometimes separated by nar-row passageways. There is little room to maneuver.

When a radio call for assistance went out about 8:30 p.m., it was an "all units" call; any available unit in the city could respond. Police throughout the city left their regular patrols and rushed to the scene, anxious to help their comrades in trouble. A radio newsman esti-mated there were 40 to 50 police officers when he arrived at 8:45 p.m. Later there were "several hundred officers," according to the *Cleveland Press.* Nearby streets accumulated long lines of abandoned patrol cars as police parked their cars as close to the shooting as possible, grabbed their weapons, and ran to lend assistance.

The battle that ensued was a combination of confusion and panic. Police enthusiastically rushed into the area without knowing precisely, or even generally, what they were rushing into. The re-sponse had largely been personal initiative rather than planned reac-tion and an orderly show of controlled force. Each officer grabbed his gun and did what he could. "Perhaps some snipers were shot and killed," a policeman recalled of his experience. "I fired, mostly at shadows." No one assumed command. There was no orderly way to report to headquarters and no way for headquarters to issue directives. Police had largely abandoned their radios when they left their cars.

. . . .

On the evening of July 23d, Henry Perryman, minister of a store-front church on Superior Avenue, was on his way to Akron, scene of recent racial disturbances, to help "cool things down." His car radio brought news of the shootings in his Cleveland neighborhood. Perryman turned around and sped homeward. He arrived back in Glenville to discover that police were firing at snipers in his own house at 1395 Lakeview.

. . . .

A fierce gun battle raged around 1395 Lakeview, lasting long after the shooting had subsided at Auburndale and Lakeview. Police reported that the snipers were firing wildly from every floor of the house. They called to a sniper in the basement to surrender, but he answered them with obscenities. At one point, according to the police, a man came out of the house and fired a weapon randomly from the areaway between 1395 and 1391. He returned to the house, and, when he appeared at a window, police shot and felled him. The shooting from the first floor stopped, but continued from the second.

Around midnight, a group of police attempted to storm the house. They got through one door; a locked second door barred them from access to the second floor. They shot off the lock but then encountered a steel wedge behind the door. Furniture and bedding were leaning against the door on the other side. They could not get to the sniper on the second floor. The body of the sniper who had been shooting from the first floor, they reported, lay on the kitchen floor dead.

"At this time," Lieutenant Miller reported at the City Hall press conference on August 9, "the house erupted in flames." The cause of the fire has not been determined, but residents of the area are convinced that the police set the fire themselves. Henry Perryman has made a plea to the city of Cleveland for compensation for the destruction of his home.

Perryman watched his home burn to the ground, the house next door (1391 Lakeview) catch fire and burn also. Police reported hearing shouts of "Omar, Omar" and "Ali" come from within 1395. . . . Fire department units made no attempt to approach the burning structures to extinguish the flames.

Among others watching the buildings consumed in flames were Councilman George Forbes, Law Director Clarence James, Walter

Beach, and three other black leaders: Harllel Jones, Wilbur Grattan, and Albert "Breeze" Forest. Forbes, Beach, and Jones, together with Baxter Hill, had been active throughout the evening trying to restore peace, trying to talk to the snipers but unable to get near because of the shooting. James had been touring the troubled area as the Mayor's eyewitness and reporter.

When the two Lakeview houses began to burn, Harllel Jones wanted to make sure that everyone had been removed from them. He, Forbes, Grattan, and Forest approached the burning buildings. As Jones got to the alley behind the houses, he noticed that the bodies of the shot snipers were still lying there. One of the bodies was beginning to burn; Jones dragged it away. Lathan Donald, still alive, was also in danger of catching fire. With the help of the other men, Harllel Jones got Donald onto a stretcher; Grattan and Forest began to carry the wounded man from the alley. According to the reports of those attempting to assist Lathan Donald, unidentified police officers (who had removed their badges) attacked Grattan and Forest, beating them severely, saying "Leave that nigger here to die." Grattan and Forest retreated without the stretcher, but managed to tell two Negro policemen about the incident before leaving the area.

All the while Forest, Grattan, and Jones were investigating the dead and wounded behind the burning buildings, Clarence James, Assistant Safety Director Frank Moss, and others remained by their cars at Beulah and Lakeview. There they became near victims of the chaos. James described what happened:

> Now there were a lot of shells exploding; it looked like they were burning shells. As I turned toward the car there were people lined up on the porches and everything, and an awful lot of police officers were there. I turned back toward the car. I heard two shots. It probably was my imagination, but I thought I heard the "zing" of one, and I dropped right down to my knees by the car. Frank Moss was just diagonally [across from me]. I could see him. He spun [around] and started to draw his revolver. . . . Boy, everybody was almost in a freeze position, and I got a little scared. . . . I made up my mind I was going to get the hell out of there.

James does not know who fired the shots, but he does not dismiss the possibility that the one that came close to him was fired by a policeman.

About this time, Grattan and Forest emerged from the alley, Forest bleeding and in pain. Clarence James and Harllel Jones took Forest to Forest City Hospital. There, James placed a call to Mayor Stokes. Stokes spoke with Harllel Jones, who was outraged over police conduct during the incident, and managed to calm him down. Later, Lathan Donald was brought to the prison ward of Cleveland

Metropolitan General Hospital by two Negro policemen who had taken him from the alley.

. . . .

At 11:11 p.m., before the fire in the Perryman house started, a call went out over the police radio: "1384 Lakeview: front door open, man wants to give himself up, wants [to surrender to] Negro policemen." A similar message went out at 12:24 p.m. This time, three white policemen, Sgt. Ronald Heinz, Patrolmen David Hicks and John Cullen, approached 1384 Lakeview to apprehend the man who wished to surrender. Fred (Ahmed) Evans emerged from the house, shirtless, wearing slacks and sandals.

The house from which Ahmed came was across the street from the Perryman house. The only times that 1384 Lakeview appeared in official police chronologies and records were the two broadcasts offering Ahmed's surrender.

When Ahmed emerged, he was reported to have asked: "How are my people?" Told that at least three had been killed, he replied: "They died for a worthy cause." Ahmed said he had 17 in his group.

When police asked Ahmed where his weapon was, he pointed to the bushes in front of the house. The police found a toga, a loaded carbine, five boxes of ammunition, and a first-aid kit. Ahmed explained: "If my carbine hadn't jammed I would have killed you three. I had you in my sights when my rifle jammed." Before taking him to central headquarters, one of the policemen asked Ahmed: "Why did you start all this?" He replied, "You police have bothered us too long."

. . . .

Thus, by 9:30 p.m., the official casualty list read: 3 police killed, 12 injured (counting McMillan, the tow-truck operator); 3 suspects killed, 1 wounded; 1 civilian killed, 2 injured. The count shows 7 lives lost and 15 individuals wounded: a total of 22 casualties.

[On May 12, 1969, an all-white jury found Fred (Ahmed) Evans guilty of first-degree murder on seven counts, without mercy. The following is from the epilog of *Shoot-Out in Cleveland*, "The Trial and Conviction of Fred (Ahmed) Evans."]

Before sentencing Ahmed, the judge asked him if he had any statements. Ahmed replied:

I fully understand the ways of life as they are now, and the truth of the matter is I have no regret. . . . I have no malice towards anyone, white people nor anyone else. . . .

This will not end by the means that have been used today against the black man who are willing, who are able, who are strong enough to stand up.

The electric chair or fear of anything won't stop the black man of today.

I feel justified in that I did the best I could. And, of course, concerning these charges I am not a murderer.

Judge McMonagle answered:

. . . If it can be said there was any defense you presented . . . it was that you did not agree with our laws, and apparently you were not bound by them. . . .

I think it is perfectly obvious that we cannot have a system where every man is his own law.

Furthermore, Ahmed had inflicted a horrible wound on the community. The judge hoped that the community, white and black together, would continue to work together for coequal status within the law.

Thereupon, he sentenced Ahmed to die in the electric chair on September 22, 1969, between the hours of midnight and sunrise.

Reaction: the Crowds, the Police, and City Hall

Take an army of policemen, especially white policemen, into the ghetto, add a crowd of onlookers, and you have created a situation ripe for mass violence.

Just north of the Glenville battlefield lay Superior Avenue, a broad thoroughfare that carries U.S. Routes 6 and 20. A crowd began to gather on Superior soon after the shooting started, barely within eyesight range of the shooting on Lakeview Road. The crowd became unruly, heaving rocks at passing cars and jeering at the police swarming into the area. When the body of a dead or dying sniper was carried toward the intersection, the smoldering hatreds of the crowd were aroused. "Look what they've done to one of our brothers!" some were heard to say.

By 9:30 p.m., the crowd had grown huge. Most in the crowd were young; by one estimate, the average age was 22 or 23. Their mood was clearly hostile. "The crowd was berserk," one eyewitness recalls, and the police were frightened; they ran from their cars "like scared jack rabbits." A police car on Superior was hit by a Molotov cocktail; there was a "whoosh" and it went up in flames. The crowd scattered when ammunition in the car began to explode. A panel truck came down Superior and turned wildly directly into the crowd. The white driver was grabbed, pulled from the truck, and beaten to bloodiness. The crowd turned the truck over and set it afire. Herbert Reed, a 21-year-old patrolman, was pulled from his car at East 124th and Superior by a gang of Negro youths and beaten savagely. Two news cars containing valuable equipment were set afire and destroyed.

As they had done on the first night of the Hough riot in 1966, the police sensed that the crowd was beyond control and they abandoned the situation. As the huge crowd began to move, it found itself free of police restraint. A few black policemen remained to prevent cars and white occupants from running the Superior Avenue gauntlet.

Mobs began to spread along Superior. Teenagers wrapped sweaters around their elbows and rammed plate glass windows of stores along the avenue, breaking them with a single thrust. "All you could hear was glass breaking," an eyewitness recalls. Gangs of looters and arsonists spread westward almost to Rockefeller Park, a buffer zone a mile away from Lakeview. At East 105th and Superior, close to Rockefeller Park, a block of buildings was burned to the ground. A store that Ahmed once had rented on Superior Avenue went up in flames, along with all the buildings next to it. Stores all along East 105th were looted. The violence spread all the way to St. Clair Avenue, more than a mile north of Superior. Sporadically it broke out on the other side of Rockefeller Park, as far west as East 55th Street and including the troubled area of Hough.

Patrol cars were dispatched to disperse looters, to answer calls of shootings, to pick up youths carrying gasoline cans or weapons. Often they had to report back "gone on arrival" or "unable to locate." A heavy rainstorm shortly after midnight offered hope of ending the violence, but the storm was short lived. The looting and fire setting continued through the night. Fire engines were brought in from all parts of the city and deployed in groups for protection against the hindering mobs. Firemen sometimes arrived on the scene to find hydrants had been opened, making it difficult to hook up hoses. They faced gangs of youths throwing bottles and rocks at them; some reported sniper fire. Eventually, some fire crews refused to answer calls without a police escort. The next day Fire Chief William E. Barry reported that the fire department had responded to between 50 and 60 legitimate fires in the troubled area during the night, most of the fires occurring along Superior Avenue east of Rockefeller Park. About 20 were "major" fires, involving two or more buildings.

. . . .

James C. Haynes was a 30-year-old stock clerk who earned extra money as a custodian and guard in the apartment building in which he lived at 1270 East 83d Street. The building was close to Superior Avenue, and Haynes was aware of the looted and burning buildings at 105th and Superior, three-quarters of a mile to the east. Apprehensive about trouble in his own neighborhood, Haynes armed himself with a pistol. Around midnight, according to his father, a gang of youths attempted to enter the building; Haynes exchanged fire with them and the youths fled. (Others say Haynes merely fired into the air and the youths scattered.) Haynes returned to his apartment, picked up a shotgun, then walked downstairs and out of the building.

What happened next has never been clarified. One thing is clear: shots rang out. The body of James Haynes was later found in an alley behind 8203 Superior Avenue, riddled with shotgun wounds, another Negro fatality in Tuesday's long night of violence.

Around the corner from Haynes' apartment, a number of young black militants were gathered at the Afro Set, the craft shop and meeting place run by Harllel Jones. Early in the evening, Jones had given assurance to Law Director Clarence James and Councilman George Forbes that his followers would not participate in the violence. He himself was traveling through the troubled area with James and Forbes, helping them in their effort to restore peace and calm with fellow black citizens. Lyonel Jones (no relation to Harllel), director of the Legal Aid Society of Cleveland, was at the Afro Set to help keep the situation calm there. As a further precaution against trouble, James had stationed a Negro policeman at the building.

Police may have heard the pistol shots fired by Haynes, or they may have responded to a message, broadcast on patrol-car radios about 11:45 p.m., that two policemen were trapped in a building on East 82d and Superior and that Negro males were setting it afire. (The source and substance of that report are further unsolved elements in the episode.) In either case, very quickly there were several patrol cars at the scene.

According to Lyonel Jones, eight policemen barged into the Afro Set, shot at the ceiling, and ordered the occupants to leave. A white captain ordered the Negro policeman whom James had stationed there to return to Fifth District headquarters. "Get your black ass out of here," he was overheard saying in response to the policeman's protests.

Then, say eyewitnesses, a patrol-car crew drove into a gas station, turned off the headlights, and began to fire in the direction of the apartment building where James Haynes lived. Another car, they say, drove into the alley behind Superior where Haynes was later found dead. Police believed they were being fired at; a patrol-car broadcast about 11:50 p.m. indicated two policemen were "pinned down" by snipers hiding in bushes in front of a funeral home near East 82d and Superior.

Law Director James, Councilman Forbes, and Harllel Jones arrived in a police car at 82d and Superior after the shooting had subsided. (James had been informed of the trouble there by the mayor's office in a phone conversation.) Another police vehicle, Car 351, was parked in front of the Afro Set. As James got out of the car, a group of young militants approached him in a state of excitement: "That's the car that did the shooting; that's the car that did the shooting [in the Afro Set]," they said, indicating Car 351.

As James approached Car 351 to speak to its occupants, it pulled away from the curb and proceeded down Superior Avenue. James grabbed the microphone from his police car and radioed the following message: "Car 351, this is the Law Director; return to the scene on Superior that you just left." Car 351 kept going, slowed down momentarily, then sped up again as James repeated his message. Then it turned into a side street.

James and Forbes got into the police car and ordered the driver to pursue Car 351 with the siren on. They turned where Car 351 turned, but the patrol car was not in sight. James called the radio dispatcher: "This is the Law Director in 8C. Will you locate Car 351?" He heard the dispatcher broadcast the message: "Car 351: your location?" There was no answer. Then James thought he saw 351 ahead of them, running without lights on. He pursued the car, siren still screaming. As he drew near, Car 351 slowed to a stop in front of him. The headlights came on. "Car 351," James radioed, "this is the Law Director right behind you. Please get out of your car and come back to me."

When the three policemen in Car 351 approached, James asked one of them, a sergeant, if he had heard him on 82d and Superior telling him to stop and return to the scene. The sergeant replied, "No; we didn't hear you." Raising his helmet, he added: "You know, we can't hear too well with these things on." Another said: "We've got the radio turned down and did not hear you call." Why, James wanted to know, would they have the radio turned down when there was all this trouble in the city? James found their answers unconvincing.

Then James asked the sergeant to accompany him back to 82d and Superior while the other officers followed in Car 351. (Only when they arrived back at the Afro Set did James realize that one of the other officers was a captain, and thus in charge of Car 351.) As they rode back, James told the sergeant about the complaints of residents that Car 351 had done unnecessary shooting. The sergeant denied the claims, saying Car 351 had just arrived on the scene.

When they reached the Afro Set, James learned that a dead body had been found in the alley behind Lakeview. He and others examined the body of Haynes, then James asked the police captain, "How did this happen?" "I don't know," said the captain; "we had just come up." James asked what had happened to the Negro policeman he had stationed at the Afro Set. The captain admitted that he had sent the officer to Fifth District headquarters, but denied that the man ever mentioned that he had been under orders from Law Director James.

Residents of the area were giving James their versions of what had happened. They told him about the patrol car parked at the gas station firing at the apartment building on 83d Street. One confirmed that spent shells were lying on the ground at the gas station. A police photographer had arrived, and James sent him to take pictures of the shells. Then James and others examined the exterior of the apartment building. "That building has been riddled with bullets," he told the policemen. "How did this happen?" The captain and the sergeant again replied that they had no knowledge of the matter since they had just arrived. People in the crowd said they had seen a patrol car shooting at the building. Concerned that the shooting might have produced casualties, James, the policemen and others entered the building to examine it. In a second-floor apartment they found that high-powered bullets had gone through windows and torn through the walls, leaving gaping holes where they lodged. There were holes above the beds of two small children who had been sleeping when the shooting started.

City officials later promised an investigation of the shootings near East 82d and Superior, probing for instances of police misconduct. If the investigation took place, the conclusions have not been made public.

*   *   *

Through the long night of July 23-24, 1968, Mayor Stokes and top officials at City Hall struggled with the decisions to be made about how to cope with the violence in Cleveland. They were hampered by inadequate and confusing information about the violence as it happened, and by the lack of contingency planning for such emergencies.

. . . .

Perhaps buoyed by its success after the assassination of Martin Luther King, the Stokes administration found itself inadequately prepared to handle the violence of July 23. Control of the situation was, in the beginning stages, left to police on the scene, and, as Stokes was later to admit, Cleveland police were inadequately trained and supplied to cope with urban guerrilla warfare. According to Maj. Gen. Sylvester Del Corso, Adjutant General of the Ohio National Guard, he had tried to get the Stokes administration to discuss measures for handling racial disturbances but had been rebuffed.

By 9:15 p.m., Stokes had decided that the situation might get beyond the control of local forces before the night was over. He called Gov. James A. Rhodes, who was attending the National Governors Conference in Cincinnati, to inform him of the situation. The Governor immediately called General Del Corso, who was in Akron, and told him to report to Stokes. Within a few minutes, Rhodes left for his home in Columbus to monitor the disturbances from there, General Del Corso was on his way to Cleveland, and the Ohio National Guard had been placed on alert.

In addition to determining the level of force needed to control the violence, Mayor Stokes knew that he would have to inform the public of the situation, to avoid misunderstanding and panic and to keep people out of the troubled area. After talking to the Governor, the mayor went down the street from City Hall to the television studios of WKYC. There he taped a special announcement to be used by WKYC and distributed in copy to other Cleveland television and radio stations. Many Clevelanders, watching a televised baseball game between the Cleveland Indians and the Baltimore Orioles, got the first news of the violence when Mayor Stokes interrupted the broadcast shortly before 11 p.m.:

> We've had a bad situation here tonight but as of this time we have the situation controlled. But we do need badly the help of every citizen at this time, particularly in the Lakeview-Superior Avenue area. Stay at home and cooperate with the police. Go home if you are on the streets; if you are at home, stay inside and keep your doors locked so that we can contain the situation.

. . . .

By 3 a.m., when General Del Corso notified him that he had a number of troops ready for deployment, Mayor Stokes had decided that the time had come to use the National Guard. Two hundred Guardsmen, together with 24 Jeeps and other military vehicles, were sent to the troubled area to patrol the streets. To each of the Jeeps were assigned three Guardsmen and one Cleveland policeman. About 4:30 a.m. the police, on orders from the mayor, were instructed to report any sniper activity to the National Guard. Looters and arsonists, said the police-radio announcement, "are to be arrested by police or National Guard without the use of deadly force." Half an hour later, the police heard another announcement on their patrol-car radios: All vacations and holidays are canceled; all personnel will work 12-hour shifts.

As dawn arrived amid a drizzle, smoke still rose from gutted buildings along Superior Avenue. Police continued to receive reports of looting and of sporadic gunfire in areas of the East Side. But the worst of the violence had abated. Cleveland, for the time being, was under control.

*   *   *

From the history of racial disturbances in Cleveland and other American cities, Clevelanders, on the morning of July 24, 1968, had every reason to expect that more trouble lay ahead. If past patterns were repeated, more violence would flare at nightfall. The authorities had to devise a strategy to cope with it.

More than 100 leaders of the black community gathered at City Hall about 8:30 a.m. to meet with Mayor Stokes. The attendance at this meeting was entirely black; not even the white members of the mayor's staff were permitted to take part. Many at the meeting had been up all night, assisting in City Hall or walking the streets, attempting to quell the violence.

Stokes opened the meeting with his assessment of the situation, then called for discussion on how best to handle it. A number of options were available to the mayor: He could impose a curfew, strengthen police and National Guard units in the troubled area, or use various combinations of force such as placing National Guard in the area and not police. Many at the meeting were concerned that if police were allowed to remain in the area, there would be further shooting. They feared that black nationalists would be made fidgety by the continued presence of the police and would begin shooting, or that if police were allowed to remain in the area, they would seek revenge for their three comrades who were killed the night before. Several spoke in opposition to a curfew, noting that if it were applied to just one area it would be resented by the citizens of that area and would not prevent outsiders from coming into the area and beginning violence again.

The meeting at City Hall produced no real consensus, and Mayor Stokes revealed no plans of his own. When the meeting broke up about 10 a.m., he retired to his office to discuss strategies with his staff, while about 20 of the participants in the meeting, most of them militants, adjourned to the Auditorium Hotel to continue discussions.

An hour later Stokes addressed a press conference originally scheduled for 9:30 a.m. He attributed Tuesday night's violence to "a gang who will meet the full measure of the law" and described the present situation on the East Side as "quiet."

> Security measures are being maintained with a minimum number of National Guardsmen on our streets and a sizeable force in ready reserve should they be needed. I have met with Negro leadership at City Hall and they have joined me in an all-out effort to make sure that Cleveland's night of terror will not turn into a riot. We are constantly re-evaluating the situation and assure that this city will not be governed by hoodlums.

The mayor indicated that he had not yet decided upon a strategy for Wednesday evening.

Early in the afternoon the group of militants returned from the Auditorium Hotel to City Hall. Now they presented a definite proposal to the mayor: They would go back into the community and try to bring it under control themselves, preventing looting, burning, and additional loss of life. They wanted a period of time to attempt this; if it did not work, Stokes could choose a different strategy. Stokes listened. He still made no commitment.

This was not the first time such a proposal had been suggested to Stokes. Bertram Gardner, who had spent the night on the streets, proposed such a course to the Mayor in a conversation about 7:30 a.m. Gardner wanted Stokes to take the police and Guard out of the area, while Gardner sent about 200 or 250 blacks into the community to try to calm feelings. He wanted only about 6 hours: from about 11 a.m. to about 5 p.m. At the 8:30 a.m. meeting, others had proposed a similar course.

About midafternoon, Stokes discussed the idea with others in a small meeting in his office. Richard Greene, director of the Community Development Department, endorsed the proposal. He felt that the black community ought to be given a chance to "pull itself together." Councilman George Forbes expressed confidence that the strategy would work. Not all were convinced. General Del Corso expressed serious reservations about the wisdom of the proposal.

When the mayor made his decision, he did not make it rashly. He had had the benefit of numerous opinions and arguments for and against competing strategies. Some options, like the curfew, had been seen as fraught with difficulties. Stokes had heard compelling arguments about the volatile situation that would be created by the continuing presence of white law enforcement officers in the black community. The "all black" strategy appeared to be the only rational policy to reduce bloodshed. In accepting it, Stokes knew he was taking a calculated risk. There would be safeguards, however. He accepted the suggestion by Richard Greene that Negro policemen function in the area as well as the black leaders. He would also station police and the National Guard around the perimeter of the area, so that they could respond quickly if trouble did arise.

Though the decision was not his alone, Stokes had to assume full responsibility for it. It was a novel strategy, one that a white mayor would have had greater difficulty in instrumenting. It was Stokes' rapport with the Negro community that brought forth the proposal in the first place and that now gave hope that it would work.

At 4:15 p.m., Mayor Stokes released a detailed plan for Wednesday night. About 6 square miles of the city were to be cordoned off until 7 a.m., Thursday morning. The southern boundary would be Euclid Avenue, eastward from East 55th Street. The northern boundary would be Superior Avenue, from East 55th to Rockefeller Park, then along the park's eastern edge up to St. Clair, eastward along St. Clair (with a small section north of it) to the city line adjoining East Cleveland. This perimeter was to be patrolled by units of three National Guardsmen and one police officer, beginning at 7 p.m. The National Guard was to retain a mobile reserve to deploy within the cordoned area should serious trouble arise.

"Normal patrol within the cordoned-off area," said the memo, "will be restricted to regular Cleveland police as directed by the Safety Director. National Guard troops will be committed to the area only if needed."

Though the memorandum did not mention that only Negro policemen would be allowed in the area, Mayor Stokes spelled out this provision in a press conference at 4:45 p.m.

> There will only be Negro policemen and possibly a Negro sheriff in the area guarding the people. . . . There will be 109 [individuals] who will represent the groups themselves and about five hundred persons who are familiar with this situation will be in the area.

All white nonresidents, including newsmen, were to be kept from the area. The mayor repeated that it was important for people to stay home and off the streets. He made two further announcements: that the sale of liquor in Cuyahoga County (embracing Cleveland) had been stopped for 72 hours beginning at 11 a.m., Wednesday; that four emergency centers had been set up in East Side churches and community centers to provide food and shelter for those displaced by Tuesday night's disturbances.

The Reverend DeForest Brown, director of the Hough Area Development Corporation, was named spokesman for the Mayor's Committee which was to patrol the streets that night. Said Brown:

> We, out of our concern, have accepted the responsibility to restore law and order out of a chaotic situation. Leaders will be out talking to the black community about its responsibility to itself.

The mayor had made his decision. On Wednesday evening black control was established for the black community.

Law and Disorder

. . . .

The Negro leaders carried the message from City Hall back to their communities, meeting with small groups to explain the evening's strategy and to organize for effective peacekeeping. At the office of Pride, Inc., on St. Clair, Wilbur Grattan, a black nationalist associated with the New Republic of Africa, addressed a group of about 30, most of whom were members of the Circle of African

Unity. Grattan had spent much of the previous night in peacekeeping and most of the day in the meetings that led to Mayor Stokes' decision to exercise black control in the black community. He described what had been discussed during those meetings, praised the bold policy that had been adopted, then turned to matters of organization for the evening. After being told by Grattan that they would receive orange arm bands labeled "The Mayor's Committee," the group worked out the problems of geographic assignments for each of them. Baxter Hill, director of Pride, Inc., closed the meeting in his office with a reminder of the significance of the responsibilities they were about to undertake.

. . . .

While the Negro leaders were hastily organizing their peacekeeping force, the Cleveland Police Department was preparing for its role in the troubled area. White policemen were assigned to work with National Guardsmen patrolling the perimeter of the cordoned area. At Fifth District headquarters, situated within the area, police climbed aboard military trucks and joked about being back in the Army. American Legionnaires served them coffee. About 100 Negro policemen (out of a total of 165 Negro officers in the 2,200-man police force) were assigned to patrol the cordoned area, using 21 patrol cars. Negroes on the county sheriff's staff were assigned to help them. White police, it was understood, would enter the area only if the Negro officers needed additional assistance.

. . . .

Through the night, teams of peace patrols drove up and down the commercial streets of the area, stopping wherever four or more people were standing around, pleading with them to disperse. Occasionally members of the Mayor's Committee stood in front of stores where windows had been broken or iron gates torn down, directly confronting the potential looters. This technique could not be wholly effective, for the Mayor's Committee lacked the manpower for permanent guards at every commercial establishment. Potential looters, some of them professionals, lurked in the shadows, sometimes for hours, waiting for the peace patrols to leave the scene. Days later they would be seen hawking stolen goods on street corners. Occasionally a looter broke into a store, setting off the burglar alarm, then hid nearby until someone came to investigate, turned off the alarm, and walked away. Most looters made off with what they could carry, but some filled automobiles with merchandise.

The Mayor's Committee observed adults, including women, among the potential and actual looters, but teenagers gave them the most trouble. Roving bands of teenagers usually were the first to break into a store, then proved unresponsive to the appeals of the peace patrols. "We couldn't control the kids," Walter Burks, executive assistant to the Mayor, recalls. "We would tell them to stop and they would walk away and you would get into your car to drive someplace else and you would drive back and they were right back with their hands in [the windows of a looted store]." Some of the troublesome youths, says Burks, were not more than 10 years old. The next day Mayor Stokes ascribed most of the trouble Wednesday night to "roving bands of young people generally between the ages of fourteen and seventeen."

An observer who accompanied members of the Mayor's Committee on their patrols recalls that some were particularly effective in their work. Harllel Jones, a young militant, wiry and ordinarily soft-spoken, dispersed a crowd at 123d and St. Clair that had gathered in front of a furniture store that had been broken into. "At 105th and Massey," the observer adds, "Harllel dispersed perhaps the potentially most dangerous crowd of about two hundred people. It took him about twenty to twenty-five minutes." Like the other militants who were particularly effective Wednesday night, Harllel Jones succeeded by making eloquent pleas to the pride of the black community. "If there was one man who stands out as having done the most effective job possible of maintaining peace," said the observer, "it was Harllel Jones."

Noticeable by their absence were the clergymen and other moderate and middle-class Negro leaders. Though a number of them had participated in the meetings at City Hall, few were on the streets Wednesday night and their effectiveness was limited. Had more moderates helped out, the members of the peace patrol felt, the sporadic looting might have been prevented entirely.

White policemen appeared in the cordoned area over the protests of the Mayor's Committee. When a pawnbroker's window was broken at East 101st and St. Clair, white policemen responded to the call. They ignored requests of the peace patrol to leave. Similar incidents occurred elsewhere. At East 123d and St. Clair, an observer recalls, an alarm went off in a furniture store.

> All of a sudden National Guardsmen and white policemen, who apparently had been stationed in East Cleveland, appeared on the scene. They started backing up toward the buildings as if they were actually in a state of emergency. Nothing had occurred and, fortunately, the Law Director arrived on the scene.

Law Director James talked to the white officers, and they left.

*   *   *

The reaction of some white policemen to Mayor Stokes' strategy of black control was made clear to those monitoring the police radio Wednesday night.

This came in response to a report of a heart-attack case within the cordoned area: "White or nigger? Send the Mayor's Committee."

When a report was broadcast that a child had fallen off a second-floor porch, the return call came: "Tell the Mayor's Committee to handle it."

When the police dispatcher requested cars to respond to a fire call, an anonymous voice suggested that Mayor Stokes "go p. . . on it." Responses to other calls included "F . . . that nigger Mayor!"

At the Fifth District headquarters, the heavily guarded bastion within the troubled area, police responded in a fury of curses and epithets, directed toward Stokes and Safety Director McManamon, when told they could not carry rifles while patrolling the perimeter of the cordoned area. A policeman there, delivering a monolog to a bystander on what is "wrong" with Negroes, gave this assessment of Mayor Stokes: "You need a sheepdog to lead sheep; you don't have a sheep lead other sheep."

The tension at Fifth District headquarters lasted through the evening. Two television newsmen who entered the building were grabbed from behind by a commanding officer, pushed through the building, and thrown out into the parking lot where other policemen shouted at them abusively. After appealing to another commanding officer they were let back in, and ultimately the first officer apologized for ejecting them.

*   *   *

At a press conference late the next morning, Mayor Stokes pronounced the strategy for Wednesday night a qualified success.

> It is our considered opinion that we made significant headway last night in bringing to an end the violence and lawlessness that has occurred on our East Side. No one was killed or shot or seriously injured during the night.

Stokes admitted that there had been trouble; he reported that 3 fires had been set, 36 stores looted, and 13 persons arrested in the troubled area. "Most of the trouble," he said, "was caused by young teenagers, roving in small bands." He expressed thanks to the National Guard patrolling the perimeter, the Negro policemen working within the area, and especially the 300 members of the Mayor's Committee "who patrolled the troubled areas until dawn to keep things cool." He announced that bus service and garbage pickup had resumed in the cordoned area and that city workers had begun to tear down dangerously damaged buildings. He emphasized, however, that more trouble could be expected.

Earlier in the morning, Stokes had met with Negro leaders at City

Hall. During that meeting the resentment over the limited participation of moderate Negro leaders in the peacekeeping was brought into the open. It was generally agreed that the peace patrols had been only partially effective; the arson and looting had not been completely curbed. Changes were needed: A curfew now might help remove the gangs from the streets; more cars equipped with radios were needed; more sound trucks would help; and broken windows should be boarded before nightfall.

While the Negro leaders continued their discussion in the City Council chamber, the mayor addressed the press conference. There he announced a change in strategy: The National Guard, he said, was being brought into the area to protect stores against looting. This change in strategy, like others he made that Thursday, was to haunt Carl Stokes for weeks to come, for it provided an indication to his critics that he had given in to pressure from others or conceded the failure of his Wednesday-night strategy. Throughout the ensuing controversy, Stokes would maintain that the strategy had succeeded because it had prevented bloodshed, and he valued life over property. Changes in the strategy, he argued, became appropriate after tempers had cooled in the black community and the protection of property could be safely entrusted to white law enforcement officers.

One of the first to criticize the mayor was Councilman Leo Jackson, whose district includes part of Glenville and who is said to represent the views of older, established Negro residents. "If you want to say what happened last night—no shootings, no sniping—was a success, then it was," Jackson told a reporter. "But if you consider the looting, the destruction, the breaking of windows, the wholesale gutting of buildings, last night's activities were a total failure."

Businessmen whose stores were victimized Wednesday night were bitterly critical of the mayor's policy. The white owner of a looted clothing store drove to the scene about 1 a.m. and could not get out of his car because of an attacking mob. A Negro policeman ordered him out of the area for his safety. At the perimeter he pleaded with National Guardsmen and police for help, but was told there was nothing they could do. The owner of a looted furniture store got the same response from police at Fifth District headquarters. A partner in a drycleaning chain, two of whose stores had been looted the previous night, had his main plant looted of clothing Wednesday night—half a million dollars' worth, he estimated. "We're wiped out," he said bitterly. "We couldn't get help. That means 70 people out of work—70 families without incomes."

White policemen were openly critical of the mayor's Wednesday-night strategy. A 30-year-old patrolman angrily submitted his resignation. When Police Chief Michael Blackwell called the mayor's strategy "a brilliant idea," there were murmurings that Blackwell, a

42-year veteran of the force, was a traitor to his department and a politician protecting himself.

Gen. Del Corso, who had argued for much stronger measures Wednesday night, declined to criticize the mayor.

> I made my suggestions but the Mayor made the decision and I am sure he did a lot of soul-searching all day. We're here to assist and cooperate with the Mayor. He wanted to use this means [citizen-patrols] and it is beginning to be productive. It is proving successful.

It came as a shock to City Hall when, on August 9, Gen. Del Corso told the Ohio Crime Commission that Stokes had "surrendered to black revolutionaries."

That same day, after the Stokes administration presented a summary of events to city councilmen and to the press, Council President James V. Stanton, considered by many to be a leading contender for the office occupied by Carl Stokes, joined in the criticism. "I find no moral grounds," he said, "for taking duly constituted law enforcement away from the families and property of that area regardless of any justification by the Administration that there was no loss of life." Stanton's charge brought a rejoinder from Safety Director Joseph McManamon. "He can't say that," McManamon retorted, "unless he means that Negro policemen aren't duly constituted officers." He added that the concentration of Negro policemen on Wednesday evening added up to the normal number of police in the area.

In the days following the Wednesday-night disturbances, support for the mayor's strategy, sometimes in the form of newspaper advertisements, came from civil rights groups, religious and charitable organizations, liberal political groups, and from Cleveland educators, industrial leaders, and other prominent citizens. A professional polling organization found that 59 percent of its respondents supported the mayor's strategy; 14 percent criticized it; the rest were uncertain.

. . . .